UNI... ...INGHAM

W... ...WN

FROM THE LIBRARY

D0274681

"India's Prisoner"

"India's Prisoner"

A Biography of
Edward John Thompson, 1886–1946

Mary Lago

NOTTINGHAM UNIVERSITY LIBRARY

University of Missouri Press

COLUMBIA AND LONDON

Copyright ©2001 by
The Curators of the University of Missouri
University of Missouri Press, Columbia, Missouri 65201
Printed and bound in the United States of America
All rights reserved
5 4 3 2 1   05 04 03 02 01

Library of Congress Cataloging-in-Publication Data

Lago, Mary.
   "India's prisoner" : a biography of Edward John Thompson,
1886-1946 / Mary Lago.
      p.   cm.
   Includes bibliographical references and index.
   ISBN 0-8262-1299-9 (alk. paper)
   1. Thompson, Edward John, 1886-1946.   2. Indologists—Great
Britain—Biography.   3. Authors, English—20th century—Biography.
I. Thompson, Edward John, 1886-1946.
DS435.7.T54 L34 2000
941.08'092—dc21
[B]   00-046685

♾ This paper meets the requirements of the
American National Standard for Permanence of Paper
for Printed Library Materials, Z39.48, 1984.

Text design: Elizabeth K. Young
Jacket design: Stephanie Foley
Typesetter: BOOKCOMP, Inc.
Printer and binder: Thomson-Shore, Inc.
Typefaces: Sanvito, Garamond

Frontispiece: Edward John Thompson. Courtesy of Dorothy Thompson.

100 223 502X

To the memory of
EDWARD PALMER THOMPSON, 1922–1993

CONTENTS

ACKNOWLEDGMENTS

My first thanks and great gratitude go to the late E. P. Thompson and Dorothy Thompson, for their kindness, hospitality, and allowing me access to E. J. Thompson's papers while they were still in their possession, and for permission to use them after they were placed in the Bodleian Library. There I had the most patient and expert help of Colin Harris and all his staff in the Western Manuscripts Department. For Wesleyan Methodist materials (Methodist Church—Wesleyan Missionary Society Archives), so essential to E. J. Thompson's story, and for permission to quote from them, I am most grateful to the Methodist Board of Missions and Joy Fox, archivist, and to Rosemary Seton, custodian of Wesleyan records at the School of Oriental and African Studies, University of London. The Rhodes Foundation Trustees allowed me to quote from Thompson's hitherto restricted reports from his three trips to India under their auspices in the 1930s, to investigate intellectual and political cooperation there. Other libraries that have been signally helpful are those of Oriel College, Oxford University; the University Library, Cambridge; the Imperial War Museum, London; the India Office Library Papers in the British Library; the Mudd Manuscript Library, Yale University; the John Rylands Library, University of Manchester; and the Watch Project, University of Reading Library. I am grateful, as always, to Martha Alexander, the director of the University of Missouri Libraries, and to her staff for their unfailing consideration and assistance.

Many persons have supplied information from personal experience and contacts: Barbara Sloman, E. J. Thompson's niece, on family background; Clifford Culshaw, on his own experience at Bankura College; Simon Kusseff, from his research on E. J. Thompson's elder brother Frank, lost during World War II; and Dr. J. M. K. Spalding, on his father's friendship with E. J. Thompson. E. P. Thompson's daughter Kate made the first sorting and invaluable card file of her grandfather's correspondence. Richard and Ann Symonds gave me much kindness and helpful instruction about Oxford history, and Maud Rosenthal provided tea and information on the history of Boars Hill. Michael Bishop, Kingswood School archivist, was unfailingly generous with school records and photographs. Clinton Seely and Andrew Robinson were always helpful with suggestions on sources. I am grateful to all of them and to the many others who have answered my letters and telephone calls.

I wish to thank the following for permission to quote from papers for which they control copyright: the Right Honorable Lord Bridges, for permission to quote from his father's and his grandfather's correspondence; Nicholas Smith, for letters of Sir Harcourt Butler; Jane Carrington, for excerpts from her father's memoir of his Indian career; the Right Honorable Lord Crewe, for excerpts from his father's letters; Mary, Duchess of Roxburghe, for letters of Lord Crewe; Teresa Smith and Janet Gnosspelius, for letters of W. G. Collingwood; Curtis Brown Ltd., for a letter from Alfred Curtis Brown; the late Leonard Elmhirst and the Dartington Foundation, for quotations from his letters and his interviews with me; the Right Honorable Lord Elton, for a letter from his father; King's College, Cambridge, for letters of E. M. Forster; William Graves, for quotations from his father's letters; Victor Gollancz, Publishers, for access to their correspondence with E. J. Thompson and for permission to quote from it; the Right Honorable Lord Hardinge of Penshurst, for letters of the first Lord Hardinge of Penshurst; Barbara Lyon, for letters of Percy Lyon; Lady Rothenstein, for letters of Sir William Rothenstein; St. Olave's and St. Saviour's Grammar School Foundation for letters of William George Rushbrooke; Dr. J. C. Spalding, for his father's letters; Lady Spender, for letters of Sir Stephen Spender; Sheila Munro, for a letter from Dr. George Workman of Kingswood School; and University of Sussex Library, for letters of Leonard Woolf.

There are regrettable and sometimes inexplicable blanks among these acknowledgments. Efforts to find executors have led to frustrating dead ends for some of E. J. Thompson's closest friends whose letters were especially influential and revealing. For instance, probate records reveal almost nothing about George Lowther; I found only a distant relation by marriage, who had no information about him. William Canton's publication copyrights were ceded to J. M. Dent and Company, who have no information about an executor. Inquiries to sources mentioned in letters or to the press yielded nothing. Requests to recorded executors for S. K. Ratcliffe brought no response. Search for executors of Frederick Joshua Fielden led from Agra University through three British solicitors' offices to the Cambridge house that was his last home—all without result. I hope that my use of those letters will cause no offense, for the friendships of their writers were indispensable to Thompson. I hope, at least, that this use may bring new information to light.

For financial assistance during this work, I am indebted to the American Council of Learned Societies, whose Travel-to-Collections grant in 1988 was, in effect, seed money for this project. For additional financial assistance I thank the John Rylands Library, University of Manchester; the University of Missouri's Weldon Spring Humanities Seminar and its Research Council for summer research grants. Nor do I forget that Selwyn College, Cambridge University, gave me a Visiting Bye-Fellowship in 1991–1992, as well as subsequent summer accommodations; and Mrs. Mary Bennett, Oxford, has repeatedly given me a home while I worked in England.

The University of Missouri Press has been most encouraging and helpful throughout the project, and I thank particularly Julianna Schroeder, whose meticulous editing tidied up lapses and repetitions. I also wish to thank both Tim Fox and Kim McCaffrey for assistance in proofreading, and I am grateful to Linda Webster for her fine index.

"India's Prisoner"

INTRODUCTION

"*India's prisoner*" is Gandhi's phrase. It refers to Edward John Thompson's 1925 novel, *A Farewell to India*. Gandhi was quite right. Although Thompson said repeatedly that he longed to be quit of India, he could not say a final farewell because he was entangled in the network of derivations, aversions, and enthusiasms attached to India's two centuries of involuntary affiliation with Britain. He was not one of those entangled in India's mysticisms, so many of which were (are) constructs of Western wishful thinking. He had a saving, if sometimes extravagantly expressed, skepticism about the British-Indian relationship, but as a child of late-Victorian England, born in 1886, he could never bring himself wholeheartedly to a view of England detached from India. He wanted only the best for India: he came to the conclusion that that best was India as a dominion within the Commonwealth.

India as he knew it between 1910 and 1946 still bore indelible marks of the upheaval that the British call the Mutiny of 1857 but many Indians regard as their first great freedom uprising. In 1858 it had resulted in Parliament's taking control of India away from the traders of the East India Company. Henceforth British India, theoretically exclusive of the one-fourth of the subcontinent under the rule of hereditary princes, was administered through two bureaucracies: the India Office in London under a Secretary of State for India, and, on the spot, the Government of India under an appointed Governor-General whose title metamorphosed to that of Viceroy after Disraeli proclaimed Victoria Empress of India in 1876. Every ten years, Parliament considered an India Bill, ostensibly a review of the state of affairs there but all too often a revelation of the shallowness of many Members' information about their Indian Raj. Meanwhile the India Office and the Government of India, even after the advent of the telegraph and the typewriter, conducted much of their business amid floods of painstakingly handwritten memoranda and reminders, formal statements of various officials, minutes of meetings, recommendations and refutations, proposals and counterproposals, trivia and strategies of vast consequence. Anyone who reads through even one year's record of these exchanges must marvel at official patience and persistence.

1

Edward Thompson was also a child of Victorian Wesleyan Methodism. His own family's tradition propelled him into the ministry, and then into the complex Indian bureaucracy as an insignificant bit of the Educational Service. His father, John Moses Thompson, a missionary in South India, utterly devoted to the Wesleyan Word, wore himself literally to death for the sake of the Work. He died in England in 1894; his widow was left with six small children of whom Edward, eight years old, was the eldest. She hoped and assumed that he would follow in his father's footsteps. When he did so out of duty and devotion to her, she failed utterly to comprehend that he had serious doubts about his relation to Wesleyanism and its foreign missions. He could not have explained them to her, and only time and experience would enable him to formulate them fully for himself. The Wesleyan ethos cast encircling gloom over his youthful years and, indeed, continued as a lingering shade to the end of his life. Its resolute sincerity commanded his grudging admiration, but its insistence upon its unimpeachable spiritual rightness alienated his affection. Wesleyanism as he knew it still had many of its eighteenth-century characteristics when, self-sufficient within their nonconformity, Wesleyans regarded themselves as "God's peculiar people" and all others as outsiders. Established society regarded them as peculiar indeed. They were heirs of those worthy farm and village folk who departed from Church of England procedure to hear John Wesley preach in the open fields. Diligence and thrift, honesty and mutual support, all of these Wesley's ethical imperatives, enabled their slow ascent from the lower ranks of a stratified society to a self-respecting lower middle class.

Edward Thompson was essentially self-educated. His formal education at Wesley's Kingswood School abruptly ended halfway up the sixth form when his mother, in desperate financial straits, removed him for work in a bank in Bethnal Green. To the end of his life he deplored and detested the memory of his five years there. He escaped by enrolling at the Richmond Theological College and was ordained a Wesleyan minister; to this he added an external master of arts degree from the University of London. He "offered" for foreign service and in 1910 went as a teacher of English literature to Bankura Wesleyan College, a missionary outpost on the remote western border of Bengal.

He did not find the Bankura Mission a congenial environment. Quickly he proved himself an outstanding teacher, but Wesleyanism's spiritual exclusiveness and its zeal for a warranty on the life everlasting had long lacerated his nerves; Bankura seemed to be only more of the same. He wanted and needed an expanding, mutually encouraging intellectual community. He wanted to be a poet and said that if he could write one really great poem he would consider his career a success. However, his Wesleyan supervisors frowned upon the writing and publication of personal poetry except on the Wesley brothers' model of hymns and other approved and "improving" verse. They did not realize that they paid his ambition an uppercase compliment when they advised one another repeatedly that Thompson was not a practical person, for after all he was a Poet, and they must make allowances for the Poetic Temperament. They could neither deny nor do without his talents as teacher. However, the conflict between poetry and piety, which began in earnest at Richmond, gripped him for many years.

His earnestness, his determination to find an intellectual home, and, while he was in India, his loneliness, attracted to him a notable series of older mentor-friends. Some of these, such as the retired journalist and editor William Canton and the soon-to-be-Laureate Robert Bridges, came about through Thompson's letters of comment or query on their published work. His first meetings with them started long and fruitful associations. Ruskin's associate and biographer, William G. Collingwood, one of the earliest of the Ruskin scholars, met Thompson through Canton. By far Thompson's most important friend and mentor in India (and later in England) was Percy Comyn Lyon of the Indian Civil Service's Educational Service and, after 1912, Education Member of the Bengal Governor-General's Council. Vigorous disapproval of the conduct of British India's English-language education system was his bond with Thompson. They refused to be reconciled to the soulless and unimaginative machinery that processed Indian young men through a literary curriculum that was designed originally for English gentlemen, which, however, as applied in India, steered the majority of Indian graduates to clerical jobs in Government of India offices. Too much of this regime consisted of memorizing lecture notes and cram-book information to be parroted back on examinations. Bengal, Lyon insisted, would be less a hotbed of sedition if it had less policing and more creative education. His outspoken criticisms made him unpopular with officials in Bengal and in New Delhi. He and Thompson also shared a genuine belief in the empire as a potential force for good and stability—but only if those in charge underwent fundamental changes in attitude and policy. Lyon was the source of Thompson's belief that India should, like Canada, Australia, and New Zealand, become a dominion within a British Commonwealth.

Thompson found an intellectual community in Calcutta, in the circle of Rabindranath Tagore, whose standing and achievements went largely unrecognized at Bankura, were known to very few outside of India, and were, even there, then little known outside of Bengal. Thompson happened to be present in 1913 when Tagore heard that on the basis of *Gitanjali*, his English prose translations of selections from his Bengali lyrics, he had won the Nobel Prize for Literature, the first such award to an Asian. A watershed in East-West literary relations, it had both political and literary repercussions. It inspired in Thompson the idea of devoting himself to translation of Bengal's vernacular writers: he would be a kind of literary apostle to the English-speaking West. Events deflected that intention, but Thompson's two critical studies of Tagore's life and work, published in 1921 and 1926, marked a new phase in the West's acquaintance with Bengali literature.

He wrote and published those studies after the Great War, during which he went to Mesopotamia as an army chaplain, and after which he returned to Bankura and a rapidly changing India. But he, too, was changed, and he realized more clearly than ever before that the missionary vocation was not—had never been—his. In all honesty he could no longer approve or accept the obligation to create converts and engage in what he came to feel was cultural subversion.

In 1923 Thompson returned to England for a peripheral assignment at Oxford: peripheral because as Lecturer in Bengali he was attached to the Indian Institute, a government-subsidized center originally intended for Indian study and exchange, but long out of touch with modern India. Indian studies at that time consisted of linguistics and Sanskrit. Thompson taught Bengali to candidates for the Indian Civil Service (I.C.S.). He quickly realized that Oxford students did not know Indian history and humanities, and, what was worse, seemed not to care that they did not know. Gradually he became known for his determination not only to broaden Indian studies at Oxford but also to better inform a British public raised on tourist stereotypes of bejeweled maharajas, secluded holy men, dusky dancing girls, objectionable temple sculptures, and glorious British victories over heathen hordes. Thompson did not exactly say to himself, "This is what I shall do," but India was what he knew best. As journalist, novelist, and historian, he began to try to correct the misconceptions. He sometimes regretted being "pigeonholed as a man who wrote about India," but he had rejected conventional religious evangelism. Now he was an evangelist for factual knowledge about India.

He would dearly have loved to have a continuing friendship with Tagore, but Tagore's personal relations were frequently erratic, and worldwide fame after the Nobel Prize made his life sometimes unbearably complex. Furthermore, he had reservations about Thompson's 1921 study of him and his work and violently disliked the 1926 book, although it earned Thompson a London University Ph.D. Still, the Tagore connection produced important ties to individuals like the philosopher Brajendranath Seal, the noted statistician Prasanta Mahalanobis, and Leonard Elmhirst, the English agricultural economist who worked with Tagore in India and later founded Dartington Hall in Devon.

At first in Oxford, where insiderness was (and is) immensely important, Thompson was dismayed to find how completely he felt himself an outsider. More than ever, he resented his loss of the opportunity while at Kingswood to try for an Oxbridge scholarship. In 1923, in Oxford's academic establishment, he was only a freelance writer unconnected to a college and tied to the fossilized Indian Institute. This feeling abated somewhat after Lyon proposed him for Honorary Fellow of Oriel College and he was accepted there. Still, with respect to advocacy of India, there were some advantages to being an outsider. His outspoken journalism, his researches into Indian history, and his novels with Indian settings in which contemporary situations and personalities were perfectly recognizable were conspicuous in the stream of comment on India. His writing brought him to the attention of Gandhi, Nehru, and other elders of the Congress Party, at a time when nationalist sentiment moved ever closer to demands for increased self-government. In his relations with them it was to his advantage that he did not belong to any political party and did not run for public office; he described himself as a liberal conservative with a tinge of socialism. In England, too, being an outsider was not altogether a disadvantage. Some officials and some Members of Parliament began to realize that he had information and contacts that they did not have and did not know how to get. It was not altogether a joke that a debate on India emptied the parliamentary benches, out of antipathies or disinterest or lack of information or all three. He was a connector and explicator at a time when Britain and India began to move inexorably apart. A caption in the *Times Literary Supplement* speaks of the " 'drip, drip effect' which led to Britain's withdrawal from empire" in the Middle East after World War II. But the drip of empire began in India after the Great War, with the Amritsar massacres in 1919, the Simon Commission in 1927–1929, and the aborted Round Table Conferences of 1930–1932. A definitive act of alienation was the Viceroy's declaration in 1939, without consulting any Indian leaders, that India was to be a belligerent in the war.

During the 1930s Thompson visited India three times with Rhodes Foundation money; strictly speaking, he was ineligible for it, but the Trustees recognized the value of his Indian contacts if Oxford were to lead in encouraging better relations with India. In 1932 he was assigned to assess the extent of "intellectual cooperation" among writers and between writers and government. In 1936 he went to gather materials for his biography of Lord Metcalfe; such a study of a past political figure necessarily involves contacts and discussions with governmental agencies. In 1939 his assignment was purely political. The Trustees asked him to see his Congress Party friends and learn what he could about their reaction to the Viceroy's high-handed declaration. He learned a great deal, and he made suggestions for improved Oxford-India relations in the future, some of which came about with the help of the Rhodes Trustees and H. N. Spalding, a generous Oxford idealist and believer in Oxford-India cooperation as inspiration and model for other universities. Thompson's reports from India to the Rhodes Foundation are published here for the first time, with the generous approval of the Rhodes Trustees.

Edward John Thompson was impulsive and impatient. His relation to India was often a love-hate relationship. He could be pessimist and optimist in quick succession, but he could admit his errors. He was always a humanist. His political journalism and Indian histories strive to keep advocacy and criticism in balance, although his sympathies are never in doubt. His novels tend to become disquisitions on contemporary issues, and the poet in him sometimes allowed the lyrical to overload his narrative, but critics often noted the eloquence of his descriptions of landscape, of flora and fauna; whether in England or India or Mesopotamia, nature's variations gave him intense satisfaction. Inevitably, commentators compare his Indian novels to E. M. Forster's *A Passage to India* and often judge that the better-written novel, but they recognize that Thompson's experience of India was much wider and deeper than Forster's. Everywhere, and especially in his letters, Thompson's style is powerfully personal; there is no doubt that the writer is a man of force and conviction.

E. P. Thompson, writing in 1993 of his father's sometimes erratic but deeply respectful relations with Rabindranath Tagore, describes Thompson as a man on "the interface of two cultures"; at a time when both cultures tried, often painfully, to redefine themselves, Thompson was an outspoken advocate of Indian self-realization. An explicator's role is not always a happy one, and Thompson was not always happy in it, but, as Gandhi had said and as Thompson himself recognized, once committed to India there was no turning back.

1

Introducing the Thompsons

Two noteworthy Indian arrivals occurred in late 1910. The more exalted of these was Lord Hardinge of Penshurst, who replaced Lord Minto, the Governor-General and Viceroy of India. At the same time, Lord Crewe, at the India Office in London, Hardinge's friend and Cambridge contemporary, replaced Lord Morley as Secretary of State for India. Furthermore, the Indian Empire had a new monarch, for George V had succeeded the late King Edward VII. Hardinge was confident that the new king's visit to India, in the winter of 1911, was a "chance that will not come again" for rapprochement and consolidation. Consolidation of British power and rapprochement with influential and "loyal" Indians were important goals, verifiable evidence of administrative success. Nowhere in India were those more maddeningly elusive than in the bifurcated province of Bengal. In 1905 George Nathaniel Curzon, then Viceroy, divided Bengal as East Bengal and West Bengal, a measure known thereafter as the Partition. It affected every aspect of Bengal's political and intellectual life.[1]

Pre-1905 Bengal, which included the adjacent areas of Bihar, Orissa, and Assam, as well as Burma, was arguably too large for efficient administration. Curzon thought that dividing eastern Bengal, predominantly Muslim and rural, from western Bengal, predominantly Hindu and with Calcutta as the capital of British India and its major commercial center, would curb Bengali nationalists' activities. It did not work that way. Bengalis saw Partition as a new effort to divide and rule, which indeed it was, "an unambiguous demonstration of the British Indian administration's antipathy to the political aspirations and cultural ideals of the bhadralok," the cultured people, of Bengal. "How thoroughly the British misconstrued the social and political forces with which they were dealing in Bengal was revealed by their unpreparedness for the outburst which their measure provoked."[2]

Only the exceptional administrator understood the Bengalis' fierce pride in their culture and their cherished mother tongue. They protested tirelessly, often violently. *Bengal* and *Bengali* became synonymous with *sedition*. Victorian England's habit of thinking in terms of social class had long been transferred to India, but with an ironic twist. England's "dangerous classes" were the ignorant and poverty-stricken, the criminal, the vagrant. In both official and news parlance, India's "educated classes" became her "dangerous classes."[3]

Those classes emerged after the introduction of a government measure of 1835 to train a corps of promising young Indians as clerks and other lower-echelon personnel to serve the English administration. On what language should this new curriculum be founded? Twenty thousand pounds were available for the "intellectual improvement of the people of this country." What was the most useful way to spend it? Half of the all-English committee charged with this decision favored English-language instruction. The other half, the "Orientalists," favored Arabic or Sanskrit. With breathtaking confidence, Thomas Babington Macaulay, who knew neither, declared that "a single shelf of a good European library was worth the whole native literature of India and Arabia." He declared that the English must now begin to educate Indians by means of the English language, which "stands preeminent even among the languages of the West."

> All [English] parties seem to be agreed on one point, that the dialects commonly spoken by the natives of this part of India [i.e. Bengal] contain neither literary nor scientific information, and are, moreover, so poor and rude that, until they are enriched from some other quarter, it will not be possible to translate any other valuable work into them. It seems to be admitted on all sides that the intellectual improvement of those classes of the people who have the means of pursuing higher studies can at present be effected only by means of some language not vernacular among them.

He became even more comprehensive. The literature then extant in English "was worth more than all the literature which three hundred years ago was extant in all the languages of the world together." He wanted "a class who may be interpreters between us and the millions whom we govern; a class of persons, Indian in blood and color, but English in taste, in opinions, in morals, and in intellect." That manufactured Indian elite would be "fit vehicles for conveying knowledge to the great mass of the population." He was supremely persuasive. English became the medium of instruction and an English-model classical and literary curriculum—as prescribed for the education of English gentlemen—was required for government-approved schools and colleges throughout India.[4]

There was a catch. Thoughtful Bengalis, quick to learn, literary minded, and after 1905, resentful of the Partition, soon realized that Shakespeare and Milton, Shelley and Thomas Paine spoke to their nationalist aspirations. Bengali imaginations easily transferred Ozymandias's stony "sneer of cold command" to those British administrators whom they found unsympathetic, and they applied Shelley's warning of the fate of empires to Britain's Indian

Empire. When Hardinge and Thompson arrived, Shelley's lesson had been well taken to Bengali hearts.

In 1910 Edward Thompson settled in quickly at the Wesleyan College at Bankura, 140 inconvenient miles northwest of Calcutta. There were lower schools, a high school, and the seven-year-old college. Edward, the most junior of the masters, supervised English literary studies in both the college and the high school. At first he was enthusiastic. He wrote that since its founding in 1903 it had outstripped "ev[ery] other Native College in Western Bengal. We stand v. high indeed with Calcutta Univ." In 1910, for the first time, it offered lower-level B.A. courses and hoped for approval to teach courses for B.A. Honours. By 1911 it would be approved in English and Sanskrit Honours for affiliation with Calcutta University: that is, allowed to set standards for other colleges in Bankura District. Edward was in charge also of English Honours. "It will mean v. hard work for me," he told his mother, "but it is worth it." He would receive Rs. 500 a month (£400 a year; European teachers in government colleges received Rs. 600 a month); with allowances, Edward received £155 a year. "I feel I shall be very happy here," he wrote.[5]

In less than a month, however, he discovered that the students worshipped extravagantly at the shrine of examination marks. Their horizon, instead of expanding, closed down on a clerkship in some government office. They seemed impervious to Edward's happy enthusiasm for the great English writers. His third-year B.A. students listened respectfully to his first lecture, on "The Ancient Mariner," "but I doubt if they were much edified. One, at the end, said they would like more 'explanation.' " Yet even with more time, how could he explain to Bengali boys, their command of the English language tenuous at best and accustomed to education by memorization, the mythologies and theologies and geographies of Coleridge's moral fable? "It is very hard," he wrote, "teaching English poetry to these boys, or anything else, for that matter."[6]

He enjoyed the work, but teaching was "full of discouragements. It seems impossible to teach them English, yet we have to believe that there is a real advantage & improvement." Personal relationships were equally puzzling. A missionary teacher must be the Christian example who leads his students to baptism. Thompson was willing, but the response was weak.

Some of the boys who seem nicest & most attractive are really the ones that will disappoint most, in every way. You never know how far you can trust these people, nor how far you understand them. They are willing to be friendly, & I believe they like me very much. But that doesn't mean that yr. influence makes any the least difference to them. And it is hard to say how far it is wise to be friendly with them, for it is certainly true that familiarity breeds contempt.

His students seemed more curious than contemptuous. The high school boys crowded at the doors of the staff room, staring "in vast groups, & gaze in simple wonder at one till the bell goes. . . . I am a show & they consider me a very rare sight indeed."[7]

He began to grasp the extent of a European teacher's power over an Indian student's life. The boys were apprehensive: how would this new man wield that power? Parents, too, anxiously assessed a teacher's ability to propel their sons into a secure niche in a government office. Edward realized that the recycling of memorized information only discouraged initiative and imaginative thinking.

> It is hard to say what to do in class. When they are doing an English text, they have native editions, packed with information, some of it misleading but most of it alright in a way. They know all you can tell them. The only thing to do is to bring home to them the spirit of the thing, which they will not grip. The whole system of this country, by which a fellow's livelihood depends upon his passing examinations, is pitiable & wrong. But it *is* the system, & we must do our best with it.

At examination time the students became literally "fevered and ill with anxiety." They refused to believe that Edward knew nothing of their standing on the examination that qualified them to take Calcutta University matriculation examinations. They thought him very strict and were "frantically afraid of me. I soothed them and advised them to chuck their worries for one evening & come to the [church] service." With mixed motives, they came in much larger numbers than usual and heard a "very fine sermon" that was "of no earthly use to the boys." If rejected for the next round of examinations they would try "to slip away to some other College with a transfer note from us, & to take the Exam from there." Bankura refused the transfers; most of the boys were poor and had to pay double fees, and the other colleges would "fleece them horribly for the favour it did them."[8]

The Viceroy soon learned that his initially optimistic view of a pacified, cooperative Bengal was overly sanguine. Two crucial measures suggested official fears of an explosive political situation. One was an act of strict control over the English-language press in India. The most recent Press Act, which included power to seize printing equipment, had been in effect since February 1910. Local government officials could seize and shut down any press that printed allegedly seditionist materials.[9]

The Seditious Meetings Act of 1907 was renewed for six months in August 1910, so that the new Viceroy might consider its continuation. Bengalis protested vehemently. Students abandoned classrooms to protest, and Edward saw the political anomalies of a missionary's position. Institutions like Bankura depended on government grants to supplement ever-insufficient

funds from home congregations. Teachers too openly interested in nationalist causes already had one foot on a slippery slope. Eventually Edward
Thompson would have to decide where he would stand.[10]

He was a second-generation Wesleyan missionary to India. His father, John
Moses Thompson, had been a Wesleyan teacher and evangelist in South India.
Son and grandson of farmers, he was born in 1854 at Scar Top, Cumberland,
and later lived near Penrith. He had no special educational advantages. His
parents were Church of England, and he was confirmed in his early teens.
For five years he was apprenticed to a drafter, an earnest Methodist, and John
Thompson began to attend the Penrith Methodist Church. Soon he began
to preach. When just over twenty, he went to the Wesleyan Theological
Institute at Richmond, Surrey. There he spent "2 happy years"; he could not
afford a third. In 1876 he was ordained and appointed to the Madras District,
and in 1878 he went to fill a temporary vacancy in Ceylon. There, in 1881,
he met a Wesleyan missionary teacher named Elizabeth Penney, from Hazel
Grove, Stockport, Manchester. They married and returned to India, first to
Negapatam, in the Madras District. The Wesleyans had two lower secondary
schools and forty-eight primary schools, with a total attendance of 2,100.[11]

In 1889 the Thompsons moved to Trichinopoly, where work had begun
in 1847 among troops of the British garrison; their first resident missionary
had arrived in 1852. The Wesleyans' mission was chronically understaffed
and underfinanced; John Moses Thompson devoted all of his considerable
energies to the good fight against the agents of darkness and delusion.[12]

In 1894, the year of his death, Wesleyan Conference minutes described
him as "an able, faithful & earnest missionary" with a "strong constitution, a
buoyant temperament, warm heart, genial manners, & asiduous devotion to
work," with mental capacities much above the average, especially in the
exposition of God's word and in administration. He was an outstanding
teacher, evangelist, and Tamil linguist.[13]

Many missionary obituaries are similar tributes to good and faithful servants. But they tell little of the frustrations and disappointments, the exhaustion and illnesses that broke those strong constitutions. Debilitating isolation
was sublimated as devotion to the everlasting validity of the Work. John
Thompson worked on in unalloyed generosity and devotion to his cause.
His coworkers admired and respected him. Nevertheless, the work was
not always congenial or even safe. Both missionaries and converts suffered
risks and indignities from antagonistic families and communities. One young
Brahmin convert was "shut up by his friends" and could not attend his
baptism. He escaped, but his brother caught him, took him home, and
kept him "a close prisoner for some weeks [and he was] frequently beaten,
& during the first five days of his confinement he had been kept without

either food or water." He escaped again, reached Negapatam, and at last was baptized. Local Brahmins held protest meetings, but nothing came of them except "angry speeches." Sometimes baptisms, and especially of Brahmins, could empty a school in protest. Therefore, the Brahmin boy's baptism at Negapatam caused dire forebodings, and "we trembled as we thought of the probable effect upon our schools. We prayed about it & left it with Him who can turn men's hearts as he will," and no children were withdrawn.[14]

Always, the missionaries felt responsible for the safety of Indians who joined them. They encouraged one another to stand firm and remember that opposition could be turned to good effect. John Thompson believed with all his heart in what might be called a doctrine of compensatory blessing. In 1885 "we met with abuse and sometimes violence. But even this turns into the furtherance of the Gospel. It attracts attention, and more are thereby brought to hear the truth." Those antagonists adopted the Wesleyans' own methods. They held rival meetings and distributed "infidel tracts"—writings of the radical polemicist and social reformer Charles Bradlaugh, translated into Tamil. This was a canny move, for mere mention of the atheist and secularist Bradlaugh, an outspoken advocate of birth control and critic of imperial expansion, only multiplied the Wesleyans' dismay.[15]

In South India the influence of the Theosophist Annie Besant supplemented Bradlaugh's allegedly evil example. Her sympathy for Indian religions, her magnetic personality, and her oratorical skills further threatened the stability of the missionaries' work. Equally distasteful was the Theosophical influence of Madame Blavatsky, "a Russian lady of rank, and Colonel Olcott, an American barrister," whose Theosophy was "characterized mainly by its hostility to Christianity and its glorification of Oriental philosophy." They had "stirred up old prejudices that were fast dying out, [and Theosophy's] teaching has a powerful fascination for Hindu minds," along with all the "wonders of falsehood." Thompson welcomed "signs of extensive defection from Theosophist ranks."[16]

In 1887 he begged the Methodist Society in London to find some generous contributor. The Wesleyans were "barely touching" the dense population around them. "Retrenchment is simply disaster, but of course that is to haunt us no more. To hold our own merely is very little better. We *must* go forward. God's hand points the way."[17]

In 1889 a more sophisticated opposition took its cue from the Society for the Propagation of the Gospel and from the premise that half-educated individuals can cause maximum disruption. A Hindu Tract Society formed "among the lowest classes of educated Hindus for the propagation of Hinduism." The Wesleyans told themselves that the new society's attempts "to stir up prejudice against our evangelistic efforts and school work" only affirmed Christianity's attraction. Nevertheless, their 1890 report noted that "increasing anti-Christian agitation is making educational work both difficult and costly." Agents of the tract society tried to break up Wesleyan gatherings. In 1891 the Wesleyans hoped that the opponents' literature "overshoots its mark and defeats its own object by its virulent and evident disruption."[18]

For John Thompson, the unkindest cut of all came from within the fellowship. Henry Simpson Lunn, ordained Methodist minister and qualified physician, arrived in the Madras District in 1887, but broken health forced him back to England in 1888. During that year Lunn, observant and articulate, circulated letters critical of Wesleyan missionary methods. "What a pitiable business this of Dr. Lunn's is!" Thompson wrote. "It seems well-nigh incredible that after spending a year in India, professedly in Mission work, he should remain so profoundly ignorant of its most elementary feature as his articles show him to be." He hoped that, like the literature of the Hindu Tract Society, Lunn's articles overreached themselves: "Out here, his misrepresentations & misstatements are doing no harm whatever, but the contrary." However, they could affect congregational support from home. His "audacity of statement, his manipulation of figures . . . will probably be seized upon as an excuse for withholding subscriptions." Thompson had to admit, however, that Lunn's criticisms were ammunition also for disaffected Indians convinced "that we preach simply because we get our living by preaching. The wretched misrepresentations of Dr Lunn which have been spread far & wide in India have given colour to this charge of 'hirelingism' for the witness against us is one of ourselves."[19]

In fact, missionaries constantly confronted charges of "hirelingism." (But a Salvation Army contingent determined to live by the poor Indian's standard was soon decimated by disease and exhaustion.) Nor was living standard the only barrier. "I cannot understand," Lunn wrote, "men who come out to this country to preach Christ, and yet are not prepared to meet an educated Hindu gentleman or native Christian . . . on terms of social equality." A "well-known missionary" (not a Wesleyan) had "silently declined to shake hands" with an Indian Christian, an outstanding public servant, the first Indian public health officer. Lunn viewed Thompson and his colleague William Findlay as gentlemen of the old school, incapable of such unworthy behavior, modest and conscientious, totally absorbed in the daily round of teaching and preaching.[20]

Lunn perceived that an isolation of their own making hampered these men of many virtues. Wesleyanism separated them from the non-Wesleyan world. Intruders like Bradlaugh, Besant, and Blavatsky sowed apprehensions that must be converted into challenge. In 1887 Lunn went to the third meeting of the Indian National Congress at Madras and quickly saw its importance for India. Thompson remained uninvolved and, it appears, uninformed.

Lunn said repeatedly that Wesleyan resources were spread too thinly. It would be wiser to close down a station than to limp along, for such attempts "must end in chaos." A closure would bring home the economic facts to Wesleyans in England. Above all, Wesleyans at home should "give up their ceaseless boasting about the magnitude of our missionary work" and stop bragging about their "'foremost place'" in Indian education: they should rather say what was *not* being done; missionaries should spend more time helping the lower castes and Untouchables. Lunn found that "the never-failing subject out here" was "the maladministration at home." As he departed for England, he reaffirmed his position as a "Friend of Missions in India": he believed in the "many earnest, hard-working, self-denying men, who are doing much to bring in the Kingdom of God on earth, and to lift degraded man nearer God and nearer Heaven."[21]

Even for John Thompson, one of the most earnest, hard-working, and self-denying, reality must break in. He doubted Lunn's sincerity, but every day he faced unavoidable facts. "Our preaching work among the heathen sometimes almost drives me to despair," he wrote in 1890. "There is so much to be done and so few to do it."[22]

All too often the burden became too heavy, however little they wished to admit it. Too much of the old Wesleyan missionary correspondence is a heartbreaking chronicle of physical symptoms ignored because of overwork, understaffing, and underfinancing; of illnesses tended too late and progressive weakening of body, if not of spirit. In January 1888 this descending spiral began to overtake John Thompson. A chill gave rise to "slight irregular pains in the back, which the doctor said would pass away as the weather grew warmer." The pains continued through February, but he never curtailed his duties. In March he suffered from "acute dyspepsia after meals," which the doctor attributed to overwork. Two days' rest seemed to set that right until, on a Sunday evening, "breathing became so difficult that I could hardly finish the service." Now the doctor called it acute pleurisy and said that Thompson had had it "for some weeks, and that it had become chronic." Fever and "congestion of the liver" followed, "& between them, the strong man was soon brought low." The doctor prescribed mustard, linseed plasters, and a sea voyage, but the patient was too weak for travel. Instead, the family spent six weeks in the hills at Coonoor, where he was "reduced almost to a skeleton, and could only just stand."[23]

Now the complexity of the family's daily life becomes clear. Three children were living: Mary Margaret, born at Negapatam in 1882; Edward, born at Hazel Grove during a home leave in 1886; and Alfred, born at Negapatam in 1887. Edith, born in 1884, lived only six months. When John Thompson was at his worst, Alfred, "a sturdy little fellow of eight months, whose health had previously never given us a moment's anxiety, suddenly began getting

fits & kept on getting them at the rate of 2 or 3 a day until a fortnight ago."
He seemed to recover, and there was always a compensatory brighter side:
"Through the dark cloud, we are out into the sunshine again, & more than
ever, our song is of mercy. . . . This sudden collapse has been a great trial to us
both. . . . Yet the time of suffering and of the subsequent enforced inactivity
has been a time of blessing, as all times would be if we would only let the
Master have his own way with us."[24]

In June 1889 he assured the London office that he was recovered—
although his chest was "not yet perfectly right," and both chest and side still
"remind me of my illness last year, though it is much less extant than before."
Now he must avoid the intense heat of Trichinopoly and cease open-air
preaching. Another chill or even a slight cold might precipitate a setback.[25]

They returned to Trichinopoly. He was no better but carried on with
pastoral duties, a theological institute, school supervision, sermons "to the
heathen 2 or 3 times a week," the general circuit work, and "a little translation
work. . . ." By April 1890 he admitted that he had "never fully recovered my
strength & vigour. . . . When once thoroughly down in this climate it seems
impossible ever to pick up again entirely without a trip home. I am seldom
altogether free from pain." The doctor cautioned restraint. In December he
was "hardly ever free from pain." He wanted to stay for twelve more years but
at last admitted that he could soldier on no longer. He asked "to be relieved
of my duties [in 1892] . . . & be permitted to return home. I have tried to
put the thought away from me but without success."[26]

Nevertheless, he struggled on. By July 1891 he was always exhausted
and in pain, "so completely worn down that there is no hope of recovery
in India, and a longer stay involves the risk of permanent disablement." He
must avoid another hot season, "& last week [doctors] pronounced a like
sentence" upon Alfred, who "has had fits literally in hundreds—three to five
a day for months together sometimes." The "fits" were certainly epilepsy, and
residual effects would be permanent. Nevertheless, two more children had
been born: Annie, called Mollie, in 1889; and Arthur in 1890.[27]

In March 1892 the Thompsons returned to Hazel Grove. The Manchester-
Stockport area had long been a stronghold of Lancashire Nonconformity,
although its state of grace seems to have been a sometime thing, with
evangelistic raids a feature of its religious life. The poor Methodists were
"most exposed because serious, and therefore worth stealing; and of all the
Methodists those of Manchester in the greatest danger, because the most
unsettled and unadvisable. . . ."[28]

Hazel Grove brought the returned Elizabeth Thompson memories of her
spiritual turning point. In 1866, as Elizabeth Penney, she had "found peace
in Hazel Grove Church," and she remembered 1873 as another landmark
year, when "revival broke out at Hazel Grove." Edward's birth there in 1886

had coincided with a tremendous jubilee to celebrate the centenary of the village's change of name from the plebeian-sounding Bullocksmithy to the more mellifluous Hazel Grove. Now Elizabeth expected the peace once found there to enfold the family in their new life.[29]

On 1 September 1892 they moved to Tranby, Colwyn Bay, on the Welsh coast, long a center of Wesleyan work among the miners of the district. There Frank Thompson was born in 1893. John Thompson served Colwyn Bay, his first and only English circuit, only briefly. The influenza epidemic of 1893 struck both parents. Elizabeth recovered, but with a weakened heart. John, debilitated by his Indian illnesses, died on 7 April 1894, two days before Edward's eighth birthday.

Among John Thompson's papers, two items stand out in poignant contrast. One is his sunny account of his first voyage to India in 1876. Utterly different is a speech that he called "Contrasts." Implicitly, he admitted that Henry Lunn was right about the unrealistic allocation of Wesleyan missionary resources. He poured out his plea in one long, heartbreaking sentence.

> In the name of God, let us try to stop this starving process, for that means the curtailment of labour that would often be promotive, and it leads to the breakdown of men & women who by years of hard work, have gained such familiarity with the language and people, as enables them to work with effect, and sends them home to English circuits to do work which others could do equally well or better, at a time when a crisis such as I believe we are sure to face with in India demands their presence there.[30]

A life invested without question ended with the realization that the investment had been mismanaged.

After his death in 1894, Elizabeth took her six small children to Southport, Manchester, to survive on a Wesleyan widow's pension and a small trust fund from the good people of Colwyn Bay; in all, about a hundred pounds a year. In 1895 they moved to Stockport. The Wesleyan environment, if comforting, did nothing to augment her income. She struggled on alone, always anxious, dreading illnesses, never certain of the next month's or even the next week's security. Faith in family solidarity and the doctrine of compensatory blessing were her armory.

The amount of mothering required in such straitened circumstances to raise six children of eleven years and under, and the dodges and devices for defending their middle-class respectability, which must not be abridged, gives anyone pause, but she had little space in which to pause. Thus meagerly equipped, she had to make their new life. Somehow, she managed.

2

DECISIONS

In 1935 Edward Thompson would publish *Intro-*
ducing the Arnisons, a narrative of growing up Wesleyan in the late Victorian and early Edwardian years. He stated emphatically that it was "*not*
autobiography, though many readers take every novel to be autobiography."
Four years later, introducing its sequel, *John Arnison,* he wrote that that first
volume

> was received as an outrage and ungracious misrepresentation; by the rest of the
> public, with a surprise that brought out the obscurity in which what used to be half
> the nation lived its life. I might have been writing of another planet! . . . Outside
> our nation there is nothing like British Nonconformity; nothing in any other
> nation can enable that nation to understand "the Nonconformist conscience"
> and outlook, which must always remain a mystery outside ourselves.[1]

Whether autobiography or fiction or both, these books represent his
effort to come to terms with that Methodist outlook and Nonconformist
conscience, sometimes as much a mystery to him as to outsiders. Cutting
himself entirely away was impossible. The Methodist imprint was forever.

Wesleyans emphasized mutual support, that in the end all might be
"saved." They earned salvation by living according to Wesley's principle that
"a Christian is so far perfect as not to commit sin" in a life of diligence and
thrift, sacrificial giving, clean living, and self-respect. Robert Moore, who
studied the Methodist community in mining villages around Durham, writes
that "respectability" was "very much a boundary-defining word." At small
"class-meetings" Wesleyans reported on their efforts to live lives worthy of
respect.[2]

John Wesley enjoined education to the fullest extent of one's resources.
Edward's education was thoroughly Wesleyan. In January 1898, aged eleven,
after the Wesleyan Higher Grade School in Stockport, he entered Kingswood
School, Lansdown, Bath. Wesley himself had founded it in 1739 at Kingswood, near Bristol, to educate colliers' children and to reclaim the colliers,
notorious for godlessness and social disruption. The Lansdown school was
its successor. Wesley designed the original curriculum. He intended its
influence to permeate the whole of the Methodist Connexion, for "the only

true holiness is social holiness." He envisaged also a supply of educated recruits to the ministry, but the original impulse came from his disapproval of other boarding schools and colleges in England and Germany. His school would impart useful and improving knowledge under the eyes of impeccably Christian masters. There were no playtimes, only constructive activity, such as supervised work in the school's garden. There were no vacations; Wesley wanted no outside contamination, even from parents—or especially from parents whose holiday indulgences could undo his good work. He was the combined board of governors, supervising bursar, and academic provost.[3]

In 1898, the constant supervision and no-vacation rules (probably as onerous for masters as for pupils) had been abandoned. The classics were taught more as literature than as grammatical study. But Edward needed more: time and encouragement to wander at will through the broad fields of English literature. However, administrators seemed not even to suspect that an adolescent boy could have such a need. He superimposed that dissatisfaction onto Kingswood's fictional counterpart, which he called "Grammand."

He was too hard on Kingswood/"Grammand." At the time, the ancient English universities were engaged in a great controversy about English literature as an academic discipline in its own right. John Gross writes, "Until the closing years of the [nineteenth] century the notion of a *critique universitaire* scarcely existed in England. . . . How do you organize the wholesale teaching of imaginative literature, without putting the bird in a cage? How do you construct a syllabus out of the heart's affections, or award marks for wit and sensitivity?" Anything so vague was "an open invitation to wander on at random, to drain the subject of intellectual content." Therefore, "teachers turn with relief to the small, hard, ascertainable fact." Edward Thompson was one of those who longed to "wander on at random." He wanted to be a poet.[4]

Some of "John Arnison's" unhappy memories were confirmed later as Edward's own. They included "a cult" of bullying, frequent floggings, rice pudding (a revolting memory for life), and lessons larded with "an intolerable deal of catechism," memorized because "the founder had prescribed it," as also "an extravagance of compulsory attendance at religious services." But his fundamental criticism was

> not its foreground of dispirited masters and ill-trained, ill-taught boys, or even its barbaric background of puritan parents. It was the dead hand stretching clammily forward, claiming to manacle and fetter after-ages while they were still living within the roses and the sunlight. The Governors of this pious foundation had never had the sense to forget its foundation (as those of our great public schools—and the Colleges of the Varsities—have long ago forgotten theirs).[5]

Perhaps, if he had not already felt confined by his mother's cherished hope that one day he would follow his father into the ministry, he would have conceded to Kingswood some of the improvements of his time there. The headmaster from 1889 to 1918 was Walter Percy Workman, who preached the Wesleyan gospel of conscientious work so successfully that in later years Oxbridge scholarship admissions from Kingswood reached a new high. But "his interests always lay rather in his teaching and the things of the mind than in the everyday life of the boys."[6]

Above all, Edward was a reader and, in this, more a son of Wesley than he could admit while at Kingswood. The tenacious influence of Wesley's own tastes in "improving" literature impeded imaginative exploration. Not until his last half-year did Edward come under the influence of a literature teacher named Frank Richards, nicknamed "Rix." Until then Edward gleaned what he could from straitjacketed English classics, denatured Shakespeare, and detached chunks of poetry inserted into grammar texts for parsing and analysis. Richards, a local preacher never ordained, assumed, without being patronizing, that if he quoted Browning he was not preaching but sharing. He was that academic treasure, a teacher who pushed pupils ahead of him so that the discoveries seemed to be all their own. Thompson, writing his Indian novels many years later, would portray his missionary Robert Alden teaching with Richards's intensity, even ferocity, of enthusiasm for literature.[7]

In 1900, Edward passed the Junior Cambridge Examinations with distinction in Religious Knowledge and English. In 1901 he took the Literary and English Prizes. He took part in Literary Association debates, where social and political discussions tended to crowd out theology. In 1901 he opposed the proposition that England was losing her supremacy: "Mr. E. J. Thompson was against the proposition, using as a chief argument the support of the colonies."[8]

Why, then, did Edward remember Kingswood unhappily? He left before he could complete the Sixth Form. He had had only a taste of the excitements of Richards's genuinely literary teaching. Soon Edward realized that if he were to fill in the gaps, he must do it alone. Eventually he discovered the Elizabethan poets. Their gaiety and ardor, their conventionalized sorrows spoke to his imagination, and he made them his models—not always to his advantage, for the influence of their sonorous archaisms stayed with him for too many years. At the time they satisfied some of an emotional need whose nature he had not yet analyzed.

In July 1902 his name disappeared from Kingswood class lists. His mother, desperate, decided that he must go to work. She had moved their home nearer London and hoped for better employment opportunities for her children. As soon as possible they must begin to earn, for her damaged heart was an ever-present reminder of mortality, and it was plain that Alfred could never be self-sufficient. She settled at 4 Hurst Road, Walthamstow, near Epping Forest, where the young William Morris in his miniature suit of armor had played at medieval legendry. There, for ten years, she maintained her family's center.

Edward became a very lowly clerk in the Bethnal Green branch of the London and Midland Bank. His duties were of the dreariest, and hours were punishingly long. His coworkers cared nothing for reading or for literary discussion. Theater and music halls, their favorite amusements, were proscribed for a Wesleyan. His supervisor's reports were favorable, but after five years he made only eighty pounds a year. He wrote poems on archaic models and corresponded with Richards but had no literary mentor close by. Weekly Wesleyan activities consumed his free time, and Elizabeth urged him to teach Sunday School. Exhaustion led to depression. He surrendered to the conviction, which never left him, that he had been cheated of an Oxbridge education and an early chance to become an established poet.

He unburdened himself most freely to a Kingswood friend, George Low-ther, who had stayed on for another year as editor of the *Kingswood Magazine.* Their friendship, grounded in literature and bounded by Wesleyanism, was close until Lowther's tragic death by drowning in 1913. Both were Wesleyan ministers' sons, and both families hoped to contribute one more to the Work. Lowther, too, was passionate about literature and dreamed of an opportunity out of which to coax a literary career, of what kind he had no idea. While Edward was at the bank, Lowther prepared for the Tax Surveyor's service and made desultory efforts at Oxford admission. He tried for scholarships at Balliol and at Trinity, without success but always with the hope that admission might rescue him from the Tax Surveyor and forestall commitment to the ministry. He tried and failed at Christ Church. He tried at Lincoln, Merton, Pembroke, and at Christ Church a second time, "my last shot at Oxford"—but "more or less half-heartedly some of them, it is true. . . . I do not see how a fellow can but lose all confidence in himself. . . ."[9]

George Lowther was a creature of the Wesleyan rigidities of that day. He vacillated between rebellion against and an emotional need for them. He had much common sense, with flashes of genuine wit. He had enormous capacities for loyalty and affection but was uncertain how and where to direct them. Socially, at home and at school, he felt a "total failure." He knew that he would feel "frightfully homesick for KS when I leave. I love the place far more than ever I did before." Leaving meant the beginning of immersion, "cum stagnation," in bookkeeping and laws of legal evidence. Edward assumed that Lowther intended journalism, but Dr. Workman disapproved; journalism, often sordid and demeaning, was no place for a good Methodist. Perhaps Lowther's editorial stint at Kingswood encouraged dreams of journalistic camaraderie and a platform from which to bring improving thoughts to others. His last trial at Oxford, he wrote, was "the nearest approach I ever felt on those occasions to *power,* the ability to set down worthy things, and the end of that,—it all combines to perpetuate that feeling of *impotency,* lack of that vital, inward energy & ability to *do,* a feeling which I am, though slowly, beginning to lose." Edward was not helpful. Utterly fed up with the bank, he wrote that he thought of offering himself for the ministry in 1907: *that* implied power and "ability to *do."* Lowther felt all the more adrift. He concluded that the decision accounted for Edward's cheerier letters.[10]

What Lowther really wanted was some occupation to support him and also leave free time for literary study. Dr. Workman suggested a primary school assistantship. The pay, some fifty-five pounds, would keep him for a year.[11]

In March Lowther found work in a primary school at Stanground, Peterborough. By June he had quarrelled with the head teacher and was back at home. He got on well with children but could not accommodate his ideas to those of a superior. He found another position at Raunds, Wellingborough, a boot-making town, thoroughly Methodist. But his heart was not in it. He had failed the tax examination on his first attempt and would have to repeat it in the following year. He would lay aside the bookkeeping manuals and turn to more inviting books. For the first time, he read Jane Austen and delighted in *Sense and Sensibility,* which he thought like "a beautiful old fragile vase, filled with finest spices." Now he decided that Dickens's characters were almost all "strong caricatures," "the veriest puppets and play actors," and his methods theatrical rather than dramatic. He read and reread Kipling: "Have you noted, his stories are all to the glory of the *boy*—his heroes are all boys. . . ." *Tess of the D'urbervilles* was "a wonderful tragedy," but he was distressed because Hardy's "fanatic with the paintpot" seemed a deliberate slur upon Methodism. Still, he worried because he enjoyed all too much these literary wanderings and feared that his great joy in the Unseen was heretical because it was "a partly aesthetic delight. . . . I am little of a Methodist except[,] I trust[,] in loyalty."[12]

Caught between his family's ministerial expectations and his chance for a "real continuous spiritual experience," he saw himself already backsliding. He longed to be "able with ecstasy to cry 'I believe, I believe.' " He told himself that the "real business of life" is to be found in "study and in effort to discover and hand on some notion of truth." He plodded on with history and envied Edward's brother Frank, now at Kingswood, studying "with the help of (more or less) efficient tutors, making his plans, with all his heart in his future work. . . ."[13]

There were physical reasons for Lowther's depression. He had a thyroid condition and a goiter so large that for many weeks he could not wear a collar; his doctor did not know what to do. When Edward kept on about his own "mainly bitter" memories of Kingswood, Lowther was annoyed. He had had "a far worse time" but remembered it in a "sunny and refreshing" way. "Moreover you *cannot* escape Kingswood. . . . Your prejudices long cherished control you, man; try to take a more outside view."[14]

Lowther's well-meant advice touched Edward on the raw and caused him in reply "so unmercifully to use the lash." He accused Lowther of an indeterminate sense of duty. Lowther fired back an accusation of "morbid introspection due to bad health . . . and uncongenial work." Did Edward think that he was the only unhappy man, that he continued "harping on your evils at KS! Well it is totally absurd & I hope before long you may begin to see it." Prejudice had twisted the "comparatively innocent" life at Kingswood.[15]

In October 1906 Edward decided that in 1907 he would enter the Richmond Theological College and train for the ministry. Tactlessly, he suggested that Lowther do the same. But Lowther was adamant. He retorted that the idea was nonsense: "I have often feared that circumstances (e.g. 3 bros. & a pater ministers) might force me against my settled conviction, but you are the first person to suggest it. I tell you if I do, I shall have missed my nook in life, and you speak on totally insufficient ground and quite off the point." Edward's last letter had concentrated on religious matters; Lowther's were all about "books and trifles, and I believe the difference in our bent is something like that."[16]

In fact, when they lectured each other about careers and ideals, they were justifying escapes: Lowther from the ministry to the civil service, and Edward from the bank to the ministry. Release explained his cheerier letters. He dismissed Lowther's contradictory opinion, that he valued academic initials too highly, for they did not "necessarily imply any distinction whatever." In September 1907 Edward left the bank forever and entered at Richmond.[17]

Elizabeth's diary entry for 2 September 1907 cites the Gospel of St. John 3:16, in which God gave to the world his only begotten Son, that "the world through him might be saved." She too gave up a son to the Work. Edward would follow not only in his father's but in those divine footsteps. She saw nothing blasphemous in the parallel. Her relation with the Savior was as close and as personal as that with her son. Uppermost in Edward's mind, however, was the fact of deliverance from the bank, which had seemed like an iron band around a growing tree. For the present, he had resolved the conflict between poetry and piety. "A considerable change has come over me of late," he wrote to Lowther in June 1908, "esp. through reading Milton. I now *mean* to be a poet. But there is no hurry—& no more short poems for me, pretty lyrics & the like, never more!"[18]

Richmond examinations in August 1908 revealed deficiency in composition, "simply because I have no vocab. & we don't do composition at college, & if we ever do any 'on our own' it is terribly hard to get it corrected." For years he would regret this handicap, which was not only a Methodist omission but a result of the assumption that composition in Latin and Greek was more important: classical ease and elegance would transfer themselves to English by some mysterious, unspecified process. "I have been depressed for months," he told Lowther. "My poetical failure is an almost negligible factor in causing this." This "failure" was *The Knight Mystic,* a pamphlet of poems published in 1907, with sonnets on the ideal knight. In euphoric moments Edward saw it as the announcement of a significant new talent, but few critics saw it at all. To him, therefore, the failure was theirs.[19]

Indeed he had other causes for concern. His mother had a constant pain in her side. Alfred was sweet-natured and affectionate but sometimes flew into unpredictable rages. He had a talent for gardening but could offer little toward family finances. Still, Elizabeth found some compensatory blessings: "He is a good lad,—&, taken as a whole, his life is not an unhappy one. He might have been blind, or a cripple, or worse still, very wicked, & I often think we have much to be thankful for that he loves his home & good things." She felt fairly secure about her daughters. Margaret was training to be a teacher and Mollie was training to be a nurse. Arthur was a clerk but wanted to be a naturalist. Frank had a keen ear for music, but he was not a scholar; another year of Kingswood's Caesar and Xenophon seemed pointless. In November 1908, not yet sixteen, he went to work at J. M. Dent's printing plant at Letchworth. As domestic support for Frank, Elizabeth moved the family headquarters to 22 Green Lane, Letchworth.[20]

Edward himself was unwell and could not get rid of "my rotten ailment," apparently hemorrhoids or fistulas long untreated. He was hard pressed for time, and his mother sometimes begged for his company when he could not leave Richmond. He felt worse when she "made the best of my disappointment, & got my quiet cup of tea." His accumulated worries revived. He brooded about *The Knight Mystic* and resented slurs from Richmond colleagues who discovered that he wrote poems: "the misunderstanding, the looks askance from tutors and ministers, the patronage, the rude, embarrassing questions, the cheap wit. But this is nothing."[21]

But it was *not* nothing. He seconded Lowther's condemnation of all review journals as "timid, sluggish, inaccurate, conventional." At last, in April 1908, a generous reviewer in the *London Quarterly Review* wrote that he showed promise "above the average of first efforts" and had an ear for the music of poetic meters. The poet would improve with maturity.[22]

He was painfully naive about the market for poetry. He assumed that a poet's sincerity must shine through his work and certify its quality. There was no one to bid him hold his hand until he had solved the imperfections that sincerity could not excuse. Nor was there yet anyone to point out that he wrote prose more easily and naturally than he wrote verse. He won a prize for an essay, "The Mass: Its Origin and Nature," for *Sunday at Home,* a Religious Tract Society publication. He considered it "execrable" and was galled because a cautious editor omitted what Edward considered the one good thing in it, "a smack at English misgovernment in Ireland." He put it out of his mind.[23]

His mother fretted more about his relations with God than about those with publishers and editors. Only Edward's love tempered the persistence of her urgings and loving admonitions. She prayed for him; he must pray for himself; his soul would be "calm & peaceful." Yet his soul was anything but calm and peaceful. The nearer the end of his course, the more he worried about the genuineness of his Call. He avoided hurting her with his doubts. He was disillusioned about his fellow students; Lowther submitted that the ignorance of theological students was "often appalling (my own is sad enough), their views narrow and their critical assumptions as confident and superior as they are ridiculous."[24]

Both young men needed more sophisticated guidance. Lowther instinctively understood his problems but did not know how to deal with them. He feared that he was a "pesso-optimist." At a peak he glowed with "effervescent joy," as when the Tax Board notified him that he had finally passed. Then he was in a panic because he feared (not unreasonably) that his poor health would summarily disqualify him. Even the threat of a setback caused him to collapse into self-hatred. His troubles, even his bad health, came of his having "no real faith. I am not '*being* saved.' " His parents were concerned but did not know how to help him. His father seemed annoyed about George's enlarged heart and an elevated pulse rate: the consequences of "self-centredness and so on." George must rid himself of that unpleasant shortcoming if he expected to be among the "saved." He longed for something or someone to lean upon. What he really meant was that he longed for someone to love and to love him. At least, he had employment. In June 1908 the Tax Office accepted him, and by July he was in its Newcastle headquarters. He now faced three years of dogged study toward the qualifying examination.[25]

Edward knew that Lowther's troubles were very real: "I understand more than you think: [the poem] Eros astray was written in my heart's blood, but not till the fight was over. I suffered agonies, spread over months, many months; & I remember, nay, cannot forget [the?] one evening when I stayed alone in my room all night, on my knees. It cost me all I had of reserve power & more, to act as I did. Yet, if expressed in words, the cause of my trouble was ridiculously unworthy, & the action I took was ridiculously simple; but who can gauge by such things as these?" Who caused such anguish remained unidentified for a decade, but he abandoned diary writing. He withdrew *The Knight Mystic* from circulation.[26]

He decided to leave Richmond after two years and to request assignment to a home circuit. From a regular income he could send his mother a little;

she sometimes confessed that she had had "nothing left until your cheque came as a gift from Heaven and set me going again." She could manage: "I am getting used to being 'hard up.' . . ." Arthur and Frank must now help. "God will help us through, we must still trust Him." When Edward proposed extension B.A. courses from the University of London, she replied that she would manage somehow: "So dear, worry no more, all is well; and all you have to do is to be useful & happy." But he did not feel useful, and he was not really happy.[27]

If a divine surrogate stood by her, it was the Wesleyan presence. Wesleyan activities gave shape to her life. Wesleyan kindnesses, often designed to reassure her about Alfred, sustained her. A farmer, "a good Wesleyan," tried him as garden helper. Another, "a great Wesleyan," promised "to keep an eye on Alfred." She tried to make time for "improving reading" and knew that she should read Shakespeare, but he presented difficulties. "Perhaps I don't appreciate Shakespeare," she wrote. "I very seldom read him, & when I do I never read far without coming to something that offends." The Brontës' sad lives depressed her. She could not feel that *Wuthering Heights* did her good, "so I got out Tennyson, & found 'The Idylls of the King' delightful reading." The *Idylls'* chivalric content must have masked passages that would certainly have offended her.[28]

In 1907, Lowther's contagious enthusiasm introduced Edward to the work of James Smetham, born in 1821, Victorian painter, draftsman, essayist, poet, and Wesleyan associate of the Pre-Raphaelites. For Lowther, and to a lesser extent for Edward, Smetham became a Wesleyan icon. He was pious, he wrote poems, he was underappreciated. Rigidly, literally, he followed Wesley's prescriptions for spiritual health: introspection, moral self-diagnosis, and absolute avoidance of self-promotion. He shrank from the hurly-burly of the artist-promoting, art-dealing marketplace. But, to make a living, he had to make himself known. He received much kindness from Rossetti and his circle, but his unresolved tensions eventually broke body, mind, and spirit.[29]

Susan P. Casteras traces Smetham's fundamental contradictions. He chafed at Methodist restrictions on his career. His family, and he himself, blamed his misfortunes partly on Methodism. He needed desperately to be loved but persuaded himself that he was unworthy of anyone's love, especially God's. When cheerful, he enjoyed art society but felt ground as between millstones: "Am I to be gradually crushed and ruined by critics, utter neglect, or collision with Methodism?" The typical Wesleyan could not afford his pictures, and the general public did not like what he exhibited at the Royal Academy. In 1877 he gave up. Overdosage of prescribed drugs increased depression. Until his death in 1889 he remained withdrawn from the outer world.[30]

None of this figures in Edward Thompson's "James Smetham's Essays," published in 1911 in the *London Quarterly Review.* He admired Smetham's style for absences of "strain, the hectic flush, the uncouth striving after effect." However, enthusiasm led him to overload his estimate by calling the essays "the greatest undiscovered country in recent prose." Nor did he avoid the hectic flush: "How noble and winning the style is!" he exclaimed. "How splendid are the dicta on the great exponents of his own art!" "How leisurely and discursive he is!" In fact, Edward's subject was not the art, but Smetham the Wesleyan.[31]

Like Smetham, Lowther measured his every act and thought against the possibility of being "saved." Salvation, John Wesley had said, was "a present thing, a blessing which through the free mercy of God ye are now in possession of. . . . 'Ye *have been* saved.' " Why, then, did Lowther not *feel* saved? He urged Smetham's religious priorities upon Edward as solution to the poetry-piety conflict. "Is there not a more or less vague notion that *art* is somehow incompatible with piety?" he wrote. He envisioned himself and Edward as a literary power in the land. "We would devote ourselves to the little known, neglected writers, we would have sparkling paragraphs; we would satirize conceited authors, we would blow reputation bubbles, we would stand up for new poets. . . . But it is all dreaming. . . ." He would be a conventional person and take refuge in his scattershot reading program. When he finally passed the tax examination, he was perversely disappointed at success: the die had been cast.[32]

He had no experience of office work and was "hopelessly at sea in the intricate business of tax-surveying"; human nature often vexed and disappointed him. He worried about the humble people, utterly ignorant of the law, who brought tax problems. An elderly butcher laboriously climbed the stairs to their fourth-floor office and "submitted to his papers being meddled with, in the childlike passiveness of confessed ignorance. . . . How wanton it seemed to drag the poor old man from his forgotten nook in the village to puzzle him with Law. What a scene for George Eliot!" Such petitioners often received scant sympathy. Other clerks, no more exalted than Lowther, seemed to enjoy striking a "pose as bounders," which was probably only inflation for their self-esteem. Some citizens swore at the clerks, some threatened revenge. The gospel of materialism suffused the atmosphere: "business, money, position, and again position, money, *business* are dinned into one's ears from morning till night." Lowther worried about errors but found some of the supervisor's mistakes more serious than his own.[33]

He ventured warily, conscience on edge, into the secular world. Friends persuaded him to go to the Newcastle Pavilion, "first time in my life to anything nearer like the then Egyptian Hall [in London]—that only once." The Royal Opera Covent Garden could not have been more ravishing to his inexperienced view. "I suppose I shall never forget my first glimpse of the stage," he told Edward. Naïveté mingled with genuine insights. "It was illuminated with uncanny brilliance, whilst the audience were in comparative twilight, and two girls, with shining gilt dresses, covered with glass ornaments, were exercising remarkable skill in manipulating a zylo-zello-Something or other; the result was striking but—not music. That dazzle is really the primary element throughout." His conscience justified the evening on the ground that there was "nothing really nasty, nothing at all nasty indeed, directly. . . ." There was indirect nastiness. He recoiled from "coon" songs "sung by a person in a tawdry, glittering dress," and a parody of a Negro preacher singing with a hiccup in the middle of a "Hallelujah." Lowther's companions loved it, but he saw beyond the dazzle when "some fragments of very badly played lowclass melodrama were made to look more unhealthy by it than otherwise they would have been, and one felt unaccountably uncomfortable till they were done." It was all standard music-hall stuff, tasteless, banal, and not "improving."[34]

But he discovered theater. When his companions decided to go to *Iolanthe,* he told himself circuitously, "I am not sure that I shall not." He went, "and enjoyed myself more wholeheartedly than for many a day. . . . I take no shame in the confession." He saw *The Taming of the Shrew.* No apologies needed, for it was Shakespeare. He thought Shaw a "jack in the box" but saw *Candida,* "a play of temperament," and decided that Marchmain's high ideals were "tainted with the snobbery which thinks scrubbing brushes and onions coarse . . . lacking moral stamina and staying power." He doubted Shaw's stamina as playwright, but on the whole *Candida* was "on the side of the angels."[35]

He ventured even farther afield. He went alone ("a bold thing for me") to a "Political Conversatione" at the Assembly Rooms. Without apologies to his conscience, he wrote, "I wish I could dance!" He became "partly used to the bare shoulders—of the *younger* ladies," but the bareness detracted from their general appearance. He dared mention none of this when he spent a Sunday with his supervisor, "a taciturn, religious man, a Plymouth Brother, having few interests save Taxes who will in time be Chief Inspector, & is of strong, dominant character." But he had a charming, lively wife, and Lowther was deeply touched when the Brother's little boy showed him affection. They played with building blocks, although the father—since it was Sunday—permitted only ecclesiastical buildings: Lowther suggested the Tower of Babel as certifiably biblical. Children were the essence of purity and sunny innocence. Easy exchanges with adults were difficult: "I hate to be habitually alone—to see everyone with friends about them and have none; to be able to vent my talk upon no-one, by reason of which it turns sour, by being kept in."[36]

He needed friends, but he would not meet those bare-shouldered younger ladies. He thought about marriage—but to whom? His loneliness was like "a cold hand at one's heart. I long for a near friend, one physically near I mean. I am very weak & very dependent on the people I love. Would God were more real to me. Pray for me." A letter from a Civil Servant Prayer Union cheered him a little; it was for young men like himself, uprooted from country towns, sheltering in pinched bed-sitters, hoping for scraps of luck and some advancement. He went to a Wesleyan class meeting, "Methodist to the core." The evening was not comforting. He returned to his tax books. He ate and slept irregularly, and his health deteriorated.[37]

Like Edward's at the bank, Lowther's office colleagues read nothing of value. He was greatly awed when he heard that one of them had served Thomas Hardy. It was a staggering incongruity: "the Shakespeare of our day" in the sordid surroundings of a *tax office*. Another clerk added insult to injury when he boasted that he had advised Adeline Sargent, the melodramatically moralistic popular novelist, and said that he saw no difference between her and Hardy. The senior tax surveyor, strict but sincere and sometimes even lovable, was "ever on the scent for what is 'interestin.' " Sometimes "his Philistinism is repulsive." Lowther mentioned Swinburne, and the surveyor said that he did not care for " 'minor poets; they are plentiful enough.' " Lowther was learning; he did not argue but said merely that Swinburne was probably much greater than Tennyson—and changed the subject. He knew nothing of Gissing or Wells, so many of whose characters shared his lonely plight. A Kingswood master had made him suspicious of all American writers. He was indifferent to the daily papers. In July 1909 he purchased his first copy of the *Times Literary Supplement,* only because it contained a review of John Davidson's last poems and an appreciation of Wesley. His interest in Davidson was not for his being, as he is now described, "the first of the moderns," but for his Evangelical background.[38]

A letter from Edward, incomplete and undated, was probably written in 1909 or 1910. "Myself, I am in a fix at present," he wrote. "I often wish I were not in the ministry; & yet was called of God. And I don't know whether to offer for foreign w[or]k or not." What he did not say was that he did not know how much of the call was from God and how much from his mother's loving wish. Her letters of the Richmond years seem serenely confident. Edward's future is Edward's choice: "I have thought of you a good deal this week, O Edward! I do so long for you to be as holy & useful as God can make you, and if my prayers can help you (& I am sure they can) I will pray for you night and day that God's purpose may be fulfilled in your life." In March 1910 she framed her vision in the form most difficult to reject: Edward would honor her by carrying on where she and his father had had to leave off: "I should esteem it an honour if the way opened for you to go to Ceylon or Burmah, for 'many waters' have not quenched my love for Foreign Missions, neither have the floods drowned it." A week later, she continued: "I wonder where your lot will be cast until Conference [and ordination], & where after. God will guide you. Isn't it wonderful how He has cared for us the last sixteen years? He has led us by a right way." Then, at last, she said it: "I am tired of being hard up."[39]

Edward knew how close to the edge they had lived and how great was his debt to her for pulling them through. Lowther's mother died, and in her life and Elizabeth's Edward saw the domestic tragedies of such women. He wrote to Lowther, "Yr. mother's history & my own mother's history forces upon me again the tragedy of most women's lives; they are lives of dull, patient, infinitely patient drudgery, lives which are stunted and starved. Men can easily become selfish, & take all & give nothing."[40]

Perhaps trying to delay, he said again that he "felt the necessity" of taking a home circuit. She swept that aside. There was no such " 'necessity,' & if you feel that duty calls you to the Foreign Field, then obey. If it is only on my account you are hesitating, you need hesitate no longer. . . . Read Sam[uel] I 27, & 28 and you will understand how I feel about the matter." That is Hannah's song of thanksgiving for the longed-for child who "as long as he liveth he shall be lent to the Lord." A week later, the die was cast. Edward would live and work in India for seven years. "I feel sure you have done right in offering 'Foreign,' " Elizabeth wrote. "You will find your sphere, & scope for your gifts on the Foreign Field. My prayer for you continually is that God would bless you, & guide you, & and make you a blessing."[41]

3

APPRENTICESHIP

Edward would be ordained in October 1910. Meanwhile he was put to good use in England. The assignments revealed new and sometimes disturbing implications of the new career.

In January 1910 he went to Stonehouse, Gloucestershire, to substitute during the illness of the Reverend Thomas Ivens, who had had a stroke that left him generally enfeebled. Stonehouse was two and a half miles west of Stroud, where the valley of the River Frome opens out into the Severn Vale. Since the sixteenth century the cloth industry had been the chief employer, but that had declined in the early nineteenth century. New industries moved in, and some of the large houses of the old cloth families were put to other uses. One of these became the nucleus of Wycliffe College, a public school for boys founded in 1882. On ground given by the college, the Wesleyans built an iron chapel, dubbed the "tin tabernacle." But it was too cold in winter and oppressively hot in summer, and also too small when Wycliffe pupils attended.

Edward was responsible for four other congregations in conditions of more or less vigor, several considerably less, but all had long histories associated with the cloth-making industry. In 1833 Wesleyans had flourished at Eastington, four miles west of Stroud. In 1910, however, Edward found them in an "extensive row over the organist's refusal to play at a recent funeral. I have spent the week stroking down the offending and offended parties. I'm afraid the trouble is not yet settled." Wesleyans at Stanley (or King's Stanley) cherished a fierce quarrel of obscure origins and thirty years' standing. Downend, thirty miles from Stroud, was "a miserable village tucked away in a crevice of the Cotswolds, an awful hole to get at, & the [Wesleyan] cause has gone to bits. The only local [preacher] is very ill, they have no organist, the members are going, everything is in a bad way. The Sunday school consists of 3 children, who don't always attend all at once. The one or two remaining members have got a fit of the blues, & no wonder." When Edward went there "& slithered about the hillside," he found "only about half the folk." He understood that the fourth chapel, at Wheatenhurst, or Whitminster, "is in a very bad way indeed."[1]

He had the sad sense of a countryside whose ancient and honorable traditions slowly disintegrated. Once-secure nooks for Nonconformity had lost spirit and courage. How could even an experienced minister breathe life into congregations so discouraged and so scattered? He discovered a basic principle of Wesleyan economics: payment would be irregular. He was responsible for his own expenses, he told his mother. "So I can send you nothing for a month, but I will then, *without fail.* . . ."[2]

He arrived during the run-up to the first 1910 general election. "Beer and bribery have been winning the elections . . . & everyone is aware of the fact." A Tory win was "unthinkable. But we do want an enormous Radical majority, that the people may at last have a chance." His liberal bent, already signaled in his "smack at English misgovernment in Ireland," now found a highly visible grassroots example of political and commercial misbehavior. The Stroud brewers sent "half-drunk men to every Stonehouse meeting, & our streets are filled with roughs." Weeknight congregations were "ridiculous, five being a huge attendance."[3]

Edward lived with the Ivens family, who were very concerned for his comfort, but he felt himself a burden at a time of family anxiety. However, he soon found that the Ivens's son Jack, whom he was asked, or had undertaken, to tutor for the intermediate school exams, threatened to become a burden on him. Edward had no separate place for his books. Jack borrowed them, "and they are all over the place." In other respects, too, Edward found the experience rather thin. "Also, I am not getting to know the people. They fight shy of me, & I never see them except at meetings; & I know hardly any of their names." Except for the Wycliffe College boys, "there is hardly any congregation." But their teachers said that the boys "listen as never before"— and not only because Edward played football with them.[4]

A Mr. Smith at Eastington, who became Edward's one close friend, said that they "had heard no such preaching at Eastington for years." Edward was not reassured. He told Lowther what he could not tell his mother, that every morning with the Ivenses he had to conduct "solemn & elaborate prayers; . . . & it is sheer hypocrisy on my part." He felt that he had lost all faith. What good were inspiring sermons if listeners concentrated on ancient quarrels?[5]

Pangs of loneliness mingled with frustrations over Jack Ivens's fragmentary literary equipment. "On Friday," Edward told Lowther, "I had a bad time. You see, I am frightfully lonely, & all day long that truculent Philistine Jack Ivens sits opposite me." *Lycidas* and *Adonais* fell flat. Moloch and Muscovy had to be explained, and "the most ethereal passages have to be paraphrased." Jack was "a good lad, a v. good lad." He asked peripheral questions, about John Donne, for instance. Invariably Edward "glowed at once, & despite previous experiences, quoted examples of Donne's unsurpassable magic"— to which Jack would reply that he did not see *why* that was so great and what did it *mean?* Edward was dismayed, however, when Jack thought *The*

Scarlet Pimpernel superior to Donne. "Enough, enough! . . . I'm a fool to argue with him."

Some of Jack's inadequate teaching had been at Kingswood. Edward thought him worth an indirect effort at retrieval. Therefore he visited Kingswood and saw Dr. Workman, who was greatly grieved because Jack had left the school:

> I said I was afraid Jack was not very fond of K.S. "Why not?" said the Head. "Well," said I, "a good many old boys are not." "But why?" asked he. I suggested that the mark-system was irksome; he pressed for information. I said I was not inclined to criticise; but he said, "these outside criticisms will help us, & I want them." I made a few general remarks. He said, "Well, I've heard these things said before, but no one has ever put it as clearly & frankly as yourself." He seemed troubled.

Apparently Edward had gone on an impulse to record criticisms, not of Jack Ivens but of the school's cultivation of English literature. Library books lying higgledy-piggledy laid their own mute charge, and a Kingswood master "lamented to me the extraordinary lack of conscience K.S. boys have with regard to books."[6]

He had lunch with Richards. "My word," Edward told Lowther, "he lives in a comfortless barn, chill & dreary (& of course bare). . . . I must say that it is a *long* time since I was as much at my ease as I was with this courteous scholarly old gentleman."[7]

The Stonehouse Wesleyan ministers disapproved of a minister who wrote and actually published poems of a personal nature and challenged him on this across the tea table, which Edward thought grossly inappropriate. He preferred the poor farmers, whose "native shrewdness and sorrow makes them wise indeed. But it is that wretched 'middle class' to which we are supposed to belong." He admired the District Superintendent, but the rest were "all so complacent, so smug in their intellectual completeness. I tell you I had an attack of nausea. I have often thought of late that I should go mad listening to the inept folly I have to answer. . . . I never felt so heartily in agreement with Matt. Arnold before as lately."[8]

Writing and publishing poems was not his only demerit. Edward now discovered that he worried Mr. Ivens, who feared that Edward had too little to do: "I am not evangelical enough for him. He worries me to death, pottering round & insisting that I now write to this local [preacher] & now go & see this old lady." Mr. Ivens's anxieties were those of an older man who had suddenly to leave his flock to a barely fledged shepherd, but his hoverings and the required morning prayers placed Edward "a thousand times on the verge of a swear, wh. wd. shock him unspeakably." He felt "madly rebellious" and also began to feel that he had "lost all faith & have become a lifeless fraud; at the beginning of this week I thought I should go *mad.*"[9]

However, he had new hope for Jack's literary education, for the lessons went a little more smoothly, and Edward experienced "a private 'glow' all on my lonesome" when he thought Jack had found an original point of criticism amid the standard summaries. There was "some repayment in helping a fellow who is becoming keen. . . . Well, I *must* escape from J. sometimes (& of course I cd. write no verse in his presence); but if I go downstairs there is the Rev. Tom. Now, I worry him, curious that!" Why, for instance, was Edward not "excitedly buzzing round, writing unnecessary p[ost cards], examining [Methodist] class books (whose contents I am *perfectly* familiar with), etc. It seems to him wicked to look over a book for more than 15 consecutive minutes. So he will come restlessly forward & (gently but firmly) place some p.c.s before me & insist on my writing instanter to some unnecessary fool of a local preacher." If Mr. Ivens went out, Edward was "(literally) in apprehension all the time. And when thy servant heareth slippered feet outside the door, thy servant sayeth a word wh. he hath had to drop for general use but still keepeth for secret. . . . Yet the Rev. Tom is a splendid fellow, & I admire him immensely. But—" Mr. Ivens thirsted, Edward wrote, "like a drunkard for conversions—& yet *more* conversions. I have loyally done my best & the last week or two has been crammed with encouragement, yet he badgers me & renders my life sometimes like a petty nightmare because I won't do my work in his way."[10]

It was a clash of generations. Mr. Ivens could no more cease what he saw as his duty than Edward could resist feeling beleaguered. If he closed his door in order to write, Mr. Ivens would comment that Edward had had "a good morning's study." When Edward was absent-minded at dinner, the family assumed that "I was continuing my studies." He felt that he would give almost anything to get away. He discharged his ministerial duties with care but mistrusted evidence of his successes.[11]

While he labored over his sermons, he fretted because "I have often found how v. hard it is to write correct English in serious efforts. It is our vile journalism has corrupted the springs of language. . . . Thus, for me sermon-writing is both practice & a snare."[12]

Some parish routines caused pain of a different kind. He had to conduct a Juvenile Missionary Meeting for children with a reputation for obstreper-ousness: it was so difficult to interest them in foreign missions. But that dwindled to pettiness beside his need to find the right words of comfort for the family of "a girl who is dying of consumption. I felt terribly sorry for the mother, there was such a look of terror in her eyes. They all know she is dying, yet dare not face the fact." At his first funeral, for a three-year-old girl who had died of diphtheria, "I felt myself an inadequate bungler as I prayed over the tiny coffin. I noticed with a kind of shock the (apparently) ghoulish interest the little children take; our first knowledge of the funeral's approach was the sudden rush of small girls within the gate; hardly was the service within the church over when there was a stampede round the sidegate to the grave. . . ." It was like the rush to keep ahead of a parade, and it left Edward feeling flat and dispirited.[13]

He had never had to submit to administrative tedium, and the regular ministerial meetings seemed unbearably pointless. "You will see," he told Lowther, "with what relief I fly to simple folk who are genuine, to shrewd workingmen & to little children."[14]

In mid-May he went to Sawtry, near Peterborough. "I am out of the frying pan and into the fire," he told Lowther. But he was generally indifferent: "As you know, I may be leaving England soon." Sawtry Methodists had little sense of denominational solidarity, and at first their outlook seemed cramped and peevish. At a public meeting a member of the audience "spoke feelingly about the excessive education of children nowadays. He complained that the worst thing—& he looked ready to cry—was when boys 'answered you back.' 'Ay, it's 'ard, cruel 'ard, that,' shouted the chairman." The complainant insisted that children were " 'that larnt' nowadays that they even pulled up local preachers if they said 'anythink contrairy.' 'Aye, they dooes that,' corroborated the chairman. His bellows seemed to have much conviction behind them. Also, members of the audience frequently held a chaffing colloquy with the speakers, & with the chairman (sometimes with him when a 'speech' was in full blast.)" There was "great good-fellowship," but where amid this fusillade of received opinions was even the tiniest opportunity to defend education as enlightenment and enlargement of mind?[15]

He struggled to come to terms with the fact of death. "For my life, I cannot see where all this facile chatter about 'smiling as if asleep' comes in. It is nothing like sleep. I always catch my breath, for I am looking ahead & I see what must happen. . . . I fear I am afraid." In short, he needed the presence of a friend and begged Lowther to come on Sunday next.[16]

His salary still came erratically. He got no living allowance, and there was little effort to make him comfortable. Life with the Ivenses had had its irritations, but they had been wonderfully kind and concerned. Sawtry folk seemed so miserly with words of appreciation that Edward decided that he was "not the man for Sawtry." He gave way to the encumbering Wesleyan conviction: failure to progress meant, not that there was still much to be learned, but that his faith was deficient. If faith were whole, would not God provide ability to learn and succeed? Edward feared that he was not a true and deserving Christian "if I go down so repeatedly before trifles, & I dread failure further on where it will be serious."[17]

Lowther had found a book that spoke to him and Edward about such mysteries of the spirit. This was William Canton's *In Memory of W. V.,* a memoir as elegy for Winifred Vita, his much-loved daughter who died in

1901 at the age of eleven, the unadorned portrait of a child perceptive and companionable beyond her years. Its simplicity appealed to Edward, who had a gift for bringing to life, in language that children understood, the great writers and their works. "Of course you like *In Memory of W. V.*," he told Lowther. "Is it not an immortal book?" He asked Canton to autograph his copy, and Canton, replying, told him that he wrote it because so many families lost children to diseases still not understood, "and so little has been said by those who have felt it that one might have thought it would have carried comfort of a kind to many more than it has reached."[18]

Canton, the son of a colonial civil servant, knew bereavement. He was born in 1845 on the Chinese island of Chusan, and when William was nine, his father died in Jamaica. The son was educated principally in France. He grew up Roman Catholic, but later turned to the Church of England. After a period of loneliness and isolation from old friends, he settled in London as a teacher and journalist. In 1874 he married, and the only daughter of that marriage, whom he memorialized in a book called *The Invisible Playmate,* died in 1877, and his wife died in 1880. Winifred Vita, of the *Memory* book, was the child of a second marriage and was born in 1890. Another daughter, Phyllis, would die in 1913. After Winifred's death he began the multivolume history of the British and Foreign Bible Society. When he emerged in 1910 from that enormous assignment, he was outside the literary mainstream and had no heart for trying to emulate the new writers. He turned to commissioned work and stories for children.[19]

Edward and Canton first met on 13 May 1910 at the Cantons' home at Berkamsted. Edward's first impression was of "an uncouth man in cycling breeks, v. garrulous . . . with a shock of white hair." They plunged at once into literary discussion. Edward now understood Canton's motive in writing for and about children. *In Memory of W. V.* was his answer to the sugary stuff that journalist "Uncles" dished up in newspaper and magazine columns.[20]

Canton struck a note that he would return to often in later years when he asked Edward to persuade any foreign missionaries he knew to "send him good copy, & especially photographs." Edward said that their best material was usually in letters. "'That's just it,'" Canton cried, "'if they would only send a letter.'" Canton was to become the correspondent, mentor, and father-figure Edward had needed for so long.[21]

Edward now knew that he would teach English literature in the Wesleyan College at Bankura, Bengal. In a burst of love and uninformed optimism he proposed that he would make a home there for his mother and Alfred. Elizabeth put him off gently: "Thank you my son for the loving thought, we cannot tell, it may be so. Time brings many changes, and if God spares my life, it may be His will that I keep a home in England to which my children may turn when they are weary."[22]

Lowther made himself Edward's agent. He tried without success to approach Macmillan with Edward's Elizabethanized play, *The Enchanted Lady: A Comedy.* This *jeu d'esprit,* part verse and part prose, written at Richmond, borrows cheerfully from fairy-tale folklore and the more lighthearted English Renaissance drama. It combines a Bohemian setting, a Polish king, a Sleeping Beauty named Irene who is sentenced to a one-hundred-year sleep, a Prince Charming named Conrad, a Norwegian court singer attached to a Prince of Muscovy, the Pope, Titania, and Puck as *deus ex machina*—and a poetic spoof of Yeats's "The Lake Isle of Innisfree." The playwright's imagination had had a fine time, but the reader soon goes astray among plot and plotlets. It is the work of an enthusiastic young man on a literary fling. Edward returned to theology and left *The Enchanted Lady* in a drawer. There Lowther found it. He took it to the firm of George Bell, who was not enthusiastic. The next day, however, Bell offered to "publish" it, which meant "print" with subvention from Lowther and Edward. It appeared in 1910.[23]

Canton, an uncompromising truth teller, said that it was undeniably an accomplishment, but "the possibilities of future achievement which it foreshadowed" were more important. Edward had the poetic temperament but not yet "the 'touch,' " and "what you need now, is a good subject," the result of life's joys and sorrows, and of much more writing. It will come in useful one way or other."[24]

As if he had only awaited the right confidant, Edward poured out to Canton his memories of two crucial and related incidents. In 1903 he had written two acts of *The Enchanted Lady* in bursts of "simply sheer exuberance." Then a revulsion had set in against work that seemed so unimproving, and "in 1904 I had a 'wrestling Jacob' experience, which lasted over many months. It was spiritual *agony:* & in ways I cannot explain the conviction came to me that I must give up verse-writing." An older friend, probably the missionary J. S. M. Hooper, urged him to do no such thing, for the eye " 'was given you to see with, not to cast away.' " Edward denied the metaphorical eye. "But I definitely foreswore verse, though I inconsistently enough kept my Mss., which were many; for a long time I believe I really wrote nothing, &—let me put it simply—I met God. But in spite of myself I used to write verse occasionally (always with a gnawing & uneasy conscience—the feeling still lingers) & Mss. accumulated." *The Knight Mystic* came from that period of prohibition and uncertainty. The completed *Lady,* after her brief bow to the reading public, retired to the wings with her well-meant borrowings from *A Midsummer Night's Dream,* the Sleeping Beauty legend, spurious Bohemian history and geography, and *Arcadia.* Canton understood: "And I too," he wrote, "have been in Arcadia."[25]

Cautiously, he approached the subject of Edward's assignment. He wrote, "So you too are going out. Take a fountain-pen and don't wait till habit and use kills the colour and the strangeness before you put down your impressions. And don't *jot* them down; write them out in full—you can't recapture the first fine careless rapture." This advice, to be repeated many times, Edward would resist by omission, while much of the color and strangeness went into his letters. "I am sorry,—" Canton wrote, "on my soul—that you are going abroad in September; but if the Voice calls go, and God bless you. One can only die once whether in India or England; and in a very true sense the chances of life are as good there as here." He offered cogent literary advice.

> Shall I give you ("all for love and nothing for reward") the best bit of literary advice man can give (though you may have got it already or may have discovered for yourself)? Never "try to write an essay," never try to acquire "a style." . . . When you want to do the best thing you can in the best way you can do it, take your pen in your hand and write a letter (imaginary or otherwise) to your dearest friend. All the graces and felicities of speech, thought and feeling are available in a letter.[26]

Edward feared that the bantering tone of his letters, which often camouflaged great seriousness, might seem disrespectful. Canton told him to write anything he pleased and as he pleased, and "there is no reason for you to worry your good soul about it." He responded with his own banter but left no doubt when he was serious.[27]

Now Edward's letters contained more narrative and discussion and less of the belligerent introspection of his letters to Lowther. Canton and Sawtry made Edward more tolerant. His sense of humor revived, and delight in humanity's foibles, as in his account of the upstanding self-respect and Methodist rectitude of the Sawtry farmer who had improved the plow and was summoned to Windsor for congratulation.

> "How ever did you manage to be so clever, Mr. Smith?" asked Prince Albert. Whereupon our Methodist worthy—he tells the tale throughout—said to himself "Now you're brought before Kings & counsellors, George Smith, & you've a-got to testify, & here's yr. chance." So he told how he had "seed things warn't right with the plough no how," & he prayed & the Lord gave him the idea. "For," he summed up, "I can't do nothing without His help." Tears filled the Queen's eyes, & she replied, "No more can't none of us, Mr. Smith." Which is as good as the question of the little girl in the grammars: "Is them sheeps yourn?"[28]

Edward found himself unexpectedly comfortable among the most unpretentious and humble of the Sawtry parish. After all, he *was* the man for Sawtry—at least, at that stage of his career. He could not have spent a lifetime there, but if at the time he was good for Sawtry, Sawtry was good for him. He belonged to the striving middle class, but now he could respect those without pretensions to higher culture and to value them above those whose snobbery made them suspect the integrity of persons who wrote and published poems. Sawtry knew nothing of that side of him, and he prayed most fervently that his cultural aspirations were genuine. When the assignment ended, he was sorry to be going. "I like these country folk immensely," he wrote to Canton, "and wd. like to get to know them & their children. But they are awfully exacting as to visiting. . . . And I am shy & busy & they are very many. The kiddies are most friendly; they always are with a parson." But by no means did all parsons have that gift.[29]

Sawtry people brought him close to the roots of Wesleyan Methodism. Their religion was limited and literal, but they stood by it and expected that it would stand by them. They were not unaware of the world beyond Sawtry—for, witness, George Smith had been to Windsor—but did not yet hanker after city sophistications.

Canton had put Edward in touch with William G. Collingwood, artist, antiquarian, Lake Country historian, and friend, biographer, and secretary of Ruskin. Canton recommended Collingwood's *Dutch Agnes,* a work of historical fiction set in Coniston and Cumbria, because he wanted Edward to know those antiquarian writings grounded in historical scholarship. *Dutch Agnes* "will illustrate what I said about your opportunities of observing a little world which seems to me almost unique, and which awaits its chronicler." Edward wrote to Collingwood, who replied that he hoped that the sun would shine for Edward Thompson "in the hinterland of Bengal."[30]

Canton arranged for Edward to meet Smetham's widow, Sarah. Lowther had sent her an early version of Edward's article on Smetham's essays. When he and Lowther called, with Canton, on 19 October, she said that Edward's theme was very good but bore "the impress of being written for a particular public," as it was—which explains why Canton asked the next day, "Why *did* you look so subdued?"[31]

Edward had still another mentor. In June 1909, while preparing for his London University B.A. examinations, he had spent three weeks in Southwark with W. G. Rushbrooke, headmaster of St. Olave's Grammar School. Methodism must have been instrumental, for Rushbrooke's family were deeply religious Suffolk Wesleyans, and he knew Frank Richards. They corresponded about metrics and metaphors. Rushbrooke wrote candid line-by-line analyses of Edward's poems. "I can't quite realise weaknesses that nearly kill," he wrote of one, "then flee before the soul, then shrivel & fall into combat." For many years Edward sent his work, and Rushbrooke replied in his meticulous fashion.[32]

Frederick Joshua Fielden, a Kingswood contemporary of Edward and Lowther, came closer to both as Edward's departure drew nearer. Fielden followed the path that Lowther so ardently desired for himself: admission to a university college, an M.A. degree, and a peaceful academic life. He had offered to help with subvention for *The Enchanted Lady:* "I have not said this before, though it has often occurred to me, because I know that you have a just contempt for those so-called friends of yours who neglected you during your years at the bank & have since been very officious in their patronage." Fielden was certain that even as a missionary, Edward could not refrain from writing poetry, "but please remember that it will not reach us unless you publish."[33]

Canton recognized Edward's tendency for uncritical literary enthusiasms, as in his praise of Smetham. He and Collingwood wrote separately about the importance of detached judgments; understanding Smetham's faults took nothing away from affection for the man. Smetham, Collingwood suggested, was "one of our poets who had not quite learnt his job: if he had got more of the technique of his art, no doubt he would have been a great man; as he is a most interesting one." Canton was more forthright: "You are all wrong about Smetham! While you were in swaddling bands I blew the ramshorn on his account, but none came to the Jubilee. I admire him, I like him—but *the greatest* master of English prose? You will see, in time, . . . that there be many masters of that same, and each better than the other, according to your mood."[34]

Edward took no offense. He visited the Cantons and preached at Berkamsted, after which the mail carrier stopped Canton in the road to say that he hoped Edward would preach there again, which would be " 'another great and glorious Sunday.' " Canton recognized Edward's skill as preacher but worried about his ability to balance work and emotions. "You are fortunate in going to the work of your choice—few so fortunate, and I, for my part, never."[35]

Canton persisted about Edward's prose, but Edward remained unconvinced: "Prose I *cannot* write; it isn't natural to me, it costs me immense fag, & is worth little when done. If I have any gift at all, it is solely in verse." Lack of tutelage in composition had frightened him. Should not really excellent prose flow as easily as the poet's verse that (supposedly) poured out through divine inspiration? His formal prose did not flow easily; therefore it was not for him. He did not realize that excellence shines forth in a well-written sermon. At the same time, in letters he poured out substantial, witty, and effortless prose. "Many things I can do with immense labour," Edward wrote, "& sometimes passably well, but only in verse am I at home. You will think this nonsense."[36]

Canton was not having this. He fired back: "What's all this nonsense about not writing prose?"

I do think you *have* a distinct gift for verse, but these letters of yours (which somehow! do not find their way into the waste-paper basket) are an ample refutation of your notion that you can't write prose. What kind of prose do you want to write? Surely not this elaborate unnatural fantastic stuff which is called a "style." I told you ages ago when you were young (and *not* biddable) that the letter-writing style is the best of all styles. It can be polished of course; and can be as full of colour and music as man could wish, without being affected. And it starts with the presupposition of truth and sincerity.[37]

Edward was to depart on 21 November. He seems to have set out in a relatively uninformed state; he had had no instruction in Bengali language or history, and he knew little about the educational system of which he was soon to be a part. A missionary conference at Cambridge was not helpful. He thought it "fantastic . . . some hours of unprofitable wind." The first speaker he thought "a solemn ass, about 30, I shd. judge, from Ceylon. He took himself v. seriously & considered no point adequately discussed until he had given his experience. The last time he rose, Walters [Richmond friend] & I behaved v. badly, bursting into an ecstatic roar; he seemed to suspect the reason & looked hurt." The chairman followed every speaker in a "heavy, latinised, rotund fashion. . . . Good stuff, but v. like suet-pudding." After twenty minutes, the speaker would add, " 'So far, brethren, I have said nothing' (pause here) 'about the main aspects of the problem now presented to us.' Then the stream bursts its temporary dam, & rolls on again, a thick volume of healthy, fertilizing, useful mud."[38]

On 3 October Edward was ordained in London. On 4 October he received his theology degree, then returned briefly to Richmond, which now seemed "the most homelike place I know. (I suppose just as we have to leave it, this old Earth will have come to feel like home.)" He then went to a meeting at the Methodist Mission House in London, very different from the Cambridge conference. A missionary from South India named Monahan "spoke as movingly as ever I heard man speak, breaking down at the end. It is not these ranting Evangelicals who are keenest on foreign Missions today, but men who are scholars & sane, men like Monahan & Hooper."[39]

The "native question" arose, and it so impressed Edward as to suggest how seldom he had heard such sentiments:

A man from S. Africa, Briscoe, spoke the bravest words I ever heard on the native problem. Was there any danger of the rising of the blacks in Africa, he was asked. He spoke carefully, as a man who weighed his words. "Not now, but in twenty years, yes. That is, for the whole of Africa. If you are speaking of S. Africa, I say yes, & that almost immediately." He gave reasons, sober & convincing ones. Monahan rose, keen & restless, with face clear-cut & eyes that somehow seem to be always looking past the things here visible. "Then do you sympathise with the national aspirations of the Natives," he asked. (Monahan was by many thought a Conservative.) "I do" came the answer, firm & low. "Regardless of the consequences to Europeans, nations or individuals!" "Regardless of the consequences." "Hear! Hear!" shouted Monahan—not alone in this. "Though mind you," added Briscoe, "I shdn't say this everywhere." I felt proud, for I knew my colleagues.[40]

This, from the young man who believed himself incapable of writing fine and fluid prose.

Finally Edward and Canton had some serious private discussion about missionaries. Canton asked whether the mistake of "these good men out in Bankura is that they 'live alone'?" Did their compounds isolate them from the mainstream of Indian life, a subtle cause of mental and physical depression? Edward must see that this did not happen to him. Canton repeated even more passionately his admonition that Edward must make the most of this experience and give a new view of India.

> What books you might—must write. . . . Here and there a missionary has given us glimpses of Indian life, but after all there is only Kipling and Flora A. Steel (a Steele?) who seem to have done anything measurable. And I *don't know* when one who has explored to any extent the folk poetry of any part of India—at any rate in the way you ought to do it, of course there are glimpses, and the French and Germans have translated this and that but who has carried on the tradition of Sir William Jones?

Sawtry, Canton pointed out, had let Edward touch "the *life* of the people," and this was a priceless preparation for India. He had "the magnetism and the gift of speech to *see* and be heard." He must also listen. The daily routine must not preempt the Indian life that "will be pressing in on you at all times and you have the energy to seize it before it escapes into the commonplace. . . ." If he failed it would be his own fault.[41]

Elizabeth's experience of India was now two decades old. Bengal was unknown territory, and she knew nothing of the political and cultural changes that already pointed toward India's independence in 1947. Edward's childhood memories of South India were principally idyllic pictures of palm trees fringing beaches that were perfect playgrounds for a small boy. No one helped him with his first great dilemma: how to square those memories with the realities of Bengal.

The day of departure was almost upon him. Rushbrooke was frankly sorry he was going. Canton wrote, "I suppose you were 'sent to me,' at a moment of which I have said nothing to you—a moment of serious crisis when I needed some one. 'Pippa' is always 'passing' in this life of ours, though it seldom happens that *she* knows anything about it. . . . I expect great things for you and from you."[42]

After a few days at home Edward sailed on 21 November. Three days later, Elizabeth wrote,

I don't think I ever knew how much I loved you until I saw the train bearing you away on Monday afternoon. Bearing you away from my care, but not from my love, & if I can no longer darn your socks &c I can help you in other ways. You were very brave, indeed I think we both were brave as we smiled each other "good-bye." . . . I am not worrying at all about you, I feel it an honour to have a son a missionary & I will do all in my power to help you by praying for you, & being happy at home.[43]

4

BANKURA

He reached Bankura on 21 December 1910. He slept little on the long train journey from Madras. At first the countryside wore no human aspect: "I watched the gray Indian country flit past like a kind of huge, impalpable wolf." He could see little, but the landscape "seemed v. bare." The 140 miles from Calcutta to Bankura took six hours, and there were only two trains a day. At 4:30 A.M. John Mitchell, Principal of the college, flashed a lantern at the window, the signal that Edward had arrived. He was taken aback to find that "the only coolies at Bankura are girls, who are like ants. They are wretched creatures, & keep up a chatter all the time." Mitchell and Edward stayed up to see the Indian dawn.[1]

The Bankura compound was "magnificent," a mile around, a government subsidy "for which we pay not one pice of rent." He found "a heap of useless letters," and one writer seemed to expect that Mr. Thompson would not last long, for it was addressed to "The Revd. etc. *or Successor, if arrived."* The college boys hung about trying to get a glimpse of him. His first impression of Bankura protocol was that "everyone is 'devilish' 'umble out here. You show yr. beastly head, & some solemn boy, hitherto unseen, salaams profoundly. You give him a haughty nod back, if affably inclined, if not, you take no notice." He felt welcomed less for himself than as a means to an end: an addition to the staff "raises the College Status and thereby adds to [everyone else's] importance."[2]

His mother had followed his progress companionably, consulting the daily shipping news and comparing it with her first voyage to India and Ceylon. She was pleased that missionaries of various denominations on board were friendly: "It is as it ought to be." She begged for details of Bankura. Did he have rooms in the main "Mission House"? Had he mosquito curtains? Were there hills or a river? Yes, there was a river, but the scenery was "on the whole tame and monotonous." The 1908 *Bengal District Gazetteer* describes the three district towns as "unprogressive, of little importance and on the whole distinctly rural in character." Bankura town, the principal civil station in the westernmost part of the Burdwan Division of western Bengal, sat in a low alluvial tract, green with paddy fields in the growing season but bleak and brown in the dry weather. To the west, the land rose to jungly rough country—not the lush jungle that Elizabeth pictured, but tracts of rock, thorny scrub, and groves of sal trees, the home of an occasional leopard or tiger and, occasionally, panthers and a bear. Edward assured her that he did not fight off wild beasts every time he stepped outdoors. The land itself was relatively thinly populated "by races or castes of a less advanced type, and into whose culture the aboriginal or semi-Hinduized element strongly enters."[3]

Elizabeth asked about non-Indian society. Were there Europeans other than the missionaries? Were there the usual district officers? What about the mission families? His letters were cheerful, and she felt sure that he was happy. His reply, however, made her think that "Bankura doesn't seem to be a very nice place, not nearly as nice as Ceylon, but the work seems to be very interesting."[4]

The Bankura District Mission began in 1870 with a school of varying fortunes. In 1889 it added a high school for English-language instruction, and by 1899 it had Calcutta University's all-important recognition and government grants. In 1903 the new college had hostels for Christian and for Hindu boys, separate in order to save Christian boys from spiritual backsliding and also from Hindu boys' persecution. It was also urgent to deliver both from temptation, for some women of dubious character had established themselves close by; not even applications to the local magistrate dislodged them.

Bankura's 1910 report announced that "the coming of Mr. Thompson gave great joy to the staff. He has already given evidence that he is not only a scholar, but an enthusiastic worker among the students." He fulfilled a "long-cherished hope" by starting a college magazine. He began at once with English literature classes in both high school and college and quickly discovered that creative scholarship was irrelevant. Examination marks were everything. When he arrived, college boys were preparing for the First Examination in Arts, which determined candidacy two years later for tests for Calcutta University's B.A. admission. The number allowed to continue was the crucial academic statistic. "We promote every boy who has the smallest claim to promotion, & only the quite exceptionally hopeless are left down." Nevertheless, "the disappointed all come in deputation" to beg Mitchell for promotion. "They bring their relatives, their guardians, their friends, to plead for them. They have the most pathetic yarns." They claimed that failure meant expulsion from home. One boy followed the college principal "half-way to Bombay, pleading for promotion." If worst came to worst, "Failed B.A." on the record proved that he had at least seen the inside of an English-language institution—a ranking with social value in Indian society, but a standing joke among Anglo-Indians. Nor was it altogether untrue that expulsion from home could follow failure, for it disgraced the entire family. "At Hindu Schools, of course, they bribe the Professors," Edward explained. "They cannot do this with us."[5]

Explicating "The Rime of the Ancient Mariner" was his initiation. Finally he thought that he "had made the thing fairly clear to them. If I have, it is a great & blessed triumph, as English poetry is a most deep mystery to the mind of the Babu." If Indians love myth, why, then, should they find Coleridge's moral myth impenetrable? Difficulties of the compulsory Scripture class surpassed even those of the Mariner. There Edward met an organized protest. They did not understand, the boys said, and one added that " 'Hindus are born philosophers!' Of course the truth is they are always anxious to get out of Scripture." The truth was that this was an inept but canny defense of indigenous culture. For Hindus, born to their own philosophy, others were superfluous. Only if Scripture lessons took effect would parents consider removing the boy to a vernacular school.[6]

John Broomfield, describing the Bengali *bhadralok*—Bengal's aspiring "respectable people"—says that "education itself became the hallmark of bhadralok status. Not every individual who considered himself a bhadralok could obtain an education. Not every bhadralok family could afford the education it desired for all its sons. But the idea was generally accepted: an education, preferably in the English language, leading to a university college in Calcutta and white-collar employment."[7]

Producing Macaulay's "class of persons, Indian in blood and colour, but English in taste, in opinions, in morals, and in intellect" was expensive. Letting missionary institutions carry part of the burden relieved government funds. Two months after Macaulay's Education Minute of 1835, money for study and publication of Oriental works was transferred to English-language instruction. Thus began the long struggle of students who never heard English at home to disprove Macaulay's argument that "no native of this country can possibly attain more than a mere smattering of English."[8]

The major universities, at Calcutta, Bombay, and Madras, were neither instructional nor residential; they set examinations and awarded degrees. The University of Calcutta opened in 1858 and became a vast bureaucracy to control Bengal's higher-education apparatus by setting uniform standards through affiliation, a certification that allowed a local college to set the standard for others in its area.[9]

Calcutta University's influence filtered into remote daily lives. Edward found an instance of this, neither unusual nor exaggerated, at the homeliest domestic level. "I had a chat with Mrs. Bannerji yestereve ab[ou]t her koka [boy]. This unhappy kid she compels to the most unremitting labour," he told Canton. " . . . Whenever it strikes her maternal heart that it is time to wallop her koka again, she goes over to him & wades into him. At one time, it is said, she used to stand over him with a cane till midnight." Edward asked her, "purely for information," if the boy's Bengali was good. "She took alarm at once, & understood me to be complaining of it. She said she wd. thrash him. I explained. Then she besought me to keep an eye (& cane) on her koka, to 'show him fear' (isn't that an expressive idiom? Or you might translate it, to 'make him see fear'), to shashon kora (discipline) him, to shasti dia (give punishment), & she waved her right arm with vicious illustrativeness. 'I also,' she said, with simple maternal pride, 'am always thrashing him.'" The Lord's people, she told Edward, must be thrashed constantly, and they must pray constantly, and "'I beat him when he does not.'"[10]

Behind Mrs. Bannerji's dubious discipline was the great fear that if her *koka* did poorly he would join the throngs of educated unemployed kicking their heels in government anterooms, or loafing in Calcutta's coffeehouses. Almost worse was being a university graduate who got only a post considered unworthy of an English-language education. In a very short short story, "The Postmaster," Rabindranath Tagore captured all this in the character of a Calcutta University graduate rejected for work in a Calcutta government office. He gets an appointment as postmaster in an up-country jungle village. He feels stranded and disgraced: stranded because he pines for Calcutta's sophistications, disgraced because his examination marks could not get him anything better.[11]

Pupils who qualified for university-level examinations flocked to the cities to study, which meant memorizing notes and summaries, alone or in one of the crammer establishments that sprang up like mushrooms. For many it was their first experience of a city. Most were from middle- and lower-middle-class families who strained their resources to the limit and beyond so that their sons could afford even Calcutta's privately run student hostels, many scandalously squalid and inadequate. Harcourt Butler, Education Member of the Viceroy's Council, was greatly worried about the health of both students and system. Education had been starved of money, he told Lord Hardinge, for "it will be on a light diet even after a big grant. . . . Our attitude of scolding, hitherto, has not been very reasonable. We cannot have anything decent without paying for it, & we have not paid." The University of Calcutta would have to take responsibility for hostels. The situation was a "scandal to the capital of the Empire. . . . And political no less than educational considerations would justify a large expenditure on this important object. . . ." It was political because discontent flourished amid these hard-pressed, overstressed, and often underfed young men. In a wrenching short story, "Rashmani's Son," Rabindranath Tagore captured the psychological and physical damage to both students and parents. A simple rural couple place all their resources and hopes in their beloved only son whose university degree will redeem the family's future. Not political agitation but illness destroys him, from overwork, exhaustion, and deprivation.[12]

As the clerical employment market became glutted, more English-educated Indians wanted to study in England. Being *bilat-phirot* (England-returned) boosted prestige even higher. Lord Crewe, the Secretary of State for India, wished to discourage this influx without political embarrassment. He feared the sudden exposure of young men, away from the conservatism of their families, to a host of new influences. He advised the King that this situation was both "embarrassing and troublesome," but they must not "announce to the youth of India in so many words that we do not desire them to come here for education."[13]

There was a philosophical division within Bengal's intellectual elite. Both factions agreed that India's troubles had begun with massive foreign conquests that introduced foreign cultures: the Moguls and then the English. Ethnic revivalists insisted that modern Bengal "must recapture the genius of the golden age of classical Brahminism," when a "strong and able elite" were mentors to Hindu society. The modernizers insisted that India must not "shut her windows upon the outer world." And then there was a third group that hoped to combine the best of the old with the best of Western culture. But what constituted the best of each?[14]

This philosophical debate was utterly remote from Bankura parents who, like Mrs. Bannerji, simply wanted the material benefits of an English-language education for their sons. They must bear the theological and familial risks of required Scripture study and instructors bent on conversion.

At first, Edward did not worry about cultural guidelines. His mother worried about his happiness. He worried about her health. "No, Mother wd. not be well," he wrote to Lowther. "She never is. It is only overwork & worry, a disastrous struggle long-continued. I shudder ev[ery] day as I think of her getting up in yr. dark February ~~days~~ mornings & her scanty sleep at night. That is why I can never save a penny till our days of depression are past (if ever)." He had "chafed and been depressed" about his poems because they brought in no money. He had found that he was less self-sufficient than he had thought: "So it is with all of us; this is the heritage of all them that fear Him!" Lowther would have to continue as his agent.[15]

His annual salary was £125. Payment was still uncertain. Was the Bankura Mission or the Missionary Society his employer? His mother wrote that she knew "only too well the tiresome way the missionaries are paid, all the years we were in India I never knew how we stood financially." Unwisely bypassing the Bengal Methodist District chairman, G. W. Olver, he wrote to William Findlay, his parents' old friend from South India days, now Missionary Society Secretary in London. Edward's salary came from the college budget. John Mitchell was not happy. The college needed every penny for a new hostel.[16]

Edward's worry was justified. The optimism that had inspired addition of the college in 1903 coincided with an all-time peak of £180,000 in the Missionary Society's annual income, but almost at once there was a precipitous drop of some £37,000. Did no one recall Henry Lunn's advice about accomplishing more by doing less? John Thompson's plea for practical compassion had carried no farther than his small audience at Colwyn Bay. Mission-station correspondence remained an unending record of human casualty: thinly veiled discouragement, exhaustion, breakdowns, and premature deaths.

Maintenance requirements were pressing. White ants devoured a building at the mission for the Santals, hill people classified as aborigines. Another was contaminated and condemned; four women had died there after childbirth. The Methodist circuit needed a *pukka* (brick-built) cookhouse to replace "a mud hut begrimed with the smoke of decades . . . it is a disgrace to us, and if a lady comes here next year I am quite sure that she will very strongly object to it." "Desperate characters" threatened to burn down a village Indian catechist's mud-and-straw hut. "We ask this man to live amongst these people and he does it gladly, but I question if we are justified to ask him to expose the lives of his family to this danger that with a little expenditure we might abolish." He too needed a pukka house—yet such expenditure meant deprivations elsewhere.[17]

Government requirements pressed hard. An Englishman was required for teaching English. A second Englishman to teach high school English was "an absolute minimum requirement." New rules demanded still more specialist teachers for economics, philosophy, and mathematics. Wesleyan policy required that all teachers, English and Indian, should be Christians, but qualified Indian Christians "of the right calibre are extremely rare, & they are snapped up immediately by the larger Christian Colleges in Calcutta." Indians should have salary equity with Englishmen, but in comparison with an Englishman, an Indian's usefulness "would be almost zero." Where were the "hosts of volunteers" reported in Europe?[18]

Bengal's chronically inflammatory politics unsettled everyone. The Swadeshi (literally, "own-country") movement urged boycotts and bonfires of European products, particularly Manchester cloth, which put Indian weavers out of work. The Government of India underestimated the strength and aftereffects of the Bengalis' long protest against the Partition of 1905: the Motherland, *sonar bangla*—"golden Bengal"—had been insulted, assaulted, and dismembered. Foreign residents were targets of resentment. Missionaries received threatening letters.

Edward exploded a bomb of sorts at Bankura when he preached on Romans 1:21–23. Verse 22 was the detonator, on persons who preen themselves upon their knowledge of God, for, "[p]rofessing themselves to be wise, they became fools." The Hindu boys took it personally. Anonymous protests appeared on the notice board calling the English teachers "the human & white-skinned gods of the College" and urging students to boycott Sunday services. An anonymous letter told Edward that the "hearts of the

Hindu students were bruised. When I came & was so genial and friendly
they 'determined to revere me.' " But the academic deity had turned viper.
Elizabeth wondered at such a choice of text. "If I may say so, I think I would
leave such texts alone until you know the people better, & until you have
an assured influence amongst them. The great thing is to win the love &
confidence of the poor boys, & through that to win them to Christ. And
this you will do I know." The row was peacefully settled, and Edward was
blithe—too blithe—about it. That incident would return as fiction, and as
expiation, many years later.[19]

Misreadings abounded at all levels. Hardinge's correspondence reveals
contradictory patterns. Some officials reported diminished unrest, effective
pacification measures, and, except for the few seditious agitators who stirred
up the illiterate masses, "the people" as solidly loyal to the Raj. Then would
come news of a political assassination, a riot, a protest meeting, a *dacoity*
(roadside robbery, kidnapping, and/or murder) by "desperate characters"
allegedly gathering money for the nationalists. Indians' loyalty was suspect
unless proven otherwise (frequently by gifts of money for government
projects). The question hovered: whom can we trust?

Wesleyans, too, made contradictory assessments. Their 1908 annual report called it "a year of unrest in Bengal, more than in any other province of
India." However, spiritual restlessness caused this new "patriotism." Indians
must realize that "a United India is impossible while deep religious antagonisms prevail, and a self-governing India is a hopeless dream on the basis of
either Hindu or Mohammedan principles." Only Christianity offered "unity
and manhood."[20]

Bankura's 1910 report was equally contradictory. The "ultra-Swadeshi
spirit had practically died out." But in fact, Bengal was a hotbed of Swadeshi
activity. Calcutta police forbade street preaching. In one Bankura District
town, an unruly crowd of five hundred shouted the banned slogan *"bande
mataram"* ("Hail Motherland") for half an hour, disrupted a lantern-slide
service, and threatened to wreck the lantern. This, the Wesleyan report
said, was "unusual" and merely indicated "the trend of Indian thought"—
as indeed it did. Edward realized that the most innocent activity had political
ramifications. When a Bengali football team, for the first time, defeated an
English military team, a Bankura instructor remarked that the victory "could
have a political bearing."[21]

Another recent recruit, a volunteer lay missionary named Owston Smith,
had preceded Edward. He had studied history at Cambridge. His family paid
his salary, which puzzled Olver; missionaries did not often come prepaid.
Then he heard that Owston Smith's eyes were so weak that at Cambridge he
had had "to have every word read to him: and that he cannot eat ordinary food
but [was] living on bread and fruit." Olver withdrew his recommendation. If

Mitchell still wanted him, the London office must be responsible. But it was Owston Smith or no one. He arrived and "seemed a very decent sort, and not as much of a crank as had been reported." He moved into the new Christian hostel, where he was expected to exert a Christian influence. Neither eyes nor stomach seemed to give undue trouble, although he welcomed being read to. When Edward (rather pedantically) tried to "instil a little poetry" into him, Owston Smith's comments were "most provoking," and his fear of the imagination dismayed Edward. His "cynicism affects his view of everything." He was "passionately sincere, but he seems to distrust everything that approaches feeling or emotion. I shall blaze out some day." Still, Jack Ivens had turned out very well, and Owston Smith might also.[22]

The kernel of Edward's Bankura experience is not in letters to his mother, but in those to Lowther and to Canton. He regaled her with human-interest stories. A boy whose " 'nuptial has been most uncongenial' " determined to devote his life to " 'meditation & knowledge,' " and if he failed to make expenses he would cast himself on "the mercy of Mr. Thompson, an English gentleman.' " There were the antics of the college's Sanskrit pundit who taught principally by cane, whose pupils were in a permanent state of uproar and disrespect. A small boy waited to help Edward up a riverbank so that he might say "with great pride & great guttural emphasis 'Good marrnin', surr,' & then went on. He had simply wanted to show off his English. Boys—& men, too—at all times of the day will put themselves to great trouble to meet you, just to say 'Good morning, Sir'; it is the only phrase they know."[23]

Edward told himself and Lowther that all must be for the best, but he knew that he had not faced facts. He had expected to find the Wesleyan community ethos transplanted. But community at Bankura seemed thin and flawed. Personal and professional worries about money and health obsessed his English colleagues. Bengali colleagues' lives and culture were mysteries. Outside the classroom English and Indians lived parallel lives, as mutually unknowable as those that most Anglo-Indian families lived by social fiat. "My Indian colleagues have been a disappointment," Edward told Lowther. "I know it wd. be alright if in time I could but get near to their real lives, as I did at [Richmond] College. But here I shall not have the chance, as we rarely meet." Several Indian colleagues "are also clearly fighting a lonely battle with a fierce refusal to acknowledge defeat. They no longer come into the open or attempt the offensive; but still they refuse to surrender the wood. . . . They stand at bay." Edward himself stood at bay. If he mentioned this to his mother, she quoted her minister: "You know you are one of the Lord's 'peculiar' people, it takes time for you to understand people & for them to understand you but I quite expect that before long we shall have you saying . . . 'Bankura is the best place to be in, & I'm a permanency here.' "[24]

To Lowther, however, Edward wrote:

There is a great loneliness in this life. I believe all is for the best; nay, I do not let myself, even for a moment, believe any other. Yet, I often think, if I dared once to face facts, I wd. find that the habit & struggle of years has been a pathetic make-believe. I do not see, I never have seen; it is only that I have willed to see, have resolved that, despite all appearance, I will see. So life has been a forlorn bravery, or perhaps a brave cowardice. But I am playing with fire, with my naked soul near the flames. So I will say no more of this.[25]

He was weary of his own complaining: would Lowther please burn his letters of the past six years? "Of course I have been sent here especially to try me. It is the first time I have been absolutely alone." No one, including God, seemed especially interested in Edward Thompson. He saw no way out except "a return to the old, everpresent mysticism which enabled me to see God." But now his "old sense of dedication has gone, the prophetic sense, the feeling that my destiny was sure. *I can no longer feel that I see what God is driving at* (I mean, not in my case—that I don't mind—but in things in general.)" He had failed the test of faith.[26]

His literary destiny was similarly obscure. He disavowed his and Lowther's old habit of exchanging criticisms of their writings. Lowther had sometimes seemed arbitrary and sententious. Edward knew that "in the past I have often seemed to patronise you; & I am heartily sorry for it—yes, & I say it was not intended, yet none the less crude & cubbish for that."[27]

Canton pointed out "that you are letting your old Wessleyan [*sic*] friend Smetham disturb you unduly. It's perhaps natural, but it is certainly not inevitable and it is far from commendable. Do not think me unsympathetic and do not think me too dense to understand." He wrote again to say plainly that Edward was only adding to his troubles, instead of "using your opportunities for a great building up of yourself. You have a poetic gift, with which you can play David to your own Saul, and why you should not use it I don't know: in reason of course and apart from your duties and obligations." There was the new world at his door, and "how mad you will be a year or two hence that you did not use this chance. . . . You see I allow you no time for introspection. Say your prayers like an ordinary mortal and leave introspection to old age." India's new world was indeed outside his door, but self-pity and social divisions stood in the way.[28]

He had thought of a remedy: a transfer to the Negapatam District, his father's old headquarters and the scene of his early childhood. His letters to Olver are quite remarkably disingenuous and disorganized. Arguments of cause and effect jumble together. He said more about himself and Bankura than he intended when he wrote that although he had been there only seven months it would be better for all concerned if he were transferred sooner rather than later.

The truth was that he feared a further drop in Methodist subsidies; as the newest recruit he would have to leave and begin anew. Instead of saying this he argued health and an altruistic concern for Bankura's work, which did not ring quite true. His discontent was *"in no sense a question of overwork."* He was not suited "to this life of alternation between College & High School." He was in continual pain from the untreated hemorrhoids. He feared breaking down and "dislocating the College work badly." He was "very fond of the boys, despite the fact that a good many low tricks have recently disgusted me; and I think they like me, though their love is not of a deep or valuable kind." He got sporadic instruction in the vernacular and then only if he found and paid an instructor. In South India, language would be no problem. As a boy he had been fluent in Tamil. Tactlessly, he told Olver that if he were ten years older, he would not mind Bankura's shortcomings, and he rushed on to admit that, having "offered" for a lifetime of foreign service, it now seemed that his "lifework" was something else, somewhere else. Negapatam (he implied) would be friendlier, more helpful, and financially sounder than Bankura.[29]

Then he withdrew his request because of "unwillingness to leave boys whom I had learnt to love," and because some (unnamed) colleagues had exerted pressure. In October, however, he renewed his request during a visit to South India. "I came here with many memories," he told Canton. An old man recognized him as " 'the Perria Dhurri's machan' (the great Sahib's son)." Which " 'Perria Dhurri?' 'Why, Tamson Dhurry.' " John Thompson's old sweeper "threw herself on the ground & passionately kissed both my very filthy boots, & she seized my left hand and kissed it. All through the interview she wept." He understood all that she said but called in a boy to translate his English. "It was a great trouble & mystery to her that I did not talk in Tamil. Again & again, she said, 'But when the dhurry was so high he cd. talk Tamil.' Of course it never occurred to her that Tamil was a thing that *cd.* be forgotten." But Tamil began "flowing back to me," everyone showed kindness for his father's sake, and "I move as nature to the place."[30]

Inspired anew, Edward resumed his transfer request. Bad health hindered his work. He was at Bankura only because no other B.A. degree man was available at the time. Tactless again, he said that in South India he could be "a real missionary, which is what I came out to be." Then, however, he did another turnabout and began to reason himself back to Bankura. He did not want to abandon "a Brahmin boy of ability" about to be baptized. He had not known that he was soon to take charge of the high school and the new Christian hostel. Hartley concluded that Thompson was restless because he hoped for the college principalship when Mitchell left on furlough. Hartley made the inevitable comparison: "I am afraid he doesn't possess his father's spirit which made him such a successful missionary." All this thrashing about was an unacknowledged effort at escape.[31]

Daily, Bankura dealt with a host of problems. The government criticized quality and quantity of the staff and threatened to reconsider Honours affiliation. "Twill be cursed awkward for us," Edward wrote to Lowther, "after all the lectures I have given & trouble I have taken, if they refuse." The government objected that Indian staff members' degrees ranked too low. "Degrees are everything out here."[32]

The college felt besieged by the government, and Edward felt besieged by the students. Their hysterical pleas for promotion got on his nerves. "You have no idea how mighty a force an educational sahib wields," he wrote. "I tell you, it touches me v. much when boys come, pale & anxious, and plead for things. I am not hard-hearted. Yet one has to be *firrrm.*" One boy's baptism was the first "in our 10 years of existence. That means trouble; & brickbats for me as I cycle to school." No more than he could tell his mother about his vocational misgivings could he tell a Wesleyan official that the boy was "one of the biggest fools in the 2nd year," reluctantly promoted and reluctantly sent on for the next level of examinations, "if sent in at all." Was the boy sincere? "One of the most disheartening things is the way the only folk to seem inclined to become Xtians are colossal mugwumps." Overriding all other complaints was the lack of genuine collegiality. This shocked Canton. "It is amazing to me," he wrote, "that men—British men—should be like this in a foreign country, that Christian men should think that is Christ-like or seemly in any way sickened me. We shall pray next to be saved from being religious men."[33]

Olver now decided that Owston Smith was "a bruised reed"; he was spiritual and earnest, but his throat was so weak that he could not lecture a full hour and thus carried a reduced load while everyone else's increased. London wanted the impossible in "far more spiritual work. . . . Largely independent of men and of money. . . ."[34]

A great distraction was about to occur. King Edward VII had died on 6 May 1910, and the new King, with his Queen, planned a state visit and a great Durbar in December 1911, as the first reigning monarch to enter the Indian Empire. The prospect threw everyone, from the Viceroy to the youngest student at Bankura, into frenzies of preparation and speculation about the customary Durbar boon. Money for free primary education? Release of selected political prisoners? No one outside a tiny circle at the center of government knew the best-kept political secret of 1911: Lord Curzon's 1905 Partition would be annulled and East Bengal and West Bengal reunited. And— most staggering of all—the capital of British India would be moved from Calcutta to a new city to be built at Delhi.

5

DISCORDS

Edward thought the King's visit and Delhi Durbar an unnecessarily exaggerated activity. Self-congratulatory celebrations never impressed him; he thought kings and potentates were "a great bore, & illogical and silly." The Durbar meant a school holiday but "otherwise it is a great nuisance." He objected strenuously to loyalty on demand. Loyalty was an affair of the heart, spontaneous and private. "Out here, everyone *has* to be so beastly loyal. If you stay quiet for 5 minutes, Govt. comes round & says suspiciously, 'Why weren't you shouting just now?' So the magistrate is v. anxious the College shd. join officially in the great procession here. But hot & dusty marches have no charm for me. If I go at all, it will be for the sake of the tamasha [fun]."[1]

Demands for exercises in loyalty increased relentlessly. "Next week we shall be celebrating the Durbar," Edward wrote. Even passing amusement flagged as the Bengali letter *s*, pronounced "sh," leaked over into English. "All day long, Bengali boys are singing 'God *sh*ave our gracious King.' "[2]

The Durbar meant unrequited expenses for the missionaries. "I believe there is a prevalent idea in England that missionaries are overpaid," Edward wrote. "Very few, I think, realise in how many different ways we are rooked for sub[scription]s for all kinds of things. . . . The worst possible way to stimulate loyalty amongst these people is by making them waste money on fireworks & tamashas, etc. As some zealous magistrates—who are anxious for Govt. notice—do." The government gave its own schools a medal for every student, a prize of fifteen rupees for the best coronation essay, and flags for 12 December, Durbar Day. Missionary schools were "practically compelled to follow suit, & all at our own expense. . . . I must say, it amuses as well as bores me to hear unhappy boys compulsorily sawing away, hour after hour, 'May he defend our laws / And ever give no cause,' etc."[3]

For the Government of India the Durbar was a budgetary and protocol nightmare. Hardinge had barely arrived when a Calcutta delegation demanded that the Royal Durbar be held there. He had already ruled that out: "I was very courteous and friendly but firmly declined to put forward their views." The Hindu Maharaja of Kashmir made the same suggestion. Hardinge told him that Calcutta had "no traditions to create any impression." A more immediate reason was fear of nationalist disruption and Hindu-Muslim clashes.

Hardinge wanted to avoid offending the loyal Indians, "which after all is by far the largest section." He wanted no "concession to noisy clamour. . . ." He wanted to create "a feeling of the deepest gratitude . . . a symbol and seal of a policy of conciliation and liberal evolution which has formed the most glorious tradition of British rule in India."[4]

Did anyone in England really understand how expensive this would be? The Durbar area of twenty-five square miles had ten miles under canvas and 239 separate camps. Every suggestion for Durbar boons touched a financial or political nerve. A tax remission? The government could not afford it. A half million pounds for technical education? This would quiet those who claimed that "England exploits India for her own benefit and especially for that of Lancashire." Unfortunately, there was some truth to that. Army commissions for selected sons of ruling chiefs of native states? Training in England might expose them to England's least desirable influences and turn them into "quasi-Indians." Something special for the police, for nationalist protesters had given them much trouble lately? Perhaps release of selected prisoners? And there must be an Honours list.[5]

The King would be crowned Emperor of India, and a coronation required a crown. Would the state crown be conveyed from the Tower? Impossible. A new imperial crown, charged to Indian revenues, would cost £60,000. Hardinge thought this undignified: could the new crown be broken up afterward? Unthinkable. (The King decided that it should go to the Tower.) There must be official artists, photographers, escorts, guests, reporters, travel accounts, and so on and on. Labour Members of Parliament asked awkward questions and charged *all* Durbar expenses to the Government of India, "an immense disappointment" to Hardinge. And everyone knew that the former Viceroy, Lord Curzon, a master of ceremonial spectacle and still active from London in Indian affairs (intrusively so, in the view of many), compared the Durbar with his own splendid Indian observance in 1902 of the coronation of King Edward VII.[6]

There were earnest efforts to respect sensibilities. Precedence of the ruling chiefs was important. The royal dais must be prominent, so that as many as possible of the common people and ordinary spectators could see the King and the Queen, who would appear on the walls of the fort to the thousands assembled below and expecting entertainment: fireworks, massed bands, pipers. The King would drive through an assemblage of the poor to be fed there, but not while they were eating, for Indians disliked being seen at their meals. This was the King's personal treat, but his gift would feed only 90,000. There would be many times that many, but turning anyone away would have a "very bad effect." It was all generously meant but had unavoidable intimations of bread and circuses.[7]

The King wanted to shoot rhinos in Nepal, which he had missed when he came as Prince of Wales in 1905. However, Nepal's king was seriously ill, and his death just then would be extremely awkward. Shooting must not seem a primary reason for coming. Would English visitors and camera-toting Americans follow him? The Maharaja of Jaipur reminded Hardinge that the King would appear too human if photographed in hip boots shooting ducks in a pond. Would he ride an elephant or a horse at the Durbar? He did not want an elephant, but two maharajas said that "an elephant is firmly bound up in the Native mind with Imperial pomp and splendour"; a horse would be "almost derogatory" to his dignity. In the event, he went shooting in Nepal, and he rode a horse.[8]

Recent elections, under the Montagu-Chelmsford Reforms, of Indian Members to provincial Legislative Councils raised more problems of precedence. Being in the central government's camp would bestow great prestige, but those in the provincial camps might feel consigned to social outer darkness. Therefore, habitual living in European fashion was the criterion for placement in the camps. Category A included those who lived habitually in European fashion. Category B, those unused to living in European fashion, would have to make their own arrangements. Category C was for those who did not live in European fashion and could not provide for themselves. But what if an Indian lived indigenously at home but coped with European customs when entertained officially? What if an Indian who lived in European fashion brought his wife, who did not? Would English wives object to the presence of Indian ladies? If Hindu and Muslim groups did their own cooking, would the odors be not only offensive but contaminating to caste?[9]

The externality of empire set the tone. The occasion was imposed from without, with the British as producers and directors. Like stage props, ordinary Indians would be moved about, for an operatic jolly-peasant atmosphere. The ruling chiefs, too, were stage props, their gorgeous jewels and apparel enhancing the extraordinary occasion, with the King always a heroic figure at center stage. On the day, however, there was only one hitch: the Gaekwar of Baroda, a principal ruling chief, made his obeisance before the dais in an "indifferent manner" that cast him into official disgrace, required a letter of public apology, and caused the *Times* to link him handily with the "advanced"—that is, nationalist—politicians with whom he had been known to associate. Otherwise all was perfect. The heart must be stoic indeed if unmoved by the phalanxes of dignitaries, the trumpets and drums, the fluttering pennons, the guards drawn up in perfect order, the hushed crowds, the solemn pace of the coronation ceremony, and the frantic cheering. There was also a subtext: India was Britain's because Britain's king is also India's emperor.[10]

The announcement of a new capital at Delhi repeated that message, and the *Times* immediately emphasized it: Britain was in India to stay. The duration of trusteeship depended on Indians' demonstrating responsibility and self-control. When that would be, who could say? The *Spectator* stated that the King, "by announcing his coronation at the Durbar, implicitly repeated and emphasized his acceptance of the trust undertaken by all English sovereigns to govern India, not for our own profit, but for the good of India." Only fools would go to the vast trouble and expense of building a new city from the ground up without intending it to be permanent.[11]

British press commentary often included derogatory comments about Bengalis. The *Times* declared that Calcutta, originally "a refuge for traders," lost most of its practical advantages to the Suez Canal, the expanded railway system, and Bombay's commercial expansion. Calcutta was "singularly unattractive," with a terrible hot and humid climate and intractable drainage problems. Its decline began after the Mutiny of 1857, when control passed in 1858 from the East India Company to the Crown and Parliament. Even worse than climate and "the drains" was "the [political] atmosphere of Bengal." The writer added an insult: "The Bengali is not only nimble-witted, but often endowed with brilliant intellectual and, above all, rhetorical gifts. . . . He more often lacks the more solid and virile qualities which distinguish other Indian races by whom, rightly or wrongly, he is neither liked nor respected." The *Spectator* took that line: placing the capital there had "given the smooth-tongued but effeminate Bengali" too great an influence on Indian affairs.[12]

Praises for the Delhi site measured a gap in cultural comprehension. Delhi, the *Times* observed, had "exceptional dignity" for both Hindus and Muslims. The new British-built Delhi would embody the old tradition of an all-India capital. The King's speech omitted the fact that the most recent pre-British imperial tradition was Islamic, and the assumption that this would delight all Indians offended many Hindus.[13]

Except for Bengalis, the Delhi announcement overshadowed the cancellation of Partition and other boons. How, asked the *Times,* could anyone regard the changes as a "reversal of Partition"? It was an equalization. Dacca, the principal city of eastern Bengal, could now hold its own against Calcutta. (But the government was disquieted when Dacca began almost at once to hold its own by demanding a university comparable to Calcutta University.) They could not say so publicly, but many officials were glad to get away from the Bengalis.[14]

There was no definite plan, however, for governing the new Bengal or for the new Delhi. Four million pounds were promised for the move—a wildly unrealistic estimate. By 1914 the "final" but far from complete estimate was well over six million. This did not include rerouted railroads, sanitary improvements, military cantonments, additional hospitals, museums, and cultural institutes appropriate to a national capital. No one could have imagined that New Delhi would be only just completed on the eve of World War II. The new, more compact Bengal required an entirely reorganized government; it became a province with a Lieutenant-Governor-in-Council.[15]

The Modern Review, the Calcutta English-language journal, warned that Hindu-Muslim tensions remained, for "if ever the Hindu-Musalman problem be solved in India—and solved it must be if ever we are to exist as a nation—it must be solved in Bengal." There was "some insularity, some provincial narrowness, some parochialism in the Bengali character," and any others' being the same was no excuse. "Our duty is to combat this failing by every means in our power."[16]

Edward Thompson, an unenthusiastic provincial observer, wrote to his mother:

> Yesterday was Durbar day; today we see that the Partition is annulled, a v. good thing. People are pleased, yet not as pleased as I expected. The truth is, the agitation against the Partition had died down so much that the Bengalis are surprised to find that they did not care about it as much as they thought they did. Brown remarks that it will be a terrible experience for them to have nothing to grumble about. However, they will soon find a new grievance. And in any case, it is a good thing the Partition is annulled; if the Durbar had passed without it, there wd. have been a frantic outcry & the King's visit wd. have done more harm than good. The other great step, the changing of the Imperial Govt. from Calcutta to Delhi, is more doubtful. The Bengalis will not be pleased, but the rest of India will probably rather like it.[17]

There was an official assumption that in any case Partition agitation had already died out. In June 1911 Harcourt Butler had told Hardinge that it "cannot last three years" and that "there are other causes for the recent state of Bengal which will not be affected by this proposition."[18]

Edward had his own ideas about the aftermath:

> Calcutta is *tremendously* sore over the capital going to Delhi. Lord Hardinge has ruined himself for ever with the Anglo-Indian population. Of course, Calcutta is sore largely for selfish reasons, but not altogether. In any case, the soreness is v. natural. . . . [Bengalis] are bucked about the Partition Annulment. But they will be frightfully sore when they discover the loss of employment in Govt. Offices that the Delhi business will entail.[19]

Indian towns and cities held their own Durbar celebrations. Edward's low tolerance for ceremony made him react with satirical exaggeration. When the local magistrate announced that Bankura's Durbar boon was the release of "22 rascals from Bankura jail, . . . a solemn hush pervaded the assembly; it was only broken by the noisy & enthusiastic claps of Owston Smith & myself." Their colleague Ambery Smith declared Owston Smith "a *most* dangerous

Radical," in fact "a Socialist pure & simple. . . . The proof always adduced is his callous conduct when the late King died. Mitchell came to him excited, with a telegram in his hand, Owston Smith being in bed. 'The King's dead,' he bellowed. 'I'm sorry,' said Owston Smith, & went to sleep."[20]

Edward after all joined the Bankura procession: "I was one of the leading citizens. The College boys marched in procession, I leading majestically yet simply attired in v. ancient & smelly clerics. I walked with grave & stately demeanour, as became a captain of so many thousands, & one upon whom the eyes of a district were concentrated. I had some grand fun." The chief representative of the District Empire League arrived late "in a wretched third-class tikka-gharri [hackney-carriage]." Edward and Owston Smith laughed aloud. "Then came our altogether absurd Judge, a silly old Bengali, *frantically* late, & was respectfully hustled by the police right up to the front, where he didn't want to come. And even the police grinned." Edward then "decided to behave myself, even though the pleaders [barristers] round me were nasally entreating the Almighty to 'shave' the King." The "thousands" of schoolchildren joined in, but "at half-a-dozen different times, consequently one heard only a wild confused row." Then, because of the distractions, he missed a scheduled church service, "thereby setting a shocking example of disloyalty."

Priorities were all wrong. A few days earlier, Edward and Brown had visited a jungle village whose poverty made even Bankura's modest Durbar celebration appear ostentatious. Edward "went over the cultivations, sampling the stuff these folk grow. They are poor exceedingly & fare wretchedly; sour weeds, it mostly seemed to me. They have a terrible lot of consumption. In nearly every hut was a boy who lay down whilst B[rown] punched his chest & armpits. They feed 'so poorly.' Bankura is the poorest district in Bengal, red desert." Their host brought parched rice, tea, and some very "musty and ancient biscuits," as well as hot milk for the "nutun sahib"—the new sahib—"but the nutun sahib politely but firmly refused it."[21]

Nevertheless, his frame of mind was reasonably constructive. He invoked Thomas Carlyle's Gospel of Work: "If I went by what I feel & see, I shd. be most discouraged," he wrote to Lowther. "But I know I am doing my best; I know I am working harder & more unselfishly than ever in my life before—so it *must* be alright. After all, I know well I didn't come into this world to write literature, but simply to do any job that was handy, from correcting Khatas [exercise notebooks] to teaching boys to play a straight bat. I believe my attitude has become permanently changed, I don't think such fits of accidie as I used to have can ever occur again. And I regard everything as *work;* that sanctifies life."[22]

This mood, at once humble and exalted, could not last, but it carried him through the post-Durbar letdown. He became Principal of the high school and began to speak more kindly of the college students. A Sanskrit Honours student intrigued him. "He is one of the old school, a boy with a great respect for his teacher. He is like an old man, with a grave dark face; & when he meets bows almost to the ground with both hands over the top of his staff. When we parted he said, almost knocking his head against the ground: 'I must beg yr. pardon most deeply, sir, for keeping you for so long a time. I am most humbly grateful for the good truths & wise sayings you have spoken to me. And I shall thank God for them." Edward had three good English Honours students, one very good indeed, who ranked fourth in Calcutta University's examination. "He thirsts for information & asks tons of questions, as Frank wd. say. When I was jawing on Anglo-Saxon literature, he laid down his pen & said: 'Sir, I must beseech you not to leave this subject till we have mastered it.' If there is anything he does not absolutely understand, he will not let it pass until he does. He aims at being 1st in the Univer[sity entrance examination]; & really stands an excellent chance." If his students did that well, "this strange underworld of Bengali students wd. talk about it everywhere, & our reputation wd. be v. great. My [lecture] 'notes' wd. become valuable on the market." When examinations approached and the boys' anxiety increased, they came to him at night for extra tutoring. He was sure that he had not helped them, but they continued to come.[23]

Edward's English colleagues were neither helpful nor congenial. Fundamentally impulsive, excessively introspective, and also frantically busy, he did not pause to analyze their relations. However, they had definite opinions about him. Olver thought Thompson and Ambery Smith diametrically opposed in attitudes and interests. Thompson and Brown made no bones about disliking each other. Thompson could not stand Mitchell. Thompson and Owston Smith had had it out and agreed that they never would like each other and must maintain an "armed neutrality." How Olver compiled all this is unclear.[24]

Edward's relationship with Owston Smith continued to be confused and troubling. When Edward returned from his South India visit, Owston Smith told Hartley that he would never get on with Thompson, but added patronizingly that he probably had abilities and would be useful. There is no indication that Edward knew about this letter, or that either Olver or Hartley investigated or understood reasons for the antipathy. Edward would be dumbstruck when those emerged.[25]

Owston Smith supervised some ninety students in the new Christian hostel. He told Hartley that they got on splendidly, that they brought him personal and medical questions—but never those about the "highest things": spiritual matters. Those they took to Thompson. Lowther sensibly advised Edward not to brood about him, for like so many devoted and earnest people he lacked imagination, which made it difficult to be charitable toward them.[26]

The "blaze-out" that Edward had predicted came not from him but from Owston Smith. It was not overtly about poetry or even the hostel boys' preference in religious counseling. Owston Smith made a petty but violent objection to Edward's habit of including "He said" when repeating another person's opinion—an honest effort not to appropriate another's statement. This was only a thin cover for another, more serious antipathy. It boiled out in a particularly painful attack and recalled Owston Smith's wariness of the imagination during their early efforts to read poetry together. Worse yet, it recalled the attacks at Richmond and Stonehouse on Edward's presuming, as a Wesleyan minister, to write and publish poems of a personal nature. This time it was Edward's newest volume of poems, *John in Prison,* a collection both religious and personal.

The title poem is a meditation on John the Baptist's transcendent experience while Herod's prisoner. For Edward, this marked a new direction. He had abandoned " 'elves and the idle glamour of the field,' but there has come knowledge of a larger country and vision of a sterner beauty." "John in Prison" was "to some extent based upon a misreading of the situation; but it must stand as it is written." It was his "witness to certain things that are being forgotten" and also his statement on contemporary poetry, which was too often "serious without hopefulness and light of joy." If reviewers missed his point, that would be less serious than his friends' "missing the sense of an informing breath and an effort beyond my power."[27]

He gave the book to Owston Smith, perhaps hoping to explain himself and thus clear the air. But he read it differently and

launched into a most brutal & cruel attack on me generally. It surpassed even his previous efforts in bigotry. He wd. not admit the slightest fault on his side, threw things at me wh. shd. have been regarded as sacred, then, referring to "John in Prison," wh. I had lent him some weeks ago & wh. he had put back in my room the same day sans a word beyond what he said when he took the b[oo]k ("I can't imagine when you found time to write all this stuff"), said, "The curious thing is"—this with a surprise in his voice wh. he cd. not conceal "from that bk. you've apparently"—then he corrected himself, lest he shd. fall into sin of charity—"that is, it seems to me as if you have had some genuine religious experience." Did you ever hear of such a thing? When I have been living here & preaching & praying for 2 years!

Owston Smith then "went on to say, that, if the stuff was genuine, I had had a relig[iou]s experience such as he had not had." Never realizing that he bared his own misunderstanding, he asserted, " '*My* rel[igion] has always been a matter of doing what I was told I ought to do.' " He then refused "to make the slightest concession or to allow me credit for the slightest wisp of religion or goodness." Religious experience for him seemed a bald competition, so far from Edward's understanding of it that he did not know how to continue or conclude the discussion. He told Lowther, "You know how terrible my faults are. But I protest to you that, since I came out here, I have fought against them, I have done my work with humility & patience. You wd. be surprised if you knew how trifl[in]g were some of the things my judge threw at me." The Wesleyan annual reports praised Owston Smith fulsomely for not taking advantage of his being a volunteer, and this "puts him above criticism." Edward, too upset to recognize that he had paid the poems a great if negatively turned compliment, sent him a "carefully-written letter" and received a reply "far more decent than I expected," admitting "grave fault on his side, tho' tacitly avoid[in]g the concess[io]n of anything but sin on mine. Still, that is much."[28]

Still, it was not enough. The collision marked a turning point. In such misunderstandings, Edward saw the conditions of his own future. The foresight frightened him. Time was flying. The bank years were a standing deficit. He was now twenty-five years old. What had he accomplished since Kingswood? Richmond and the University of London had given him solid and respectable qualifications but had led him to this Bengal backwater that offered little companionship and less intellectual challenge. He was a little happier after Arthur Spencer, a Kingswood friend, came to Bankura. "Young Spencer is a promising addition to our staff," Ambery Smith told Hartley, "& Thompson has now settled down & is doing excellent work."[29]

Owston Smith had not settled down. He began a six-month effort to escape. A letter to Hartley contained a clutch of contradictory reasons for leaving: a missionary was no more important, after all, than a magistrate. He was thirty-five years old but could not marry on a Bankura stipend. Did the Wesleyans keep some of his money back? He had an offer of eight hundred or perhaps a thousand pounds from Calcutta University and an offer from another town. Mitchell advised him to accept one of them. Still, Owston Smith did not want to leave the college in the lurch. Hartley could not understand why he wanted to leave when he had been so valuable. He could not return if another job turned out to be temporary.

In February 1913 he accepted a Calcutta University post. In March he decided to stay at Bankura. In May he told Hartley that Edward Thompson was his greatest burden, a hindrance who should have been a help—not Thompson's fault, he added. In July Mitchell told Hartley that Owston Smith was "a man no one can understand." Mitchell blamed Edward, as Owston Smith's bête noire, for his dissatisfactions: Thompson was "an excellent fellow in many respects. He is a poet of some ability & has an exceptional knowledge of English literature & especially poetry, but he is conceited & [Owston] Smith cannot put up with his conceit, & I rather think that this is the reason why he is not so happy here as he would have been. . . . On the whole we are a very happy family, but the conceit is there. Still even he is improving & he has this merit he keeps us alive—he is *irrepressible.*"[30]

No one worried about Edward's reasons for unhappiness, or why insecurity might appear as conceit. It should have been clearer that Owston Smith was drifting and that Edward was trying with all his might not to drift. On one crucial point they agreed: they wished belatedly for professional guidance. Owston Smith told Hartley that in early years he probably would not have known what to do with it. Just a year earlier, Edward had told his mother, "Why didn't I ever manage to go to Oxford or Cambridge? I believe, if I had only known about things, it cd. have been done."[31]

His mother's anxious love oppressed him, and it increased as her long weariness bore down and drove her efforts to guide her other sons, particularly Arthur, into the Wesleyan way. When she confided this to Edward, he warned her to expect changes as they grew older. She must have more rest and "some distraction from housework." Borrowing from Canton's advice, Edward urged her to write out memories of her own experience of growing up Wesleyan, which would be "an immense rest & refreshing of yr. mind. Also, we have all long known that you tried to do too much. Of course you must trust us. It's not the slightest use worrying." Then he addressed the subject all-important to her but restrictive for her children: her overriding concern about their immortal souls, and her too-obvious contrivances for keeping them good Wesleyans, as when Arthur for the first time took the collection at a Sunday service, "a little thing," she wrote, "but if we can bind him by invisible chains to whatever is good & lovely & true, so much the better." He was cross and unhappy because the family had left rural Letchworth. City life was easier and more interesting for Frank, since Dent's plant had moved to London, and he sang in concerts of the Alexandra Palace Choral Society. Elizabeth thought she understood Arthur's unhappiness when away from the country and his naturalist pursuits, but that was how things must be. For the first time, she could pay expenses, which was impossible at Letchworth. Arthur could attend evening biology classes. He found compensations: he took up marathon running, competed seriously, won prizes, and joined the Naval Reserve.[32]

She marshalled reinforcements. Her minister, Mr. Maltby, was keen to " 'get hold of' " both Arthur and Frank for Sunday afternoon Bible classes. He had little success, although Elizabeth thought they were being "drawn gently toward the Truth." She thought Frank "a bit of a Socialist, for he has a big picture of Lloyd George on his bedroom wall." Young men's opinions at church meetings "would have greatly shocked many orthodox ministers in the old time," but Mr. Maltby would frown or snub questioners, thank them for their frankness, say why he disagreed, cut off discussion, and go on with his own ideas.[33]

Lowther, too, was useful. He visited regularly and hoped that the family might take him in, but Elizabeth felt that she must keep a room free, particularly for Mollie when she came home exhausted between private-nursing assignments. She thought Lowther a good influence on Frank and on Arthur, who just then was a creature of contradictions. He had talked about "having a jolly good shot at" preaching. At the same time he wanted to go to a theater or music hall: would it be all right, Lowther asked Edward, if Arthur went with him? "The only objection (apart from the question of your Mother) appears to be that it might take time better spent in his special [naturalist] employments."[34]

Edward wanted no part of any campaign to chain Arthur, visibly or invisibly, to Wesleyanism. His letter must have grieved Elizabeth, but it was his long-delayed declaration of independence from her hovering concern.

> As to the salvation of us, that's no particular business of yrs. & in any case you cant do much beyond pray. You need not worry. If Frank isn't all right, I dont know who is. You seem to get great comfort from what you imagine to be my state of mind. Well, as you must know, my views are not yrs. in all things, & v. possibly some of them, if you knew them, wd. shock you. But what's the good of worrying abt. opinions? I confess my contempt grows for them. If you have no cause to worry abt. me, what possible cause can you have in Frank's case? In all the essential things, in modest & unselfish simplicity of life & in quick sensitiveness of religious feeling, he's worth fifty of me. Be quite sure of this, that plenty of folk belong to Jesus Xt whose opinions & habits are v. different from yrs. or mine. Where will you find a better girl than Annie [i.e., Margaret]? In my opinion, she has quite as much religion as it is healthy for a young girl to have. What if she does sometimes seem to think more abt. Charlie [her fiancé, Charles Pilkington-Rogers] than abt. God? Does it matter? Not a bit, I believe. It is natural, & I am sure God wd. have it so. It will be all right in the end, in the end [*sic*].

What did it matter, he asked, if Mollie sometimes "talked lightly of her work"? Her unselfish nursing relieved much human suffering. He, too, had talked lightly of his work, "but if any man thinks that prevents me in a perfectly genuine affection for these students whom I denounce[,] pouring all I have out & wearing myself down, he's a mean little soul who knows nothing of human nature. I know perfectly well that my master wont press my remarks too hard but will look at other things. He knows that my work, for all its limitations & folly, has cost me something, just as His cost Him everything." Margaret did not "talk too freely of deep matters to us. It's all right." In purity of spirit Margaret "has been . . . only beaten by Alfred, who has worked hard & not grumbled & without any admixture of self. Arthur, too, will be all right in the end. Again, I assure you, you have nothing to worry abt. We don't talk religion to you, that's all. I loathe & detest talking abt. religion, & you are the last person in the world I shd. talk abt. it to. Arthur & Frank are the same. When they begin to be pious snifflers, then get worried but not before." Both Mary (i.e., Mollie) and Margaret had "a sight more genuine religion" than Elizabeth suspected. She must discard the idea that "everyone who dies in a certain condition drops into a hot bath"—if it were true, "it would be wicked & the act of a fiend. Even if the Bible teaches it, it isn't true. What matters is the main trend & tenor of a life's effort. . . . You have lots to live for yet. And we are all right."[35]

Methodist social and spiritual disciplines had helped Elizabeth through the impossible years, and she could not imagine living without them. Edward caught her state of mind perfectly in *Introducing the Arnisons:* "Something was done and achieved, with each day that saw [the children] to their beds. And God was with her, she was sure of that. She prayed, in language unvarying through the years, as she gathered them for evening worship, that they might 'all meet an unbroken family around Thy throne in Heaven.' " If her children backslid, what of that vision of heavenly reunion? Even at the risk of hurting her, Edward must get free. One's spiritual autobiography, like loyalty, was the heart's own concern, spontaneous and private.[36]

His letters became so strained that Rushbrooke sent a cable whose whole text was "Courage / Rushbrooke." Then he wrote to say that he had cabled because Edward's last letter showed that he was "in deep waters or in low water or in hot water or (a fish) out of water, and I could not reach you by wireless or phone." He was not at all certain that Edward ought to be in India at all, for his letters showed "overstrain, overwork, overweariness, & I think of overstay in that parched & soul-parching land." He must fight to repel dejection.[37]

By this time Canton and Rushbrooke had met and no doubt pooled their misgivings. Canton's letters combined the poetry-piety and verse-prose dichotomies with stern discussion of problems inherent in Wesleyan spiritual introspection. He did not, he wrote, want Edward to be a " 'littery man,' but I don't want you *nei*ther to smother any creative gift under Wesleyan prejudices or futilities. As for your prose, much that is in your letters could not be bettered." He knew Edward would bitterly regret his refusal to keep a diary. Canton never expected a *Vita Nuova,* but "even now you have lost your English eye for Oriental colour, and the things that 'erst' gave you a thrill seem now deadly commonplace." He scouted the Wesleyan idea of insurance against sin. "Still I will venture to say that I think you would be happier in your gardening and more successful with your flowers if you would not pull them up by the roots to see *how* they are getting on." Introspection is "only a form of egotism" and is "not a mood to be encouraged in *any* one at *any* time.... Even bothering about our sins is egotism, and of a very rotten kind." Edward should keep his eyes on the Ideal "*without a thought about the*

Ideal, or about our eyes, or about pressing onward." That, Canton thought, "may not be Methodism, but it is the right thing."[38]

Another letter opens, "Dear Edward the Flagellant": unfortunately, the scourge often fell on " 'Lo, (the poor Indian.)' " When, he asked, "did I say that I did not like your verse? . . . I did say your prose (in some of your letters to me) sometimes got itself into the happiest of periods; and if—this I add now—if you would write your essays as letters, you would compass some delightful essay writing. Hear me miserum!"[39]

This barrage did offend Edward. But Canton did not retract a word, although he hoped that Edward would not think that he wrote only to annoy. On occasion he had "deprecated your looking at human nature and life through *ultra-ascetic spectacles; . . .* Wesleyanism ought to be proud that it can raise men still to ascetic heights, dangerous as those heights may become."[40]

Edward told Canton that knowing him had "confirmed me in the resolve that came to me before, to live *humanly.* I believe in no other fashion can we make men grateful to God for us."[41]

Edward returned to work and duty. He tried harder to understand Indian cultures outside Bankura's narrow orbit. He visited his Wesleyan colleague Woodford among the Santal hill tribes. "He has become almost as much a junglewallah as his flock; believes profoundly in bhuts [ghosts], & is hesitant anent witchcraft. . . . Many chats had I with the simple jungle folk," Edward told Canton. But sometimes Edward's efforts at cultural enlightenment were more puzzling than revelatory. When a *zilla* (district) school played football against Bankura, Edward was shocked and puzzled when the zilla boys clapped and cheered when a Bankura boy accidentally tripped him. "Yet I have not only done them no harm, but have more than once done them courtesy & kindness." At Bankura, zilla schools had a reputation as hotbeds of sedition, bad manners, and "silly Hinduism," and Edward felt "a distinct atmosphere of opposition" in every class he visited there. But *why* this scorn for a sportsmanship that was not merely an English importation but also an expression of human decency? He had underestimated the relative political and intellectual sophistication of zilla schools and was amazed to find the most advanced class reading Thomas à Kempis. The show pupil was told to talk about the book. "In a parrot fashion, like a smart kid doing a recitation, he announced: 'Though I do not approve of the doctrinal points, nevertheless I have a high regard for *that* book.' His tone was so impudent & combative that it rattled me, & I held a brief dialogue with him, riddling & scornful!!!" These boys, or their Hinduism, were being " 'innoculated.' This is the kind of thing Hinduism is everywhere doing. These boys fancy these ethics are Hindu. It feeds an already bursting complacency." On the chalkboard was "a chunk of greasy, nauseating piety. Hinduism at present is built upon a bog of bunkum & cant."[42]

He had to live with the incongruities of England's vaunted civilizing mission. British sportsmanship, believed to embody a universal ethos of decency, was turned upside down. Ancient Hinduism had been untrue to itself by appropriating Christian ethics without understanding them. Were these really fruitful ways for East to meet West? The more he contemplated such maladjustments, the more he wondered whether a better way even existed. The conflict of cultures seemed so complex, so unfathomable, and after all, so insoluble.

6

FORGING A CHAIN

The reunification of Bengal was set for 1 April 1912, and the ensuing weeks were an interim of rumor and reassessment. The choice of the new Governor was the overriding subject for speculation. "Bengali newspapers were busy with the time-honoured British Indian sport: picking the new Governor. Their editorial tips were delivered with the usual air of authority, but for once all were wrong." Lord Crewe, as Secretary of State for India, chose Lord Carmichael of Skirling, who had been Governor of the Madras Presidency since November 1911. He had a reputation for liberal views, and he knew that his appointment was "intended as a public demonstration of the British Government's determination to pursue a new policy there." He went to "reconcile the dissentious communities and put an end to terrorism." He must appease both Bengali nationalists and disgruntled Calcutta boxwallahs, who felt excluded from political and commercial affairs.[1]

The Calcutta English, Crewe told Carmichael, now seemed more reconciled to their new status. However, there would be "a noisy and violent minority, more angry with Hardinge than with the new Governor[,] represented by *The Englishman* [Calcutta newspaper], who will more probably expend their wrath on Hardinge, moreover, than on the new Governor." Hardinge advised Carmichael to "ride them with a light hand"—and "all the more as their mouths are sore for the time being." He would find the Hindu Bengalis immensely civil, "and delighted about the new province," but some property-owning Bengalis in Calcutta were sulky. Carmichael must not take the expressions of Bengali feeling too literally and must not become "enthralled by the Bengalis," as disillusionment was sure to follow. Muslims in eastern Bengal, a majority in the former province, were very sore about the Partition annulment. Carmichael should improve education so as "to run them even weight with the Hindus" instead of allowing Muslims "an advantage in the handicap." Historically, the Muslim community, fearful of non-Muslim interference with Islamic schools, had resisted English-language education, had fallen behind in employment and economic advancement, and now made belated efforts to catch up. Crewe was confident, however, that Hindu-Muslim antagonisms would eventually ease "and that the task of the Police will be far easier."[2]

Carmichael replied that he did not "jump at the proposal" of Bengal but accepted it as an interesting challenge. Where possible, he would avoid using the punitive police, who caused fear and resentment. Unfortunately, dacoities continued, especially in eastern Bengal; also unfortunately, the offenders were often educated young men. Bengal needed more intelligent rather than more numerous police. Many were recruited outside Bengal, and only a few had more than a superficial knowledge of the local language. Educated criminals and undereducated police were a dangerous combination.

Carmichael had to appoint a new Director of Public Instruction for Bengal. It was not a good moment for poking that bureaucratic hornet's nest, for a Parliamentary Commission to look into Indian Public Services was even then in India to hold hearings and prepare reports. Slowly, very slowly, the effects of the new educational appointment would filter down through the bureaucracy.[3]

Meanwhile Edward Thompson, a very small cog in the educational machine, looked more closely at Bengal beyond Bankura. He realized how stubbornly the color line persisted, not only between English and Indians but also within Bengali society. He had noticed that Bengali journalists were "*v.* jealous on this point of colour. Once they were white, & still like to think they are, speaking with scorn of the aborigines. They are *v.* petty on the point—Well, they say, so many Indians go to England that we know all abt. the English[,] & 'their vaunted superiority' is seen for the myth it is." Therefore derogating the very dark Santals and cataloging English failures fortified self-esteem. This page of Edward's letter is strenuously penciled and the remainder scissored off.[4]

There was no one at Bankura with whom to discuss the subject. English and Indian staff still kept carefully to themselves after working hours. The Reverend Clifford Culshaw remembers that his brother, who arrived in Bengal as a missionary in 1927, was "one of a small number who tried to identify themselves with Indians by adopting Indian dress and a more or less Indian style of food and living. . . . He was told that whatever he did he couldn't disguise the fact that he *was* identified with the ruling race." Mr. Culshaw himself, when he came to Bankura in the mid-1930s, tried the same thing but gave it up "for various reasons." Political differences exaggerated cultural difference, and the Englishman continued his "tradition of isolating himself from what was after all an alien society. (I am not defending this, merely stating it as a fact.)" Life was difficult in "small communities with companions they did not choose, and in a tropical climate they got on one another's nerves for all their Christian aspirations, exaggerated eccentricities and imagined slights where none were intended." As at Sawtry, Edward Thompson was more comfortable among the country people than with Bankura's expatriate English or the half-Anglicized Bengalis.

"Thompson strikes me," wrote his son, "as some kind of outsider, a go-between on the margin of Bengali culture whose station in English culture was unsure."[5]

Edward's acquaintance with Bengali literary culture began slowly. It is difficult to assess the extent of his acquaintance with the literature, but it is certain that encouragement to explore was not forthcoming at Bankura. Where were the Bengali poets whose work Canton had urged him to investigate? He heard names mentioned, particularly that of Rabindranath Tagore, but he had not met one whom he would call a true poet. In fact, an ancient poetic tradition flourished all around him. This still exists in the lyric verses and songs of the Vaishnava sect, which remains particularly strong and characteristic in Bengal. Vaishnava *sankirtan,* public antiphonal singing and dancing in praise of the god Krishna, were a familiar sight in Bankura streets. Edward encountered some Vaishnavas, "a party of haribollers. A man was running (dancing) along, shaking a sort of dull cymbals & shouting in rhythm 'Bol Hari Bol' (Speak, Hari [Lord], speak). Then he wd. turn to certain kids, acolytes, & they replied in a slightly different rhythm. A regular cathedral chant business, in the open air of course v. common here." The leader, then his acolytes, threw themselves at Edward's feet: "I wonder if they took me for an incarnation of Krishna."[6]

The lyrics explicate the essence of Vaishnava belief: Krishna as reincarnation of Vishnu, the Preserver. *Bhakti,* or worship, is the offering most welcome to him: this was what Edward had observed in the street. An intricate oral tradition, many centuries old, inspires Vaishnava worship in ecstatic singing of lyrics from a vast collection that clusters, in many thousands of variations, around a central metaphor for the loving relation between God and the human soul. Modern scholars have recorded many and have collected others that survive in written form, but uncounted numbers have been lost to fires, floods, wars, and the appetite of white ants.

That central metaphor has passed into the daily speech and literature of Bengal. The relation between God and the human soul is embodied in the god Krishna and Radha, his favorite among his milkmaid companions. At its heart is the concept of *viraha:* separation. Eternally Krishna and Radha seek each other and seem as eternally to just miss meeting in the darkness: so God and the soul eternally seek each other. Once in a very, very long while they meet, but meeting and revelation are always fleeting and leave only renewed longing. Another version of the story points a moral lesson: when each milkmaid believes that Krishna loves only her, he hides so that none can find him, for selfish conceit prevents spiritual communion.

A Vaishnava lyric is a miniature drama. A narrator-observer, who is also narrator-commentator, preserves a discreet distance between reader-audience and the speaker of the lyric lines addressed to the lover/God. The poet writes himself into the poem as listener-explicator, with a thoughtful comment in a final couplet called the *bhanita*.[7]

No one at Bankura explained that Vaishnava *bhakti* was not just a pagan exercise, but a two-way conduit for personal salvation. Yet all around were Vaishnava metaphors and images. Boatmen on Bengal's rivers rowed to Vaishnava songs; village workmen hauled and hammered; housewives cooked and wove; children played to songs on the Vaishnava concept of the human soul in endless search for a personal relationship with the Eternal. Of all this Edward Thompson, a poet, as yet knew almost nothing. Clifford Culshaw advises that "the Vaishnava tradition did not arouse any *scholarly* interest in my time though we were aware of it because of Bengali texts we read for language exams: the fashion swung like a pendulum in missionary circles in attitudes towards Hinduism. . . ."[8]

With Partition annulled, Bengal as a political entity changed literally overnight. Edward felt that he, too, had changed. He was quieter, less irrepressible. He heard that the college students complained that he did not mix with them in the old way; he seemed "to care more for the schoolboys. I told him it was true." Much, however, was suppressed. There had been a "face-chopping incident" when he came unexpectedly upon a visiting school inspector "messing abt. with our b[oo]ks." With an unpremeditated swing to the jaw he had knocked the interfering inspector flat. The boys carried him out, Edward apologized and explained, and apparently there were no hard feelings, for the inspector's report was excellent. But "a shock does make a difference. Also, I have temporarily got tired of a thing so onesided, of being frank & getting no frankness in return. But the chief thing is the physical exhaustion that comes on everyone in this climate. I am no longer fresh from England." He preferred the high school boys who as yet aspired less to a superficial Western-style sophistication. He wished for more men fresh from England—not ministers, but men like Canton and Fielden whose motivation was belief in the value of their work.[9]

He did not know that events in London had already laid the foundation for an important but paradoxical friendship and a momentous change in his associations and ambitions. He was to be a link in the chain that marked a vitally important modern exchange of East-West literary influences. That began on 13 January 1910 at the Royal Society of Arts in London, with a protest against government policy for art instruction of Indian students, to the effect that India had handicrafts but no fine arts. The protester was Ernest B. Havell, retired Principal of the government's Calcutta School of Art. This policy, Havell said, attracted principally "the flotsam and jetsam of the Anglo-Indian university system." They went to art school because they could find nothing better to do, and money spent on them or their works was wasted.[10]

Presiding was Sir George Birdwood, who had done much to improve standards for India's handicraft products but denied the value, even the existence, of indigenous fine art. He rejected Havell's argument, saying that all so-called Indian art was either obscene or utilitarian, and that the iconic figure of the Buddha was no more spiritual than a boiled suet-pudding.[11]

This outraged the painter William Rothenstein, who had come with two like-minded friends to support Havell. Rothenstein was passionate about the welfare of artists and curious about enduring traditions in art. He had acquired a collection of Mogul paintings, at three shillings each, that the British Museum had rejected. He proposed, there and then, an India Society to educate the British public about India's fine arts, music, and literatures. The India Society began to plan lectures and annual private publications for its members.[12]

A crucial link in the chain was a lady of whom Thompson had never heard and would never meet: the expert copyist, Mrs. (later Lady) Christiana Herringham. In 1910, while Havell and Rothenstein attended the Royal Society of Arts in London, she was in the Ajanta Caves near Hyderabad, practicing what they preached: copying what was left of the neglected wall paintings that Buddhist monks had executed probably between the first and sixth centuries. By the thirteenth century the monks had disappeared, no one took an interest in the paintings, and successive British governments had left them to disintegrate amid damp and darkness, bat droppings, and smoke from campfires of wandering tribesmen.[13]

The second link in the chain dated from the winter of 1910–1911 when Mrs. Herringham returned to Ajanta, and Rothenstein traveled with her, first to see Ajanta, then to seek other examples of Indian art, and, he hoped, to meet living Indian artists. With introductions from Havell he met two brothers named Tagore, one of whom was Havell's successor as Acting Principal at the Calcutta School of Art. They were exactly what Rothenstein had hoped to find: Indian artists in the Indian tradition, using Indian motifs instead of slavishly copying European art. He met also their uncle, Rabindranath. Rothenstein, like most in the West, had never heard of him and had no idea that he was an educator, poet, playwright, and novelist: a one-man refutation of the assumption, analogous to English ignorance of Indian fine art, that Indian vernaculars produced no serious, artistic literatures. To Rothenstein in February 1911, Rabindranath, with his full white beard and flowing robes, was simply a wonderfully beautiful artist's subject, and he made a set of portrait drawings that would embellish frontispieces of international editions of Tagore's work.[14]

In 1912 Rabindranath came to London. Feeling lost and alien, he remembered Rothenstein, who in the meantime had gathered information from Bengalis in London about Tagore's standing in Bengal. Did he have any of his work in translation? Tagore gave him a small blue notebook, his English prose-poem versions of lyrics from several of his Bengali volumes, one of which was called *Gitanjali* (Song-offering). Rothenstein, enchanted, sent copies to Yeats, then gathered his friends, leading figures in literature, journalism, and the arts, to meet Tagore and hear Yeats read from the manuscripts. The poems evoked genuine enthusiasm but also some confusion about Tagore and Indian spirituality. Were these religious poems or love lyrics? What almost no one knew was that they derived from the Vaishnava tradition and could be read as either or both. Was their provenance "poetry or doctrine"?[15]

Among those who met Tagore at Rothenstein's home was Charles Freer Andrews, who had been a Church of England missionary with the Delhi Cambridge Mission since 1904. Andrews had a paradoxical personality; he possessed a tremendous capacity for work but required an inspiring friend or father figure as focus. Hugh Tinker calls his biography of Andrews *The Ordeal of Love;* for him, love was an ordeal, a burden, and love of that kind can become burdensome to its object. He was in England, had long wanted to meet Tagore, and had rushed about London hoping to find him. When they met in Rothenstein's drawing room Andrews was moved to make obeisance—to kneel and touch his feet, but Tagore forestalled that by offering his hand. Quickly Andrews produced an effusive article for the Calcutta monthly the *Modern Review.* It begins, "Rabindra was in London!" He hailed Tagore as "the new luminary which has come upon the horizon of the West." But he failed to explain adequately the Vaishnava sources for the poems.[16]

Tagore's introduction in England was a lesson in how not to present a poet to a new audience. The poems as they first came to Rothenstein were sometimes awkward, with unnecessary repetitions and errors of syntax and usage. Manuscript copies passed among Rothenstein and his friends, none of whom knew Bengali. Everyone had suggestions, and Yeats, with very fixed opinions, became the arbiter. Ezra Pound's unequivocal views made the mix even more complex.

The new India Society published the poems as *Gitanjali (Song-Offering),* its members' private publication for 1912; a trade edition followed from Macmillan in 1913. Yeats wrote an effusive introduction that exaggerated Tagore's standing in India, for in fact he was then virtually unknown out-side of Bengal. Even there he belonged to a circle of scholarly individuals whom many regarded as rarefied, not to say dangerous, intellectuals. Yeats's impression of Tagore came not only from their meeting at Rothenstein's but from several Bengalis whom he met in London, who were thrilled that their countryman got such English notice and were eager to confirm Yeats's romantic impressions of poet and poems. They had stirred him, Yeats wrote, "as nothing has for years," but he could never know the life and thought

behind them "if some Indian traveller will not tell me." Yeats's informants—
"my Indians," he called them—waxed eloquent about Tagore's spirituality
and his premier standing among Bengali poets. Thus Yeats fell into the trap
that still catches many in the West: the West is irredeemably crass and crude,
and the East is so spiritual that money and position are meaningless. Yeats
said to one of "his Indians": "We have to do so much, especially in my
own country, that our minds gradually cease to be creative, and yet we
cannot help it. . . . Four-fifths of our energy is spent in the quarrel with
bad taste, whether in our own minds or in the minds of others." In other
words, the West lacks the spiritual force of Indian creativity. Where Yeats's
Indians failed him was in not explaining Tagore's Vaishnava contexts. He
touched upon them but did not follow through: "Lovers, while they await
one another shall find in murmuring [Tagore's verses], this Love of God a
magic gulf wherein their own more bitter passion may bathe and renew
its youth." He concluded with paeans to innocence and simplicity, and a
catalog of images from the Radha-Krishna story: flowers and rivers, conch
shells, monsoon rains, parching heat, a boatman playing a flute like Krishna's,
waiting lovers: all, Yeats says, mirroring "the moods of that heart in union
or in separation." This was as close as he came to full explanation. Did the
Indian informants tell him more than he used in the introduction? If so, it
was an opportunity lost.[17]

William Rushbrooke was in Mentone, where he met the Bengali philosopher and close friend of Tagore, Dr. Brajendranath Seal. He lent Rushbrooke
a copy of the India Society *Gitanjali.* Did Edward Thompson know "this
modern bard and seer, as they deem him?" Rushbrooke asked.[18]

Edward knew something, for he had met Tagore's friend Lokenath Palit,
who from February 1912 to March 1913 was district and sessions judge for
the Bankura District. With him Edward was reading Tagore's Bengali poems;
it was an elementary crash course in *rabindra-sahitya,* or "Rabindranath
literature," and was, in fact, his serious introduction to Bengali literature.[19]

By July 1913 Canton had seen reviews of the Macmillan edition of *Gitanjali* and had a context for Edward's letters about Tagore. "Mighty cocky
you are about your superior knowledge of Rabindranath," he wrote, "and
mighty impatient with our insular ignorance. Really we *have* heard of your
Brahmo Samaj—much as we have heard of Philladelphians and Plymouth
Brethren and Wesleyan Methodists: but we did not know that Rabindranath
belonged to any of these interesting denominations. For my own part my
only knowledge of the gentleman was contained in Yeats's introduction,
but with my usual critical flair(!) I told you it was impossible to accept the
pomes [*sic*] as Hindu pure and simple, unless Indian religion had been grossly
misrepresented." He decided that they were "essentially Christian in their

feeling"—a common Western conclusion in the absence of more precise knowledge.[20]

Edward already knew the difficulties of theological communication. A first-year college student, with "the hungriest eyes I ever saw," was "always popping up with questions abt. the soul & future existence." He asked about rebirths, and Edward was only "beginning to see how terrific the battle will be & how unequipped I am." When he seemed to sidestep the subject, the student said, "with the greatest pathos imaginable, 'You are our guru, & you can easily explain these things.' " Edward felt hopelessly inadequate. "What can I do? I cant see why much of their nobler belief shd. not be perfectly consistent with a true loyalty to Xt." There must be a key, but where? On New Year's Day 1913 his students made an interesting attempt at synthesis. "Today," Edward told his mother, "our Xtians had a sankirtan— that is, a dance & howl-song through the town." It was their adaptation of Vaishnava sankirtan, with the singing and dancing praising Christ instead of Krishna. Edward had promised to join them, "but they were so long in starting that I had to come away again."[21]

As long as Elizabeth did not question the state of his soul, Edward's home correspondence went smoothly. Some family conditions had improved. Frank still worked very long hours at Dent's London plant, but his health improved, and he hoped to attend evening classes and qualify for a better job. Arthur had rooms in Letchworth and was again close to the countryside. Alfred, a warehouse courier for a clothier, was proud and happy to make modest contributions to the family budget. However, Elizabeth's ideas of Edward's responsibilities at Bankura were sadly out of date. She could not comprehend how much modernization had changed India, or the fact that he was so tiny a part of so huge and intricate a bureaucratic machine. It was all quite unlike her memories of Negapatam. In Canton's words, "It is amazing how many people, growing old, do not perceive that everything is changing about them, and that the younger generation insist on being measured for their own clothes and having them cut after the latest fashion."[22]

Edward found it difficult to mediate between his realities and his mother's outdated memories. Those Indian universities, she told him, "mustn't pile too much work on you. You'll have to say to them—what Alfred said to his manager one day—'I'm not afraid of work, but I'm not a mule.' " She thought that Edward was only homesick for English greenery. She knew he was tired: "India is a country for the trial of nerves and temper, some people return home better & some worse for the discipline." He must get away to the hills. She knew that life in India was difficult—"India ruins people's lives"—but he was gaining experience and growing intellectually and spiritually, "& don't worry if you are not as 'smart' as you once were, 'smartness' is over estimated in these days. . . ." She knew he was "fighting a battle, but you are on the winning side."[23]

That widening distance from his mother weighed upon his spirits. Canton thought it "ten thousand pities that you have not some sympathetic colleague," and why did some men, "especially missionaries—hold aloof from each other as they so often seem to do." Edward's two-year review was imminent, and he was torn between extending his service and resigning and going home. Canton begged him "not to act hastily in any way. I protest vehemently against you making sacrifices in any case, . . . and yet it may be the divine order of things that you should fulfil your contract—whatever it may have been—well and thoroughly—but don't be a fool in the wild dream of being a saint." He said it "bluffly but not, I hope unkindly." Then he dropped all pretense of tact and bore down hard on the fact that so many missionaries, lest they seem disloyal, hesitated to consider the business element in their professional relations with a headquarters committee:

> Look here, these lunatics are getting too much. What more does any society want from any man but "loyalty"? Surely that word means everything. I cannot believe you have lost faith in the eternal verities. . . . What do you mean by a good Wesleyan? If they, having scrutinized you for two years, pass you, it seems to me you are just making yourself an unnecessary nuisance. . . . Next, don't you see that all this relationship between you and the mission is a business speculation. If you had been an unlikely person, would they have sent you out? . . . The only proper way to deal with this is the business way. All goings out of young men are speculations. It is in the cards that the man may change, that he may die, that he may prove unfit. I beg and pray you will not act hastily in any way.

All this inspired a notion of furlough in England and perhaps study for a further degree. If the opportunity came, take it, advised Rushbrooke, who doubted "whether you ought to be in India at all" and whether Edward could find the right kind of wife in India: "So come back speedily."[24]

In fact, Bankura had become somewhat more satisfactory. Olver had settled up Edward's accounts, and he was somewhat better off than he had thought. He and Arthur Spencer enjoyed reminiscing about Kingswood and Richards. Owston Smith was still there, but that animosity was at least dormant. In 1912 Edward had failed his first try at the Bengali examination but in January 1913 passed it triumphantly. His Bengali address received "an astonishing report, easily the best we have had for years. It says my accent is excellent, that I speak the language with ease, & so on." His mother's congratulation was rather deflating: "Your father spoke Tamil 'with ease' & his accent was 'excellent,' & in this respect as in others, you are proving yourself a worthy son of a worthy father." His father's example had deposited him at Bankura, and he did not appreciate the reminder. Was not the credit his own? In July, however, he received an excellent two-year service report.[25]

Late in 1912 he began a correspondence with Robert Bridges, who would become Poet Laureate in July 1913. Edward had pointed out an erroneous reference to Stonehenge in Bridges's introductory essay to an edition of Keats's poems. Bridges had implied that Keats actually saw Stonehenge as a "natural picture." He wrote to Edward, "No doubt you are right about Stonehenge. . . . I did not know that Keats never visited Stonehenge, and if my essay had had a biographical intention this reference to Stonehenge w[d] have been a bad error." He kept it, however, as "for the reader's purpose the word Stonehenge is very valuable, and I doubt if I sh[d] have changed it. . . ." Edward had also mentioned Bridges's *Milton's Prosody,* a work extremely important to Bridges in view of his intense interest in prosody, rhyme, and scansion. In three closely written pages Bridges explained the genesis of that book. He wrote it, he said,

> to oblige a Clarendon press editor who wished to prevent his scholars from misreading Milton's blank verse by mispronouncing words so as to make them "scan." As students read it (and it had an actual effect on verse writing, and even started Stephen Phillips's reputation) I added to the new editions of it further statements of fact, until my wife said that the book had got appendicitis and critics spoke of my "theories." I have no theory, unless it be a theory that Milton made out for himself a systematic prosody on Chaucer's basis with the hope of being able to render English prosody sufficiently strong to be without dispense with rhyme. The main proof of this was in his definite rejection of the "supernumerary syllable" in mid-line—and this demonstrated fact, which has been quite unrecognized, alone separated all M's early work from his later.[26]

Bridges wished next to write on "*poetic form* and intended to take Shelley for my text: but his metaphysic prevented me" because he thought it "too childish or unconsidered for serious treatment." Still, when asked to write the introduction to the Keats edition he decided "to say the few things that I had to say on *poetic form.*" Edward had mentioned pedantry in poetry, which Bridges thought "the most useful field for poetic criticism. Poetry pure, cannot be taught: but the essentials of any artistic technique can, and they should be reasonably exhibited." He was always ready to expound his ideas on prosody; still, it was a generous letter to an aspiring younger man whom he had never met.[27]

However, Bridges's comments on Tagore in England suggested again that Yeats's *Gitanjali* introduction had failed to convey the most essential information. "We have been very much interested with the English poems of a Buddhist Mystic, Tagore,—which have been published in England lately with a preface by Yeats. Have you seen them? There seems a possibility that Asiatic poetry both Indian and Japanese will be influencing English literature—and Mysticism of all kinds is getting fashionable in some circles, in reaction, no doubt, to the cold materialism of the 19th century scientists." Tagore in England, Bridges had heard, had made a pleasant first impression, but he did not know "whether my Indian sympathies made any but the geographical link with you? I suppose it is the geography which has led me to mention Tagore."[28]

Bridges wrote next on mutual influences of Asia and the West, but his ideas on Hinduism (and on Wesleyanism) were still foggy. "Did I speak of Tagore as a Buddhist?" he asked. "I am afraid that I do not understand the modern Hinduism. But I suppose that a great distinction is the deism of the Hindus." Edward's information about Tagore was "very enlightening to me—I am afraid that I could not tell you what a Wesleyan is—I have the vaguest notion." He did, however, have a timely notion about Indian students in Oxford and their increasing social separation from the English of the university and the town. Bridges "had always done my best to promote every sociability on equal terms, which is what is needed—but the number of dark undergrads has increased very much of late, and in the case of Indians, this has not improved the situation, both because it multiplies the occasions of misunderstanding & due to their own distinctions among themselves, & also because they have more facilities for holding themselves together in exclusion from the English." Some Indian students came to his home on Boars Hill, and he hoped that his hospitality was beneficial. Tagore's visit to England did good, also, "for they saw him welcomed and honoured." When Tagore returned from America in 1913 and came to Boars Hill he was "charming, friendly and modest," but Bridges prophesied that as cultural distinctions became "blessed by civilization, everything promises to become hybrid, or at least it seems as if some of the most specialized humanities must go under." What he had seen of the English vulgarization of Christianity was not encouraging. However, he did his best to promote cultural exchange: he had just arranged for a Japanese visitor "to hold forth on the poetry of his nation at the school of English Literature in Oxford. I hope it may come off."[29]

His letters encouraged Edward. Here was a new correspondent whose life revolved around poetry and who showed an intelligent (if incomplete) interest in India. Edward's Bengali examinations were behind him, and the two-year evaluation was more than favorable. His outlook promised to be, if not exhilarating, at least one that he could live with. He persevered.

7

REQUIEM

In Edward's absence, George Lowther made conscious efforts to expand and enrich his life. The Tax Service now assigned him to various London areas, but his professional experiences were often depressing and disillusioning. Persons of public standing fell precipitately in his estimation. Sidney Low, Literary Editor of the *Standard,* had "acted like a baby. I spoke to him with all the courtesy I knew & he answered like a petulant child. He thought he was showing independence, & so forth; instead, he excited my contempt." Lowther was weary of "constant bickering between official and public, the eternal parrot cry of injustice & curse Lloyd George and on the other side the perpetual nagging for 'thoroughness' and 'efficiency,' which simply means more irritation of the public. All this grows worse & usage does not make it any less ugly & depressing. An approximate justice is the best one can hope for, but the system is such that the rogues come off best & the honest men are wearied to death." Outside the office, he saw more than he had imagined of the seamy side of London and hoped he would not become insensitive, for "innocence of spirit is of the Precious Things," and only sensitivity kept man from becoming a beast.[1]

He detested superficiality. In June 1911, London's preparations for the coronation of George V did not impress him; he agreed with Edward that such things were an overdone bore. Special buses took out-of-town visitors to view the decorations. Fleet Street was full of "fripperies" and "open-mouthed strangers, staring up at the gaudy trappings."[2]

He returned to literature as refuge and endeavored to catch up with recent developments. He read John Davidson again, as poet and not for his Wesleyan background. He wished he knew more about Yeats's experiments in speaking poetry to the psalter but hated to see so fine a poet "pottering with stage-effects like a child with bricks and soldiers": a waste of time and talents, surely? However, the Irish literary renaissance fascinated him, and he urged Edward to share his interest in Synge.[3]

Reimmersion in literature revived uncertainties. Should he risk an effort at becoming a journalist and literary critic while he starved in a garret? Canton curbed that by warning against the overenthusiasm that often led both Lowther and Edward to sweep aside whole generations of writers and critics for their favorite of the hour. Edward agreed: perhaps they were still handicapped by some remnants of Methodism. Talk of literary careers always threw Lowther into premonitions of a "new zone of life" and impending crisis (there *was* a crisis: the final tax examination was a few weeks away). Again he felt isolated but brushed it off. Still, how could he "be of use" by writing? He had lost confidence in his ability to write marketable stuff, for journalism was the captive of advertising. If he could become established as a successful journalist he would again propose a biography of James Smetham.[4]

Now Lowther took up Canton's line of advice to Edward. Richards had found *The Enchanted Lady* "repelling by its antiquated form." Inspired by Synge's plays, Lowther suggested that Edward try more modern dramatic subjects, not problem plays like Shaw's and Ibsen's, not verse dramas, but "prose plays of modern life" like Synge's. What about some of the "fine material which makes your Stonehouse letters (to me) the most valuable series I have? And there is topical work of this kind in India too doubtless." Canton was right, Lowther now thought, that Edward was one of those who could not help writing poems, but recent work did not seem to spring from "overmastering inspiration." Quantity was unimportant: *only faith in the medium mattered.*[5]

Determined to become a more social creature, Lowther sampled further the non-Methodist world. He defied the Wesleyan prohibition against card playing and went to a whist drive, bound "if I can, to overcome this social gawkishness." He went once to the races at Cheltenham Chase and admired the bookies' sprightliness without realizing how much of it was contrived image. He took up tennis, which went poorly at first because others avoided a beginner. A more serious drawback was the difficulty in thinking what to say to girls as they sat between the sets. However, he persevered and improved—at least, in the game itself. He had a swimming lesson, only the second time he had been in a pool. In June the *Oxford and Cambridge Review* accepted an article and invited him to a contributors' dinner at the home of Oswald Dawson, its editor. Lowther declined, "through funk & partly because I hadn't an evening suit." He went to a dancing class and felt that it had done him good; he met "one oustandingly nice girl there & we got very chummy."[6]

These social experiments were another effort to face up to changes in his religious position. Could he justify indulgence as sheer and sensual pleasure, as opposed to spiritual "improvement"? Was dancing really as beneficial as worthwhile reading? Thoughts of sex were ever present; must brains and sex be always at war? The place of sex in the good life overbore even religious scruples; he told Edward that he found the pressures of sex more insistent each year. He was twenty-six years old and still shrank from the fact of women's sexual attractiveness. He met a girl he had known as a child, now in long skirts and with her hair pinned up. She was still sweet and commonsensical, but he had liked her better before she grew up. As little girl she had seemed comprehensible, a playmate. Grown up, she was a conundrum and a mystery. He wondered, can there be purity without celibacy? What *is* purity? It could not be regulated or judged in relative terms. If excessive indulgence is wrong, is not all indulgence wrong? When he read poetry, "the soil and the flesh are present with me too insistently." He felt "dragged away by hot, seductive soft hands which I cannot resist, and the calls of the spirit grow faint in the distance."[7]

He took two definite steps, one toward a long-deferred ambition, the other a new and unlikely one. In April 1913 he applied for admission to a B.A. Pass degree through a universities extension program. He wanted to study English, Economics, Classics, French, and the origins of the English language. He knew that he got at intellectual truths by intuition, not by study. However, now Edward need not urge him to try again for a university degree, for Lowther was determined on it.[8]

Next, he surprised especially himself by joining the Territorials. He became Gunner Lowther of the Gloucestershire Royal Field Artillery 3rd Battery. He had had riding lessons, and now his acquaintances knew why. He did not want to be a soldier but believed that a nation should have such a force: if one had opinions one must act to support them. In May 1913 he was in camp at Pembrey in western Wales and discovered that he enjoyed it: "For the first time in my life I am learning something of the manage[ment] of horses." There were six men in his tent, one "a religious man" from his office. Some old stagers were chronically drunk enough to keep them thickheaded. The waste of food and the appalling manners in the mess shocked Lowther, who would have taken a stand on the subject if he had been longer on duty. Camp ended with a jolly time in a pub; his companions were rough, but he enjoyed himself. He received some results of his applications for the B.A. degree: Latin was "very promising," Greek was "nix."[9]

Frederick Fielden's companionship compensated somewhat for Edward's absence. "You are right that talking to him wd. do good," Lowther told Edward. "It *has* done *me* good." Fielden's regard disproved Lowther's conviction that there were "divisions" between him and all his friends. Fielden, a steady and quieting influence, had "suggested it might be all on my side in the other cases too." At Kingswood they had "once or twice got sadly askew, owing to my invincible hatred of explaining myself & to his strong practicality." Fielden had seemed to have "a spice of Philistinism" but was "not quite so barbarian when I got to re-know him." By 1913 each had smoothed over whatever the other regarded as rough edges.[10]

Fielden's surviving correspondence with Edward begins shortly before Edward left England. Fielden had a Kingswood memory of Edward: "I wish

I could see your apologetic figure hurtling itself through the doorway with that curious sidelong gait. . . ." "Apologetic" and "hurtling" perfectly catch the essence of Edward's personality: uncertainty and impetuousness, not greatly changed since Kingswood. Fielden could not yet afford Cambridge college fees but stayed with his parents in the town, read diligently, and earned a modest income as an Extension Lecturer. Like Lowther, he felt that he had been "made for something" but was only marking time; unlike Lowther, he felt that he could not wait upon God for the solution. By August 1912, Gonville and Caius College accepted him with a scholarship of sixty pounds a year.

In the summer of 1913 Fielden and Lowther planned a week's walk among the Lakes. Lowther was depressed and lonely but brightened up after they met at Windermere. Their holiday ended tragically at Flautern Tarn near Ennerdale Bridge. On 30 July, as they rested on the hillside, some two miles above Ennerdale, Lowther proposed a swim in the tarn in a hollow at their feet. Lowther was "splashing about & calling 'Murder' and 'Help!' & pretending to be very cold—you know his playful way." Actually, the water was "delightfully warm. The hot sun had been on it for days & there are no deep currents, I should think." Fielden swam across, about thirty yards, and Lowther called out that he wanted to join him but made no move to do so. Fielden swam back—but on his right side with his ear in the water so that he neither heard him call nor saw him disappear. "So far," Fielden wrote to Edward, "I have nothing to regret, but now I did a foolish thing. Instead of looking for bubbles or a swirl of the water or anything I stampeded up & down yelling—then ran up the bank thinking I might see some one, then came back & dressed, then ran off to get help, which proved to be 2 miles away, tho' of course I didn't know that then." When Fielden returned with help and ropes, Lowther had been in the water for almost an hour and a half, "so of course by then there was no hope." An underwater shelf dropped off abruptly, and Fielden thought that Lowther "got tired, & tried to bottom, then found he couldn't & not realising that because of the steepness of the slope a stroke or two would have brought him into his depth, got frightened & lost his head & in his splashing got his mouth filled with water & went under."

Others blamed Fielden, "and I think so myself, I don't suppose I shall ever forget hauling his body out of the water." If only he had not proposed "that fatal bathe, or if I had been swimming on my left side instead of my right, or if instead of losing my head & rushing for the help which proved nearly 2 miles distant I had waited till the water cleared & tried to pull George out myself!"[11]

Lowther never saw a letter of 17 July from Edward. On 22 July he wrote again with, in retrospect, a painful irony: "No letter from you to answer. My correspondence has been so in arrears that you must suffer for this week."

News of Lowther's death came by sea mail, and Fielden's letter of 1 August arrived very late. On 6 August Canton wrote, "It depends on which letter you open first, as to who breaks to you the lamentable news that will reach you by this mail. Our dear old friend Gunner has left us." Canton had received a "gay postcard from him" from Borrowdale, of Wordsworth's desk and school at Hawkshead. On 4 August Mrs. Canton, while reading out bits of news, had "suddenly stopped with a great Oh! and stared at us. It was a very short report of the accident." Thoughts of Lowther had been with him ever since. "Fielden will tell you how it happened. I fancy it must have been heart-failure caused by the intensely cold water. Not an unhappy death, but lamentable to those who loved him." Lowther's last postcard had finished curiously: " 'Yours at greater peace than of late, Gunner Lowther.' In any case it is good to think that he was in a happy frame of mind at the end."

Edward was not comforted, and Canton, whose only surviving daughter, Phyllis, had died in June, wrote again: "You begin to *know*, now one of the catastrophes of life. Death is a thing like pain—no observation or reading or sensibility can put you in touch with it; ~~until it has~~ it must ~~happened~~ happen in your own experience—I mean an experience in which you are so concerned that in a sense you die too." Even worse was "the hopelessness that dries up the wells; and even then suddenly without notice, the wells are again full of water for a moment." Canton thought it all nonsense that Fielden should feel to blame. Edward *should* mourn. "I have never been able to understand why it is *unmanly* not to forget our sorrows. That must surely be an apology for the shallow natures that never cared. . . ." But Edward should make no sudden move. "Don't, if I may venture to say so, be too hasty in anything you think of just now. Take time to think calmly."[12]

George Lowther was buried in the small cemetery at Ennerdale. A dedicated Wordsworthian, he lay near the spot where Wordsworth placed Leonard's grave in his poem "The Brothers." He left unfinished the more spacious earthly life that he had only begun to envision and make his own.[13]

Frank Richards and Edward wrote obituaries for the *Kingswood Magazine*. Six months earlier, Richards and Lowther had spent a day together, and Lowther had "outlined his plans of work for the next two years. Even then they seemed to me of far less importance than what he was already himself: his heart was as simple as a child's, he was sound and true throughout." Talent was slowly ripening, but "he had showed as always a genius for friendship." Edward recalled that after 1906 their friendship became close, during his own "period of extreme depression and disappointment, and I was not keen on keeping up my connection with K[ingswood] S[chool] or with any part of my old life." Lowther, although often depressed himself, "ignored all rebuffs, and with unremitting patience and affection brought me to better thoughts." When Edward received the news, he had "cycled into the jungle; it somehow seemed that, if I got away from men, Lowther would come to me." That feeling slowly faded, "but I know that whatever I have done for years has been done with a view to his approbation. He has been the voice of God to me. 'Othello's occupation's gone.' "

Edward recalled their own visit to the Lakes and was glad that Lowther, so sincere a Wordsworthian, was buried there. Edward had seen "how fast his character was mellowing, how steadily the tides of God's peace were flowing into his soul," so that now it was "hard to understand that I did not see that the end was preparing. It is all clear now, and he has gone home because he outstripped me."[14]

8

EPIPHANY

George Lowther's death left a great empty space in Edward's life. With him, too, Lowther had walked among the Lakes. Lowther, who had visited the Thompsons regularly, was a link with the distant family. "It seems funny," Edward had written, "to think of my people living & working in England while I can't see them. I suppose they are really all right. One tries to imagine them, doing this & that." Lowther had felt distant from his family, and the Thompsons became substitutes. His valiant efforts at a conventional social life produced no new and abiding friendships. A brother married Fielden's sister, but that brought Lowther little closer to his own family. Fielden, not Mr. Lowther, arranged for burial in Ennerdale churchyard. Edward's memorial is *Ennerdale Bridge and Other Poems,* published in 1914.[1]

At such a time Elizabeth's gospel of compensatory blessings was too much a giving-in to the inexplicable, of which death was the most inexplicable. The Wesleyan machinery for spiritual reclamation and growth seemed an unproductive consumption of time. Edward told her that the Wesleyans' May meetings, their annual stocktaking, would not "excite me much nowadays." A London furlough during which he might work for an advanced degree was impossible. Not even writing verse was helpful. Canton still urged him to use materials at hand and to take himself less seriously. "The things you throw off jocosely," he wrote, "are to my liking, much better than what you set down too yearningly."[2]

In the spring of 1913 Edward had gone to Burma. "This Burma visit has not done me a scrap of good physically," he had told Lowther, but "mentally I am a richer, much older man. I have been seeing life, as someone has said Kipling (& why not Masefield) writes of it, with a *capital Hell*," some of which was Englishmen's misbehavior. Canton was dissatisfied. "Lord," he wrote, "what endless material I should have at my pen's point if I could see all you have seen." Had Edward jotted down anything? "You can't *remember* everything; take my word for that." Edward should have been alarmed when Canton wrote that he seemed to view "the *subject of Burma* from the missionary point of view. Of course each of us sees things as we are given to see them and that's the end of it." He had wanted "more impressions of the *people* and

85

the *country*—the fresh suggestive things you saw and heard about *them.*" He never imagined that Englishmen there were worse than at home, for conditions "allow them apparently to be *more 'frankly* animal' than at home; but a walk through Piccadilly or Regent's St is quite enough to display the animalism, if not the frankness; and the newspapers tell what one can't actually see. Of course in Burma the white man is more conspicuous."[3]

Canton told Edward that if he would "explain how that same Tagore comes to be, you would do well. A Rev. C. F. Andrews had something about him in July *Contemporary [Review]*, but it does not seem to explain anything, and I don't see how Tagore originates out of anything I have seen of Indian poetry or of Indian religion."[4]

Andrews no doubt puzzled others besides Canton. Like Yeats's ecstatic introduction, his article played to readers susceptible to sentimental orientalism. He does not explain that the English *Gitanjali* is prose versions of Bengali poems with strongly disciplined rhyme and meter. "The heart of Bengal was felt throbbing with human passion in the poems of Chandidas, and overflowing with spiritual song in the beautiful legends of the Chaitanya period." But *what* legends? *Who* was Chandidas, *who* was Chaitanya, and *when* was "the Chaitanya period"? Furthermore, a government already distrustful of Tagore's liberalism could have read Andrews's peroration as seditious: Tagore's vision of "golden Bengal"—sonar bangla—was that of "a united people raised from the dust to sit with kings and princes."[5]

Edward outlined an English poetry anthology for Bengali high schools, "a decent selection. . . . All the present ones are about as rotten as they can be," but as the high school Principal, he had little time for this. His students' mistaken ideas were no longer amusing. Scripture papers read "exactly as if the boys had been taught Scrip. by some determined enemy of xty. instead of by Chandra Babu, our native minister."[6]

His Bengali hostel superintendent used Edward's funds for his own debts. If Edward sacked him he would never recover any of the money. "It is v. disappointing," Edward wrote, "having Xtians like this." Meanwhile, Olver wired from Calcutta when Bridges became Poet Laureate in July: "Brydges [*sic*] who is he why laureate / can you send two columns."[7]

India and Lowther's death were Edward's real troubles: "I cant tell you how India gets on the nerves & depresses. This eternal loneliness, this everlasting blazing sky & baked landscape, make one nearly lunatic. I'm sure I don't know why folk are such fools as to leave their own land, esp[ecially] for my sort of work & terms of service. Seven years is a fearful period, 3 years too long." He could not forget the delay in the news of Lowther's death. "The keeping me unaware of Lowther's death was kindness, I know, but it has worked out pretty cruelly. . . . The true kindness is to cable out." He begged Elizabeth for news about Lowther: "I have not seen him for 3 years & I feel as if I did not know the true L. He had altered so much & so finely that I feel out of touch with him as he was at last. . . . I never knew about his paying for Frank"—for singing lessons. "I am glad he was friendly with you all before he died."[8]

It was high time for something restorative to happen. Happen it did: he met Tagore. He went to Shantiniketan, but the school was in recess, and Tagore was away. They met first in Calcutta.

> I saw Rabi Babu himself. He is tall & frail-looking & wears a scarlet robe; he is v. dignified & gentle. When I sent my card in at the Tagore's [*sic*] big house, he rec[eive]d me at once; most sahibs wd. keep a stranger waiting a few minutes, just to show their importance. There were 2 secretaries, v. ordinary-looking babus, in the room all the time; they were a nuisance, I felt, but one had to put up with them. He said he had met [Lokenath] Palit in Eng[lan]d [during the summer] & heard a great deal about our college. He begged me to come to the Santiniketan again & when his boys were back; I promised. Then I asked him if there was any chance of his coming Bankura-way. "I shd. like to," he said, v. simply. "If Lakshman [i.e., Palit] were there, I wd. But I know no one there." So I said "Will you stay with me?" "Thank you," he said. "I will."[9]

Patrician, polished, so apparently cosmopolitan, Tagore was entirely different from any Bengali whom Thompson had met. E. P. Thompson reminds us that "Bankura's middle-class was known for its conservative, sanskritized traditions." To them, Tagore would have been a dangerous radical. His early schooling had been so unimaginative that it made him a chronic truant; his elders finally had him taught at home. That, with the family's varied talents and interests, made him a Bengali original.[10]

Edward had some twenty minutes' talk with him and thought him "a most noble saintly fellow. . . . As you probably know," Edward wrote, "he is a v. great poet; so far as I know, the world's greatest living poet. He is a member of the Adi Brahmo Samaj, a profoundly saintly man."[11]

In 1913 Tagore, although surrounded by friends and associates, was essentially a lonely man. His wife and two of his five children had died. His life had three foci. At the family home in Calcutta he saw visitors and conducted business. The Shantiniketan property had long been his devout father's rural retreat. The school there was Rabindranath's protest against his own formal education. It drew upon the ideal of the *tapoban,* the ancient forest hermitage where chosen pupils gathered to be schooled by a master teacher. Shantiniketan sounds idyllic, and in many ways it was, but it was a continuing drain on his resources.[12]

Shelidah, the family estates in riverine East Bengal, remained Tagore's retreat. He had lived in Calcutta until his father decided that his poet son needed practical experience and sent him to East Bengal where he lived until

1901 and proved himself an excellent estates manager. For the first time, he was close to the *ryots*, the peasant farmers, of eastern Bengal. He observed their good times and troubles, wrote down their songs and stories, noted their idiosyncracies and strengths. He incorporated this invaluable material in fiction that spoke for the East Bengal peasant to the intellectual elite of Calcutta.[13]

In 1913, however, the English *Gitanjali* created a public beyond Bengal, beyond the India Society and its friends. "You must be prepared," Rothenstein warned while Tagore was still visiting in America, "for a more clamorous reception than you met with before." Replying from Chicago, Tagore struck a note often repeated: "The people in this country are hearty in their kindness but there is a rudeness in their touch, it is vigorous but not careful." American kindness was unconvincing, and "therefore I could not take any delight in it as I did in your country." He had met a few sincere Americans, and perhaps his own reticence was to blame. Perhaps, more accustomed to English reserve, he concluded that Midwestern heartiness had no real heart.[14]

Early reviews of the India Society *Gitanjali* were few but good. Rothenstein had twice delivered additional manuscripts to Macmillan. The critic and author Charles Whibley again was Macmillan's reader; he liked additional poems in the *Gitanjali* style but thought the rest of very uneven quality: essays and stories that "for the present may be neglected," and "plays or dramatic pieces which consciously or unconsciously recall Maeterlinck, which are of undoubted interest." Publishing everything would be an "artistic mistake. Here, indeed, the half is larger than the whole." George Macmillan advised proceeding by stages.[15]

Macmillan's edition appeared in March 1913. On the whole, reviews still followed Yeats's lead. In 1912 the *Athenaeum* had pronounced *Gitanjali* of "trance-like beauty; . . . appropriate to the vein of essentially Oriental mysticism which supplies throughout the poet's imagination." It was the mystical East with a vengeance; the writer obviously knew nothing of the fiery Tagore whose essays, lectures, and patriotic songs had so antagonized officials during the Partition protests. In 1913 the *Athenaeum* kept to its line of "serenity which is one of the lessons most needed by the restless peoples of the West." Cultural self-abasement was another theme: "We go back and forth between pure theory and scientific experiment."[16]

In London Ezra Pound and Tagore had had a long talk about prosody, and Tagore sang a few of the poems that he had set to his own music. Pound saw a parallel with the troubadours of twelfth-century Provence. However, unaware of Vaishnava philosophy, he gave Buddhism credit for the poems' serenity. They would "change the prevailing conception of Buddhism among us. They are closer to what we call Taoism." Pound was puzzled when Tagore sang his *"Sonar bangla"* (Golden Bengal), which during the Partition protests became an unofficial Bengali anthem. Pound almost understood it as a highly emotional patriotic rallying-song: "It is 'minor' and subjective. Yet it has all the properties of action." But he fell in with the political assumption that an Asian country cannot (or should not) possess a concept of nationhood: *"Sonar bangla,"* he wrote, must be the Bengalis' "Marseillaise, if an Oriental nation can be said to have an equivalent to such an anthem."[17]

By November 1913 Tagore was back at Shantiniketan. Thompson was there on the fourteenth, when Tagore heard that he had won the Nobel Prize for Literature. This time Edward heeded Canton's advice and on the seventeenth wrote an account of the visit. Tagore gave his guest a batch of manuscripts, "new translations," and asked Edward to "improve their diction and rhythm." They had a wide-ranging conversation. Tagore spoke of his old feud with Calcutta University over his use of the Bengali vernacular for serious poems. Students put them into "chaste" Bengali—the sanskritized literary Bengali, a compulsory revision that wrecked rhyme, meter, and metaphor. He complained that "the preponderating *babu* element" at the university banned his books as textbooks. "I happen to know this is so," Edward wrote. "There has been a dead set against him."[18]

They spoke of Yeats's notion that Tagore was "applauded by a unanimous populace." Not so, Tagore said, for " 'I have been an unpopular poet. They say we Tagores are not like other Bengalis but are like a separate nation in the nation. Bengalis always complain that my poems are obscure.' " He thought that Yeats should have made even more corrections.

Edward played cricket with the boys; at their request he addressed them in Bengali and in English. They praised his Bengali, and "I felt more at home than I had yet done in India and we became great friends." While at dinner with them, "a hubbub arose": telegrams had brought news of the Nobel Prize for Literature. "I was nearly dancing with joy," Edward wrote. "I would not have swapped being the one outsider there on this night of madness for anything."

The boys went mad. They didn't know what the Nobel prize was, but they understood that the gurudeb [great teacher] they adored had done something wonderful, as indeed he was always doing. They formed ranks and marched round the ashram singing their school-song "Amader Shantiniketan" (Our Santiniketan). Rabi and I were sitting on the sofa, and they went past when they saw that. But they would not go past the second time but gathered at the door. I went and looked at them. They had gone wild. I called to Rabi, "You'd better come." He came. Then a frenzy of worship seized them and they, one after another, threw themselves down and touched his feet. . . . I could have done it myself almost; but I am an Englishman and have a stern contempt for the fools who pretend they are easterners.

Rothenstein was elated at the glorious outcome of his interest and efforts: "I open the Times and a great shout comes from it—Rabindranath has won the Nobel Prize! I cannot tell you of the delight this splendid homage gives me—the crown is now set upon your brow." The shout was Rothenstein's, for the two brief notices in the *Times* were scarcely that. They were somewhat bemused: "hereditary versatility . . . [a]dministers his own large landed property . . . successful journalist and historian . . . has been known to sing his own verses to his own music." Swedish papers "express some surprise at the unexpected decision of the Swedish Academy. . . ."[19]

"I shall get no peace now, Mr. Thompson," Tagore told Edward. He confessed to a low opinion of missionaries but refused at first to believe that Thompson was one of them. "They say," Edward remarked, "that when a man's a padre, it leaves a mark on him and you can spot him anywhere." Tagore said, "There's no mark on you." Edward had "made about 300 pencillings in nearly 150 poems." Tagore was "at sea on the definite article." Repetitions caused monotony. Unnecessary words made the rhythm sag where two clauses met. Tagore admitted, "I am not at all at home in the language and cannot judge of rhythm." When Edward was uncertain, Tagore began to sing. "He said he had a very bad memory for verse. He would sing the whole poem through till he got to the line; then he would ask me my opinion as to its translation. . . ."[20]

Edward mentioned the verse anthology. They left it with an apparent understanding about collaboration. Tagore asked him to write at once to Macmillan "and make arrangements, using his name any way I chose." Edward departed feeling that he had had "one of my most intimate experiences. It is no exaggeration to say that I loved him long before the evening was done. They told me that he misses his English friends and had greatly enjoyed the day. His parting injunctions were that I should pencil [corrections to his translations] as much as I liked."[21]

"For Edward Thompson," his son says, "this was a moment of epiphany. . . . But the premonitions of future misunderstandings can be detected in this first encounter." His visit was pleasing and flattering, but did Tagore really like "the curious mixture of diffidence, homage, and cheek—the assumption of equality in the republic of poets?" Tagore never followed through with collaboration.[22]

Edward had little sense of conventional religious mission, but his Wesleyan upbringing had engendered an evangelist who needed a message. Bengali literature, with which the West had only the most fragmentary acquaintance, could be his cause. Benita Parry describes Thompson as a man with an "impulse to mediate." Proselytizing for Bengali literature was more than an impulse; it was a mission requiring energy and evangelistic fervor.[23]

One month later, Tagore wrote a strangely contradictory letter. He had

been "absurdly oriental" and apologized for misleading Edward, whose kindness had prevented perfect frankness. Despite his deficient English the
work must be his alone. Then he adverted to his distrust of missionaries:
they lacked imagination—Edward already knew this too well—but perhaps
Edward was an exception. On 27 November Tagore again decided to use
most of Edward's emendations. On 1 January he accepted all of them,
saying that they greatly improved the rhythm. He asked Edward to suggest
stories for translation. On 13 January he promised a future talk about them,
but on 18 February he wrote that Edward's interest in translating them
was "premature." This time he stated plainly that all profits from *his own*
translations went to the school. Still, adequate translation was beyond him
without help from an Englishman "with literary abilities." Andrews, who
knew "very little Bengali," was now to be that man. If Edward had not been
so much under Tagore's spell he would have either called a halt or insisted
on a clear agreement.[24]

He pressed on, however, still believing that Tagore, though contradictory,
was not just being polite and that eventually they would collaborate on the
anthology. He wrote to Elizabeth about the "verse for schools that Rabi and I
are doing together (*together* means *I*)." Tagore did not write again until New
Year's Day; he was off on a "boat-trip" in search of some rest.[25]

He needed that riverboat respite. An uproar of Bengali attention had
followed the Nobel announcement. Certainly Edward was more welcome
at Shantiniketan than another congratulatory visitation: "Over 500 of Rabi
Babu's most distinguished compatriots journeyed up to Bolpur by special
train some time ago [23 November] to congratulate him on the Nobel award."
Some were genuine friends, but most were "the gentlemen who had been
busy attacking him for years & they simply use his greatness as a means of
self-complacency. He wasn't a bit pleased to see them & took the trouble
to tell them so, in his beautiful simple manner. And now there's trouble,
no end of trouble. A poet who speaks frankly & doesn't pander to their
ridiculous self-complacency is not popular with the Bengalis." There was
irony in congratulations on attention from the West, from persons who had
attacked him for excessive Western influence.[26]

Canton perceived that something had happened to Edward. "You have
been another man since you met Tagore," he wrote. "Why? He and the cold(?)
weather have wrought miracles. How? Don't you see you are a creature of
nerves and impressions and that instead of reading letters sent you you read
into the letters sent you. Thanks to the Indian poet, even this screed may pass
unchallenged and unsuspected of scornful irony and resentful displeasure."[27]

Canton had seen only *Gitanjali.* "His prose translations are so good that I
can hardly believe he could better them by making them into English verse.
At any rate they are as beautiful as need be, and in this form have a singular

freshness. I hope he has variety, for there is always danger even in so good a thing, of monotony." Like Pound, he puzzled over reference to Bengal as "Mother." If the "eternal East" is "unchanging," how could Indian breasts harbor the very modern sentiment of patriotism?

> Is this another western notion picked up with Christianity; or has a real change come over the "unchanging East"; or have all our writers of books about India not seen what was under their eyes, and told us the thing that is not and was not? Hatred of the foreigner is common everywhere (even in Whitechapel); but most of us have been taught that patriotism, as we understand the word, was a sentiment long extinct, if it ever existed, in India. Indeed as a rule patriotism is found, or was, in comparatively small countries well defined by seas and mountains and woods and great rivers. And how does the Mohammedan element get on with this Bengali patriotism?[28]

Canton had touched the heart of the matter. English preferences leaned subtly toward Muslims because Islam seemed more comprehensible than Hinduism. Islam and Christianity believed in one God and lived by one holy book, while pagan Hinduism worshipped a plethora of gods. Therefore Hindu opinion suspected English rulers of partiality. Could the Government of India create conditions in which the "Mohammedan element" would co-exist with Bengali patriotism and with non-Islamic India? Pleasing everyone all the time seemed impossible.

On 17 January Edward went to Calcutta in hopes of finding Tagore at home. He was still away, but Edward was received "joyously, not to say effusively," by Nagendranath Ganguli, a son-in-law, who said, " 'Father-in-law is always talking of you, so we all wish to know you.' " Rabindranath's nephew Abanindranath, one of the artists Rothenstein had met in 1910, was equally cordial. Edward was charmed and thought him "far more Bengali than Rabi." His studio was impressive with "Indian antiquities such as I suppose can hardly be seen together elsewhere. There were many old mussalman & rajput paintings." They pressed him to stay to tea, but he had to return to Bankura.[29]

On 28 February he returned to Calcutta to discuss the short stories. This was unsatisfactory, for "sometimes he wants me to translate them, sometimes he wants to do it himself, as he says his sch[ool] is hopelessly in debt. I saw him on Sunday [1 March]. It was most inconvenient to go down, & every visit to Calcutta costs at least £1—this cost more—but I felt I cd. not refuse. The old fellow was v. pleasant, more cheerful than I have known him. . . . He again asked me to translate his short stories. . . ." That "sometimes . . . sometimes" should have been a warning. Tagore had said plainly that remuneration from *his own* translations went to the school. But Edward was quite swept away, and Canton noticed that he now wrote nothing about Bankura people: "They have got off your nerves completely now, I take it—I wonder if you have got on to theirs since these Tagore developments. Body 'o me! But you are a quick-change artist."[30] Tagore seems not to have realized that the best of his stories from the 1890s were extraordinary examples of the short story as radical departure from the leisureliness of Victorian fiction. He was unjust to himself when he told an interviewer in 1936 that his later stories had "greater psychological value" and did not deal with "problems." Thus to dismiss the best of the earlier stories as having less psychological value and no social or political content was a serious underevaluation.[31]

The modern short story, by Frank O'Connor's definition, deals with "a submerged population group." Tagore's best stories examine the lives of Bengal's submerged groups: the ryot; the traditional housewife; the abandoned child; the university student who carries all his parents' aspirations; the Bengali trying to be an imitation Englishman, who makes himself look foolish and strews all around him the wreckage of others' lives. "The short story," writes William H. Peden, "brief, elliptical, and unwinking, tends to ask questions rather than to suggest answers, to show rather than attempt to solve." Thus reading an incisive story, oblique and open-ended, can be hard work, since it forces one to explore social and psychological regions that one may wish, consciously or unconsciously, to ignore or suppress. Readers must *think;* therefore it is eminently useful in times of social stress and suppression of freedoms. Many of Tagore's Bengali readers preferred to avoid the social and domestic issues dissected in his stories.[32]

Tagore's great skill with the best of his short fiction was not accidental. He read widely and variously in foreign authors. He knew a wide variety of French writers through his brother Jyotirindranath's Bengali translations: Gautier, Anatole France, de Maupassant, the Goncourts, Zola, Daudet: all experimenters with the more concentrated modern short story.[33]

Tagore's judgment of professional acumen was less reliable, for he turned over to Andrews not only some of the translations but also business dealings with Macmillan. More serious than Andrews's "little Bengali" was his lack of literary judgment. His worshipful attitude toward Tagore determined that whatever Tagore wrote must be canonical. Thompson admired the man but approached the work with enthusiasm for it as literature. The enthusiasm faded as their relations became more complicated. As E. P. Thompson points out, if Tagore was tired and overburdened, so was Edward Thompson at Bankura. If he were to translate for Tagore, he must plan accordingly.[34]

9

INTERIM

During the spring vacation of 1914 Edward took a two-month furlough at his own expense, in part because of increased tension between himself and his mother. Her letters were gloomy and pessimistic. Wesleyan affairs, always to her a personal concern, had gone badly. In 1913 income was down and the Missionary Society in debt. Guiltily, she reflected that her former South Indian colleagues were still at work there, while "here have I been toiling & moiling for 20 years, and badly enough has my work been done." She concluded that she had benefited neither herself, nor her children, nor her church.[1]

Edward perhaps excepted, the present generation seemed to lack an adequate sense of a great cause that called for sacrifices. Now there were changes even in him. She begged him not to desert his "poor Bengali boys," for "God's will is *always* best." But "the girls and I" thought "indecent" some remarks in his letters. They were probably only slangy, but they marred her idealized picture of her missionary son following in his father's footsteps. She tried to understand: she knew he was weary, but he must not let India lower his standards. Would he perhaps "like to go into Vernacular [street-preaching] work?"—the attraction least likely for him.[2]

His missionary future still seemed uncertain. If the London office "takes no responsibility for me," what happens, he asked Hartley, the Missionary Society Secretary, "if the College did not have the money?" "Then," Olver had replied, "you would have to go home." Elizabeth heard about Edward's letter to Hartley and fell into a panic. (Edward seems never to have grasped the range of the denominational grapevine.) She thought that he had been disrespectful to a Wesleyan elder. He must not write " 'nasty' letters" to anyone, especially not to Hartley, her friend for twenty years: "You young folks are too hot-blooded, too impetuous & impatient, you need to calm yourselves, & to possess your souls in quietness. Your mother has a busy time praying for you all. . . ." She could not understand that Edward's impatience was that of a whole generation. It was the more painful because the love was mutual.[3]

Her letters increased in length as her anxiety grew. She was sorry he was lonely, but there was a compensatory blessing: loneliness is bearable if it "brings us nearer to the Best Friend of all." Was he in some spiritual trouble? "I feel you are in peril of some kind or other, indeed I am sure you are." Prayer for him was some consolation. She became morbidly possessive. Would he please address her as "*My* dear mother"—not just as "Dear Mother," which could address the Mother Superior of a convent "or anybody's mother. I often wish you would acknowledge me as your very own mother." The tension grew when he mentioned a dancer. She was terribly hurt and charged that he did not know how much she loved him, but "it was so unexpected that you should be intimate in any way with a dancer." She had rewritten her first two pages; Edward had returned them, and she had burned them along with his last letter. If he had seen a demonstration of classical dance, to Elizabeth that would have connoted temple-dancers and prostitution. She was glad he had said what he thought, but "we seem to see some things from a different point of view. . . . Sometime, somewhere, these misunderstandings will melt away, & until that day dawns we must have patience with one another & love must never fail."[4]

Rumblings of war also accounted for the brief furlough. Insidious German propaganda kept turning up in India, such as an unidentified passage for translation from Hindi to English inserted into a recent Calcutta University examination. It praised Germany as "the center of art and science" and claimed that most of the best books taught in English universities were "mere translations" of German books. Indians who ignored Germany were "badly dyed in English colour," Oxbridge instruction was not "true teaching," and study in England was pointless.[5]

The Government of India feared uprisings of the warlike tribes beyond the Northwest Frontier. A prompt army counterraid repelled invaders from Afghanistan. This was the way to handle such outbreaks, observed the *Times,* for it "saves the necessity of an expensive expedition" and showed that "there is a power in hand ready to strike sharply." The Government of India, always mindful of the 1857 "Mutiny," was less complacent: were full-scale invasions imminent from Afghanistan and Russia? The Afghan border was a boiling kettle with a too-tight lid ready to blow. It distracted from greater issues and gave Bengali extremists an excuse for sedition. Crewe thought that systematic surveillance might curb crime in Bengal, although similar measures had not worked in Ireland. Carmichael sent an army detachment to eastern Bengal, to show the flag. Fortunately, the soldiers behaved well.[6]

The spirit of preparedness caught up the Thompsons. Arthur was in the Naval Reserve. Mollie considered army nursing. Englishmen in Bengal were required to join a defence training unit of some kind. With Bankura's civil officers and the missionaries Edward joined the Chota Nagpur Light Horse— without horses but with new, special-design rifles.

The whole matter, as it appears to me, is that I'm not entitled to expect other men to defend me if I'm not prepared to risk my own life in the same [way]. If we must have war, it seems to me that every able-bodied man shd. be liable. . . . All this makes for security & takes away the chances that we shall have a 2nd mutiny. . . . I'm not going to let other fellows engage to do that for me wh. I wont do for myself or them. It isn't decent.[7]

Edward's English furlough was too brief for him to test the literary current. Canton, Rushbrooke, and Collingwood, his mentors, knew that they were lingering Victorians, of a tradition increasingly foreign to the "hasty readers of a newer time." They pointed Edward toward the future but could not tell him where to go thereafter. Canton knew that literary time was passing him by, but he did his best to keep up. On 8 January 1914 he had attended the opening of Harold Monro's Poetry Bookshop in London. Monro and Edward Marsh, patrons and encouragers of younger poets, saw their work as heralding the next new movement: pictorial representation to replace general impressions, which they saw as "decorative art." They intended to escape Victorian sententiousness and *fin de siècle* affectation to "establish a new orthodoxy in the place left vacant by the death of Tennyson." The best known of their protégés were Rupert Brooke, John Drinkwater, John Masefield, Walter De la Mare, Siegfried Sassoon, and D. H. Lawrence. Georgian poetic reputations survived unevenly, but they and the Poetry Bookshop inspired a wave of new interest.[8]

The opening illustrated the advance of generations. Canton observed the audience much as more conventional elders observed the coffeehouse poets of the 1960s. He wished Edward could have seen "the array of young fellows and young women, all apparently of the warbling feather. . . . I should have greatly liked to lift off the lids of some of the simmering or seething girls who were there, and there were several Sapphos who had long passed the summer of their days, and who might have had yearning stories to tell." Still, his tolerance for the unpredictable prevailed.

Naturally I am chary of criticizing. It is so easy to say things which, instead of stimulating, discourage, and so do mischief. At the same time it is worth remembering that whatever is said in honest criticism is worth considering: not because A or B says it, but because what A, B or C thinks hundreds of people *like him* will also think. We are (nearly all) representative men (and women)—so commonplace are we! Of course my criticism [of Edward's poems] broadly amounts to this, that "I wouldn't say that," or "I think that would be better, put differently," or "That is inaccurate, untrue, unauthorised, unintelligible."[9]

Edward had no congenial center like the bookshop and no mentor like Marsh. He clung to a poetic vein where he felt safer, but he needed a more crisp and colloquial idiom, such as came so effortlessly in his letters. Tagore's influence also tended to isolate, for he too was out of touch with the currents into which friendly circumstances had thrust him in 1912 and 1913. For Pound, Tagore remained "the sensation of the winter [of 1912–1913]." Nor did Tagore seem fully to understand the importance of Yeats's poetic innovations. In his Bengali essay on Yeats, he dwelled principally on parallels between Indian and Irish politics and on how poets may be national spokesmen, but Yeats became impatient with poems in the *Gitanjali* vein, with regret for what he saw as Tagore's lost opportunity. In 1916 he told Macmillan: "Tagore is not a master of facile English for English religious readers, but master of very arduous measures whom they read as a tongue that is not his."[10]

Tagore's English poetic diction was not a beneficent influence on Edward. He needed a more crisp and colloquial idiom, such as came so effortlessly in his letters. Tagore, even in informal English letters, kept to old-fashioned circumlocutions, orotund and stilted. Contemporary readers were unlikely to persevere to the end of such passages. Again, in 1917, Yeats told Macmillan, "Now I had no great heart in my version of his last work *Fruit-Gathering*. The work is a mere shadow. . . . He is an old man now [he was fifty-six] and these later poems are drowning his reputation." Thus Tagore stood at an angle to possibilities of new direction. The coming war would jerk Edward out of old habits and Bankura isolation, but it isolated Tagore from English influences that might have been salutary.[11]

Edward had obeyed Tagore's instructions to write to Macmillan about the schools anthology. In England, he followed it up, but the project hung fire because Tagore had been ill, protested that he did not know English poetry well enough, and felt, quite rightly, that his name should not be on the title-page if another did most of the work. Textbook adoption in India was crucial to sales; Macmillan wanted his name, but he admitted that it "carried no influence with Calcutta University. . . ." In fact, "for some months" Tagore had been too busy to even look at Edward's suggestions.[12]

Edward sent Canton a translation of one of Tagore's stories. Canton thought it was "more interesting than convincing. In other words the work is better than the material—at least to an average English reader." Edward defended it, and Canton replied, "And are you too among the mystics? I don't see where *I* come in. But peradventure that is the best test of the mystic—quien sabe?"[13]

The story was "*Jibito o mrito*" (Living and dead), translated as "Living or Dead," in which a young widow raises a brother-in-law's small son during his mother's illness. One night she has a sharp pain in her chest, falls into a coma, and is pronounced dead. Before cremation can take place, she revives and makes her way home by slow and painful stages, terrified and convinced that she is her own ghost: "her existence perplexed her. . . ." At home she finds the child ill and feverish. If she really is a ghost, none can see her caring for him. He asks, "Did you die, Auntie?" When she says yes, he says matter-of-factly, "Do not die again." But a maidservant and the mother see her and faint, and the terrified child bursts out, "Go away, Auntie, go away!" She does: to prove that she is not dead but living, she drowns herself in the well.[14]

Did Canton miss the point? Like many Western readers, he read Indian stories as "tales" of the supernatural. He had seen a translation of another of Tagore's stories, which may have been "The Hungry Stones." He thought it "the usual haunted-house . . . a Puck story. . . . How is it that all stories of this class as a rule run to the useless, the trivial, or to the tricky and wicked?" In fact, *"Jibito o mrito"* is not a ghost story, but an analysis of superstition's grip on unsophisticated minds and of a popular mysticism that usurps the place of reality. Tagore hoped to encourage self-analysis, but this is not one of his best-constructed stories; in the Bengali original, division into brief sections prevents smooth transitions; still, the atmosphere of fright and self-doubt is as oppressive as Tagore intended.[15]

Before Edward left England, he and Bridges met for the first time, in Oxford on 4 June. Bridges enjoyed the evening "greatly" with several hours of "quiet before dinner and had good evening."[16]

When Edward sailed on 23 June, Elizabeth was too upset for tears. The difference between her missionary commitment and his own assailed him when she wrote that he was "doing a great work for Christ in India, & I am glad." Mr. Maltby, her Wesleyan minister, refused to give him up for lost: one made allowances for the loneliness of a missionary's life, the climate, heathenism, and idolatry. He and Elizabeth still concentrated on capturing Arthur for the church, but he escaped to Epping Forest on Sundays until time for the evening service. He "pines for the country," Elizabeth told Edward, "& it may be he will find God in the Forest."[17]

The Great War began while Edward was at sea. He found Bankura in upheaval and anxiety. Owston Smith had gone to a government college at Patna. Now Bankura needed a man not only for history but for economics and philosophy. For years Mitchell had held out against philosophy, "but Indian students *will* have philosophy, though they are not really capable of intelligently understanding its essence & purpose." The Viceroy shared this concern. He had "read students' note-books containing beautifully written essays on Mill, Burke, Spencer and others, and yet these young men have been quite unfit to discuss any point with me owing to their insufficient knowledge of English. It is a parrot-like education, which must be absolutely valueless, and I do not see how it is going to be altered."[18]

Mitchell and Olver were close to despair. Currency was restricted, and Bengal banks refused paper as payment. News was heavily censored; they had little idea what was happening at home. Skimping was already daily practice. The Reverend A. R. Spooner was due from England but did not meet Calcutta University standards for teaching B.A. History. Bankura might lose its grants, "without which we cannot exist as a College. . . ." Mitchell juggled staff and appointments without flexible money. Several of the missionaries' wives were in an extreme state of nerves.[19]

India's entire east coast was also in a state of nerves. The audacious German light cruiser *Emden* prowled up and down from Calcutta to Madras. Ships required government approval to leave Calcutta. Trade was paralyzed, and businessmen were agitated despite reassurances from Carmichael, who remained at Darjeeling. There were no warnings about dangers in the Bay of Bengal, and faith in the Intelligence Department waned rapidly. Would Indian dissidents use the situation to their political advantage? In September the *Emden* shelled the Madras beaches. On 10 November, to everyone's relief, an Australian cruiser sank her, but other German marauders were loose in the Pacific, and the *Times* called for better protection for British shipping there.[20]

War revived old issues about Indian volunteers for the army and especially about regular army commissions for Indians. And what about Muslim sympathies if Islamic Turkey entered the war? A Muslim had told Hardinge that " 'their heads are with us but their hearts are not.' " Many believed that Germany was Turkey's true friend: Turkey in the war could threaten stability in Bengal. Carmichael hoped that Hardinge would keep troops there unless urgently needed elsewhere. No one then imagined how many Indian troops would eventually be spared to augment British forces in Europe and the Middle East.[21]

On 11 August Hardinge ordered the army to accept Indian volunteers. However, senior officers must be regular army Englishmen, and Indian should not outnumber English companies. English volunteers, "who have strong feelings and prejudices," must learn to accept the Indians, or there could be riot or even mutiny. Officers must respect Indian soldiers' anxieties about caste customs and restrictions.[22]

By 3 September Hardinge relaxed a little. There was such indignation over the London Cabinet's idea that Indian troops be used only for garrison duty in Europe and the Mediterranean that Hardinge had "fairly rattled Crewe with indignant telegrams." The Cabinet backed down and requested "far more troops than we had originally contemplated." Muslim loyalty was admittedly a problem in view of the Turkish problem, but Indian Muslims were "so disunited and broken up into cliques, that they do not present a really serious danger, even if they wished to be troublesome, which I do not believe to be the case." Almost a greater problem was getting the India Office in London to say who was responsible for what in this war effort.[23]

Edward's home news was of the family mobilizing. Margaret and Charles Rogers decided to marry at once. Mollie prepared to go to Flanders. Arthur went to the HMS *Dreadnought*. Frank trained with the Artists' Rifles. Elizabeth, patriotically resigned, found refuge in sentiment and religious faith. "Now that this just and righteous war for us to fight has been thrust upon us, as one man the Nation has united together. . . . It cheers us to read of India's splendid loyalty. . . ." She could not blame the Kaiser too much, for "one can never forget that his mother was an English Princess." Mission funds would suffer, but perhaps, as compensation, "God intends the seed that has been sown in heathen lands to come to life & vigour without the further aid of missionaries."[24]

Edward's contacts with Tagore had been sporadic since February 1914. Tagore had rejected Edward's proposal to translate his stories as "a little premature." Edward apparently apologized for his audacity, and Tagore replied with a lament about Shantiniketan's debts. Edward translated a long story, apparently *"Megh o roudra"* (Cloud and sun). Tagore put him off with the usual deprecation of his own knowledge of English. Canton advised him not to worry too much about Tagore's retreat: "Possibly the poor man may be passing through some mental storm, of which we know nothing."[25]

Unfortunately, Edward's relations with Tagore were still entangled with hero-worship (his own and others') and hopes for an enduring association. During 1915 Edward was drawn into a morass connected with Robert Bridges's wartime anthology, *The Spirit of Man*. The affair eventually involved Longmans, the publisher; Macmillan, who administered Tagore's permissions; the Society of Authors as legal adviser; C. F. Andrews as éminence grise in Bengal; and Yeats, Rothenstein, and Edward Thompson recruited as expediters. It encapsulated not only Tagore's doubts and defensiveness, but also the difficulties of literary exchange across cultural barriers.[26]

Since their Oxford meeting in 1913, Bridges's relations with Tagore had remained cordial, and he admired Tagore's modesty. In June 1914 Bridges told Tagore that he had met Edward Thompson, "the young Scotch [*sic*] missionary, who spoke of him and described "something of your way of life," and "indeed it is his telling of it that has given me confidence to write as I do: for I guessed from what he said that you are likelier to overvalue my sympathy than to underrate it." He hoped that the Nobel Prize "may not encourage your countrymen inordinately to write their poetry in our foreign language, especially as their success shd they succeed wd be oldfashioned. You must advise them."[27]

When war began, Bridges was "terribly smitten down at first, with something like rage, but I hope that I am getting more placid." As Poet Laureate, he was already uncomfortable about having to write to order. In 1915, with the European war already longer than anyone had expected, he designed a collection of serious, inspiring verse more dignified and enduring than the jingoistic concoctions of versifiers in the daily papers. He would emphasize poems rather than poets; titles and authors would appear only in an index. The selection would be for all time, universal in appeal and also intensely personal. He wanted to include eight poems from an edition by Tagore and Evelyn Underhill of poems by Kabir, the seventeenth-century Muslim weaver-mystic. Bridges wanted also three poems from *Gitanjali.* Number 67 from that book, in particular, became the crux of a long-drawn contretemps.[28]

At issue were the ethics and legality of translation and an author's rights of ownership. Bridges wanted to make "verbal alterations" in Tagore's texts, to correct what he considered awkward syntax and inconsistencies of diction. Number 67 in *Gitanjali* apostrophizes an Eternal Being and begins, "Thou art the sky and thou art the nest as well." Bridges thought that from line to line a lofty tone sank to the colloquial. He designed his "verbal alterations" to keep that ecstatic tone and the devotional tone of the King James Bible. His desired effect is clear if one compares Number 67 from *Gitanjali* with Number 38 in *The Spirit of Man.* He added a penciled note to the file of correspondence, that in his sequence the poem "stands between Plato & Aristotle & it was necessary for the solidity of my b[oo]k that it shd not stumble in that place." Tagore's was free-form prose-poetry; on principle Bridges disliked undisciplined verse; the title of a 1922 essay (originally intended as a subtitle) says it all: "Humdrum and Harum-Scarum: A Lecture on Free Verse." He intended to do Tagore a service by presenting his work to best advantage at a time when adverse criticisms of his poetic style increased.[29]

Now began a labyrinthine correspondence about who had, or had not, given permission for what. Bridges asked permission for his "verbal alterations." Tagore thought that Macmillan would agree, since he had "no personal objection" and "no real critical apprehension of the musical value of English words." Then he back-pedaled: readers who already knew the English *Gitanjali* might resent changes in a beloved text. He must rely on Macmillan. Bridges thought that Tagore overestimated "the familiarity which English readers have with his book."[30]

Rothenstein suggested that Tagore feared offending Yeats, who had made the early revisions. Bridges wrote to Yeats, who was not at all offended. Inspirational books sold well in wartime, so why were Tagore's poems selling less well? Bridges thought Tagore's popularity in England "a matter of fashion"; a publisher must agree: "That seems to me the practical point."[31]

Macmillan gave permission *if* the poems appeared in Tagore's published English, and Macmillan continued to refuse Bridges's changes. Tagore's communications to Macmillan and Bridges continued equivocal. Bridges appealed to Herbert Thring, Secretary of the Society of Authors, who pointed out that copyright applied *unless* a translation were from the original text: in this case, the Bengali.[32]

Rothenstein went to the heart of the matter when he pointed out that Tagore feared charges in India and in England that the English poems were Yeats's work. He suggested further that Andrews had caused the impasse because "his admiration for Tagore is a little too uncritical." Andrews, Rothenstein wrote, "was sweet & well-meaning enough, but without any sense of literature and very little of the masculine side of life. He flatters the sentimental side of Tagore, & does not understand the more natural side of his nature—the best side, in fact. . . . I wish he had not become so famous, & people did not regard him as a saint. He isn't that at all. He is a very human and delightful person, witty & observant, & the saint's halo has been stuck behind his head by slaves—certainly not by his equals." Finally, Tagore admitted to Bridges that he did fear being disloyal to Yeats. Andrews told Macmillan that he thought Bridges's alterations quite outlandishly inappropriate.[33]

Now Bridges appealed to Thompson as a man on the spot and suggested that Tagore was " 'being influenced by some one.' " Edward replied that that someone was indeed Andrews, who "for months" had intercepted his own letters to Tagore. When Edward finally got a letter through, Tagore was penitent, and Edward wrote what he meant as "a tactful & kind letter." Tagore read it to mean that Edward was " 'hurt' " and, inconsistently, broke off all relations. For Edward, the letter "made all further intercourse between us impossible." A few weeks later he met Tagore's son Rathindranath, who knew all about the problem of Number 67 and "came as a sort of ambassador" for a long talk. He said that his father "had had a v. bad time mentally[,] at one time being resolved to leave India & go to Japan. That was when he wrote to me." Rathindranath said that his father knew that Bridges's alterations were improvements. Dr. Seal was supposed to arrange a meeting with Edward but forgot all about it, and Tagore "swooped off to his wayside nest at Shillida." However, he now wrote kindly to Edward to say that he had told Macmillan to let Bridges do as he wished.[34]

Besides some thick correspondence files, what came of all this agitation and irresolution? Macmillan had played by the rules. Bridges made his changes. Still, it may be doubted whether many, if any, readers laid the two versions side by side and assessed Tagore's reputation accordingly. Bridges assumed that he and Tagore dealt as poet to poet and understood each other's literary assumptions, but Tagore had encountered a Poet Laureate with a commanding personality and strong convictions. Finally, Tagore really could not judge Bridges's alterations. Uncertainty paralyzed him under the epistolary bombardment from the Laureate and Rothenstein, to whom, if Tagore had only remembered it, he was even more indebted than to Yeats.

Edward gave Bridges a further explanation for Tagore's state of mind. "Rabi has greatly changed for the worse in one respect," he wrote. "He was always v. touchy under criticism; but now he is rabid if a word of disparagement is breathed, broods over it & resents it as injustice. He is spending his time writing & printing personal 'apologies,' in verse & prose." Another reason for disquiet was a knighthood proposed for June 1915. Honors, particularly those for Indians, were carefully checked and balanced for maximum effect and for risk of public criticism. In 1914 Lord Crewe had heard (from Andrews?) that Tagore would not turn down a knighthood. Andrews should sound out Tagore. In a long and repetitive letter he reported that "the Poet" was so shy that he would dread the publicity. A knighthood certainly had its perils. His critics could ask why he was thus honored. His friends could accuse them of jealousy. Those who had criticized his Nobel Prize could criticize again for too much sympathy with Western ideas and avidity for Western honors. And was the knighthood a bribe to forestall criticism of government policies from one who had criticized freely in the past? The knighthood was announced on 3 June. Four years later Tagore would renounce it, as his personal protest against the massacre at Amritsar.[35]

Edward soon had other concerns. In June he had a brief but restless holiday in the hills at Coonoor, the scene of his father's worsening illness and of the beginnings of Alfred's troubles so long ago. "What is this," Canton wrote, "about being 'off the teaching tack altogether before the year ends?' " He knew that Edward thought about enlistment but passed it jokingly. "Going to be a Maharaja? Or to marry a Begum, by gum? Or starting as an Indian pote [sic] with a tom-tom and a Nobel prize? . . . I am curious. However, don't jump once before you have looked twice, and again twae."[36]

Edward wrote to his mother: "The thought of Frank enlisting brings a pang to my heart. Yet I wd. not have us as a family do a scrap less than our best. If a thing is God's truth, it must be lived by, worked for, if necessary died for. My own decision waits. Am I to cling to my tame life here, useful but safe, or to prove myself no thin-blooded weaver of rimes but a man no whit less than those who cannot play with silken words?" The Missionary Society disapproved but could not forbid his going. "It isn't the Front I would avoid; but I do shrink in distaste from the long months in an Indian garrison town, as one of a mess, the junior of all with nothing but routine & distasteful tasks. But poor Frank! He always has struck me as such a frail, delicate flower. But, if all are dying as they seem to be,—what does anything matter?" Alfred would be all right, for "no harm can come to him on ocean or on shore. But I am v. different, for harm comes to me continually, & comes from within." He worried less for himself and more about Arthur on the high seas, about Frank going to France, about his mother, and about the zeppelins over London.

Everyone else was "facing hell for my sake, while I live in ease." His mother must trust in God, and he would "trust my countrymen wh[ich] is perhaps the same thing."[37]

In July the officer in charge thought that the government would probably consider Edward more useful at Bankura, for "students are inflammable material," and if they caused trouble those who knew them would be best able to talk them out of it. Edward replied that he would do his duty.[38]

The college closed for October holidays, and his students honored him with heaped flowers and garlands. Edward asked whether they would spend their time writing poems and painting pictures. No, they said, for they were all *bokas* (fools). "This touched me, so I said, 'Oh no, you are not. I call you bokas, but you know what I mean.' 'Yes, sir,' they chorused. So finally we parted with great friendship & much salaaming & politeness all round. Just before we went, Mohini exclaimed, 'Sir, how white yr. hands are!' At this they all roared.' "[39]

Edward ended 1915 working in famine relief, for a bad crop and inflation had decimated the villagers' resources, and he could set a good example for his students: "One sees some pretty bad things." Still, he knew that these had been good years that would not come again. "I think I have inherited yr. sadness," he told his mother, "so that, though my students think greatly of me, I pass my days with little lightness of heart. I save others, I believe, but I have never been able to save myself. . . . I can do everything except support with courage this constant . . ."[40]

There, incomplete, the letter ends. In six months he would be in Bombay, a captain in the army chaplaincy.

10

"CHAPLAINING"

Percy Comyn Lyon now became another mentor. He would not displace Canton. Canton's was the world of literature past. Lyon's was that of Indian politics boiling furiously in the present. Born in 1862 and thus twenty-four years Thompson's senior, Lyon was educated at Oriel College, Oxford, and entered the Indian Civil Service in 1881. He had dealt with land record and revenue in Assam and East Bengal. In the reunited Bengal he was Education Member of Governor Carmichael's Council, from 1913 until retirement in 1917. During an inspection visit to Bankura, Lyon was impressed when Edward spoke in a meeting, then visited his class. Lyon's admiring note in the visitors' book "made me blush, esp[ecially] when I saw my teachers smile as they read it. My teachers unfortunately know me." In March 1913 Lyon invited Edward to Calcutta. Edward assumed that Lyon was interested in him because his only son, who wrote poetry, was at the Front.[1]

In April 1916, Edward visited Lyon again in Calcutta, and Lyon wrote a letter that told as much about himself as about Edward:

> My note to you was a poor return for what you have given to my boy and still less for what you have said about myself. For my part I am sorry, very sorry, that we shall not meet again for a long space. I am sure you did me much good during your stay. You brought a breath of truth with you, most salutary for a poor official, and you revived in me tastes and ideas which were sick from long neglect. But what you have said is so much more than I deserve that I feel that you should know me more, in the interests of truth!
>
> Indeed, I am proud to know a man who has your gifts, so the kindness is by no means all on one side. So don't be afraid of friendship. . . . Though I think it might perhaps help you a bit just at this time, through some of your troubles.[2]

Visits to Lyon at Calcutta brought other contacts. Edward and Dr. Seal translated "about 10 of my Ramprasad songs together." These would be published some years later as *Bengali Religious Lyrics,* but with Arthur Spencer, not Seal, as collaborator. Edward met the botanist Dr. J. C. Bose and "young Mahalanobis," who had just returned from a brilliant career at Cambridge and for many years would remain a principal friend.[3]

Lyon made no secret of the fact that his superiors did not consider him a team player. What was his offense? He too often dissented from government policy. He believed that the bhadralok moderates had helped to preserve order and therefore deserved more recognition and more responsibility. If Bengal was out of step with the rest of India, that was because it was politically advanced; it must now become India's pacesetter. In 1916 Lyon drafted an official note, "an epoch-making communication to India on the present political situation in Bengal," with recommendations for postwar policy: "But if only I can give my words the strength of my convictions I should be able to make something of it. I wonder what it will be like when it has got through our Council?" He thought it liberal and broad-minded, cautious and practical. "And yet—I am very diffident over it, though I think a good deal of it in my own heart." The time was ripe for a new policy. Such a chance would not come again.[4]

His official note might indeed have been epoch-making if the government had taken heed. It not only ignored the advice but harshly criticized the adviser. Broomfield calls the note "a warning disregarded." Its gist was that merely keeping order was no solution. The educated groups had been patient and cooperative, but their patience was not inexhaustible. "They are already learning to identify themselves with the masses," Lyon wrote, "and are spreading their own distrust of British rule amongst them, and they will ultimately carry the people with them in their demands that nationalist views should be introduced into the government of the country." The war presented an opportunity to adopt a broad and constructive reform policy. "Otherwise, our proposals will lead inevitably to coercion followed by an administrative collapse, and it may then be too late to guide the political evolution of the country along any safe and peaceful course."[5]

"What Lyon was demanding," Broomfield says, "was not simply reforms but a revolution in British thinking about India." He invited his I.C.S. colleagues to acknowledge "the superior capacity of the bhadralok, to admit the legitimacy of nationalism, and to transform the political role of the Indian bureaucracy." The central government advised Lyon to put his time and energy into restoring order in Bengal "instead of trying to teach the Government of India its business." He had committed the cardinal sin of disregarding the hierarchical order of procedure.[6]

Lyon advocated dominion status within the British Commonwealth. Carmichael agreed, but that only convinced the so-called Old India Hands that "these two senior members of the Government of Bengal were fundamentally unreliable." Broomfield says that in May 1916 the Government of India considered asking both to resign. In fact, as early as 1913 the Viceroy had pressed Lyon hard to retire early and go home; a knighthood was dangled as inducement. Lyon was candid about wanting the title, for he had seen knighthoods go to persons of lesser achievement, and the honor would enhance his effectiveness in civilian appointments at home. Carmichael told Lyon that if he left at once he would urge Hardinge to bestow the knighthood. Lyon refused to leave before retirement in 1917.[7]

In 1914 Hardinge tried again to force Lyon to retire. He rejected Carmichael's idea that Lyon might go if he got a knighthood in England. This was not in the package. Hardinge approved Carmichael's idea of a more conservative man on his council to counterbalance Lyon's influence. Still, no title was forthcoming.[8]

In 1915, however, Hardinge had to admit that although he thought some of Lyon's associates were questionable, the contacts sometimes proved useful, as in settlement of a constitution for the new University of Dacca. Later in 1915 Hardinge wrote that the government of Bengal was the worst in India, principally because of Lyon. He thought Lyon and his ideas a very present danger to the Bengal government.[9]

Did Thompson realize that he was the friend of a dangerous man? If so, it would not have mattered. Unlike many in high office, Lyon was approachable. Unfortunately, even small private efforts to encourage Indian self-esteem did not always turn out well. They led Lyon and Thompson into a bothersome involvement with Harihar Das, an ambitious collector of eminent persons. He was writing a biography of Toru Dutt, a young Bengali woman writer. For her day she had singular literary enterprise and intellectual curiosity. The manuscript needed much revision and a concluding chapter, which Das wanted Edward to write. Das and his book became an intermittent nuisance until its publication in 1921.[10]

Harihar Das was a minor disturbance compared with events abroad. "I feel ashamed about the war," Edward told Lyon. "One can do nothing. The obvious thing for a fool to say is, write about it. But the thing is too serious for literature. . . . I will not turn living agony into literature; neither will I talk about glory till we are through with the business." He needed an "objective subject." He outlined a university extension course for Europeans in Bengal. He even thought about an unpaid year after the war in which to found an English-language journal for Bengal, on the model of the London *Spectator.* But objectivity was difficult, for "a man living alone in the East gets driven in on himself. . . ."[11]

In August 1915 he applied for an army commission. He wrote to Hartley: "It is my duty to tell you that I have applied for a commission in the Indian Army Reserve of Officers." He was able-bodied, unmarried, and unengaged; "I can ride & shoot." He was the very last man to want to fight, but those who survived this hell were "the men to whom I must preach when this war is finished." He would remain in the ministry, although "my action is sure to be misunderstood. . . . I have applied, that is all." The Wesleyan Committee might take "whatever action seemed right to them."[12]

His mother wrote that he was doing "such important work where you are amongst those Hindu students, that only a *very* clear call would justify your enlisting." He was aware of Bankura's staffing difficulties, but always there was the thought of his brothers soon to be in the line of fire.[13]

Most alarming was the army's determination to enlist Alfred. Time had disposed of the notion that the war would last a mere six months, but was it going so badly that men like Alfred must be sent out? His fate hung fire for more than a year. Mr. Maltby accompanied him to the army medical examiner, and he was rejected. Elizabeth believed that if he had gone alone he would have been taken; if she and Margaret had gone, "neither she nor I would have been taken any notice of." By November 1915 Elizabeth felt that she had finally persuaded the insistent recruiter to leave Alfred alone. She changed her mind about ministers who enlisted: the country's need was so great that if they saw that as duty, they should go.[14]

In March 1916 conscription replaced voluntary enlistment. Three times between March and November Alfred was called and rejected. In November Elizabeth went with him and stood by while two doctors examined him. She explained about his childhood seizures and his doctor's warnings that great excitement would renew them. The next morning Alfred returned alone with a doctor's letter, was kept all day, and returned at night "in a perilous state of nervous excitement." He thought he was rejected, but then came an order to report for induction. A determined Elizabeth, his papers in hand, went to the induction center. This time she made the army take notice of her, and at last the matter was settled. The whole heartless story amazed and outraged Edward. He read her account with "mingled amazement & contempt. There's no question if he'd belonged to a working man's family, he'd have been enlisted. If they're pressing men like that into the Army, it seems to me time we ceased gloating over the Germans putting into their firing-line mental deficients. The thing's a disgrace to all concerned." If the army was that deficient in compassion, chaplains were all the more needed.[15]

In May 1916, Edward had met Thomas McClelland, Olver's successor as Bengal Methodist District Superintendent. He had heard that a Wesleyan chaplain in the Bombay hospitals had gone to the Mesopotamian campaign, and another was needed at Bombay immediately. Hundreds of Indian wounded from Mesopotamia passed through those wards every day, and "Mac put it to me." It was during vacation, and he felt that he should do what he could, although "chaplaining's not my line at all." The mission would spare him for a month. By 1 June he was in Bombay being measured for a captain's uniform, saluting and being saluted and finding it "a bit queer, as it is." Soon he was convinced that not only was one month's service on loan a paltry contribution, but he should follow his brothers and request field service.[16]

McClelland found him a baffling case altogether. What gave him this notion? He was a poet, that was what. Poets were quixotic and therefore unreliable. He gave Hartley the stock Wesleyan explanation: "He is a Poet, so it is not easy for a prosy chairman to follow his arguments in justification of the step he has taken." McClelland was sure that he could have convinced Edward that anyone with influence over inflammatory Indian students was "worth a dozen Subalterns to the Empire." In all his years with teachers and students he had never met anyone like Edward. When he suggested that Edward use his holiday to assist at Bombay, did he perhaps hope that that sample of army life would send him back to Bankura breathing sighs of relief?[17]

It did not happen. Two more Wesleyan chaplains left Bombay for Mesopotamia, and Edward asked for a Bombay extension. McClelland approved, but Mitchell refused. "If he had heard & seen what I have," Edward told his mother, "he'd have realised that we *must* do something." He understood Mitchell's reluctance, for he would have to take over English Honours and the hostel, which advertised "English supervision." In uncertainty Edward spent "3 of the worst days I ever had," then wired that he would return to Bankura—but then came a generous letter from Mitchell to Lyon, who had intervened to point out that Edward was doing important government work. Still, he regretted leaving his students and the Bengali language just when he hoped to settle to steady work at translation.[18]

If he could not get an extension, he *would* try for Mesopotamia. Hartley refused, but the War Office repeatedly asked for Thompson. Hartley agreed, but then he heard that two more Wesleyan chaplains were leaving England for Mesopotamia. He resented his missionaries being "commandeered" when others were available. He gave up all responsibility for Edward, who told McClelland that rather than miss going to Mesopotamia, he would resign the ministry and join the Indian army. McClelland did not know whether to take this seriously. Again he invoked the poetic temperament as explanation: a taste of army field discipline would straighten Thompson out. "I've severed my connection with Bengal & I feel bad about it," Edward wrote to Lyon. "Poor old John [Mitchell] writes miserably. He rose to scratch because he hoped I was going to the Gulf; & now he finds he has been treated with scant courtesy, & that I am here just for an incessant round of preaching & visiting. He writes that he feels we have been 'had.' " Edward's excellent teaching was Bankura's key to more university admissions. "And John says he daren't let on to the clerk or students that I'm not returning. 'It will have to leak out somehow.' "[19]

Mrs. Mitchell upbraided Edward for leaving the comfortable home she had arranged for him and for ignoring her husband's sacrifice in letting him go. Lyon intervened again and wrote to both Mitchells, who were only somewhat mollified. "I really pressed it home," he told Edward, "as I felt deeply on the subject, and his letter echoes the tone I took, to some extent. . . . A general regard for you shows itself throughout it." Lyon wrote, "You know you are of real use, that you are doing three men's work & that many a poor wounded fellow will go without the kindness and help which you can give him, if you knock up. So treat yourself as of some value & avoid such needless injury to others." Fielden, who now taught English literature at the University of Lund, felt keenly that Sweden was a backwater; his peaceful life there "throws into very strong relief the heroism (I can use no other word) of your life at Bankura & the nobility of spirit shown by your latest step."[20]

Edward and the Viceroy had arrived in India at the same time and now both prepared to break away. Hardinge was very tired and was already a year past his term. His elder son had died in England after injuries in France, and Lady Hardinge died after an operation. Austen Chamberlain had succeeded Hardinge's old friend Lord Crewe as Secretary of State for India; his letters are cordial but lack the fraternal warmth of exchanges with Crewe.[21]

Edward went to Bombay. The work there, he wrote, was "unending. Even now men die steadily; & the sick drift through in their weekly hundreds. . . . There are rumours of a huge battle impending up the Gulf, & they are clearing the wards." His army ecumenical education began. He discovered the pointlessness of denominational divisions. In the wards he had to "drift in on C[hurch] of E[ngland]'s & R[oman] C[atholic]s, as well as nonconformists. In fact, there were only 2 Wesleyans in the gang I saw. After all, my padreship is something worth keeping. Just because I happened to have a dog-collar on, ev[ery] man welcomed me & talked as frankly as cd. be. I have seen some bad things already." He worked with Frank Hart, Wesleyan minister in the Bombay area, and "for the life of me, I don't know how Hart and I are going to get through the work. We make no distinction of creed; & I for my part don't feel it good enough to say 2 or 3 commonplaces & then hurry to the next bed." The General made him a government chaplain, which somewhat improved upon his meager Wesleyan salary. "We have tommies in here at ev[ery] hour, they drift in and want to talk. There's an amazing amount of simple, Methodist religion in many of these chaps. I don't know what to do. What are 2 men among 5000 wounded, some of them passing through for a day or two only? Then there are the dying, & the funerals. . . . I'm here for a month; if things are impossible now, what'll they be when Hart's alone again?"[22]

A few days later he visited the English officers' ward. They received him politely, "but with not a soupçon of suspicion at first," for he was "obviously able-bodied and they've no use for padres, as a rule." Edward had "just enough tinge of the gentleman about me in spite of being a nonconformist missionary, to break down or modify their attitude, if I get 5 minutes." But it was the Tommies who needed him; with them he was more comfortable.

More and more he realized Lyon's value. He reinforced Edward's views on "the absolute need for drastic revision in Education, & on certain lines, unless we are to have v. great trouble indeed." Famine relief work had "brought me into more intimate touch with the agricultural folk who crawl on that hard soil. And one cries, with King Lear, 'I have ta'en too little thought of this.' " He was "proud to feel I was considered a friend by any man who really cared for Bengal & its people." With increasing conviction he shared Lyon's vision for India's future as a dominion in a British Commonwealth.

Now that Edward was away, kinder things were said about him at Bankura. In short, he was "a very useful man here," a good teacher with a good knowledge of the Bengali vernacular and "considerable influence" over students. However, Mitchell, who valued mechanical aptitudes, doubted that Edward would be a successful officer: "He is inclined to be dreamy—being a poet—& is not reliable. He is absolutely unpractical, a more helpless man in practical affairs, viz. organising, building, plan making & practical mechanical matters generally I have never met." He did not explain how Thompson managed to be so useful despite a poet's dreaminess and impracticality. But he told Lyon that he had never before seen Thompson "so enthusiastic about any work."[23]

There were only fourteen Wesleyan chaplains for the entire Mesopotamian campaign. Elizabeth was now happy to think of Edward as a chaplain, "& there is nothing artificial or put-on about your religion." The patients' gratitude tore at his heart. They were "abjectly grateful for trifles, when they ought to spit at me for letting their poor bodies be broken in my stead." Many visitors trooped through but passed on after a quick look. Patients told Edward that " 'they don't stop like you.' I feel as if I want to cry sometimes." These were working men who had slaved away during peace "that I might scribble pretty rimes, & now they face shrapnel & machine guns & bayonets, while I——" It was tragically incongruous that they should apologize for giving trouble.[24]

Bits of unfinished literary business followed him to Bombay. Somehow he wrote the chapter for Harihar Das's biography of Toru Dutt. Lyon had paid Das's typist but soon regretted his generosity, not because Macmillan turned it down but because Das burdened Edward. He continued alone with the poetry anthology, but war played havoc with permissions correspondence. He thought about editing Marvell some day, but Canton dashed cold water: "Who will buy it?" He saw little human interest in the poems, "though his cadences and rhythms are taking."[25]

Macmillan had Tagore stories that became *The Hungry Stones and Other Stories,* and those that became *Mashi and Other Stories.* Macmillan had given them to Whibley, who found that they needed "v. thorough revision"; therefore they would omit translators' names. It now transpired that, in all,

Edward had worked on all or part of thirteen stories. He wrote Macmillan "a perfect snorter of a letter." He was equally angry with Tagore: "Because of his hypochrondriac fancies, I gave up ev[ery] moment of my time when I was ill & pretty wretched & M[ahalanobis] was away" and could not check his translations. Now Macmillan had allowed someone to make the stories feebly Kiplingesque. Canton reminded him again that he had entered the project without clear conditions: "Don't be an unmitigated idiot! You take a hand—all for love and nothing for reward I suppose. . . . Then you fall foul of the publishers and send *them* a 'snorter.' Well, I hope you have repented by this time."[26]

"At the same time," Whibley wrote to Macmillan, "I confess that there seems a danger of Tagore's spoiling his market by overproduction." Macmillan might as well publish, but "what becomes of the legend of the exclusive and secluded poet?"[27]

In April 1916 Tagore promised some finished work, then departed for Japan on a missionary expedition of his own: an ill-advised attempt to revive a common spirit of Eastern spiritualism. England was really his desired destination, for he missed the literary company and admiration he had enjoyed there. If he could not reach England, he would go lecturing in America. "I haven't the slightest doubt he'll say some not v. helpful things to his long-eared friends," Edward wrote.[28]

On 28 July 1914 Austria declared war on Serbia, and Turkey asked Germany for a secret alliance if either went to war with Russia. At this unstable moment England seized two battleships being built for Turkey (one already completed and paid for in part) in Tyneside shipyards. When Britain, mindful of her own naval needs, refused to return them Turkey signed the alliance with Germany. Thus "this simple piece of piracy on the Tyne," as Barbara Tuchman calls it, led to the Dardanelles campaign, with British, French, and Indian forces against Turks under German generals.[29]

Concern about Indian Muslims' sympathies for the tottering Ottoman Empire became even more urgent. As the Indian Muslim had told Hardinge, his head was with India, but his heart was with Turkey. Hardinge was apprehensive, therefore, when he sent more than a million Indian troops to Europe and the Middle East, not only that he might deplete home defense forces, but that Muslim soldiers might desert to the Turks and thus encourage Muslim sedition at home. He could only trust the Indian people not to take advantage of the emergency to cause trouble. "It was a big risk," he wrote in retrospect, "but I took it" despite warnings from the cautious. "And my confidence was not misplaced."[30]

The ill-advised campaign for Gallipoli from May 1915 until January 1916 was intended as a quick strike, a tour de force of military derring-do. This was as unrealistic as the 1914 estimates of the war's duration. The Turks knew the peninsula's hellish terrain of sharp ridges, gullies, and precipices that so surprised some of the English officers because many of their maps were obsolete, inaccurate, or unavailable. Naval support, communications, and medical services were lamentable, and many died for lack of care. Supply lines broke down. Conditions in the field worsened, while the War Council in London met barely once a month. Generals were at cross-purposes, and on both sides men died at the rate of thousands a day. At last, after eight and a half months of misery, heroism, and death, the British gave up. They never reached Gallipoli. None of this can be romanticized, however valiant those who fought there.[31]

Gallipoli's lessons went unheeded in Mesopotamia. Sir George Buchanan, port management expert summoned from Burma to Basra, had to fight for a hearing and a chance to apply his specialized knowledge. Again there was a shining prize in the distance: the fabled city of Baghdad. Again transport and medical services were too little and too late, and the deficiencies became a public scandal. English propaganda and lying reports from Mesopotamia gave the impression that all was under control, but civilian letters filtering through to Chamberlain told the truth. He told Hardinge that whatever he heard, conditions were far worse. There were no hospital ships; sometimes the wounded were carried downriver on filthy steel decks of barges that had just transported horses and mules. There were perhaps three or four doctors for each three thousand or four thousand wounded. Being so few, the doctors could not get a hearing in high army quarters. There were too few ambulances, and a dozen stretcher bearers had to convey three hundred casualties five miles to an aid station. It was, Chamberlain wrote, "barbarous."[32]

No one in India or in London had assessed the crucial river transport, or the radically variable depths of the river at different seasons. Many available boats proved unusable. The field army from India, says Sir Llewellyn Woodward, "had no aeroplanes, no wireless, no motor transport, and little telephone equipment," for attention had concentrated on Russia as the major threat to India. Organization was crazily inefficient. At Basra forty unloaded ships sat in a line eight miles long. "Ocean-going steamers," Woodward wrote, "which could cross the bar of the Shatt-al-Arab [Basra's port] discharged their cargo into native boats," and Basra had no cranes and few warehouses. Ships were loaded haphazardly at Bombay, their cargoes often unknown. A ship laden with heavy cargo had a derrick and crane for unloading—"but the crane was at the bottom of the ship with the cargo on top of it."[33]

And so on. Hardinge's pleas to London for additional men for Mesopotamia brought only calls for more Indian army troops for Europe. By June 1915 the British force had advanced ninety miles up the Tigris to al-Amara. By September they had occupied the city of al-Kut—but were five hundred miles from their base at Basra. On 22 November they were eighteen miles from Baghdad, but the Turks forced them to retreat to al-Kut. There the British force remained under Turkish siege until 29 April 1916, when they were finally starved out and forced to surrender. Ten thousand men, many never seen again, became prisoners.

Lyon was in Bombay when Edward had arrived there. They had talked late into the night, and Edward told his mother that what Lyon knew or conjectured about the Mesopotamian campaign was "a fair eye-opener to me. There'll be a howl of rage, when the English public knows. . . ." Mail was heaped up at Basra, and hospitalized men in Bombay had received none for three months. He would try to get it forwarded. He had heard "that the Gulf fighting had been worse than in Flanders or the Peninsula, but c[oul]dn't believe it. I now know that it was."[34]

He pulled all the wires he could touch, for assignment to Mesopotamia—Mespot, in soldiers' parlance. On 29 July, a telegram ordered him to prepare immediately. On the thirtieth he was in the Persian Gulf, the only chaplain aboard the hospital ship *Liberty* and assigned to the British Field Ambulances of the 7th Field Battalion. "I don't anticipate anything, of course," he told Lyon. "But the place is in a fearful mess with diseases of every sort; & I have discovered in talks with the men that the only padre who's any good to them is the man who shares all their risks." As a newly fledged minister in days that now seemed inconceivably distant, he had believed that he was "not the man for Sawtry" but had discovered that after all that was not so. Now he was about to test whether "chaplaining" was indeed to be his line.[35]

11

COMBAT

In *Across the Dark Waters,* novelist Mulk Raj Anand depicts an English bishop of an Indian diocese who visits a mixed British and Punjabi company on the Western Front. He is everything that Edward Thompson as chaplain abhorred. His natty appearance is an indecency amid the muddy squalor of the trench. In his smarmy self-confidence he entirely misses the point of the Tommies' snickering ridicule and the Indians' honest puzzlement when he addresses "the Tommies mainly and giv[es] up the heathen for lost." The bishop, who had come "to cheer the troops up and not to be flippant," launched—quickly, for he must not be late for lunch with the general—into his repertoire of patriotic platitudes and an English sermon incomprehensible to all the Indians except one who has attended a mission school. The officer makes of him a show specimen and asks him to tell the bishop what he has "learnt of Christianity." The boy crosses himself and rattles off an English prayer "like a parrot." When the bishop says that the prayer earns a plenary indulgence, and the boy adds that it applies also to souls in purgatory, the Tommies, "who had been marvelling at this sepoy with unbelieving, humorous faces spluttered into a laugh."[1]

Bishops in trenches seemed to attract irony, and Edward soon found that most soldiers were not interested in religion. Robert Graves, in trenches in France, heard a sergeant remark that the " 'niggers' "—the Indians— were "right in officially relaxing their religious rules while fighting." Graves noted "scant respect" for the Anglican regimental chaplains and found them remarkably out of touch with the soldiers, for they were "under orders to avoid getting mixed up with the fighting and to stay behind with the transport. . . . On a quiet day in a quiet sector, the chaplain would make a daring afternoon visit to the support line and distribute a few cigarettes, before hurrying back." One officer got rid of four Anglican chaplains in four months and applied for a Roman Catholic, for they were "not only permitted to visit points of danger, but definitely enjoined to be wherever fighting was." Robert Bridges told Edward, "I wish all the parsons w^d go out to fight. I don't think anything else w^d save them. The prayer composed by the Bishop [of London] for use during war was beyond description bad." An Anglican bishop came in uniform to visit the Indians at Basra, and although Edward liked him, he thought it "rather absurd" of him to wear a Major-General's collar-facings, and there was a touch of denominational condescension: "He can't quite rise to speaking of other churches except as 'bodies'; but there was no other trace of the patronage."[2]

"But the Great War was more ironic than any before or since," Paul Fussell says in *The Great War and Modern Memory.* "It was a hideous embarrassment to the prevailing Meliorist myth which had dominated the public consciousness for a century. It reversed the Idea of Progress." How but with irony and satire could one face the fact that guaranteed improvement accepted and even worshipped in Western civilization, would collapse when shaken catastrophically?[3]

Mesopotamia was a catastrophe, the scene of an inglorious siege and surrender, an ill-advised, ill-fated sideshow to the European war. Mesopotamia, now Iraq, was vague in English minds except for biblical and archaeological associations with the Tigris-Euphrates junction as the "cradle of civilization" and, perhaps, the site of the Garden of Eden. Military planners resented the Mesopotamian campaign, intended as a diversion to pin down Turkish forces who, with German officers and advisers, were the enemy in Mesopotamia. It also drained away resources needed in Europe.

There were 675,391 Indians serving in Mesopotamia. The Fifty-first and the Fifty-third Sikhs fought with the Second Leicestershires, to whom Edward Thompson was attached. Most represented traditional India, being "almost exclusively," DeWitt Ellinwood says, from peasant villages and Northwest Frontier tribes. The North Indian soldier was generally in good health, taller than the average, uneducated but intelligent, and not politically minded "which was part of his appeal to the British." He was already tradition oriented but "did carry some elements of change in his tradition or experience." Caste and convention accustomed him to a hierarchical structure; to this the army added its discipline and the life-or-death necessity for cooperation. If already in the Indian army, the peasant soldier was used to being moved about and, even within India, meeting cultures other than those of his village.[4]

In the first week of August 1916 Edward Thompson reached Basra, today Iraq's second largest city and the principal port on the western bank of the waterway at the Tigris-Euphrates junction. Small streams filled the low-lying terrain, but desert determined the capricious climate, which could vary from enervating heat by day to bitter cold at night. Ancient Basra had been a center of Arabic culture: poetry, science, commerce, finance had flourished there and it had been a military center. By the fourteenth century, however, neglect and Mongol invasions left little of the original city. In 1668 the Turks took it and by the nineteenth century had made Basra an important trans-shipment point. In 1916, as Buchanan discovered, the harbor was left undeveloped.

On 10 August Edward wrote from Basra that he had been in Mesopotamia one day less than a week. He had hospital duty with the Seventh Mesopotamian Field Army but could not say exactly where. He would embark three or four miles above Basra, to proceed upriver on the Tigris. The food was plain but reasonably good and the forks were clean—"wh. is more than they re in many a C'cutta burra-sahib's house. . . ." He had an English orderly, a butcher in civilian life. Edward and another Wesleyan padre, Percy Brunt, had fourteen cases of "comforts for the troops." On 20 August they were near Sheikh Saog, and Edward was glad that he had come and felt that he would do better work here than at any previous period of my life. If that is so, it wd. be a crime to wish me elsewhere. And my being here not only means a change when I was wanting one v. badly, in ev[ery] possible way; but I think it will mean furlough in Eng[land]; much sooner than otherwise." But I get no news. For all I know Berlin may have fallen, & the war may be over." He got about on horseback, but the horse was clumsy and jolting, unlike Bengal's more congenial mounts. He had been asked to start a reading room at the rear and would do it, although it meant giving up his nice tent "and the glorious power of bathing under cover when I was *dirty*. . . ." The general wanted him to organize hockey matches. "I'm finding my feet famously," he told his mother. The hockey games were a lot of trouble, but he got to know the men. "And, as these men will probably have to hop the parapet some day, it isn't much one can do in return. So I have done my work joyfully. Still, it's pleasant to know that my General knows I've done it & appreciates it" and had said so several times. Edward also conducted his first field funeral, for a man who had died of sandfly fever. Edward himself had a spell of it that put him in the hospital. "The Devil made this country," he wrote, "& did it when he had plenty of spare time on his hands. And he put his lovingest, carefullest work into the sandflies." Edward made friends, "not of the old intimate sort—that I don't expect, & hardly want—but still friends."[5]

Canton had not abandoned efforts to persuade Edward to keep a diary. "Perhaps *now* you will have the sense to take a note of first impressions and experiences. Perhaps you won't, in spite of what you have learnt of how much you have lost of your first impressions in Bengal." *Was* he writing down impressions? "You call that journalism; I call it common sense." In fact, Edward kept a Mesopotamian diary and was greatly alarmed about it when his belongings became scattered among three different locations: "I'd rather lose all my kit than that." Those notebooks became his book, *The Leicestershires beyond Baghdad.*[6]

The Basra Operation had begun with landings in November 1914. By the end of September 1915 the advance up the Tigris and the capture of al-Kut were complete. Then came the ill-fated attempt to push on to Baghdad; the repulse and the enforced return to al-Kut, and two failed attempts, between

January and March 1916, to relieve the Turkish siege there. A third attempt in April, succeeded, and the British, regrouped and resupplied, planned their push up the Tigris to Baghdad.

Edward's first conflict was with the camp hierarchy. His reading room was off the beaten path but at the center of a controversy. A Quartermaster Major who had seemed "frightfully keen" about the idea, got into "a desperately quarrelsome mood" and decided that Edward had been " 'setting up an opposite shop' "—a " 'rival institution' " to the Church of England reading room more than two miles away. Edward denied that his was either rival or narrowly denominational and said, "I'm sorry, but it's nothing of the sort." His tent was inconveniently far from the center of things, for "a padre's shd. be the accessible tent in the div[ision]; mine is the inaccessiblest." Nevertheless his reading room gave the men "somewhere to sit & keep from gambling. This is the rear camp, where they have all the fatigues & work, & they can't be expected, after a hot & heavy day, to walk 2 meters." He was indignant that anyone thought he wanted an exclusively Wesleyan reading room as a place to snag converts. That anyone should think that "I'm going to fag myself out to get a proselyte out of a man who next week may be blown to bits is too insulting for characterisation. The probable explanation is that [the Major] had been having a bad time with the General. The only other, that the C. of E. man had been making mischief, is too mean to entertain."[7]

In fact, among the chaplains he found "good fellowship that is pleasant beyond words. Padres have an excellent name here; & we have an extraordinary variety of most interest[ing] and able men." The Church of England padre "took me straight into his tent & set me beside him at mess, & has been awfully decent in ev[ery] way." The Roman Catholic chaplain was "a joy, & we get heaps of quiet fun in the Mess." The American Y.M.C.A. man and the Presbyterian, Wesleyan, and Catholic padres worked together admirably and any suggestion about competition was good for a joke: "They pretend to anticipate rows, but as a matter of fact our coming together has done good." Edward was obviously surprised that the senior Church of England chaplain "makes no distinction, & runs our affairs as if they were his own men's. We take services & funerals for them, & they for us. You see, in war we can't go on ordinary lines. Unless we all lend a hand, the work can't be done."[8]

This revelation inspired an ambition to do for Christian missions in Bengal what the Basra padres had done for him. He would be an explainer, an explicator, an opener of horizons. He wrote to Lyon: "My exper[ien]ces here, where all have vaguely heard of Bengali 'sedition' & have persuaded themselves they hate the Bengali & where officers nearly always misunderstand & despise India & missions & literature & . . . —have convinced me, so that I will work & work until I get it done, that the Xty. wh. *knows* what Xty is . . . & yet loves and tries to understand India, is strongly represented." He revived his idea of

journal for Bengal on politics both national and international, on literature
and the arts: "We must have our Indian *Spectator* after this war; & Seal must
help, & the 2 Lyons, father & son, & Canton, & Rabi[ndranath], & Mitchell,
& E[dgar] W. Thompson, & all who love His Kingdom. The establishment of
his will be my next job; & I am working for it even here in Assyria. And I
don't care a damn who runs it, once it is run & well run." It was a flight of
editorial fancy and an unrealistic notion of a successful team. What brought
it on just then, besides the euphoria of Basra's unexpected ecumenism, was
Lyon's retirement in 1917. "So why should you go?" Edward asked. Lyon was
Edward's "own one link with the official mind" and was essential because
the project must coexist with the government's Press Act, and "if it becomes
possible for you to stay, then no one will rejoice more than I shall." Edward
forgot Lyon's reputation as a man dangerous to the bureaucracy.[9]

Lyon still disapproved of concentration on police work to keep Bengal
steady. In a long letter to Edward, he wrote that "very large and generous
reforms, making for real self-government, will alone help us, and we shall
do well to grant them & not wait to have them forced from us. . . . I have no
doubt that our policy must be a bold one, and yet I fear that the traditions
of the Bureaucracy & the I.C.S. in India do not make for boldness." He
had even less faith in the boxwallahs. "They are, in the mass, temporary
sojourners in the land, with no knowledge of, or sympathy with its peoples,
and their gradual disappearance from the country would be by no means
the irretrievable calamity that they themselves would assert." They had
developed resources, but their profits went abroad. The Bengal government
would "have my head on a charger" if they knew what he really thought.
Many Indians trusted to promises about future self-determination, but if the
British only went on "tinkering with the machinery of administration, while
maintaining law and order by means of special penal enactments, we shall
have bad trouble in Bengal." Lyon left on 8 April 1917, and the Government
of India remained unforgiving. He went without a knighthood.[10]

On 13 December 1916 the push began to recapture al-Kut. It is in what
is now eastern Iraq, where the Tigris branches to the south. Edward, now
assigned to brigade headquarters, started up the Tigris with the Seventh
Division operation that lasted until 25 February 1917 and ended with the
British again in possession of al-Kut. He knew that "big events will be going"
that would be history before Canton received his letter.[11]

In mid-December, during a week of Turkish bombardment, he came
under two kinds of fire, one bureaucratic, the other potentially fatal. While
arranging a hockey match, a much-needed bit of relaxation behind the lines,
he "sailed into v. heavy weather" with a headquarters officer. He felt sick
about it, but the next day the General, who had already complimented his
effort, said that he could not be "sufficiently grateful for the trouble I'd taken."

Then Edward came literally under Turkish fire for the first time. He wrote to Canton, what he would not have told his mother: "I was in between them [the English guns] & the Turks. . . . My horse went crazy! I wasn't v. greatly afraid. If I'd been afoot, I'd have dropped into a communication trench." On 6 January he wrote that he had seen the trenches and graves where the Leicestershires "last April tried to dig themselves in in the hellish fighting" during the third and successful but still deadly attempt to relieve al-Kut. The empty trenches and the filled graves made the war more real than even the live fire. "I hate Mesopotamia," he wrote.[12]

He told Elizabeth not to worry; there were a lot of fights nearby, but he was "as safe as in India." As for distant bombardments, "we listen unmoved; the thing lost all novelty for us last December." Now another battle began, and nine German officers with the Turks were killed. "I am glad with all my heart. The whole affair is distressing to the last degree; but it has to be finished. I am going to waste no more sympathy on the Turk. He had no call to butt into this show, & he's cost us directly a good 200,000 casualties, in the Balkans & Gallipoli & here." But a total withdrawal of understanding went against his nature, and he continued: "The Turk is fighting his best, a losing battle but a gallant one. It is an awful pity he's not on our side. If he had been, we'd have wiped those wretched Bulgars out of the planet. The Turk's been a fool; but, when all the truth is known, perhaps we may see that our own diplomatists & politicians were the bigger fools."[13]

But he had no mitigating regrets for gallantry misplaced in Europe:

Never, whilst I live, shall I forget the devilry wh. thought of men & their destinies as pawns & let this organised murder loose on the world. I think I have got past the ranting, passionate stage; this is the deepest & most sorrowful resentment I have known, & it grows. Had I the power, I wd bring it home to Germany in blood for blood.

I wish to see no man more die up here. These deserts have drunk enough of our blood.

The little I have known of being under fire makes me feel almost as if Frank's life was lost already. I never refer to Frank when I write home. But no one can get away from the thought of the gallant boys in Flanders.[14]

Frank's life was indeed soon lost. Edward's letter must have been on its way when Frank died in France. He was a Second Lieutenant, promoted from the ranks, with the Civil Service Rifles attached to the King's Royal Rifles. When he heard rumors of Indian assignment, he had told Edward that he would rather go to France. He went, on 18 August 1916, in good spirits. Elizabeth had given him his father's brandy flask in a most un-Wesleyan state: "full of brandy!" He found association with his men "the most extraordinarily steady in human affection I have ever known." Most, he said, had had good jobs as civilians. Because he came from the ranks, "I was determined, that if I could, I would make things as easy for them as was compatible with duty." They had worked harder for him than he had expected and had done small personal favors, "and that is a thing to be greatly treasured." He died on 13 January 1917 near Ypres when a sniper he was trying to hit had found him first.[15]

For the family it was the bitterest irony, in a conflict replete with bitterness and ironies, that the news came unexpectedly by radio and that it was Arthur who received it on the HMS *Dreadnought.* Lyon sent a cable. "It is very bad for his mother," Edward replied, "& she will hardly survive it long; & for his fiancée. And it will be very hard on his bro[ther]s & sisters, esp[ecially] the brave lad in the North Sea, who was close chums with this bro[ther] &, moreover, has only recently heard of his closest friend's death in France. I do not know how he can carry on."[16]

To his mother Edward wrote, "I loved and honoured him beyond words; & no one cd. know him & not love him. Now I must try to comfort you & myself, Mother. In the first place, there is nothing to regret, so far as he is concerned. Nothing. In all these years, we never saw a trace of selfishness in him. . . . I know something of what he must have gone through in France, & this knowledge troubles me. But I know he was never left to himself. And, even in the first flood of grief, I knew that God had answered my prayers. For from the first I had prayed that his life might be spared; but first of all & most of all, I had prayed that his mind might be kept from fear, from the sudden terror that even our bravest can hardly escape always, & from loss of self-control." He was grateful that Frank died instantly, never to know what worse pains so many others suffered before being summarily labeled "Died of Wounds." "Our boy, the dear laddie we knew, never had any part with 'the fearful or the unbelieving'; therefor he was where he was." So Elizabeth must comfort herself and Frank's fiancée, whose grief was doubled, for her brother had died in France. Edward could not write to the rest of the family just then, but would she show this letter to Margaret?[17]

Elizabeth's reaction was a terrible numbness. Margaret was greatly concerned because she had not once wept. Canton went there immediately and tried to reassure Edward that "your mother seems to me to live already almost as much in the life to come as she does in this, and to be borne up on an unchanging trust in God. And I have no fear for her." Tears would come later. "The natural sense that she will never see him, never speak again in this world will come upon her as the first shock passes away, and tears will come with it." Arthur wrote to Edward, "There is one thing brother whatever happens we'll stick together as a family as we always have done, and Frank's memory will always be fresh. . . . I can stick it, and when this ghastly business is over I think you will find that I shall be a better man from the experience." Margaret, who taught in Ipswich and was a volunteer in the recruiting office while Charles, too, was in Mesopotamia, wrote the kind of letter that helps to clear away old resentments. "I wish I could make you see your life as it appears to us at home. Don't you *know*, dear brother, what we all think of you?" They knew what he had given up when he left Kingswood for the bank. They knew his gifts, though she could probably never fully know "all that the giving up of a university career meant to you yet I know in part & appreciate the huge sacrifice. You have always been our eldest brother 'big boy' as Frank used to say—& we all owe a tremendous portion of our happiness to you."[18]

Edward had two weeks' leave to Basra, then learned that his division had fought in the battle and capture of Sannaiyat, from 17 to 24 February. He was "as sick as I can be, that I was absent from my place just when most needed." Elizabeth would rejoice, but he would be "sorry all my days." There was only a slow boat from Basra. At al-Amara he saw the two thousand Turkish prisoners taken at the Dahra battle in February. Again he forgot his resolution to expend no more sympathy on Turks and again thought of them as dupes of the diplomats. "They were fine ruddy faced men, v. like the best class of British workmen. I felt sorry we were fighting such men. They had been through sheer Hell, & seemed quiet & self-possessed. Their bearing was v. noble. This is in many respects the ~~greatest~~ noblest battle of the war. The 2 bravest nations in the world are fighting here, with unexampled courage & terrible persistence. That Sir Edward Grey shld have squared the Turks somehow. I'm inclined more & more to think he was a mediocre chap."[19]

Sir Edward Grey, as Foreign Secretary, was more limited than mediocre. He was fatally uninformed about the Balkans and the Middle East. "So non-cosmopolitan, so English, so county, so reserved," says Barbara Tuchman, "he could not be regarded by anyone as a mettlesome mixer in foreign quarrels."[20]

The push to Baghdad began. The Turks retreated northward, and Edward was beyond range of shell or bullet. "Germany will either have to let Baghdad, & presently Turkey, slip; or else she will have to send away help she cannot spare from herself." He allowed himself to think that the end was near, that he would be home "this year," that peace would mean furlough in England. "War," he wrote, "is an even sillier game than I had thought."[21]

Baghdad fell on 11 March 1917, but the Leicestershires pushed on toward Samarra. In April Edward's brigade, the Twenty-eighth, was in two hard battles: on the 21st and 22nd at Istabulat, and on the 23rd and 24th to occupy Samarra. In the first the Turks overran the aid station that Edward had set up on his own, with one orderly and more than a hundred wounded, of whom fifty or sixty were Turks. Guardedly, he told his mother that it was "a strenuous time." He had started the aid station because "there was very great need." He and his orderly worked "like slaves" until their hands were "red with blood to the wrists; & I saw many horrible sights without even realising till afterwards that they were horrible." He had probably saved "some lives & many operations." His commanding officer had been "very grateful," had thanked him for "*very* great work."[22]

The more detailed account went to Canton. Edward's battalion doctor had gone forward to a man hit in the stomach, then "sent along a message for us to join him. We went on another half-mile, & came to a place of ruins & mounds, some ancient city of the paynims aforetime." The 350 men of the Twenty-eighth Battalion "calmly walked across the plain, took 250 unwounded prisoners & 7 guns," which they could not hold but sent the wounded back in "batches of 20 to 40 in charge of a couple of men or so. The Turks counterattacked, & all afternoon the fight went on for the guns." The doctor then left his wounded with Edward and

went forward, leaving me to get them away. But my place developed into a second dressing-station. The Turk shelled my ridge very heavily, hitting every slope but ours. We had to remove the wounded to a better shelter behind. We picked them up & ran. I carried little Westlake; & just as we reached the edge of the open, a 5.9 burst at one side, & a sheet of wind & metal swept over our heads. Not a man was hit, fortunately. Then we had a busy time. The men hit at our side came in; men came down from the front. Wilson, our d[octo]r, did the fractures & sent flesh wounds to us. Indians who missed their way to their own Aid posts came to me. The artillery adjutant asked me to look at a man who had been hit by the shelling which cleared us out of our place (to wh. we came back, keeping only the worst cases in the other shelter). I came; one man had all his brains blown out, but the man next [to] him was still breathing, so I had him brought in.

Then the wounded Turks came to him, "a pitiful crowd, most horribly smashed by shells, begging for water, touching my feet & saluting." Edward and his "most excellent" orderly (his name was Dobson), too hard-pressed for fear or disgust, gave them water and dressed their wounds "and my hands were soon steeped in innocent gore." They worked all night and sent back fifty wounded, "ours & Turco, at midnight." Transport was scarce, but they returned all of their casualties "some hours before any other regimental Aid Post got any but walking cases away except by their own stretcher-bearers." The next day Edward tramped five miles before he found five ambulances, "wh. I just took & brought back. So we got everyone away. I can't speak frankly here; but the medical arrangements failed, that's all there is to it."

But, as I sat through that night of bitter cold, listening to the wounded & with no covering except towards dawn, a waterproof I borrowed from a dead boy beside me, the insanity & hellishness of it all burnt deep. If only for those gallant & broken Turks who crawled about my feet & begged for water, I wd. never forget the guilt of those who brought this thing to pass. The fighting men have no hate; & the wounded suffer and die side by side.[23]

Edward wrote *The Leicestershires beyond Baghdad* to correct an official omission:

> The Mesopotamian war was a side-show, so distant from Europe that even the tragedy of Kut and the slaughter which failed to save our troops and prestige were felt chiefly in retrospect, when the majority of the men who suffered so vainly had gone into the silence of death or of captivity. . . . The men in Mesopotamia did not feel that this was unnatural. We felt, none more so, that it was the European war which mattered; indeed, our lot often seemed the harder by reason of its little apparent importance. Yet, after all, Baghdad was the first substantial victory which no subsequent reverse swept away; and it came when the need of victory for very prestige's sake, was very great.[24]

The journalist Edmund Candler, a teacher and traveler in India, reported from Mesopotamia as "Eye-witness." With another Indian Division, the Seventh Meerut, he followed the push to Baghdad along the Tigris bank opposite that occupied by the Leicestershires. Authority allowed no mention of specific units, and Candler was bitter about the censorship. Edward's sources for *The Leicestershires* were his own experiences, his diaries, regimental diaries to which he had access, and conversations with officers. If Mesopotamia was a sideshow, "if our fighting was on a smaller scale, we saw it more clearly. . . . We were not a fractional part of an eruption along many hundreds of miles [as in Europe]; we were our own little volcano. . . . Nor can any front have had so many grim jokes as those with which we kept ourselves sane through the long-drawn failure before Kut and the dragging months which followed."[25]

He selected for his book, as the first of the two Leicestershire campaigns, the two-day battle for Istabulat on the road to Samarra, and the battle for Samarra itself. Their fighting along the right bank of the Tigris ran parallel to the only completed stretch of the Berlin-Baghdad Railway, which ran eighty miles from Baghdad to Samarra and was a key in the German campaign to subvert and control the Middle East: "If we could capture this the Turk would have to supply his troops from Mosul by the treacherous and shallow Tigris." The Samarra campaign was a series of smaller engagements to keep the Turks permanently out of action.[26]

The Leicestershires is both valuable and touching for its awareness of events proceeding uncannily parallel to those of antiquity. As Fussell notes, only soldiers from the classical tradition of English public schools could be so aware of that parallel. On the first day of the contest for Istabulat the Leicestershires had battled up to an ancient wall that became a burial ground for many. That wall, even at such a dire moment, evoked its history. It was the

Median Wall built by the ancient Medes, "old in Xenophon's time; he speaks of it [in the *Anabasis*, Book 2] as twenty feet in breadth and one hundred feet in height. Once it was the border between Assyria and Babylonia, and must have stretched to the Euphrates. Even now it runs from the Tigris far into the desert. It has crumbled to one-third of the height given by Xenophon. The semblance of a wall no longer, it is a mighty flank of earth, covering tiers of bricks." Xenophon's army had moved along its northern side, as did the Leicestershires in their turn; references to Xenophon and sightings of places familiar from his history marked their progress. As they "calmly walked across the plain," the wall hid them from the Turks but did not protect from their shelling. As they sat there in reserve, a fellow officer, whose company had "a certain unattractive duty assigned to them on the extreme left," predicted that the Median Wall "would be shelled to blazes, which seemed pretty probable." Thus Turks in the twentieth century, entrenched among old mounds of no discernible historical provenance, would try to destroy that which was already ancient four centuries before the birth of Christ. In its truncated state it survived, but some of the men stationed there did not. The Turks knew the exact range, for German archaeologists had worked there for many years and knew the wall brick by brick.[27]

Edward's diary note for the Leicestershires' sighting of the Tigris reads only "Men's delight to see river." In *The Leicestershires* this became: "We came suddenly upon Brother Tigris, basking in beautiful sunlight, becalmed in bays beneath lofty cliffs. In this dreadful land water meant everything: we had had experiences of thirst, not to be effaced in a lifetime. Away from the river men grew uneasy. The river meant abundance to drink, and bathing; everywhere else water was bad or the supply precarious." Therefore neither shells nor bullets "prevented men from greeting so dear a sight. Standing on the beach of imminent strife, in act to plunge, men cried, 'The Tigress, the Tigress!' " Xenophon sprang again to mind,

> from the book so often near to thought in these days: how Xenophon, weary and anxious with the restlessness and depression of his much-tried troops, heard a clamour from those who had reached a hillcrest, and, riding swiftly up to take measures against the expected peril, found them shouting *"Thalatta, Thalatta."* Seafaring folk, the most of them, they had caught, far below, their first glimpse of the Euxine, truly a hospitable water to them, since it could bear them home.[28]

Shakespeare, too, was wryly apposite, *The Life of King Henry the Fifth*, a multipurpose text. It answered their need for irony and sarcasm as relief from depression and exasperation, the filth and vicious sandflies, the no less vicious Arab tribesmen who looted graves and unburied bodies, the dust storms and heat that bedeviled sleep. Edward inserted an epigraph from the chorus: "Behold, as may unworthiness define / A little touch of Harry in the night," with a comment from a fellow-soldier: "If I thought Hell was worse than Mesopotamia, I'd be a good man."[29]

Sometimes Edward and fellow officers traded Shakespearean tags so aptly that a sarcastic recitation cleared a deep cloud of depression. Someone wished for reinforcements "from the immense armies which our papers bragged were being trained at home." Someone else replied:

> "Oh that we now had here
> But one ten thousand of those men in England
> that do no work today!"

Edward commented: "Swiftly that immortal scene of the English spirit facing great odds invincibly, followed, passage racing after passage": " 'God's will! I pray thee, wish not one man more!' " When they recited the lines in which Westmoreland declares that those with no stomach for the fight should depart, "laughter cleansed every spirit present of fear, and the shadow of fear, misgiving. Nothing less grimly humorous than the notion of such an offer being made now, or of the alleged consequences of such an offer, in the instant streaming away of all His Majesty's Forces in Mesopotamia, could have made so complete a purgation. Comedy took upon herself the office of Tragedy." They continued to trade lines, from the ironies of " 'His passport shall be made, / And crowns for convoy put into his purse,' " which promptly "towered to an ecstasy of sarcasm" in " 'Gentlemen in England, now abed, / Shall think themselves accursed they were not here.' "[30]

The death of Major the Earl of Suffolk, as he manned a gun on the first day of the battle for Istabulat, dismayed those who knew him and evoked from Edward a Shakespearean context as epitaph for a brave man greatly respected: "It seemed strangely mediaeval, as from the days of Agincourt or Creçi, that Death, scarring so many, but forbearing to exact their uttermost, should strike down so great a name and one that is written on so many pages of our history." Once more, lines from *King Henry the Fifth* released the moment's tension with the laughter that is the last resort before despair: " 'We would not die in that man's company, / That fears his fellowship to die with us.' "[31]

"So laughter ended a terrible day," Edward wrote in Old Testament cadences: "Next day our tiny band was the spearhead of a handful of fifteen hundred bayonets, who caught the Turk in his fastnesses, wrested guns and prisoners from him, and slew and broke his forces so that they recoiled for thirty miles."[32]

Buchanan speaks of "the ubiquity of the native of India," hard at menial work everywhere in Mesopotamia, "either in a labour corps, or as a sweeper, looey bearer, saice [groom], follower, cook, motor driver, or mess servant, and without him it would be difficult to carry on the campaign." The Sikhs' record with the Leicestershires testified to their forward actions. The severity of [their] losses is eloquent testimony. . . ." Edward wrote, [The Fifty-third Sikhs] lost their four senior officers, killed." The stoicism of one with terrible wounds, and the sympathy of his fellows, long remained with Edward. "Now he lay with scarcely a moan, while Sikhs gathered round and gave such consolation as was possible, an austere, brave group." The man died that night.[33]

Edward particularly admired the Roman Catholic Father Bernard Farrell, "slaving, as he had done all night," in the hospital tents. An English bishop was an exception to his official rule when he came from India to consecrate graves, a dangerous mission, for some had been booby-trapped to discourage Arab grave looters. Edward and others looked on apprehensively, lest "the good Bishop might find, even in Mesopotamia, Elijah's way to heaven, fiery-chariot-wise." Unfortunately, he forfeited some of that credit when he returned again to preach. He intended his mission to be a "bucking up [of] the spiritual side of things generally," but there was "some awful profanity, evoked by his compulsory church parade on a weekday at 6 A.M., I do not know of any effect his visit had in my own brigade."[34]

Edward, and some other officers, respected Turks who were not only brave soldiers but also dignified prisoners. During the battle for Samarra, a machine-gun officer and a Red Crescent orderly surrendered to Edward, but neither the aid station nor the Sikhs nearby could take them on. So Edward set out with them "on our tired trudge to Samarra." Along the way he and the officer discussed, in French, the course of the war. Edward wrote, "In every way one spared a brave enemy's feelings." He pointed out to the officer that "last year they had won; now it was our turn. 'That is so,' said he. This thought comforted him, and the memory of their great triumphs before Kut in early 1916." Edward begged scraps of food from men marching past and shared with the Turks. "I expressed regret for this march on empty stomachs. 'C'est toujours la marche,' said the officer, shrugging his shoulders." Along the way Sikh troops took them for three prisoners, and Edward for a German, until a fellow officer "cantered up and hailed me," at which they recognized him and a sympathetic laugh "ran down the column, with the words 'Padre Sahib.' " At Samarra he handed over his prisoners to an English General with the request that they be well fed. "Then a pleasant thing happened. The Turkish officer stepped quickly up to me, saluted, and held out his hand. I saluted back, and we shook hands. They were good fellows, both officer and orderly, and carried themselves like free men."[35]

The Leicestershires explains, besides his character at life-or-death moments, a great deal about Edward Thompson as literary person. As Canton insisted, it was so obvious that prose was indeed his natural voice. A factua account of battlefield movements and units can be the most stultifying o literary genres but comes alive in the right hands. Robert Rhodes Jame: achieved that in his *Gallipoli.* Edward achieved it on a smaller canvas in *The Leicestershires,* in which personalities characterize an entire unit. The account flows effortlessly. The wry embellishments of his epistolary style which may seem only flippant or ill-natured, here give force to feeling that would destroy if not deflected. Due credit to the Leicestershires drive: his narrative. He names individuals, brigades, and battalions, always with admiration for their ingenuity and bravery.

Many commentators mention his skill as a nature writer. In England and India flora and fauna were refreshment and renewal. In Mesopotamia, either extremely marshy or extremely arid, nature's relief was doubly welcome because so often unexpected. Marching toward action at Beled, the Leices tershires came upon such a spot. Edward wrote of it as a happy discovery but even here nature's way turned into the way of war.

> Splashing through the marshes, we came to undulating upland, long steady slopes, pebble-strewn and with pockets of grass and poppies. The morning wind made those uplands extremely beautiful. . . . As we approached them, the ruffling wind laid its hand on the grasses, and they became emerald waves, a green spray of blades tossing and flashing in the full sunlight. As we passed, the same wind bowed them before it, and they were a shining, silken cloth. The poppies were a larger sort than those in the wheatfields, and of a very glorious crimson. In among the grasses were yellow coltsfoot; among the pebbles were sowthistle, mignonette, pink bindweed, and great patches of storksbill. Many noted the beauty of those flowers, a scene so un-Mesopotamian in its brightness. We were tasting of the joy and life of springtide in happier latitudes, a wine long praetermitted to our lips; and among us were those who would not drink of this wine again till they drank it new in their Father's Kingdom. After Beled we saw no more flowers.[36]

The transition from shimmering natural life to imminent death and to life hereafter, whatever that may be, is so smooth, so inevitable, and New Testament cadences enter in so naturally, that implications of rhetorical contrivance fall away.

The Leicestershires proves that "chaplaining" was indeed Edward's line. No amount of third-hand reporting could duplicate the immediacy of his descriptions: the battlefield aid posts, the voices of isolated wounded Turks crying out in the dark, the miseries of long marches bedeviled by heat and thirst. He seldom mentions his church services; when he does, the common condition is his text. On the road to Samarra in high summer "my morning service was swathed in dust, one swirling misery, and I was sore tempted to preach, foreseeing the days to come, on 'These are but the beginning of sorrows.' " He refuses to be pious. One duty was a lecture on Mesopotamia, and he spoofed its success as "a terrible lecture on Mesopotamian history, which, from first to last, I delivered over fifty times. Latterly envious tongues alleged that I had to ask units for a [church] parade when I gave this lecture. But those who said this lied saucily and shamelessly."[37]

Harihar Das's biography of Toru Dutt pursued him literally to the battle-fields. After all the fuss about the last chapter, Das had omitted it because Edward did not declare Toru's work perfect in every respect. "Yr. old pal Harihar continues to excel himself . . . ," Edward told Lyon. "It's quite all right; & I'd rather be left out." But why Das insisted "on my keeping the letter of an unwilling promise when he now so quietly moves it aside, I can't say." It was useless to be cross with him; he meant well but "don't know no better." He could do as he pleased, but it was presumptuous of him to want to send it to the *London Quarterly Review.* Edward preferred to see to his own affairs.[38]

Robert Bridges wrote letters of encouragement and liked Edward's poems that became *Waltham Thickets and Other Poems,* published in 1917. "I think you have done quite rightly," he had written when Edward decided to enlist, "and will find a great reward." He thought the poems' "mixture of heroism, poetry & natural history is rich and rare. . . . You seem to do 3 things well," he wrote, "—Soldier padre & poet. . . . An *immense* quantity of incompetent verse is being thrown out just now—most of it very poor indeed, but it seems to be in answer to a demand." Bridges's son Edward was fighting on the Somme, and his father was restless: "It is no fun being 72 years old, and sitting by the fire, and realising how dependent one is on common comforts, while all the young fellows whom one most loves are facing every kind of pain and danger." He had addressed an audience of working men at Swindon, and although it seemed a success he came away thinking that it was all relative: he was "more fitted to fight than to make speeches."[39]

Canton had asked for a " 'verbal *picture*' of the region you live in—summer & winter." Edward, again the nature writer, sent a long description of the country around Sannaiyat, and of some rural English flora and fauna among the arid unfamiliar and remnants of antiquity. In the banks of the winding Tigris lived "great, broad-faced, whiskered voles." Among plants that survived on the sandy plain was tamarisk that covered it "with pink bells, like a heath"—but thorny, "following Eden's curse." Falcons and buzzards sat at the edge of a marsh, but plovers and coursers ran on the plain, owls and partridges in the brush. There were a Persian robin or two among hoopoes, wagtails, and green bee-eaters. Where Edward sat, there were only a few stunted mimosas—"& sand, sand, sand—'miles & miles & more bloody miles!' " There were no villages at Sannaiyat: "They had all gone."[40]

"With mixed feelings" Edward received news of his Military Cross for conspicuous bravery under fire. He actually tried to forestall it. "Nothing I did was one-quarter of what the most ordinary combatant had to do, as part of his normal duty," he told his mother. "Yet the doing of it established me in the regiment; & I shd. hate to lose the place I had won, by being in any way noticed or rewarded. It is better as it is, to be accepted by brave men as a true fellow & equal. Nor do I want any sort of distinction."[41]

Nevertheless the citation symbolized the fact that "the men have an altogether new friendliness since our 3 battles together—so much can a 'whiff of grapeshot,' endured in company, avail—& officers have dropped the patronising kindliness they give a padre. Our most antipadre officer has told me that, 'as long as I live, I shall remember the way you pushed our wounded off,' & yesterday my mess elected me M[ess] P[resident]. The old notion that a padre is a man who keeps ten miles beyond shellrange & then turns up to preach when the fighting's all over, is dispelled. And for this, if for no other reason, I wd. go through that terrible day again. My task was easiest of all, during those hours of heroism & suffering. But I was there; & it suffices." The distinction helped also to revive his mother. Canton wrote that it brought her "down to the earth of this day and has roused her to the fact that she has other sons, and that they are doing fine work, and that she should try to live a little *with them.*" Canton had met some army officers with "the rather rotten attitude some of your officers appeared to take toward Nonconformist ministers. One in the little eye for them! Really this spite and jealousy and cock-sure exclusivity of the Anglicans (of many of them at least) makes one sick of all their pretensions to represent Christ."[42]

A bad letdown followed, and the month of May seemed the darkest Edward had ever known. The formulaic requirements of his religious duties seemed "increasingly hard, & even distasteful. There is so much that is stereotyped about the business; the style of thing expected from one. My life at B'kura hid this from me—largely. There I was a teacher, mainly; & I love teaching, & I have not the least doubt that it is the thing I can do best. There is no stereotyped long prayer to be got thro[ugh], no text on wh. to hang the sort of thing they call a sermon. You have yr. subject & you talk & are talked to. There will be a lot to reconsider when the war's over." When he got that English furlough he would "neither preach nor address Sunday Schools. But I want to lie on the grass & talk to any friends who remain & to have a good look at heather & maybloom."[43]

Fever and dysentery accounted for the lowered mood. Probably he had been ill throughout the April battles. He avoided the hospital because the senior chaplain was already short of staff. Now Edward was exhausted and weak, and he got a month's leave to India. Just hanging about at Basra waiting for a passage made him feel a "moral pariah" until he saw two of his wounded men at a church service who were "really most absurdly pleased to see me, as I them, & it bucked me no end." He had not realized how intimately that battle experience had stayed with him. One of the men had been at the Istabulat aid post, and again there burst upon Edward's inner eye the "regular roof of shells above us all the time. Our guns were just behind us, blazing away; & the Turco guns were trying to find our guns."[44]

While Edward waited for a ship he read *Mr. Britling Sees It Through,* in which H. G. Wells creates a suburban British Everyman who at first denies the possibility of Britain's going to war, then endures it along with everyone else on the home front. Edward liked the book "with reservations" but did not put it anywhere near where "yr rhapsodists do, with the Master books of the Ages, a little above the Bible & a lot above Dante." The befuddled but staunch Mr. Britling as typical Englishman was too manufactured, too neatly inserted into the English class roster, to be really satisfying. He spoke more for H. G. Wells and an abstract England than for Edward Thompson and those like him. Edward's thoughts kept returning to the waste, the idiotic mismanagements and insults to the human spirit, but the longer he waited for a ship, the more he feared that on return he might get a base assignment. There were "swarms of padres" coming out who longed to be at the front. "If they'd once had a taste of it, they might not be so keen."[45]

He had seen it through, had seen through it, had secured his place, and had no intention of giving it up to someone else who might cut and run at the first shell. Edward the soldier was fortifying his hard-won ground.

12

REVISIONS

Even before the April battles and the onset of dysentery, Edward's health had been poor, and "the last 3 years have overstrained me, in every way," he told Lyon. "I worry too much; but I can't help that." He fluctuated between hopeful estimates of the war's end and the dreary certainty that no one foresaw it. In any case, he would "overhaul my whole position, & to decide on the work of the next few years. But the first thing I must have is *rest*. For the present, I can carry on. I love India too well to be able to leave it, especially as I believe—indeed, know—that I am of more use to India than to England. But I sometimes think I cd. do best, under the circumstances, if I had some job—at any rate, for a time—in connection with Indian students in Eng[lan]d. Such a post was suggested to me in 1914, & I was asked if I wd. care for an interview with Asquith. But it seemed best & loyal to go back to Bankura." He needed Lyon's advice.[1]

Indian students in England were a nagging concern of both the Government of India and the India Office, which maintained a social center in London and an adviser to offer academic counsel and keep the students from being too lonely—and as much as possible to discourage involvement with English girls. The government felt, resentfully, that its efforts were unappreciated. In 1914 a high India Office official complained that the center seemed not only unpopular but the target of active suspicion. It was expensive and well meant, but many Indians felt distrusted and spied-upon. The India Office suspected that they blamed its agents; it blamed Jinnah and his Muslim followers. The India Office did indeed keep informed about Indian students who were too friendly with nationalist agitators or with the few nationalist sympathizers in Parliament. Wartime tensions only fanned the flame.[2]

Edward's proven rapport with Bankura students would have made him an excellent candidate for such a post. However, his outspokenness and his friendship with Lyon, had the India Office looked into that, might have scored against him. In later years he would take unofficial interest in Indian students in England.

Two spells of serious dysentery got him leave to India in 1917. He went first to Calcutta. Three hours' talk increased his respect for Brajendranath

Seal, who insisted on double-fanning him the whole time and had prayed for Edward every day. "He is eagerly for us & our cause," Edward told Canton, "always provided there are no annexations or indemnities after the war." He thought Seal too idealistic, for "he is no politician, & he thinks 'indemnities & annexations' are a penal measure, a kind of grabbing of a naughty child's cake. We must leave all to the unfolding of Time & Time's Master." Seal and Tagore sometimes disagreed, especially about the rightness and necessity for the war. Seal pressed Edward hard for details and an impartial report on the performance of Indian troops. "I think," Edward wrote, "there is no one on this planet with whom my relations are more entirely satisfactory than this v. dear friend." A little later, he wrote: "It is interesting to see how different are my relations with these 2 great Indians, Rabi and Sil [Seal]. Rabi is the greater writer[,] Sil the greater mind & greater man."[3]

He was always uncertain of his relationship with Tagore, who seemed to assume that a poet was a free agent in the conduct of personal relationships. This went down well with persons as uncritically worshipful as Andrews, but it alienated others who had to balance genuine admiration with responsibilities assumed on his behalf. The contretemps over *The Spirit of Man*, which Bridges regarded as a test of tenacity, was an example. Did Tagore unconsciously assume that the West, having enriched itself at the East's expense, now owed debts to India?

Edward saw Tagore during his leave, "tho I had meant giving him the miss." But Seal had insisted, and "at the eleventh hour I looked him up. Rabi looked better than I have ever seen him. He was v. nice. I quoted to him what Sil had just said, that the political situation was far better than a year ago. He smiled & said he can't understand Sil's opinion, implying also, that he set no store by Sil's thought in these matters. He said it was worse; & talked to me of the deportations"—Indians suspected of sedition, some of them former Shantiniketan students, exiled to the Andaman Islands in the Indian Ocean. The sentences would shadow their careers for a lifetime. Nor was that the only cause for protest. Lord Chelmsford, Hardinge's successor, faced a huge wave of criticism about government foot-dragging over full implementation of the Montagu-Chelmsford Reforms.[4]

Those were the outcome of the five-months' tour of Lord Chelmsford and Samuel Montagu, Undersecretary of State for India, through British India. Broomfield neatly summarizes their report to Parliament in July 1918. It asked for "a greater devolution of power by the Home Government to the Government of India, and by the Government of India to the provinces." Indianization of the services should proceed more rapidly, and provincial legislatures and the franchise should expand. More government services should move to the legislatures. This horizontal structure, known as dyarchy, replaced the vertical imperial structure. The I.C.S. disliked the plan intensely.

Must they "obey the dictates of high-caste [Indian] politicians?" What job security had they if "subject to Indian political control"? What of order and justice if bhadralok politics muddled the police and the courts? Separate electorates for minorities, especially Muslims, was an issue that would grow and grow until it became the rationale for Pakistan in 1947. The I.C.S. most disliked "the thought of a politician being pitchforked into their tidy bureaucracy."[5]

In other respects, too, Tagore's affairs went badly in 1917. In 1916 he went from Japan to America, since England was still unreachable. His American lectures drew large audiences, but he was seen increasingly as the focus of an unthinking sentimental cult. His lectures on nationalism, and this war in particular as its consequence, were in fact his public wrestling with the meaning of the word *nation*. After he returned to India he wrote to Rothenstein:

> I suppose it is one of those words whose meaning is still in its process of formation. If you really mean by that word the peoples who have the consciousness of a common tradition and aspiration then why do you exclude us Bengalis from its category? For you are never tired of reminding us that we do not belong to a nation. When we try to understand you we find that our tradition and aspiration are of a different character from yours—it is more religious and social than political. Therefore it seems to me that the word nation in its meaning carries a special emphasis upon its political character. Politics becomes aggressively self-conscious when it sets itself in antagonism against other peoples, specially when it extends its dominion among alien races.[6]

If he had adopted this more exploratory tone in America he might not have so offended those who took his statements on nationalism as unwarranted and ungrateful. His book sales declined so that by 1919 Andrews would demand to inspect Macmillan's books. The Macmillans were indignant. If Andrews wanted an audit, Tagore must pay for it. The trouble arose, wrote George Brett of the New York firm, "solely because, owing to Tagore's alleged activities in this country, and perhaps in India also, the American public made up its mind that he was pro-German, or pacifist, or both, and for a time ceased buying his books, in fact, the sales fell off to practically nothing, and we even had to take back from the booksellers considerable stock of Tagore's books previously sold to them, and for which they could find no sale." Not only Wesleyans found poets baffling: Maurice Macmillan replied, "We must make allowances for a poet."[7]

Edward found Tagore's mood disquieting. "Taggory is doing a mighty deal of preachment these days, not to say scolding," he told Canton. "I've just given him a hint to stow it. Amid much that is striking, there's a deal of shallow knowledge. Pity he's turned preacher." Tagore often attributed his actions to unidentifiable forces. His political reentry in 1917 was "some unexpected freak of fate" that caught him in "a dust storm of our politics. . . . I am more convinced than ever that a poet might do worse than write mere verses." Rothenstein told his brother, "I see Tagore is being dragged into Indian politics—a bad thing for a man with so little decision as he has."[8]

During his Indian leave Edward spent two pleasant weeks at Darjeeling, where he "began badly" when he offended against a local military dress code; its stringency increased according to distance from any battlefield. "I had just got out of the train; I was correctly dressed for Busra [Basra], Baghdad, C'cutta, or Bombay; when a stuffy old fool in mufti came up, & said 'What's yr. name?' Taken aback, I told him. (He had no right to ask it, in mufti)." He identified himself as a Colonel and said: " 'You are wearing shoes, & stockings' " (instead of boots). Edward apologized and pointed out that he had just arrived. "He was in a most beastly wax, & went off, muttering 'Captain Thompson, H—m, Captain Thompson.' " Edward, "frightfully ratted," went on to his hotel but found the officious colonel there, "& he passed me with a black scowl because I hadn't changed my shoes in the streets." Edward decamped at once to another hotel, but there he found posted "their fat-headed local rules about officers' dress." The paragraph forbidding " 'shose' " was blue-penciled. Edward tore it up and threw it on the fire, "thus adding sedition to the sin of insubordination. The only other officer there applauded; & we became two untrammelled souls."[9]

The self-satisfaction of the vacationing civil service wives was equally fatuous. Edward heard two of them discussing him. One said that Thompson, a missionary, knew Bengal well. Said the other, " 'He never was a missionary; he's been stuffing you.' " First lady: "(glowering) 'I thought he was stuffing me' "—after which she cut him dead as a convicted liar. Lyon had gone, still considered "the most unpopular man in Bengal—most scurvily sent home without a knighthood, after being 2nd man in Bengal."[10]

Edward finally found peace in the Darjeeling Jail House, not because of offenses against the dress code, but because the keeper was an old acquaintance who sought him out and insisted that Edward stay with him. This brought him into Darjeeling's social whirl. He detested officious memsahibs who swept aside his social obligations to fix up other engagements—he being a single man obviously on the loose. In hindsight, he decided that these women were "all right enough," but "I think the East spoils women far more than men."[11]

Nor could he fend off Harihar Das, whose demands penetrated even unto "the Hills." He now wanted after all to include Edward's chapter on Toru Dutt, signed, although Edward had asked that, if included, it be unsigned. Further, Das had wangled an introduction to Lord Curzon, and he pestered Edward "to do a petition" about the book.[12]

Edward visited Bankura briefly and received "the utmost kindness from Brown & Spooner, & all my students." The next day he left for Bombay and Mesopotamia, somewhat refreshed but still not feeling really well. However, he did not want to relinquish his front-line job. He had "formed the most extraordinary admiration along the lines for the ordinary soldier."[13]

By 31 August he was in Mesopotamia, "the vilest place I ever struck, without any sort of competition. Even Manchester is preferable." At first he was with a Seventh Army regular division, which he found "v. uphill & disheartening work" where religious traditions were "just the 'good form' of having occasional Church Parades & the necessity of belonging to the Establishment & of being a Tory." Then he relapsed into dysentery and the hospital, but by 13 September he could deliver his lecture on the history of "this utterly loathsome land" to an audience of generals, one of whom slept intermittently, then woke with a jerk and became a most enthusiastic listener. "Some audiences," Edward noted, "might have snored."[14]

He returned to the Leicestershires, "to the end of time, for me or them or the War." The reception from some senior officers was "chilling, but all was different when I ran into our subalterns. Nothing cd. exceed the warmth & kindness of their welcome. . . . I find they take it for granted that now, where they go I go & there is no more stiffness because a padre is with them." A rough old Irish sergeant-major said that he had observed a battlefield incident that proved that Edward was not a " 'blue funk' " despite his confession that he was always in a blue funk in emergencies. "But I consider this compliment, from such a quarter, is worth v. much more than many of the *Mentions* or decorations. The memory of it will do a good deal to keep me cool in any tight corner in wh. I may find myself hereafter." If any superior officers were frosty, they were not of his world, and the air warmed among the lower ranks and common soldiers.[15]

Early in November 1917 he was in two more battles and spent seven hours clearing wounded from the battlefield, but "our tiny side-show seemed more insignificant than ever" after the bad news of the Allies' reverses in Italy. During part of a very cold night he "marched with my friends of the 53rd Sikhs," and also with them was "Sarcka, the excellent Yank who ran our Y.M.C.A., carrying a camel-load of cigarettes" who announced, " 'the sensation I am about to go through is one which I wouldn't miss for worlds.' . . . I bided my time, knowing how unpleasant the first fifteen minutes under shell-fire are for even the bravest." The Turks tried for the range of "us who formed the doctor's retinue," but the troops raced forward and "consequently the doctor's party got the benefit of most of this early shelling." The Leicestershires and Sikhs, speeding ahead, took the Turks by surprise. "If the doctor stopped to bandage a man, we had to run to keep touch with the regiment." Edward worried about pockets of fifty or sixty wounded left behind with medical personnel. It was suggested that Sarcka stay back with them. " 'No,' he said sturdily, 'I'm going on.' And go on he did, and was shortly afterwards distributing cigarettes under heavy fire," and "when he justified his place by a score of deeds, from cigarette-distributing to bandaging the wounded, public opinion rejoiced and accepted him, known for a comrade and a brave man."[16]

Media manipulation of the news is not new. While Edward and a doctor looked down at a Turk who had died of terrible injuries, an official "cinematograph operator" turned up to film him, then proceeded to "stage-manage the place." When an ambulance arrived for an injured Turk, the cameraman ordered it to back up, then to "run up smartly, while the man was to be lifted in, equally smartly." He bade Edward and the doctor stand beside the dead Turk, so "somewhere or other, a film has been exhibited, 'Wounded being collected on Mesopotamian battlefields.' " They were vastly relieved when the cameraman left. Edward was grateful not to have seen another casualty that still harrowed his memory: a Turkish sniper stationed in a stack of thornbushes with sandbagged seats at the center. The Leicestershires had bypassed him, but when they returned he had been horribly hit, "had dug a hole in the thorns, and buried his head; I suppose to escape the flies. His legs were waving feebly. It was right that he should be left to the last, as he had no chance of life, and nothing could be done for him in any way. But never did I feel more the utter folly and silly cruelty of war than when I saw this brave man's misery." When they passed him again, somehow he had left his thorn stack and had crawled some hundreds of yards before dying.[17]

During the battle for Tekrit a few days later Edward fell ill again but stuck it out with his unit. The Turks retreated, and the Leicestershires moved downstream. "Fritz," the German reconnaissance airman, disappeared after (it was said) dropping a message, "Good-bye 7th Division."[18]

Edmund Candler asked Edward to correct his account of the Leicestershires at Istabulat and Samarra, for his history *The Long Road to Baghdad*. Edward liked Candler very much, found him interesting and "broad-minded for an Englishman." For a later version Candler included all that the censors had forbidden earlier, including a statement that politics had overborne strategy, for "our policy was one of opportunism." There was no valid reason for advancing to Baghdad and beyond, once they had the port of Basra and the Abadan oil fields. "It was the old story of vague and ill-considered policy," vacillation, dissipation of resources, compromise, and ignorance. Every soldier in Mesopotamia cursed the bureaucrats. Indian administrative thinking was long outdated and was responsible for the many thousands of unnecessary deaths. The War Office took over in February 1916, but it was too late for too many.[19]

On 23 December 1917 the Leicestershires were back at Basra, amazed after so much desert to find "willows in their winter dress, gold-streaked, and the brooding blue above the waveless channels." They were sobered as they again passed "the tall feathery tamarisks above the Norfolks' graves and trenches" near Sannaiyat.[20]

On 4 January 1918 they embarked and on the seventh were on the way to new campaigns. Nine months later they were "swinging through Beirut in the old, immemorial fashion, though foot-weary, and singing, whilst the people madly cheered and shouted. But it was not the old crowd." Some were gone forever. Some had gone to France. Edward went to Egypt.[21]

He reached Cairo on 22 January 1918, posted to the Egyptian Expeditionary Force. He had signed on for another year from July 1917, after which he intended to go to England. His plans ran afoul of chaplaincy administration. The Wesleyan chaplains who had come from India at the urgent request of the principal chaplain were unhappy about salaries, for they received less than those from England, got no allowances for uniforms, and had irregular contracts that caused endless confusion about leaves. Edward expressed himself "rather recklessly," and another chaplain said the same thing, "but with more commonsense in the matter." Edward thought that it amounted to the mixture of church and state: when a man became a bishop, or a principal chaplain, "or anything, nominally religious but, officially connected with the State, the official swamps the religious. If this war has done nothing else for me, it has made me the most convinced nonconformist in English-speaking places. . . . [O]rganised Xty will soon be fighting for its very existence."[22]

The unquenchable Harihar Das still pursued. He had begun to touch Edward for money: "Ever since I knew him, he has been without any visible means of support except his acquaintances." Das also "immediately commanded" Edward to introduce him to Canton and to persuade Tagore to persuade Macmillan to take his book. "I think he is the most persistent person I ever met," Edward wrote to Lyon, "as well as the coolest—& now writes upbraidingly." Edward did not turn him away, for Harihar Das was an Indian, and the West had enriched itself at the expense of the East. From the depths of some historical subconscious, he too was saying, in effect: *You owe me.*[23]

In Cairo Edward was at a casualty clearing station. Now preaching duties and bedside visiting were a letdown. "So my 'Story' is at an end," he wrote to Elizabeth, "& I become a tame cat at a hospital." He missed the Leicestershires. He told Canton, "No one cd. be jumpier than I, or loathe the whole business more; but war, war with the boys about you, was better than this chatting from bed to bed. I must get back to divisional work, in a few weeks." During his last visit to the trenches, his large audience had sheltered from shells in a huge dry watercourse while he talked for an hour and a half. "Everyone was there. One stern C. of E. officer told me he came unwillingly, but 'the force of public opinion' constrained him." The men told Edward that a Church of England padre in his old division was much disliked: if they got rid of him, would Edward stay? He declined to get involved but hoped to rejoin them after a few months' rest. However, replacing him at Cairo was difficult because no other Wesleyan wanted his job, for it included Indians and only a handful of Wesleyans.[24]

He reflected that his going to Mesopotamia had probably cost him the Bankura College principalship: "If so it means I haven't the chance I hoped for, of influencing Indian thought & education. I shall probably have to take my own way; not for the first time." He would resign the chaplaincy, be demobilized, and have that English furlough before returning to Bankura.[25]

He got himself transferred to Jerusalem. There his plans underwent a great revision. He met Theodosia Jessup, daughter of William Jessup, of an American Presbyterian missionary family of many generations of Princeton University graduates and founders of the American College at Beirut. Theodosia was a Vassar graduate with an M.A. degree from Columbia Teachers College. Now she taught Arabic and French to members of the Red Cross Commission and helped to run an orphanage. She was pretty and vivacious, energetic and efficient. Admirers surrounded her. To her, Edward seemed quite a new type: affable and good company but more serious-minded than her American admirers: not exactly handsome, but attractive in his seriousness. His manner implied both self-confidence and depths of thoughtfulness; he was also great fun in a group. He was an experienced veteran, and he wrote poems. If this was not love at first sight on his part, he wasted very little time. On 2 August Edward wrote to ask "Dear Miss Jessup" not to worry: had he been hasty, his feelings too plain too soon? He had thought that only his books interested her. He had spoken only because times were so uncertain. Then he tried to explain the provenance, neither lengthy nor lurid, of his heart's affairs. He had loved a girl who loved a mutual Kingswood friend. They quarreled, she turned to Edward—for a while, for she was not a constant nymph—and he, doing the honorable thing, sent her back to her lover. Here at last was explanation for the "Eros Astray" sonnets written at Richmond in 1909.[26]

This explained also some oblique letters from Canton in 1915 and 1916. A friend's wife had come to India and, on her husband's recommendation, looked up Edward and become a profound influence. "Egeria seems to have wrought many miracles in a short time," Canton had written. Canton pointed out to Edward that she had made him "revise your opinion of women's intellectual limitations" and had made him " 'ashamed of your habits of self-analysis.' " His advice only made Edward "insufferably headstrong and cantankerous. . . ." Well, Canton had concluded, "Egeria" would do him good, if only as contrast to the "mission ladies of Bankura." He was less likely to settle down with "a frowsy mission lady" and be haunted day and night by memories of "Egeria."

That friendship could not last. Bankura's missionary wives became intrusively suspicious. "Ladies don't do that sort of thing," Canton wrote, "*Christian* women ought to be ashamed of such pernicious spite." The local ladies' gossip hastened the end, about a year later, and Canton advised Edward not to be too hard on "Egeria." She had taught him much that he would never have learned from the mission ladies.[27]

The "Egeria" episode, Edward told Theodosia, had been "a dazzling experience, for a man living a very lonely life." He and the unnamed lady rode together and read Sophocles, and he worshipped her and wrote a little book for her. When she tired of him, as of everyone, she wanted to keep it. He wanted it back so that he could burn it. Eventually, he did so.[28]

Relatively naive, pessimistic, largely self-educated but brimming with undeveloped possibilities, Edward now saw in Theodosia much of what he had missed. By 18 August he was "an accepted lover." Theo, however, was less liberated than he had thought. The next day "she was worried, & we went back; now, I don't know where I am. Nowhere, apparently; or worse off than before. She's dead afraid of making a mistake." An older confidante somewhere gave her "the sweetest, most sentimental & according to the best early-Victorian standards but (I suspect) hopelessly beside-the-point advice." Theo had "poise and sense, but she knows nothing of the world." Her Red Cross colleagues seemed to accept him as hers, and she made him deliver lectures and "show off as a sort of performing bear." Her confidante was not the only one "beside the point." Victorian rhetoric of romance framed Edward's amazement that a lady as exquisite as Theo had stooped to him. No English poet except Browning, he thought, had been so lucky. He told Canton not to worry "about her being a mission girl." He had never expected to find a wife with charm *and* brains and love for God. He had called her "Theo" before she indicated that that was acceptable, which every true gentleman knew was not done.[29]

His battlefield confidence ebbed away. He worried that his "low nervous state might annoy her." If he seemed conceited that was only his front for "a world that has no use for a poet and idealist, who therefore has to pretend that he is other things." Was being a Wesleyan minister a false position, and would she be happy in Indian work? On one point he was firm: "I will never permit any girl to take the risks & duties of wedded life with me, unless I can see my way clear as noon to ensuring her days free from care." He hated preaching, but he loved Theo and for her sake was willing to labor on.[30]

Suddenly he was ordered to France. To his immense relief, that was cancelled. He began to plan a furlough, perhaps his last chance to see his mother alive. "She is now old," he wrote to Hartley, "& my brother Frank's death was a very severe blow, & she has been ill this summer. So I think I may definitely state that I shall be home next spring, & my wife with me."[31]

Theo's friend Dr. Marshall Brown, in peacetime the chairman of the Princeton University Lectures Committee, pressed Edward to lecture at Princeton for a few months and offered to arrange the same at Harvard. It was seductive, but Edward decided that academically he was nowhere near ready for such an appointment. It would pay well, and it might enhance his reputation as a poet. But he could not see how at that stage he could honestly accept it. It was as well, for at that point he would have been as a sacrifice thrown to academic lions. His honesty saved him.[32]

The Princeton suggestion sharpened the old disappointment about the education he had missed. "I've always regretted, fiendishly & rebelliously & enormously, that I have no connection with either of our older universities," he wrote to Lyon. Perhaps he could take a two-year Oxbridge "research" degree. But, "I am afraid I can't get *2* years."[33]

Canton was not surprised at Edward's "little expedition into the regions of Maya" and wished him luck. Certainly Edward should not marry a "mission girl (unless she was a 'pagan')," and he rather liked "the notion of an American girl (or Americanized); she might do wonders with you which you would not do with any one else. . . . Don't be in a hurry. . . . Don't believe that if you don't get what you want today you won't ever get as good or better." He was not unsympathetic about "the new Egeria," but Edward must not be too lyrical or too tragic or "press a one-sided suit." He suspected, rightly, that Edward was not widely experienced in matters of the heart.[34]

His advice came too late. Edward and Theo were engaged and planned to marry in March. "She's the most fascinating, clever, vivacious Amurkan girl imaginable with the wildness still about her of those Lebanon hills where she lived till over 20 years of age," Edward wrote to Canton, "& she's going to do no end of good." Would Canton write to Theo—but he must not "let on the harm you know of me." Assuming (or hoping) that Edward would not return to Bankura, Canton told Theo that England was not Lebanon or the United States but was a good place to live. She had, in effect, taken Edward off his hands. "The last—how many years?—I have tried to 'bring him up' in careful and seemly fashion. It is a feather—nay a plume—in my cap that your approval of him shows I have not wholly failed."[35]

Edward went to Beirut to meet Mr. Jessup, a difficult journey because fighting there had left the city famine-stricken, and the road was strewn with dead ponies from "the miserable flight of the Turks. . . . It's rotten, to belong to a beaten army." He liked Mr. Jessup very much and found him "the sturdiest & sternest Teutophobe I ever met. My diatribes—felt, not spoken— are milk-merciful to his." At the American College everyone, including its president, greeted Edward warmly, which delighted Theo. While he was there, the war ended. Events then moved quickly. Edward and Theo were married on 10 March and had "five perfect days" at Aleppo. Theo then left for

Letchworth to await the beginning of Edward's furlough. He went for a long walk across Galilee, then to demobilization camp. On 3 June he embarked at last, wonderfully happy but still not well. Rheumatism brought on by the months of field conditions declared itself again, and he felt in need of general repairs.[36]

At Letchworth Theo began to see her husband from his family's point of view: "Edward's own mother says that he 'takes a bit of knowing'—but how worth while that 'bit' is we have both found out," she wrote to Lyon. Edward was home by 16 July. They would return to Bankura in January. But before they could get away, the ineffable Das caught them at Letchworth. "The number of wires he has managed to pull is amazing," Edward wrote to Lyon. "He believes supremely, with sublime simplicity, in INFLUENCE." Edward stood it all, "except his patronage. This drove me crazy." Theo wanted to box his ears. Das advised him to " 'keep working away, for ten years perhaps, & fame will come to you.' " He intimated that Edward might get a government job, or perhaps an examinership at Calcutta University—Edward had already refused this annually. Das left behind a mass of Toru Dutt's letters, which Edward had promised long ago to read. In a way Das's visit did him good, "for he showed me things I had been forgetting." Fundamental facts, perhaps, about the complications and consequences of imperial involvement.[37]

A few days later Das overreached himself, and Edward at last rebelled. He had estimated the number of publishable letters but refused to correct badly typed manuscript pages. "Three times," he wrote to Lyon, "have I revised that [biography] ms. I did a long chapitre also. I have read thro the letters (v. many). I have drafted an appeal to that man of wrath, Nathaniel Curzon. I have advised on many points. I have paid typing bills. . . . I have finished."[38]

While Edward considered his future with the Wesleyans, the Bankura Wesleyans considered his with them. Mitchell had retired, and the college was now six men short. Qualified Indian Christians, paid only twenty-five rupees a month, wanted government jobs. Brown thought that the new emphasis on science would "*make* a student think" instead of relying on memorized notes. He did not say that students who thought scientifically might think even less about religion. Now Bankura wanted Edward back by July despite his being "somewhat unreliable or rather irresponsible." However, a wife should set him straight, for "if she be the right sort of lady she may make all the difference to Thompson and give him that steady influence which is all that he requires."[39]

The Bengal to which he would return was not the Bengal he had left. Brown told Amos Burnet, a new Missionary Society Secretary, that the college was peaceful. There were "no evil effects from Mr Gandhi's crack-brained [Non-cooperation] scheme. I do not think that the boycotting of schools and colleges will take on at all in Bengal." It was a serious miscalculation. The political atmosphere had changed drastically after events that, to many in England and in India, seemed random upheavals but in fact were tightly, logically linked. They had already changed the old imperial relationship beyond repair.[40]

13

AMRITSAR

While the Thompsons were still in England, the Jallianwala Bagh massacre at Amritsar in the Punjab further poisoned India's relations with Britain. It became the companion piece to bitter memories of 1857's events, which the West calls the Mutiny and Indians prefer to call the Uprising or the First War of Independence. It shook Edward Thompson's inherited faith in the empire as a viable force for good; and it heightened his misgivings, already rooted in the manifest deficiencies of the educational system, that the governing of India had taken a wrong turn. Amritsar was a tragedy for England as well as for India. Broomfield writes that it "brought a storm of protest from all political groups in India. The Moderates pointed out reproachfully that nothing could be better calculated to lend colour to the Extremists' assertion that within the Jekyll of the reforms lurked the old Hyde of repression." However, the storm was not immediate, for reliable information was suppressed for too long. Those who advocated strong-handed control had another argument for increased policing.[1]

On Sunday, 13 April 1919, a crowd variously estimated at fifteen thousand to twenty thousand unarmed Indians, among them some women and many youths, gathered to hear nationalist speakers in a tightly enclosed space called Jallianwala Bagh. The object was to encourage a *hartal* (a semireligious nonviolent day of fasting and no work) to protest the Rowlatt Act of 21 March 1919. The Rowlatt Act, intended to curb revolutionary conspiracy, severely curtailed civil rights such as trial by jury, and it authorized draconian measures for threats, real or apparent, of seditious conspiracy, or of extreme emergency as defined by the Government of India or a provincial government. Sir Michael O'Dwyer, Lieutenant Governor of the Punjab, defined the Jallianwala Bagh gathering as both conspiracy and threat of sedition and violence.[2]

It was not a random irruption. Since at least 1905 local protests had caused the Punjab government to close newspapers, deport or imprison leaders of public protests, and ban public gatherings. Helen Fein, in *Imperial Crime and Punishment*, examines Jallianwala in the context of imperial interpretations of authority, violence, and civil disturbance, when official policy and behavior reversed the received definitions so that *victims* became *ulprits.* Jallianwala, like the 1857 Mutiny, marked a nonreversible turning-point in British-Indian relations.[3]

Thus not all of the troubles at Amritsar in 1919 are chargeable to the Rowlatt Act, which required the Government of India's approval and in fact was never formally invoked. However, such threats only stoked already-smouldering fires. Indian leaders who had tendered goodwill felt rejected. The Rowlatt Act seemed to negate good intentions implicit in the Montagu-Chelmsford Reforms and their recommendations for Indians' wider participation in government. Sir Michael O'Dwyer claimed that "[t]o expose the falsehoods about the Rowlatt Act employed to excite the ignorant mobs, we had hastily printed and distributed tens of thousands of copies of an explanation of the Act. . . . These copies were torn up or burned publicly, for those who were behind this lawless agitation knew that it could only thrive on falsehood." But how many of the 160,000 persons in Amritsar city, many illiterate mill workers, could read those circulars, even in vernacular translation?[4]

In the Punjab, successfully nonviolent hartals took place on 30 March and 3 April. Gandhi, only recently prominent as a Congress Party leader, used the hartal to substantiate his philosophy of nonviolent protest: *satyagraha* or "truth-force." The government forbade his entering the Punjab or any other province on such an errand. He was arrested and thus was not at Amritsar on 13 April 1919. The Punjab government quietly removed from the city two leading local Indian organizers of hartals. On 10 April as many as forty thousand rallied for a hartal and release of political prisoners. Mounted soldiers stationed at the British quarter fired without warning and killed some twenty to thirty persons. Public buildings were looted and burned, and five Englishmen died. The suffering icon for that day, and for years afterward, was a Miss Sherwood, a British missionary dragged from her bicycle on a side street, attacked and beaten, but saved by several Hindus nearby.[5]

Sir Michael O'Dwyer was an old-line imperialist who regarded Indians per se as dangerous and untrustworthy: only stern authority curbed them. The events of 1919 were "the Punjab Rebellion." He blamed "the slaves of catchwords, and empty but high-sounding formulae," Indian politicians and the Indian "educated classes"; and Fabians, Theosophists, and Indian extremists in London. Any instability, real or imagined, awakened in him the siege mentality that his generation had inherited from the 1857 Mutiny.[6]

On 11 April he welcomed Brigadier General Reginald Dyer, who had comprehensive authority to restore order. There were no overt incidents on the twelfth when Dyer arrested "about a dozen ringleaders of the mob" or when his eight hundred troops marched through the city, although "people spat on the ground and muttered nationalist slogans as the soldiers marched by." However, "there is no evidence" that Dyer's warning of 12 April was published. He did not know, until four o'clock on the afternoon of the thirteenth, about the Jallianwala meeting. He went there immediately with armed Sikhs and Gurkhas in two armored cars with machine guns.[7]

A *bagh* is a garden, but Jallianwala was only a bleak and rather rubbishy enclosure. Many there seemed to regard the gathering as more social than political. They did not riot. They sat quietly on the ground listening to speeches. Dyer's armored cars could not negotiate the narrow entrance so the soldiers stood on a mound overlooking the enclosure. Without calling for dispersal or warning of intention to fire, Dyer ordered them to begin and continue firing. In panic the crowd rushed toward the few narrow exits. Dyer claimed later that he thought that they were massing to counterattack. The soldiers fired "almost 1,650 rounds" at the struggling crowd.

The government moved with delayed deliberation. Not until October and November did an investigative committee with a British majority convene with the Scottish jurist Lord Hunter as the chairman. There were also a Punjab District Committee and a Congress Party Subcommittee; the latter met separately because the government refused to release key Indian witnesses from prison. The Hunter Committee reported in October 1919. O'Dwyer stated that he had warned, "by beat of drum" on the morning of the thirteenth, of military force to be used against "unlawful acts." He then heard about the meeting but thought that in view of his measures there would be no insurrection. Figures varied, but the Punjab government's home-military records cite 379 dead. More than 1,000 were injured. One Indian author lists, by parent age, caste, age, and residence, 381 dead. Most were between twenty and fifty years of age. Most were from Amritsar city or district, which contradicted charges of extensive outside agitation. The dead and the wounded were left unattended because a six o'clock curfew kept rescuers away, under threat of being shot. One woman described, for the separate National Congress committee, how she defied the curfew to get inside and move her husband's body to a "dry place, for that place was overflowing with blood." She sat all night by the body, beating off dogs with a bamboo stick. There was no water or first aid. Much later Dyer claimed that "they had only to apply for help. . . . I was ready to help them if they applied." Obviously, they could not apply, and no rescuer could apply because of the curfew. To whom could they have applied? Neither Dyer nor anyone else was at hand to hear them.[8]

Could Dyer have dispersed the crowd without firing? Yes, he said, but they "would all come back and laugh at me, and I considered I would be making myself a fool." He wanted to *punish* the crowd *so that they could not laugh at him:* "My idea from the military point of view was to make a wide impression."[9]

How much of regrettable English behavior in India sprang from fears of looking foolish? So carefully separated from Indians they were, that they did

ot know how often Indians laughed at them in private. E. M. Forster, early
A *Passage to India,* has Dr. Aziz and his Muslim friends joining in "bitter
in" at their English superiors. Because the official English so often lacked
sense of the absurd and could not laugh at themselves, Indian fun at their
xpense often turned bitter. General Dyer could not see that he exemplified
basic fact about the British Raj: almost as much as Indian rebellion, the
nglish feared Indian laughter.[10]

From 15 April to 11 June martial law prevailed in five of twenty-one
unjab districts, with summary courts, floggings, confiscations of property,
nprisonments, and hangings. Cultural insults added to the injuries. The
ne most bitterly remembered was General Dyer's "crawling order": Indians
ust crawl on all fours along the street where Miss Sherwood was assaulted
n 10 April. Other orders forced them to *salaam* or touch noses to the
round before Englishmen. High-caste males had to do street sanitary work
nd lawyers had to do menial tasks. Students selected apparently at random
ere expelled or lost their scholarships. The list of ingeniously insulting
enalties is very long.[11]

Selective press censorship, in both India and England, was possible be-
ause candid reporting was made impossible. The *Times* reported on the
eaths of the five Englishmen at Amritsar on 10 April. Until December
ere were no forthright statements about a massacre of Indians. Anodyne
atements such as "All quiet at Amritsar and Lahore" masked that omission.
he *Times* called the Rowlatt Act only a "pretext" for provocation and Gandhi
nly "a misguided and excitable person, who is used by others as a stalking
orse," not "in any sense dangerous." Montagu and the Viceroy were dupes
f unpractical idealists who knew neither India nor the Asiatic atmosphere.
Last Sunday"—13 April, the day of the massacre, was only a "renewal of
isturbance" at Amritsar.[12]

Thompson, like everyone else in England, was left in the dark. He knew
nly, when he wrote to Lyon about a week later, that something terrible
ad occurred. "Why is there no *Friends of India* association—Europeans
etached & impartial? I am expressing myself badly. But we do need *some*
ay by wh. ~~moderate &~~ *fair* men can find a voice."[13]

Edward may not have known when he wrote that Tagore, as his personal
ct of protest, had notified the Viceroy that he wished to relinquish his
nighthood. He did not act immediately because for him, too, Amritsar
ews was scarce and fragmentary. Andrews tried to gather facts. He hurried
o Delhi and Simla but found Chelmsford "cold as ice with me, and full
f racial bitterness." Andrews told an official that the government's "moral
restige" had never been lower. The reply was that, on the contrary, it had
ever been higher. That man did not know, Andrews told Tagore, "what
oral prestige means." Andrews went to the Punjab, but his train was

searched at Amritsar, and police removed him and sent him back to Delhi
On 12 June, after martial law ended, he reached the Punjab and for th
first time got firsthand information, a shattering account by a Jallianwal
eyewitness.[14]

Indian politicians could not or would not promptly protest. Disgusted
Tagore acted alone. On 3 June he sent the Viceroy a letter of impressiv
dignity and restraint. He knew that it would be regarded as an insult t
England, from an Indian to whom England had condescended when plent
of homeborn English gentlemen hoped for knighthoods.

"Your Excellency," he began: "The enormity of the measures taken b
the Government in the Punjab for quelling some local disturbances ha
with a rude shock revealed to our minds the helplessness of our positio
as British subjects in India." The act had neither political expediency no
justification. When the news "trickled through the gagged silence," th
rulers, "possibly congratulating themselves for imparting what they imagin
as salutary lessons," ignored the people's indignation. Most of the Englisl
language papers in India praised this "callousness" and even poked fun a
Indians' sufferings while suppressing statements from "organs representin
the sufferers." Pursuing vengeance, the government had been false to its ow
"noble vision of statesmanship." Therefore he must speak up and take th
consequences.

> The time has come when badges of honour make our shame glaring in their
> incongruous context of humiliation, and I for my part wish to stand, shorn
> of all special distinctions, by the side of those of my countrymen who, for
> their so called insignificance are liable to suffer a degradation not fit for human
> beings. And these are the reasons which have painfully compelled me to ask
> Your Excellency, with due deference and regret, to relieve me of my title of
> Knighthood, which I had the honour to accept from His Majesty the King at th
> hands of your predecessor, for whose nobleness of heart I still entertain great
> admiration.[15]

The letter deserves a place of honor in epistolary history. Gone is th
metaphorical overkill frequent in his English letters and essays. Regret an
blame are perfectly balanced, and deference does not grovel. Patience ha
run out at last. Someone must speak for those unable to speak for then
selves. If the comparison with Chelmsford's predecessor did not wrench th
Viceroy's conscience, he was indeed a man of ice.

Andrews sent Rothenstein a copy of the letter. "How can I not approve c
it?" Rothenstein told Tagore. "You have not put off, but have put on dignity
Tagore replied at once, saying that the most painful part of India's trial wa
the lack of opportunity "to redress our wrongs." Meanwhile his school wa
his best comfort: "So, in order to forget that this life is a nightmare I have t

serve these little boys I have gathered round me, teaching them elementary things and telling them stories."[16]

"He had never wished for the knighthood," Edward wrote seven years later, "but the pain of having to repudiate what he knew had been meant as recognition and an honour was very acute. Still more acute was the pain of disillusionment. . . . He had always believed in the essential fairness in the British character." He knew that other rulers could have been much worse. "A tired and unhappy man, he felt the world going wrong all about him."[17]

Whatever else happened, Edward now had a wife to support. Literature would not make them a living. He shrank from relying on Theo's American income. She tried to keep alive the idea of the Princeton lectures, but he could not spin a career from so slender a thread. Bankura was the one certainty.

His distaste for pastoral formalities had become a settled conviction, although he discharged his duties willingly and well. At Wycliffe College he had won the boys' confidence. At Sawtry his congregation appreciated both his kindness and good preaching. In Mesopotamia soldiers came to his services without orders. At Bankura, however, preaching was a tool for conversions. Undermining another's faith now seemed unbearably presumptuous, even despotic. Disposing of his students' Hinduism would not dispose of their social and educational disadvantages.

Bankura and London conducted a "Where's Thompson?" round-robin. Hartley had not seen him. McClelland still thought him an unsuitable college principal and relied on "the possibility of the steadying influence of a wife"; he would not oppose an appointment as Acting Principal. Hartley agreed that he was not the ideal choice, but Brown really needed his furlough.[18]

McClelland had good reason for alarm about the Wesleyan institutions. A Government of India index of censored books would "affect missionary propaganda of almost every type." The government refused to discuss the matter. Just three days after the Jallianwala massacre McClelland seems to have known no more about it than did Edward in England or Tagore in India. Terrible events had occurred, McClelland told Hartley, but he too meant the riots on 10 April, "a regular orgy of destruction at Lahore and Amritsar." He blamed everything on Gandhi's noncooperation. "Apparently, the Government is waking up to the seriousness of things. . . ." The government did its best to keep everyone else from waking up to the facts.[19]

Finally Edward saw Hartley and indicated that although he was still badly in need of rest, he would shorten his own furlough in order to liberate Brown. Edward and Theo finally secured passage and arrived at Bankura on 17 April 1920. She was pregnant, and to avoid the hot weather she went to Darjeeling to await the baby's birth in August.

By then the Hunter Committee's report was public knowledge. Edward found at Bankura "not a scrap of interest" in politics. "Even Amritsar is not mentioned much." However, "Rabi is on the ramp throughout India against us. I can get no reply from him, tho I have written. Possibly he has wiped all English acquaintances off his list, save Andrews. . . ." Ten days later Tagore did write. He said only that he would go soon to lecture in Europe for money to expand the Shantiniketan school into an international university as Visva-Bharati. He hoped to attract foreign scholars to live there and lecture, teach, and translate. It was a brilliantly progressive idea. In 1920, however, Tagore's was an uphill effort, undertaken impulsively and with public relations poorly prepared. He was in low spirits but would return "happier and more fit for my vocation of life."[20]

In that same letter he resumed his vague importuning that Edward translate the short stories, particularly "Cloud and Sun." His translations did after all "retain the delicate bloom of the original to a great extent." Very little of others' work pleased Tagore; and, most frustrating, he could not define his dissatisfactions. It was *The Spirit of Man* all over again. There was still no mention of remunerating Edward.[21]

Before he could settle to work, Edward became involved in an Amritsar protest. Pro-Dyer hysteria was rampant among Anglo-Indians. The London government equivocated, and Lyon thought that its actions were "all right," for if the Cabinet spoke out, there would be "a crop of resignations in India. Hence a certain amount of *camouflage* and soft sawder." Dyer had had "no wise committee at his elbow" and was "bound to go wrong, and as he clearly thought black lives were cheap he could not see how monstrous it was to mow a crowd of Indians down in the way he did." The delay in disclosure "should have been avoided at all costs, even if the disclosure preceded the formal inquiry. But we always seem to do the wrong thing where 'Indian sentiment' is concerned." The terribly wrong thing was giving comprehensive power to a man of such limited understanding. Lyon prophesied that "the Amritsar horror will be the text for hundreds of inflammatory speeches during the next decade, while it has reduced the moderate Indian politicians almost to despair. I don't forget the differences between Punjabis and Bengalis, but surely we managed things better in Bengal?" Yet he, too, misjudged when he praised O'Dwyer as "the greatest ruler that India has seen for many years. . . ." O'Dwyer, in old-fashioned imperialism and racial intransigence, had approved, then tried to excuse the tragedy. In leaving responsibility to the unstable Dyer he had in effect abdicated his own responsibilities. For O'Dwyer the issue was survival of the empire. Even Lyon underestimated Amritsar's consequences. For much more than a decade Amritsar remained a text for Indian resentment.[22]

Worst of all for Edward was the consolation fund of twenty-seven thousand pounds from Dyer's imperialist sympathizers. A "missionaries' manifesto" protested it. At first he refused to sign because it was poorly phrased. He sent a substitute document that became the published version. "Now I am held up to reprobation as 'unBritish,' full of 'maudlin sentimentality' & other dreadful things," he told Lyon. "As for my own countrymen, I am ashamed of them. . . . At present Andrews & I seem the two most unpopular Englishmen in India. . . ." The Anglo-Indian English Association was only "a tory annexe, to express racial prejudice." Theo reminded him that people's minds were made up, but he refused to give in. It was abhorrent "that there might be English folk who declined to abdicate their dear-bought inheritance, of thinking and speaking for themselves."[23]

By far, "the women have been the worst." A lady who signed herself only "Englishwoman" produced "the most ferocious letters, with a sweeping disregard of reason, & with a quality of insolence that a man never seems to think himself entitled to use. What happens to my countrywomen out here?" When the Dyer case seemed closed, Edward dared to hope that the old Raj had come well out of this matter. "The English rule is still the sanest & fairest on this globe, after all." But the next day a virulent antimissionary letter showed again "that there is no class so hated & misunderstood by Europeans as missionaries." Indian Christians, too, were dismayed at the behavior of those Englishmen, nominally Christian, who excused Dyer's actions.[24]

Dyer's supporters longed, like E. M. Forster's Chandrapore Collector, for "the good old days when an Englishman could satisfy his own honour and no questions asked afterward." What most angered the Dyer-O'Dwyer supporters was that critics dared to question their judgment. *India As I Knew It*, the title of O'Dwyer's autobiography, tells it all: India as British property, its status unquestioned and unquestionable, belonged to a past tense.[25]

Disturbed as he was about events, Lyon nevertheless tried, from his British vantage point, to keep Edward on balance. "On the other hand," he wrote, "—and it is well to have the other view in mind—much of the violence & hot-headed talk is due to apprehension for our womenkind in lonely stations in India; and one can understand how hard it is for most Englishmen not to lay exaggerated stress on the dangers to which anti-British agitation exposes them." He knew of extremists who had blanketed the ignorant masses with leaflets urging them to "nameless atrocities against Englishwomen with an unreasoning hatred" for all Indians. It would be better if the women were not there. European women in Eastern countries "would be altogether a mistake, did not their absence lead to other evils which are hard to contemplate." The eternal question was whether the English should be in India at all except as "temporary sojourners."[26]

For I.C.S. men the "eternal question" was that of lifetime career investment. They worked hard and sacrificed much, and now their achievements slid toward an unexpected future that they did not understand. Advice from their early, optimistic days was often contradictory. Should they "keep the native in his place" or assume that a gentleman was a gentleman even if his skin was dark? How could the young I.C.S. candidate, with a bare minimum of trust from his charges, keep Indians in their place? Alas, Indians did not always "think the more of" the I.C.S. man who tried to keep them in that undefined place.[27]

Many in the I.C.S. did not really understand what educated Indians wanted nor did those Indians, often blindsided by government actions that *they* did not understand, always know how best to frame their demands. Dyer and O'Dwyer were akin to Forster's Collector, who declares: "What you've got to stamp on is these educated classes, and, mind, I do know what I'm talking about this time." When Dyer stamped with bullets on the crowd at Jallianwala he stamped on those he considered the unwitting dupes of "these educated classes."[28]

Those educated classes wanted more responsibility for their national future. What then of the civil service, a privileged career for generations of middle- and upper-class English? Now Lyon hesitated to encourage young men into the I.C.S. "It will be hopeless work if he is to be subordinated to a Government which distrusts him and will listen to any racial misrepresentation against him—to say nothing of striving to keep him back in order to promote Indians." Lyon continued to hope that the younger men would help the Indian Moderate Party, "with all their faults," to build upon its strengths. He thought that among those he met in England "an encouraging tendency towards independence of view is emerging." He hoped to secure "their confidence to some extent. But I lie low and leave it to them to make the advances—I think that is the best way to lull their ridiculous suspicions of the ex-bureaucrat!"[29]

Hate letters to the missionaries continued after publication of their "manifesto." Edward wrote to Canton: "We are hav[in]g a savage & increasing outburst of racial hatred. You in Albion can have no conception of the blaze & baseness of passions out here." Of two principal English-language papers the *Englishman* was "just savage, racial bigotry—the planter at his lowest & most selfish. It frankly wants shooting of niggers all round." The *Statesman* (Calcutta), which had published the "manifesto," was better but backed off after "one feeble attempt to stem the tide," in fear for its circulation. Most of the letters were anonymous, the women "far more virulent than the men even, & write with a particular sweep of insolence. . . . India is one ramp. That missionaries shd. *dare* to have souls & opinions of their own! Anonymous anger fumes & avows that it is no wonder that missionary work gets so little support from the European community out here. Spiteful letter after letter hopes that 'next time'—i.e. when there is a mob row—we shall be massacred. Then we shall know, you see. . . . If you were in India now you wd. not dare to speak to me."[30]

Perhaps, he told Lyon, the manifesto had been "bad tactics" and himself "a fool for butting in. But what is one to do? Once in a while writing to the papers really makes a difference in India where there is no other way of touching opinion. . . . As you know from experience, when a man is absolutely alone in India these things do worry him if he is at all sensitive."[31]

Lyon was not surprised that Edward had had a large part in the manifesto. "The very vehemence with which it was assailed by the irresponsible should assure you of its value. I don't agree that it was 'bad tactics' to publish." Edward had helped the Indian moderates: "There are so many reasonable and right thinking Indians who have been driven to despair by the exhibition our countrymen have made of themselves in this affair, and it is essential that they should be assured that there are many Europeans who think with them." He understood how such an event weighed upon a man as solitary as Edward at Bankura, and he was sad about "the way in which so many men of my own [Education] Service are unable to see straight in such a matter. . . ."[32]

Of abusive letters received, a retired English soldier wrote the one that most riled Edward. "He accuses me—never having seen me, but having gathered all this from the very temperate letter I wrote . . . of being a coward, living a sheltered life during the War, 'while Dyer defended me,' of being greedy, self-indulgent, 'living in a nice house,' with 'well-fed belly' & 'money to burn,' going to the hills directly the hot weather comes on, of pandering to natives in my sheer funk, of educating 'the sons of dhobies [washermen] & sweepers,' so that Indians desert 'the simple plough of their forefathers' & are unwilling for manual labour. Dear, dear!" Worst of all was the charge of "my cowardice, & the fact that I have no knowledge of serious danger. He warns me that 'next time' (there is an Amritsar rising) I shall be wiped out & he personally rejoices in the prospect."[33]

Canton advised him to give the letter writer a "straight answer," "by no means hiding the M[ilitary] C[ross]." Edward must "challenge the *anonymous* indignation-person, and blow your own trumpet a little." "I do think," Edward replied, "the military brain is the thickest & silliest in the world. I see the Yanks have been running amuck in Haiti. One often feels that the best thing all these great civilised nations cd. do is to leave other folk alone & try to manage their own affairs."[34]

Collingwood did not know, he wrote, how to deal with the Indian— and Irish—troubles. There was too much disconnected talk on both sides. Everyone was "simply in for a run of storms—politically & socially as well as meteorologically—and there is nothing we can do but sit tight and try to mind the boom when the boat goes about."[35]

John Moses Thompson, father of Edward John Thompson. Courtesy of
Dorothy Thompson.

Kingswood School, Bath. Courtesy of Kingswood School.

Frank Richards ("Rix"), Kingswood School English Tutor. Courtesy of Kingswood School.

Dr. W. P. Workman, Head of Kingswood School. Courtesy of Kingswood School.

Margaret Thompson, sister of Edward John Thompson. Courtesy of Dorothy Thompson.

Mollie Thompson, sister of Edward John Thompson. Courtesy of Dorothy Thompson.

Alfred Thompson, brother of
Edward John Thompson. Courtesy
of Dorothy Thompson.

Frank Thompson,
brother of Edward John
Thompson. Killed in
France in World War I.
Courtesy of Dorothy
Thompson.

Arthur Thompson, brother of Edward John Thompson. Served on the HMS
Dreadnought in World War I. Courtesy of Dorothy Thompson.

Edward John Thompson (second row, left), at Bankura Wesleyan College, West Bengal, with Indian staff colleagues, ca. 1915. © Bodleian Library, Oxford University.

Edward John Thompson as Chaplain with the Mesopotamian forces, British army, World War I. © Bodleian Library, Oxford University.

Mesopotamian war scene, as observed by Edward John Thompson and company doctor. © Imperial War Museum.

Edward John Thompson with his mother, Elizabeth, and wife, Theodosia, at Buckingham Palace, at his investiture with the Military Cross, 1919. Courtesy of Dorothy Thompson.

Portraits of Rabindranath
Tagore by William Rothenstein,
Calcutta, 1910. © Lucy Dynevor.

William Rothenstein and Rabindranath Tagore, London, 1912. Photo by
John Trevor, Hampstead. Courtesy Mrs. Alan Ward.

Theodosia Thompson. Courtesy of Dorothy Thompson.

Frank, Theodosia, Edward Palmer, and Edward John Thompson, at Scar Top, Boars Hill, Oxford. Courtesy of Dorothy Thompson.

Percy C. Lyon. Courtesy of Barbara Lyon.

William Canton. Courtesy of Dorothy Thompson.

Gandhi visiting the Thompsons at Boars Hill, Oxford, 1932. Courtesy of
Dorothy Thompson.

Edward John Thompson (to left of fireplace) with Fellows of Oriel College, Oxford, Senior Common Room. Photo by S. Shah Khan. Courtesy Oriel College Archives.

Elizabeth Penney Thompson, mother of Edward John Thompson, ca. 1923. Courtesy of Dorothy Thompson.

Elizabeth Penney Thompson and Frank Thompson, at Islip, ca. 1923.
Courtesy of Dorothy Thompson.

Frank, Edward John, Theodosia, and Edward Palmer Thompson, at Scar Top,
Boars Hill, Oxford. Courtesy of Dorothy Thompson.

Edward John Thompson. Courtesy of Dorothy Thompson.

Edward Palmer Thompson. Courtesy of Dorothy Thompson.

Saunders Close, Bledlow, Buckinghamshire, the Thompsons' last home. Courtesy of Dorothy Thompson.

14

BREAKING WITH BANKURA

Waiting on tranquillity at Bankura was difficult. The atmosphere was tense because of politics and because of personal relations. Edward, Brown, and Spooner ran both high school and college. Brown was the more cordial, "but S[pooner] never speaks to me. He sits half-round the table, looking at B, to whom he addresses all his remarks. If I ask a question, he rarely answers, & then not for some time. So I have given him up. He and B. are the closest chums all day long." At tea together, they ignored Edward while he served them. They became increasingly secretive: "It isn't my idea of missionary work," Edward wrote. After the other two arranged and, without him, attended a "secret prayer-meeting," Edward "blazed up" at Spooner and said he was fed up with not getting answers to questions "as if I had no right to an interest in things." Spooner took on "his grave tone of laconic rebuke, his best sermon-silky timbre," and sided with Brown. Edward said that if Brown could not see that they were heading for disaster, he should be put right. Spooner and Brown had "a mysterious confab" after Edward went to bed. He began to see that, sooner or later, he must decide whether he could stay at Bankura. Canton advised him to be as cool and civil as possible, to preserve a sense of his character as a missionary and of the mission's claims upon them all. He was setting the course for the remainder of his stay at Bankura.[1]

Theo was lonely and depressed at Darjeeling. She wanted Edward to join her, but the college was still in session: "Nor wd. an Indian prof. ask a month off, so I can't." Nor could they afford the expense. He reminded her, not for the first time, that "a missionary's life, in all the essential humanities, is a hard one." He asked her not to send her relations "such a glowing picture of our feudal splendour, our servants & meals. You have a job to get folk who've never experienced it, to realise what has to be given up and gone through. These Indians have no faintest conception of it. They think we have a good time." Theo had spoken "bitterly" of his ambitions, but his only ambition just then was to get through the day. She urged him to come and stay after the baby came, but he admonished her that "there isn't another missionary of all our lot who can afford to do things so expensively." Every day he wondered: should he have returned? Undeniably, Bankura was not

ood for his poetry. "Just as Rabi found in Engl[an]d that poetry had deserted
im, so I feel in India." He loved the jungles, but English woodland was what
e really needed.[2]

William Frank Thompson, named for Theo's father and Edward's lost
rother, arrived a month early, on 18 August, and Edward went at once
o Darjeeling for a few days. Theo would stay on with Frank until the cooler
veather.

Edward rediscovered the difficulties of explicating Browning. "Life in a
ove," companion piece to "Love in a Life," only baffled his students. "These
haps know nix of women, except as a creature who serves & cooks &
s handed over in marriage. All these complex ideas are strange to them. I
on't know if it's any use teaching them." However, the syllabus prescribed
Browning, and next week would be worse. He must teach "A Grammarian's
uneral."[3]

The students were in no mood for study. Gandhi's noncooperation fi-
ally "invaded our hitherto peaceful province." The majority were opposed,
ut "the violent minority howl all moderate opinion down," and "relays of
rators" worked up the students, who devised a supremely impractical "sig-
natureless petition" that the college be "nationalised," refuse all government
grants and hand everything over to a "University of National Education. . . . a
parody of C'cutta University." Brown, who usually reacted to such initiatives
by shouting them down, received the petition courteously and requested a
day for consideration, but only 40 of 450 students backed the project, and
t fizzled.[4]

Nevertheless, the administrators were really alarmed. Woodford reported
hat the Bengal student world was "in great ferment now." Calcutta University
students struck. Outside agitators came to Bankura, satyagraha propaganda
was everywhere, and the college had to close for two weeks. Brown seemed
o lose all heart. Edward heard him say that of the seventy students about to
ake the university's matriculation examination, "he loathed sixty of them; &
hat there wasn't one he wd. like to come into close intimacy with. The
heathen, of course, is always faulty, judged by any standard of ordinary
decency. But just now he is uppish. . . . *Now,* if I were to heap coals of fire
on a heathen's head, I shld be prosecuted. . . ."[5]

One morning, while orators agitated outside, only twelve of Edward's
sixty-five students came to class. "These were unhappy & were watching
the mob outside nervously. Then a professor, who has been playing hard for
popularity ever since he came, resigned, wildly cheered." The troublemakers
were "a handful of students from other places, whom we allow to come to
a college wh. was built for the folk of this district, who put this pistol to our
head. Not a single [parent or] guardian has said a word." The rebels wired
to Gandhi and to the Calcutta University extremists for support, and the

" 'patriotic press' " fumed about the college's " 'unreasonableness.' " Brown held a council of war. Then, with the college closed, he ordered home within twenty-four hours those not preparing for Calcutta University examination. His action "filled the rebels with dismay," for they had intended to boycott classes and hold " 'meetings,' getting inflamed & rec[eiving] orators from outside." At home, "each 'hero' had alone to meet an irate guardian, it will be a much cooler experience than shouting down a mob of 500." It might blow over, but the faculty had begun to feel that "these people are not worth working for. . . . I don't think Brother Gandhi's movement can go far without violence. There's enough cause for anxiety even here, though not dismay." Brown had handled the situation as well as could be done, but the strain was severe.[6]

Seeing no end to the breakdown of collegiality, Edward concluded that his usefulness at Bankura was over. He sent the Missionary Society his resignation. He spoke generously of Brown's "great knowledge of the language and people and his administrative gifts." His principal reason was that the college now turned from the arts to sciences, "and it is right that it should." He knew that his absence had strained Brown and Spooner. He must stay on, "in simple honour," until they had furloughs. "In 1923, then, I ask to be withdrawn from this field altogether. My usefulness here is done."[7]

Canton thought the letter more temperate than he could have written under the circumstances but thought that Edward blamed himself too much. His colleagues had behaved badly, but why chuck the Indian mission field? Rushbrooke suggested teaching at a preparatory school, but that would be starting where he should have been twenty years earlier, "with 20 years less resilience." Now he must support wife and child. Goudie, the Missionary Society Secretary, did not seem to understand: surely Edward was not leaving India? They would just wait until 1923. Predictably, out came the Wesleyan indictment. Woodford told Goudie, "You need to allow for the Poetic Temperament in all his communications." He admitted that Brown did not treat Edward with "sufficient consideration" even though he was "too wrapped up in his literary work. . . . Thompson is not a practical man." Edward told Canton, "I can't tell you what a sense of relief it is to have come to a decision as to my 2 colleagues at B'kura. They are the angriest & most injuredly indignant men that ever lived. I was never so sure in my life of being overwhelmingly in the right. It is assumed that I am suffering from a mood, wh. will pass. This is mistaken."[8]

He had always known, from the beginning, in the depths of his heart, that it was all a mistake. Only the teaching was right. The preaching, the obligations to pull in converts and retrieve wanderers, had overtaken him after his escape from the detested bank. He had done his best, for his mother and for Bankura, but he could not live with the knowledge that he was disliked—although he knew that when he himself felt dislike, he showed it. Lack of collegiality was only one reason for his leaving. He felt that he had not been forgiven for a supposedly long holiday at the war, and therefore he had been for the past year shut out from society.[9]

Most important was the fact that neither Theo nor the baby was well. At Bankura, Frank was almost continually ailing. When the weather turned hot in 1921, Theo took him again to Darjeeling. Edward thought that he had "never felt the climate and other things more." He really did not see how she and Frank could "stand another 20 months of this most poisonous & detestable land." Somehow they must get a vacation in the hills, "a ghastly expense" but unavoidable.[10]

The political situation worsened. Noncooperation and Swaraj ["own rule"] supporters openly threatened Calcutta shopkeepers who sold Western goods or refused to close for a hartal. The government declared volunteer groups illegal and began wholesale arrests. Indian neighborhoods filled with police and troops with machine guns. All the colleges closed until the end of the year, while the European quarter prepared "on the grandest scale" for a visit from the Prince of Wales. "To a visitor," Woodford told Goudie, "Calcutta seems very gay just now; but her heart is very sore, and I fear her back is up."[11]

Fortunately, Edward had a distraction. He had long thought of writing on Tagore's work. There was still little objective criticism. Edward did not think highly of Ernest Rhys's kindly book published in 1915. Rhys used what Tagore himself had provided of autobiography and what was then known of his work. He wanted to "relate [Tagore] both to the old tradition in India and to the new day anticipated in his writings." Edward wanted deeper examination of Tagore's strengths and the reasons for adverse criticisms. Canton's reaction emphasized what was missing in discussions of Tagore: "I don't know what has been written about Brer Taggory, but I hope you will make your book an interweaving of biography and literature. A literary man's life should surely be as much 'literature' as 'life,' and any critical (or landscape) book about him should show the one mingling and producing the other—unless there be weighty reasons to the contrary." How did Tagore represent or depart from his contemporaries? Edward must explain the poems. "Those Vaishnava Sakta [devotional] warblers are birds of unknown feather." Translations should be accurate but not too literal: "One wants to understand and feel about a poem translated what a nation understands and feels about the original. Them's my sentiments."[12]

In fact, between 1920 and 1922 Edward wrote two books on Tagore. J. N. Farquhar of the Y.M.C.A. Press in India wanted a volume of forty thousand words for its Heritage of India series. At the same time, Edward hoped that Oxford University Press would publish a longer literary biography. The two publishers agreed that the Y.M.C.A.'s Association Press would handle the shorter book for about a year. Oxford would then handle both books. However, Oxford began to cool off. "And they say we can't get round Macm[illan]'s, *re* quotation, without 'enormous expense.' I do not know what will happen."[13]

He began the shorter book in August 1920, blowing hot and cold about it from week to week, and even from hour to hour. He was often sick and tired of Tagore, but when he read his early letters or early poems, "I am all admirat[io]n & sympathy. He *was* a fine chap despite his preoccupat[io]n with himself & not unpleasant egotism. But in these latter years I cannot away with him." He had read some fulsome articles on Tagore's American visit: "It's a foul, vile, ugly picture. Some things cannot be said now, least of all by me. But POSTERITY will say them, & say them with pretty decided disgust." Tagore had scolded the West for its love of comfort—yet traveled in a private compartment with an English secretary and " 'scoldings at seven hundred dollars a scold,' " as an American paper put it. "Andrews fondly imagines that I'm putting together a rapt gazing at the master's face. There will be a few shocks. I'm aiming at someth[in]g bigger—a real contribut[io]n to truth." Sometimes the book seemed an albatross, but then it would begin to promise well: "I think I can do a more valuable b[oo]k than I thought."[14]

Rabindranath Tagore: His Life and Work appeared in 1921. Part 1 is biographical and ends roughly with the turn of the century. It urges definition of Tagore within the Bengali literary tradition, a descendant from Sanskrit literature and from Vaishnavism. Part 2 deals with the varied activity of the later years.[15]

E. P. Thompson sees flaws in his father's book, but in at least one important respect it broke new ground. To escape the adulatory appreciations since the Nobel Prize, Edward "adopted the stance of an admirer but [also] of a critical interpreter. . . . Uncritical adulation he saw as inverted patronage." Edward's own early poetry, which found obscure publishers and had few readers, was in one part

> observant nature-poetry and another part of intense mystic questioning within a dissenting Christian tradition. Yet it had, even in its own time, a curiously old-fashioned, almost "sanskritized" feel to it. It reminds one that Thompson, while a voracious reader, had been largely self-taught, and then had gone to his lonely post in Bankura, with a few literary correspondents, most of them men of an old generation.[16]

This same "curiously old-fashioned" flavor, a certain stateliness, suits this book about a subject who sprang from a splendid ancient tradition that became bogged down in Sanskritized formalism, then created a synthesis o open new literary vistas. Buddhadeva Bose, a leading Bengali poet of the post-Tagore generation, calls Tagore a "phenomenon . . . our Chaucer and Shakespeare, our Dryden and our equivalent of the English translators of the Bible. . . . He has created language. . . . His verse and prose, his fiction, drama and song, his poetry and his humour are mutually linked and dependent; one is beautiful with the other's aid. His greatness is the greatness of the whole."[17]

Tagore's successors found it very difficult to break away from his style and rhythms, even those of his daily speech. His metaphors passed into the vernacular. Buddhadeva means quite literally that Tagore "created language." The academic pundits especially hated *Kshanika*, published in 1900. Its title means "momentary," "fleeting." Its influence was not fleeting: it was a turning point in Bengali literature. Tagore dropped the heavy Sanskritized forms of elite literary Bengali, particularly the two- and three-syllable verb endings, and wrote in the simpler Bengali of everyday use. He eschewed epic themes and spoke of human love and village concerns and daily life. The pundits tried to punish him by putting *Kshanika* poems on Calcutta University examinations, to be put into "correct, literary Bengali," which of course destroyed his wonderful cadences. Edward provides a fine vignette of a Bankura pundit reacting to *Kshanika*. "He ramped about the school like a leopard with an arrow in his side. The Bengali was so shockingly bad! He was seventy-five years of age, but his voice was tremulous not with age, but with anger." Younger Bengali colleagues and the generality of Bengali linguists 'raised a howl of sorrow. They are howling still." This alone, Edward thought, should dispose of Yeats's misunderstanding of Tagore's poems as universally adored in Bengal. Neither Yeats nor Rhys had realized the "sharp division of opinion of Rabindranath, and the intense dislike with which his name is regarded by many of his countrymen." Alas, their misconception had "gone abroad and won such acceptance that it seems hardly worth while trying to show its falsity. Yet false it is."[18]

Edward predated Buddhadeva Bose when he wrote, "*This epoch has been Rabindranath's as emphatically as that of Dante was his, and far more decidedly than Shakespeare's was his. He has had no Ben Jonson.*" Many Bengalis chose to be offended by a section headed "Bengali Opinion Provincial." "The extreme narrowness of Bengali life," Edward wrote, was due to caste restrictions for everyone and purdah for women. Hinduism forbade travel abroad. Bengali commerce was "in the hands of foreigners"; this led to both restriction and excess: "Bengali thought is so provincial that any Englishman who praises Tagore is at once called his 'disciple,' since the popular opinion cannot understand that a man may admire intensely and yet keep independence and critical detachment. The Nobel award was commonly understood to mean that the world's opinion had sent him to the

head of the class, with the corollary that his race also now 'led all the rest.'
Bengal needed what Tagore tried to be: the example of successful synthesi-
of old and new, indigenous and foreign. Edward particularly deplored the
cult of discipledom. In fact, he feared that he himself would be "labelled and
libelled" as a Tagore disciple.[19]

Edward told Canton, "What did vex me was a shabby & ungenerous lette-
from Seal, to whom it is dedicated. Anyway, the book isn't going to be
neglected." Seal's letter upset him much more than he admitted; they did
not meet again for fifteen years. Many other Bengalis took his considered
evaluations as attacks on Bengali culture. "Just now," he told Lyon, "these
people won't stand any criticism, however mild." The book sold steadily
in Bengal. Abroad, except on the Continent where he was still a postwar
enthusiasm, "the Tagore slump has gone further than I ever dreamed." But
Edward knew that his book had value "& also that he is by no means a
negligible poet." Being part of a missionary series told against it, and that
"awkward little preface about it being for 'Indian students'—who never buy
the series at all."[20]

One of the most severe criticisms, in the Calcutta journal *Modern Review*
which had published the first English translations of a number of Tagore's
works, did not appear until March 1922. The reviewer dwelt on passages that
had so irritated Bengalis. Where was appreciation of Tagore "as a *Bengali*"
Why did Thompson not show "why so unworthy a people as the Bengalis
were considered worthy by God" to have among them a few men "who
could stand comparison with at least second-rate occidentals . . ."? Thus the
reviewer only confirmed Bengali provincialism.[21]

From Tagore himself Edward received "a long, somber, but gracious letter."
He was sure that it was " 'the best book yet written' " on his work and was
sure that Edward had tried to be fair. But he was plainly hurt. Edward doubted
whether he could have written one as good in the circumstances.[22]

Although still without a publisher, he went on with the second book. It was
useless now to ask Seal for advice, "since the heinous guilt of my tagorisation
made me a heathen man—& a publican. . . . So that is that." He hoped that
eventually this book might get him a London University Ph.D. Meanwhile
the first book did amazingly well: "It is admitted now, even by Bengalis, that
it has put the subject on a new level & scrapped every preceding scribble." A
letter from Dinesh Chandra Sen, a notably conservative Bengali folklorist and
literary historian, particularly pleased him. Sen wrote that he "had read my
Tagoriad with great pleasure & admiration, that he esp[cially] admired my
'clear-headed judgment & mastery of details' & that I had 'done full justice
to the poet, without falling into the exaggeration of a biassed partisan.' So I
am in a fair way to be canonised, after being stoned."[23]

He decided to limit the new book to the poems and plays, perhaps because those were his own favorite genres, but also because of the vastness of Tagore's output. He wrote steadily. "But when a man's verse & drama are close on 100,000 ll., it is an appalling job, & will take far longer than I hoped."[24]

Tagore could not help very much. The aftermath of his European and American lectures had caused the rift that Rothenstein kindly called "a passing breeze." It was much more. Tagore's frenetic pace prevented the leisureliness that had fostered the English friendships of 1912 and 1913. He stayed only three weeks in England. Rothenstein had recruited influential persons to advise and raise money for Visva-Bharati. But Tagore, convinced that official England had turned against him, rushed away to the Continent. He sent Rothenstein a long resentful tirade, insisting that Continental praise did not influence him, for he had a "natural power of resistence [sic] in me against intoxication produced by praise" and believed that "the breath of official suspiciousness can blight in a moment my cherished scheme." He accused Rothenstein of having sold his soul to materialism. Rothenstein, deeply hurt, replied that Tagore was quite wrong: British officials did not wish to interfere with Visva-Bharati. He made "needless difficulties" for himself and should save his energies for the task ahead. It was unfair, if English friends wished to help, that "you should put extra should refuse [sic] to smooth some of the difficulties in their way." These were harsh words from a man who cherished friendships as Rothenstein did. The correspondence ended in March 1921 and did not resume until Rothenstein took it up again, to Tagore's manifest relief, a year later.[25]

Leonard Elmhirst, the eminent English agricultural economist and, later, founder of Dartington Hall, met Tagore in America in 1920 and would join his agricultural project, Sriniketan. Elmhirst wrote in his diary in 1922: "The poet is not always a Philosopher, and sometimes his natural bitterness against certain gross aspects of British imperial behaviour peeps out from under his normal philosophical calm. Among the British in Britain are some of his very best friends, but as a nation they have never accorded him the kind of public ovations and popular enthusiasm that he met with recently on the Continent of Europe and especially in postwar Germany." In 1967 Elmhirst still recalled him as "an eminently grabbable person" who too often "allowed the wrong persons to grab him." Eventually Tagore would recognize such errors, but damage was done. However, Dutta and Robinson point out that Tagore was not being altogether paranoid. There were indeed past incidents of British interference in his affairs abroad.[26]

Mahalanobis told Edward that Tagore returned from Europe terribly down-hearted and fearful that Visva-Bharati was a mistake. He had begun to think that his own countrymen would obstruct it. Bengali politicians either for or against noncooperation fought to enlist him and tried simultaneously to corner him in Calcutta. Tagore slipped away and left them wrangling with each other. At Shantiniketan, too, some of the teachers had embraced Gandhi's ideals, a wounding failure of loyalties. If Edward should see him, Mahalanobis asked, would he try to cheer him?[27]

Tagore's troubles were part of the general predicament, for, Edward wrote, "every year it gets more manifest that we cannot keep the Empire unless we have a real citizenship to offer, to those who can conform to certain conditions. You do get the Indian who is worth an army commission just as you get the Indian who can become a first-rate scientist or doctor. It shld. be our glory to make more, & yet more, of such as the time passes. . . . Meantime, we chatter about democracy—a vile word—, & the U.S.A. will not allow negroes to exercise their votes & we refuse the right of landing in various parts of the Empire & have only just thrown open real commissions in the Army."[28]

Such references to the United States offended Theo, and Edward was not always tactful. She did not understand that that "vile" meant democracy betrayed. He assumed that she shared what he intended as wry amusement at Americanisms. The problem had been building for some time. At Port Said in 1919 he had met an American who was pretty and energetic but had the " 'Murkan' drawl badly, & is very short of ideas. Talks in the strangely pseudo-correct epigrammatic fashion yr. highbrows seem to cultivate." Such teasing quickly sours if the recipient's mood is wrong. In the summer of 1920, Theo objected strongly to similar comments, and he begged her not to take his "fooling words" so seriously. When he joked about Americans he did not even think about it in reference to her. However, she took it personally and could not seem to distinguish teasing from seriousness. But he *was* serious when he wrote that "yr own great peace-lov[in]g country, lest the League of Nations notion shld. prove to have some kick in it, . . . has resolved on build[in]g a fleet wh. will ensure her 'world primacy.' She is truly at last 'first in peace, & first in war, & first in the hearts of the rest of the nations.' "[29]

Especially perturbing was the American misconduct of race relations. In the *Crisis,* the magazine of the National Association for the Advancement of Colored People, he found the damning statistics of lynchings. He assumed that Theo's social conscience would revolt from such enormities when he wrote that just up to 1914 there had been 2,662 lynchings without trial. A related account in the *Modern Review* made him feel ashamed and helpless. Americans got upset over Ireland and India, but he had never met one who cared about lynching atrocities. In 1921 he begged Theo, again at Darjeeling with Frank, to really care, not to "look indulgently on a thing simply because it's American." There were so many big-hearted Americans that the world had "the more right to ask why a country so powerful, so full of idealism, with an altruistic energy that flows over to the ends of the earth does nothing."[30]

Theo wrote cross notes in reply. "If tomorrow's letter is like yester-day's and today's," Edward wrote, "I shall take the hint that you wish our correspondence to drop." But not writing was too painful, nor could he drop the subject. There was no long-distance solution to such unproductive wrangling. He could not let a day go by without sending something. He sent reproof for "shabby, loveless little notes," while he wrote long, loving letters. He had "no hint of your mind, so do not know if an appeal is any use." She sent still another "hard letter" in which she said that she was set on Frank's being educated in America. He replied that she would not understand why he rebelled at that and why he did not care about nationalism as she did. For good measure, he reminded her again that on a Wesleyan minister's salary they could not have everything. Certainly, she was not accustomed to Wesleyan frugality.[31]

She was more conventionally American, less sophisticated than he had realized. Both were naive and uninstructed in the mutual adjustments of marriage. He agreed to her summers in Darjeeling with Frank, then he asked plaintively why she must be away all and every summer. He grieved about missing so much of Frank's growing up. As for Theo, she had had to cope with a quick succession of challenges: a new husband, a first pregnancy, and the new environments of Letchworth, Bankura, and Darjeeling.

Edward was miserable with overwork and loneliness in Bankura's blazing heat. He must have faced hints that Theo was not after all "the right kind of lady" for Bankura. His health deteriorated further. He had still more surgery for fistulas and a protracted stay in the hospital because the trouble had gone on for so long. Dysentery reoccurred. He had nightmares about being bombed from the air. He got into a panic and imagined some esoteric strain of tuberculosis. He reflected that he was at just the age when his father "began to go to pieces, & it began just as with me, with persistent low-health when there was no chance of any relief or help." His mother wrote querulous, unhappy letters. He was sorry that she was lonely, but why did she always have to tie it to God's will and the welfare of his soul? "But I do get tired of her narrow mindedness," he wrote to Theo. "That was a rotten theology in wh. we were brought up. The government of the world as we can see it is bad enough. But that old crude God who sent folk to everlasting Hell because they didn't believe this or that bilge . . . ! I hate the thought of it, & can't speak strongly enough. And here's mother eternally worrying herself as to whether I am sound theologically, or Margaret, or . . . I don't think she worries so much about the girls. Then I get these silly letters every now & then. O drat! Aren't one's real worries bad enough?"[32]

Fortunately, tensions relaxed as Frank's health improved after a year of nearly despairing of his life. Edward thought that he behaved better than the other English children, who seemed very spoiled: "a v. nice little boy, though I say it myself. His mother has brought him up well, & he is a miracle of pleasantness, compared with most kiddies out here."[33]

For some time, however, Bankura had seemed "never in a worse state." Spooner thought that noncooperation explained students' indiscipline. "But even he is now alarmed. . . ." Edward wished with all his heart that his students would do as Tagore had done: draw inspiration from their surroundings. He hated it when they sat "like silly, passive buckets, wait[in]g to be pumped into, just ask[in]g for 'notes' wh. they can learn off by heart—that for half these things they cd. get best what they want in their own experience, or the open air. There's cloud & trees & sunlight—the tank, the green mohur [trees] outside their classrooms—; but these are not 'in the syllabus,' so they don't care to see them. Ah, qualis artifex pereo! I might have been a success if I had taught a western audience."[34]

Finally, a different dilemma reinforced Edward's decision to leave Bankura. Brown at last left for his furlough, and Edward became Acting Principal. When he checked accounts he stumbled upon irregularities of nearly ten thousand rupees and two hundred rupees due on an unpaid account. The deficits were Brown's, incurred on behalf of an unreliable local Bengali entrepreneur. Woodford and Spencer confirmed the irregularities. Woodford explained that the culprit had been the mission's first Brahmin convert, and Edward now understood how Brown had "persuaded himself that [the man] was far more precious than mere mission funds." Woodford thought that this was why Brown, in a "final explosion," wanted Spooner to oversee accounts. Edward was deeply disillusioned. Now he found that Brown had figured in a number of lawsuits on the man's behalf and had seemed willing to do anything to clear his bad debts. It was a sad case of loyalty gone awry. Now Edward understood why Brown and Spooner had frozen him out and why Brown had been "savage" about letting him see the accounts. Nor did relations improve with Brown away. Spooner now monopolized Spencer, until he and Edward seemed to have only Kingswood memories in common.[35]

Edward had had more than enough: his mind "was settled long ago, but if it had been necessary to put any lid on, this does it." He was sad to leave after so many years, but he could not face another year as colleague to a principal whom he no longer respected.[36]

The London headquarters could not believe that he was really going and offered assignment to another Wesleyan college in India, but Edward wrote that the Bankura career had been a sad misjudgment and he "could not risk a second mistake of this magnitude." He dared not spend his life on "a sterile effort or going with the reputation of being a man who cannot work with anyone else." He said that "most missionaries seem to me too autocratic to be good colleagues," and missions must have men who would work efficiently in "freedom and elasticity of opinion & personality. . . . At present, men's lives & characters are wasted, as well as money."[37]

From the Y.M.C.A. Publishing House, Farquhar wrote, "It is very sad to lose E. J. Thompson, for he is not only a brilliant writer: he is the one man here who is in the heart of the cultured Bengali society, the only European who knows all Bengali literary and artistic people. We shall miss him very seriously. . . . Perhaps he may yet return."[38]

He did not return. The post of Lecturer in Bengali fell vacant at Oxford, and Edward took it. Theo was thrilled, for if anything could approach Princeton, Oxford was that place. She and Frank went to relatives in Beirut while Edward found a home for them. On 23 January 1923 he sailed for England.

15

OXFORD AND ISLIP

Oxford was his third and last escape. Exhausted from the years of feeling a divided person, he was in full flight from Wesleyanism. E. P. Thompson says that "what must be stressed is the *intermittent character* of Wesleyan emotionalism." Did the son, when he wrote of Methodists in the eighteenth century, have in mind his father's dilemma in the twentieth: "It is the paradox of a 'religion of the heart' that it should be notorious for the inhibition of all spontaneity. Methodism sanctioned 'workings of the heart' only upon the occasion of the Church; Methodists wrote hymns but not secular poetry of note; the idea of a passionate Methodist lover in these years is ludicrous. ('Avoid all manner of passions,' advised Wesley.)" Edward John Thompson was a passionate man, in love and in all other commitments. He mistrusted inhibitions of spontaneity, which was why Bankura's wariness of the imagination was so dismaying.[1]

This third escape was different. At Richmond and Bankura others had gone before to prepare a place and a discipline. In Mesopotamia also discipline was preordained. At Oxford Edward had to prepare his own place, and the reward was meager: £160 a year plus £15 for each student tutored in Bengali. In the first term he had one student.

Edward knew, abstractly, that to feel oneself a genuine Oxonian, one must be an insider with college membership or a university appointment. He was outside the social and professional network that facilitated such connections. His miscellaneous educational background had no public-school or Oxbridge cachet. Oxford's Bengali lectureship, attached to the Indian Institute, was a utilitarian device to facilitate the I.C.S. The institute, however, floundered amid unfulfilled hopes, and the I.C.S. was losing its appeal, and the postwar atmosphere, Richard Symonds says in *Oxford and Empire,* was that of "diminuendo" in the long enthusiasm for imperial effort. Most of the new university students were ex-servicemen, "many of them disillusioned with appeals from King, Country, and Empire." The League of Nations appealed more to idealists. Enthusiasm and support for missionary work declined; doubts increased about the wisdom of " 'taking away the natives' souls' " and giving them " 'a false copy of English political ideas.' " Edward Thompson knew too well the corrosive effects of trying to turn Indians into imitation Englishmen.[2]

He now discovered how difficult, in the interwar years, it was to speak up for India. He did not consider himself an orientalist: one with the authority of specialized knowledge and experience. His only authority had been that vested in him by the Missionary Society, to teach and make converts. It was true, as Canton kept telling him, that his skepticism about the missionary ethos was a useful perspective upon its weaknesses. In England, however, so many had so little accurate knowledge and no experience of India, that willy-nilly he became an authority by virtue of simply having been there. His tendency to question everything saved him from smugness, but it swung him between belief that the empire was a good thing and conviction that it was making a mess of administering India. Edward Said, in his dissection of orientalist studies, distrusts interpretative authority because "it is virtually indistinguishable from certain ideas it dignifies as true, and from traditions, perceptions, and judgments it forms, transmits, reproduces. Above all, authority must be analyzed." But Thompson's experience of Bengal was his stock-in-trade, so to speak. He had no breathing space in which to pause and analyze.[3]

His arrival at Oxford from Letchworth in February 1923 was bleak. He told Canton that Bridges, Gilbert Murray, Yeats, Masefield, and an assortment of university dignitaries had met him at the station. In fact, it was spoof and a bit of invented bravado, for his arrival was quite unnoticed. Bridges did not yet know that he was in town, and only later would he become acquainted with those others.[4]

Quickly, he had to find a place for Theo and Frank. Oxford was shockingly expensive, and no one at the Indian Institute seemed prepared to see or welcome him. "I felt sick at heart," he wrote to Theo in a long journal letter, "as I realised what a rotten job I'm in for, & how poor. It's depressed me all day." Cambridge had six Bengali-language students to Oxford's one. The clerk at the Indian Institute suggested that he go home and begin in the next term: "I said No." His predecessor seemed eager to be rid of both him and the job. Edward did, however, begin to feel easier, after a brief talk with him, about his own command of Bengali. He came upon a Wesleyan church, at least a point of reference. The minister was effusive and referred him to an " 'awfully nice lady' " who had rooms. When Edward saw her he was glad that she had nothing available. He tramped about all day and returned to Letchworth that night exhausted. The next day was the same. "I'm not v. cheerful," he told Theo. "This is a good place for the young & the wealthy. But I have a merely nominal connection with the University, & a pay that will hardly pay rent. We shall need all our courage, to stand even one year."

Imputations of "authority" commenced: the Wesleyans seized upon him for the Wesley Society, for a social evening, for a talk about Tagore. He did go to a gathering of Wesleyan students at Merton College, and their keenness impressed him. He met his "class," and found the student's pronunciation "hideous" and uncorrected; he had no decent dictionary and believed that none existed. Edward learned, however, that his pay would be raised to £260—others would not teach for a basic salary of £160. The government, not the university, would pay him.

After another weary day searching for rooms, he began "to understand' why women students are so unpopular. Several places cd. have taken me, but—they had women in already, & the women's colleges folk refuse to allow them to have men as well." At last he was referred to two maiden ladies who admitted him for three weeks to their home at 120 Bainton Road. A woman theological student lived there—"v. plain and unattractive, so don't worry, sweetheart." Edward got in on tolerance because he was a lecturer, not an undergraduate. "So I breathe, instead of being on the tramp again." Room and meals were three and a half guineas a week—more than his present annual pay. "I had come to realise the *extortionate* charges for rooms & rent here; & how absolutely less than nominal my connection with the University is. Felt as hopeless as cd. be."

He had heard that Oxford looked after its own "in a quiet fashion." Perhaps he might garner a degree "& other jobs, after a time, if the *Tagore* wins reputation." Literary work sent from Oxford might have a better chance. They could make interesting friends. There were wonderful local offerings in drama, music, lectures. The colleges possessed scholarly contacts. A dinner at Queen's College was brief but pleasant; he does not say who invited him. A. A. MacDonell, the Professor of Sanskrit, asked him to dine at Balliol, which was more satisfactory. When they retired to the Senior Common Room, he was " 'too scared' to do justice" to the fruits and sweets and had only a bit of port. He sat "(by accident) next to the Master, a famous history scholar" who at first seemed "obviously too conscious of his fame to unbend to a lexurer in Bengali," but Edward was mistaken. The great man "was a really decent chap, with immense knowledge, of a remarkable number of subjects. He's v. keen on the Crusades, & got quite excited when he found I knew Joinville, & remembered some of the fine passages there. He talked of every blessed thing under the sun."[5]

Both Edward and the institute were outsiders. It had had worthy intentions. Monier-Williams, its founder, had been justifiably concerned about the many Indian students studying unsupervised in England and those in Oxford with no college affiliation; I.C.S. probationers studied Indian languages without instruction. A debilitating academic feud crippled the institute's usefulness, between Monier-Williams and the distinguished Max Müller, whose studies had established Sanskrit as the third major classical language. Monier-Williams had defeated Max Müller for the Boden Chair of Sanskrit, and the two who should have cooperated in founding programs of Indian studies were bitterly antagonistic, and hostesses took care not to invite them to the same dinner party. Monier-Williams intended the institute to be residential, a study and social center for meetings of East and West. He proposed the idea in 1875, and in 1883 the Prince of Wales laid the cornerstone. The building was completed in 1896. Max Müller thought that the money should be used for research and fellowships instead of for "bricks and stuffed animals." Symonds says that Monier-Williams's election to the Boden Chair was "a tragedy for Indian studies at Oxford," for Max Müller turned away from Sanskrit to philology and comparative religions.[6]

The East India Company, which belonged to pre-Mutiny India, defined Monier-Williams's philosophy. By 1858, parliamentary supervision and the I.C.S. had replaced the Company's administration. The institute was sadly out of touch with changing times and far from its founder's intentions. It was not residential. The lecture and social programs had lapsed. It had a library and a museum, which Curzon, then Chancellor, damned in 1909 by saying, " 'That the collection is visited annually by more women than men is a sufficient condemnation of its retention here.' " Eventually its fine art objects went to the Ashmolean Museum. The library passed under control of the Bodleian Library. The stuffed animals decayed.[7]

The institute might have fared better, Symonds says, "if the teaching of Indian History at Oxford with which it was associated had been more scholarly and imaginative." The first Reader appointed held the post for forty-eight years from 1864 and taught only the history of British rule in India. He "believed that British Rule would provide the framework for the evangelisation of India, just as Roman Government and Greek philosophy had provided the means of converting the ancient world to Christianity." The next Reader had no particular interest in India but did beg the university to add Indian humane subjects. Opposition to Home Rule for either Ireland or India clouded the views of another. When Edward arrived, the Reader was Sir Verney Lovett, a retired I.C.S. man who had served on the Rowlatt Committee but saw no connection between that act and the surgence of Gandhi's noncooperation. Oxford seemed to have nothing to say to a man interested in modern Indian literature.[8]

MacDonell advised Edward to begin seriously on Sanskrit "& is going to give me advice & all the help he can. He suggests that I put my name on some colleges' books, & do a degree." But Oxford residence would be obligatory and beyond his means, "whereas now there is a chance of going to [live in nearby] Abingdon, or Cumnor, or Islip." Besides, he was sick of cramming. "If I can study Sanskrit & Bengali in a general way & bit by bit make some reputation & room for my writing, I think I cd. be happier & usefuller." He needed to revise the longer Tagore book for submission to the University of London. He would postpone housing decisions until Theo arrived.[9]

In 1923 both city and university were in transition from their ancient character of academic and market town to academic and industrial, the latter the result of the Morris automobile works that grew from origins in a bicycle shop to a plant producing more than fifty-five thousand cars in 1925. Automobile traffic and outdated tram service already crowded the old city. By 1921 there were 67,290 new residents, largely industrial workers who lived distant from the university. Therefore Oxford, as decorously as possible, experienced boomtown pains. The colleges preserved their old ways, but the Never-Never Oxford of Max Beerbohm's *Zuleika Dobson* was more fantastic than ever.[10]

A number of landladies refused children, and another refused anyone without his own servant. Edward finally found two fairly spacious rooms at 18 Park Road. "This is a cruelly expensive place," he wrote to Theo, "& everyone says the only chance of getting a house is building one. If one lives out of Oxford, one is out of things. . . . If we lived 3 or 4 miles out, we cd. have a house of our own, & I cd. cycle in daily, wh. I shouldn't mind. But it wd. be a thin time for you, as you wd. have to cycle in too." They would have a real family life, but it would be harder to make Oxford friends. With two thousand pounds, they could build a house, but they did not have two thousand pounds. Theo, who was with family in Beirut, suggested that he give his mother an Oxford holiday. He replied that he could not afford it. Besides, "I really shd. be lost, alone with her all day. I *can't* talk religion." The Letchworth Wesleyan minister wanted him for Easter services. Such demands devoured time and left him feeling deceitful and hypocritical. He must get out of the ministry.[11]

Indian obligations pursued. A former Bankura student was in Oxford studying Thomas Otway and hoping for a Ph.D. Edward feared being called in to help. Why did Indians not draw on their own rich literature instead of trying to exploit obscure English subjects? Bankura parents begged him to persuade their sons to stay out of noncooperation. The ineffable Harihar Das turned up at New College. In 1921 Oxford University Press finally published his biography of Toru Dutt, with Edward's problematical chapter as "Supplementary Review," complete with his reservations about Das's "marks of carelessness," and, more seriously, "lack of sympathy in the author." Das wanted to know, did Edward's lectureship pay well? Edward was certain that he had tried for it.[12]

Robert Bridges was greatly surprised to learn that Edward was in Oxford. He and Mrs. Bridges welcomed him warmly and often at Chilswell, their home on Boars Hill, six miles out of Oxford. Bridges had a comfortable private income, but even without it he would have ignored current fashion. He had very definite ideas on music, foreign affairs, translation, publishers and critics, religion. He wanted, his biographer explains, to achieve "something [in English] that was parallel to and not imitative of classical verse," which led him to experiment with quantitative verse without obvious stresses. "The experiments that Bridges made for the rest of his life were attempts to gain the best of both worlds. . . ." His plays, on Renaissance and Shakespearean models, lacked general appeal, but he believed that art, particularly the theater, was duty-bound to give children some sense of "the poetic aspects in life." As Laureate he avoided out-and-out political poetry whenever possible. He was a dramatic figure in the streets of Oxford, very tall, neatly bearded, wearing a broad-brimmed hat and cape. Edward called him, affectionately, "the Pontine Bob" or "the Pontifex."[13]

During an early visit Bridges read aloud "a good deal of his unpublished poetries. Said this modern *vers-libre* was all rubbish." He had a feud with American editors. " 'You know,' he said, "'since they've got all the money, we ought to send them the manufactured article, in the shape of poetry. But they won't pay what I ask. But I'm going to fight them.' " It was a point of honor.[14]

Bridges's company was invigorating, but nearly everything else worried Edward. Theo wanted another two months in Beirut. Again there was an exchange of sharp letters. She seemed not to comprehend his difficulties. His health reports were bad, the result of malaria and dysentery, of poor care or none in India. His eyes gave trouble, and reading Bengali and Sanskrit scripts strained them. His mother's health seemed worse; she was more in bed, was more deaf, muddled questions and answers, and there was "nothing to talk to her about." "I suppose," Edward told Canton, "Frank will feel that about *us* some day." He went to a Church of England service, and Elizabeth was unhappy for the rest of that day. Theo wanted him to come to Syria: impossible. Her contribution to their budget was nearly spent, and she had no idea how expensive England was. Now it transpired that he would receive only £241, not £260 for the year. He began to understand the urge to suicide. Theo wanted a furnished house and a trip to America in 1924 so that her mother could see Frank. The United States, Edward replied, was even more expensive. She became defensive again and took it out on Bridges's views on poetry in America. If she delayed it would be too late to share urgent decisions about their arrangements. The exchange became ever more petty. She came, but apparently because the last straw was that he had gone cycling with a girl he knew.[15]

Once Theo and Frank arrived in May, the air cleared. After six weeks in the two Oxford rooms, they moved to Islip, where the River Ray ran past the property, and they had a few yards of fishing rights. The rental included a servant. The Oxfordshire countryside, tourist-poster green and prosperous, was idyllic and refreshing. Islip, clustered about an ancient church, village green, and pub, seemed the essence of old England. There was a Wesleyan chapel, but Edward kept his distance.

The Robert Graves family, who had been there since 1921, were their near neighbors. They lived in World's End Cottage, last in a row of attached stone cottages, which ended at a meadow that sloped to the river. At once the entire Graves family—Robert, Nancy, two small girls, and a boy—came to call, in a canoe. Unconventional and independent, they were a contrast, to say the very least, not only to Bankura society but to any other the Thompsons had known. Nancy, artist daughter of the painter William Nicholson, was an unapologetic New Woman who kept her maiden name, refused to wear a wedding ring, wore breeches instead of skirts, and refused to go to church or have her children baptized. Graves had married Nancy in 1919, for love but also as mental and physical refuge from the terrible battle memories that he would describe in *Goodbye to All That.* Robert enrolled for English at St. John's College. He too found Oxford crowded; property owners, who had had few tenants during the war, now tried to make up for lost income. Ex-soldiers changed the leisurely prewar atmosphere to that of seriousness-in-a-hurry. Graves, as a married war veteran and undergraduate in poor health, got permission to live in a cottage on John Masefield's Boars Hill property. Briefly, Nancy operated a small general shop there. It flourished at first, but they were hopeless managers of time and money; after six months it was bankrupt. They moved to Islip.[16]

The Graveses were very interesting neighbors. "It is v. rarely a day passes without their coming in. I think he's an awfully nice fellow," Edward told Lyon. He called Graves "the sepulchral Bob." Indeed, at that time Graves had plenty about which to feel sepulchral. War memories, old injuries, and constant need for money dogged him. Work for the B.A. went badly, and he dropped it; he found the university's emphasis on eighteenth-century literature sterile and outdated. "In Graves's case," says a biographer, "two years of studying the eighteenth-century poets hardened dislike into loathing." He began a bachelor of letters thesis, but that did not come easily, for academic style was uncongenial. He was a classicist who wanted to use classical sources and styles in his own way. Edward looked on in amazement as Graves "continues to *pour* out verse & prose at an incredible rate. He'll beat Tagore if he lives only a few years more. And he finds publishers for every thing, & an eager 500 subscribers to buy numbered and signed copies at £1.1-."[17]

Edward read Graves's philosophy as making "no distinction between subjective and objective, knowledge & reality, & that if you think a thing is true it is true." This went against everything that Edward had been taught about honest poetry. He was amazed to learn from Graves that Edmund Blunden wanted to meet him. Blunden had told Bridges that " 'Thompson's a better poet than most folks imagine.' " Edward had assumed that the Georgian poets had never heard of him and could not quite believe in Blunden's interest: "I thought I was simply unknown & ignored; but apparently, to hese Georgian poets I've been a jest & a mock, standing for a pretender who wrote Methodist poems & tried to fit in their charmed circle."[18]

A working poet as neighbor was stimulating (although Edward wished hat he liked Graves's poems more). The Thompsons found the Graveses "delightful people, & we admire their pluck & straightforwardness v. greatly. They apologise for nothing, but go ahead frankly." Others, especially Robert's mother, thought there was a good deal to apologize for, and not only Nancy's feminism. When Theo heard that Graves bathed the children and did much of the housework, she "said warmly [to Bridges] . . . 'Then Mrs. G. must be a brick.' Whereat the pontifical one responded grimly, 'In this case I think it's *be* who's the brick.' " Edward commented: "Seemly, Mrs. G. (who keeps her maiden name) paints and rests" while her husband "buys & peels the taters, sets the table, washes up, & then bathes & puts the babes to bed after wh., by the light of the stars, he composes his lofty numbers." Soon, however, Edward retracted this, and "we hold they are both bricks. Miss Nicholson does quite as many chores as Robert." In return, the Graveses appreciated the Thompsons. Robert described them to his mother as particular new friends in Islip: " 'our closest neighbours here of the educated class'; he 'a north country man & a Wesleyan Minister; a very good man,' who played in the [local] football team; and she 'American & has lived a long while in Syria.' " The two families regularly shared picnics, holiday dinners, guests, and children's parties.[19]

Edward had told Edgar W. Thompson, a Missionary Society Secretary (and his godfather), that he wished to resign his ordination in order to escape the continual demands to preach and serve on deputations; area churches seemed to regard him as an unemployed floater. On 25 July 1923, he went alone to a Wesleyan meeting at Bristol and submitted his request, and "my case was passed by the Conference." In October Edgar Thompson kindly asked whether Edward really intended resignation: was nothing salvageable? Could his lectureship be a " 'ministry of reconciliation' " to interpret India to England and England to India, "the latter perhaps in a lesser degree?" If he was "at liberty in your own soul as a Methodist minister" he need not resign. Edgar Thompson promised to fend off the "mosquitoes" and begged Edward to think it over again. He was *not* at liberty in his own soul and did not change his mind. Ministerial status fettered his sense of himself as an honorable man.[20]

Of Elizabeth's opinion of his action, there seems to be no record. Perhaps disappointment was too keen for words. Nor of what Mr. Maltby thought about it, for Edward was the Thompson who got away most publicly. Edward wrote to Canton:

I am no longer a Wesleyan minister. The situation was becoming more and more impossible. I got requests daily to take services, all over the shop; & folk looked me askance, a parson who—as is well known—has nixes to do, yet who wd not preach all over the place. We can't run any more than this one experimental year, *on a deficit.* Which means I've got to get some work done, extra, for wh. I shall receive some payment. . . . I was never meant for a parson, & I've been guided to work that I can do far more usefully.[21]

While he was in Bristol, Elizabeth first visited Islip. She too had no idea of the difficulties of Oxford housing. She thought their house a makeshift, too much like the old farmhouse where she grew up. They were "very game to put up with such an old-fashioned type of place. Once she said, 'My word, Theo! To think of *your* living in a place like this!' but added hastily, 'Of course I like it quite as much as these newfangled homes with tiny rooms.' " One day while she was there, Theo (again pregnant) kept the Graves children: "Our taking away the children was a blessed relief to their dad who was feeling miserable and who, I hear, promptly went to sleep where he lay on the living room sofa" until the children returned two hours later. A few days later Theo gave all the children their afternoon tea. While she adjudicated divisions of milk and cookies, "every one else sat around—'Robert' flinging himself, to my anxiety, on Frank's bed. I don't know whether that frail affair is warranted to carry eighteen stone!" He "tried to convey to me something of the amazingly vital and revealing conversation that they had yesterday at their house, lasting from 12 to 6 P.M." with a visiting philosopher and a "psycho-medic. . . . He said he was still exhausted by the mental strain, but it had been wonderful." Theo was interested, but four children were "a pretty effective bar to conversation of a sustained character."[22]

Proximity to the Graveses was not always easy. In August, when Theo was away and Elizabeth was caring for Frank, Nancy did not come, and no one explained why. The situation deteriorated:

> Robert lay on our floor, reading, while those kids ramped. Katherine [*sic*] swayed to & fro in a drunken[-like] ecstasy, taking my books & shying them all over, seizing anything within reach & hurling it on the hard floor, crushing my cigarettes; David ramped in his own way; Robert ignored them, while Little Ma & I were worried. . . . Jennie alone stood wistfully, drinking in the gramaphone [*sic*]. That kid's v. attractive. Then she sunk down beside her father, & said "Father, I want to say something. I do wish we had a gramaphone." Poor Bob went red. They'll find presently that the kids demand a normal life. At going, David tried to bag all Frank's things, & did bag a small tin dipper, wh. Frank has been mourning ever since. . . .
> Robert was v. distrait, & not over-friendly. As you have noted, he's moody. He said, in a queer way, "Nancy's in bed today again." Said she was all right. I fancy they've had a huff. Fancy they often have.[23]

Edward made himself welcome in Islip, not by preaching, but in cricket and football. The schoolmaster, a Yorkshireman, wanted him to lecture to the Men's Institute. Edward suggested as a topic either Tagore or the Mesopotamian campaign. The schoolmaster chose Mesopotamia: "Then 'that other name, is it the name of a poet or some sort of writer?' I told him about the Nobel Prize, & he was interested to hear what it was." The schoolmaster had a recent Oxford degree and was writing a diploma thesis on North Oxfordshire. Edward asked, "Geology?" No, a bit of everything. The schoolmaster read down a list. What about fauna? " 'Oh, rabbits, & the usual sort o' little things.' But what he has really been sleuthing down is whether there used to be a wool trade in Oxfordshire. He found no evidence whatsoever, & is disappointed. 'You see, ah thowt ahs'd joost try to work up a little problem of me own.' Isn't that delightfully like your thesis-writer? In a universe bristling with thesisable problems, really worth yr. worry, they 'work up little problems' of their own!"[24]

Occasionally, Edward met more sophisticated persons at the Graves home. Edith Sitwell made a distinct impression: green dress, bobbed hair, a combined resemblance to Elizabeth Barrett Browning and Alice Meynell. She seemed very shy and when introduced Edward "didn't get a word out of her." He was sorry not to hear her talk, for her small talk must be all of "apes & Macaws & Yucatan, & Jonah & Melchizedek."[25]

The Thompsons did not always know when to take Graves seriously. One day Robert disappeared after playing football, and Theo suggested that he was having a bath. One of his admirers, who was helping with the children, was deeply shocked. " 'Oh, no,' she said, 'I'm *sure* Robert wouldn't *think* of having a bath without Nancy. They always have their baths together, & they make such a social event of it.' I hope the story doesn't shock you," Edward wrote to Canton. "The remark was made in all seriousness & it seems to me illuminating. It's an amazing, loveable, irresponsible, gay, happy, selfish, annoying, childish & childlike household."[26]

Nor was association with the Graveses always entirely safe. Some time later, Nancy's father gave her an automobile. She drove it for three days, then took Theo for a drive. They smashed into the sidewalk, lost a wheel, stopped, left the car, and proceeded to Islip on Theo's bicycle. "I am lucky not to be a widower," Edward told Lyon.[27]

The Islip interlude, however, soon ended. Although Edward pictured publishers at Graves's door, the literary agent James Pinker at his command, and poems going out and money coming in, the prospect was not that rosy. By 1924 the Graveses had four children under six. Robert's books sold in the hundreds, not thousands, and he was so desperate for money that he took on the most miscellaneous hack work. He came in, "v. blue these days," then suddenly told Edward what a hard time he was having. "It's perfectly absurd," Edward wrote to Canton, "trying to carry on by poetry alone. . . ." Early in 1925 the arrival in the Graveses' midst of the American poet Laura Riding marked the eventual decay and destruction of their marriage. In January 1926, with Robert hoping for financial respite, the Graveses and Riding left together for Egypt and Robert's short-lived academic career at the University of Cairo.[28]

On 4 February 1924 Theo fell on the stairs, was rushed to a hospital and, without harm to either, Edward Palmer Thompson was born and named for his father and an uncle of Theo's. Until he entered the army in World War II, and always within the family, he was to be known as Palmer.

Elizabeth came when Theo and Palmer returned home—and gave Edward a shock. In Oxford she "broke the holy habit of a lifetime, by going to a theatre to see *Hamlet*. She justified herself by saying they were not *actors & actresses* but undergrads. But—despite my effort to hide *The Times* from her—she discovered from it that the Queen & Ophelia were professional actresses, brought in specially. So she will be 'put back in the queue' as Margaret has it." In fact she was in terrible danger of falling two places back on the Golden Stair. She had been "handling" cards at—of all places—the Maltby's! She did not try to justify this to Edward; he knew it only from Margaret.[29]

Now the Islip house really was too much a makeshift. The Thompsons moved to a house called The Cottage, on Boars Hill. Briefly, Edward became more optimistic. The publisher Ernest Benn offered some editorial work and wanted assurances that he would stay in England. Whether to stay on in Oxford was the great question. MacDonell wanted him there for the sake of oriental studies, but "the trouble is, as he admits, that no one cares a pin about Oriental studies, least of all the University, & there isn't a living in them."[30]

Lyon pressed for an honorary M.A. for Edward, but it fell through. "My M.A. turned down is, of course, partly because of India's low place in esteem," Edward told him, "partly (even) because of dislike & political resentment at the back of people's minds. . . ." Edward felt more an outsider than ever. "What I feel most," he told Lyon, "is that I must continue outside the University & all its colleges—though nominally a Lecturer of it,—unless I consent to accept undergraduate status—which I decline to do, at my age & with my record of work." There was a "bad schism" between persons like MacDonell, nominally attached to the institute but belonging officially to the university, & "those who are really Indian Govt. There is no one to fight for Oriental Studies, & to insist that they be a respected & integral part of the University which ought to be the greatest in the world. As far as I can judge—& I am writing more frankly than I should, unless to a friend and unofficially—, every thing is in a mess there. The library is in a mess, the Indian students are as un-understood & as much a breeding-place of discontent as ever, & there is no attempt to make the University & the public take India seriously." Discontinuity and ineffectiveness resulted

rom renewable one-year appointments like Edward's, so that "you have to
ill them up from retired men of means," with haphazard results.[31]

M.A. status rejected meant an end to the Thompsons' dream of a house on
Boars Hill. Two weeks later, however, Lyon got the honorary M.A. approved,
so that Edward could now "count as a member of the University." Lyon's
houghtfulness was unfailing. He introduced Edward to Gilbert Murray,
another Boars Hill resident. Edward was pleased when Murray called, to
walk down the hill with him: "His modesty, simple friendliness, & lack of all
logmatism were most winning."[32]

In February 1925, Lyon arranged for Edward to be an Honorary Fellow
of Oriel College. At last he felt included, a bona fide member of Oxford
University. He and Theo now asked an architect to investigate requirements
for a site on Boars Hill. By November they had their own house and called
it Scar Top, after the farm near Penrith where John Moses Thompson had
grown up. The house is still there, expanded at either end by later owners
but essentially as the Thompsons knew it: a comfortable residence on two
and a half sloping acres and, at the back, a splendid view of their own land
through generous windows: a long, broad slope with woods at the bottom
and a view across fields and woodlands to the Chilterns. It was an ideal
setting for two growing boys. The Thompsons were in Oxford to stay.

16

THE OTHER SIDE OF THE MEDAL

Edward now had to reposition himself with respect to India. Being India-returned was as disorienting for him as being England-returned was for many Indians. He knew best an isolated corner of Bengal, poverty-stricken, conservative, outside the mainstream of Indian affairs. Exasperation had jostled admiration, and he often doubted his right to be there at all. Still, he had something of value to contribute to British-Indian understanding.

Bengal was the key. In the press, in public meetings, in missionary conferences, in club smoking rooms, the British perspective on India returned sooner or later to political assumptions and stereotypes that originated in or derived from Bengal. The Bengali as seditionist and troublemaker was a common analogue for Indian unrest.

In 1922 Lord Lytton, inspired by Montagu's reforming zeal, became Governor of Bengal and discovered that the I.C.S. resisted the Indianization of government. Financial shortages hampered legislative change. The Moderates suffered a serious defeat in the provincial Legislative Council elections because of divisions among the bhadralok. They failed, Broomfield says, "to realise that there were two levels in the politics of the reformed orders: the upper level of the more sophisticated bhadralok and the lower level of the new mass electorate."[1]

Percy Lyon still maintained that quick solutions, such as arrests and deportations, were useless. "Masterly inactivity," a breathing space, was essential. He advocated "what most people would condemn as mere weakness & shuffling evasion—play for time. . . . But if no one is given time to think, and the Moderates are violently dealt with, they will 'buckle and break' and help us not one whit."[2]

In 1924, Oriel College Provost L. R. Phelps asked Lyon whether the system of government in native states might restore stability if imposed throughout India. No, Lyon replied, for "divide and rule" would result. The British had ignored the tide of Indian opinion, and worse, had failed to "conceal a supreme contempt for Orientals of every class and race in India, and that is a very unsafe foundation for any permanent structure." He had just read *A Passage to India,* set in the state of Behar, which he knew well. Lyon thought hat the novel "exaggerates the narrowness of the average Englishman in ndia; but it suggests at least some of the reasons why Indians do not love us."[3]

Edward realized how little the English knew about India, and how little hey cared that they did not know. Was it even worth his while to write bout it? Canton had observed: "Curious, but I don't know a book that gives even a *list* of Indian authors, poets and literary folk." The English common eader, asked to name Indian writers, would have been hard pressed to think f anyone besides Tagore, if indeed even he came to mind.[4]

In 1924, *Rabindranath Tagore: Poet and Dramatist* got Edward a University of London Ph.D. degree. Whether because of the degree or the Oxford ddress, he began to find more prominent publishers. Harrap accepted his *Cithaeron Dialogues,* which had drifted about for a decade: "Tis the first ime any respectable publisher has taken any buke [*sic*] of mine at his own harges." The six *Dialogues* are a pleasant experiment with Ciceronian, Platonic, and Socratic forms. They attracted little notice.[5]

He indulged in a brief spell of playwriting on themes from ancient Indian history, but the most interesting has a contemporary setting. This was *Atonement,* set in a Baptist missionary college in a Bengal country town, whose Principal speaks in Thompson's voice, even to phrases recognizable from his letters. It reproduces with unerring accuracy the cadences of I.C.S. wives' nattering complaints, their husbands' nostalgic justifications of the British Raj, and the Indian characters' arguments for self-determination. n *Atonement*—the Sanskrit word is *prayaschitta*—the definitive action s an offstage riot and massacre reminiscent of Amritsar. Resolution, the opposite of General Dyer's, occurs through discussion and arbitration. A noncooperation leader embodies Andrews's sincerity and earnest effort to ameliorate social injustices. Edward seems to offer here his own atonement or derogatory comments about Andrews. In fact, many English characters atone with some recognition—often limited and reluctant—of contradictions inherent in their very presence in India; almost all of the Indian characters recognize contradictions between their resentment of the British presence and its undeniable benefits. The play might have been called 'Contradictions."[6]

The Y.M.C.A. asked for a third book on Tagore and a life of Akbar. Edward declined both. It was more important to find a publisher for *Rabindranath Tagore: Poet and Dramatist.* Jonathan Cape thought it a " 'very important book' " but feared that Edward's past record of sales did not promise "sales commensurate with its importance." Would Thompson supply a subvention of one hundred pounds? Thompson did not have one hundred pounds.[7]

For some time he had not heard from Tagore, who now traveled almost nonstop. In the spring of 1924 he went to China, and not only Thompson and Rothenstein noticed his separation from former friends. Dinesh Chandra

Sen wrote sorrowfully that Tagore now seemed to care less for poetry and more for money raising and was losing popularity even in Bengal. During farewell address on the eve of departure he sat garlanded on a high dais and scarcely mixed with old friends and associates. Sen thought it wiser not to repeat what was being said about the occasion.[8]

Andrews went with Tagore to China but remained behind when he went to South America. He was further hurt because Tagore chose Leonard Elmhirst to accompany him, a particularly bitter pill, for Andrews resented Elmhirst' close working relationship with Tagore at Sriniketan. In 1970 Elmhirst told this writer: "Remember that all kinds of people were determined to put the Poet and his mind into their own pockets. Inadvertently, and without my making a bid for him, he walked into mine. Hence every kind of jealousy was set up without my being conscious very often of what was happening. . . ."

Tagore was invited to Lima in 1924 for a celebration of the centenar of Peru's independence from Spain. He was to visit Mexico as well. The postimperial aspect of the Peruvian event attracted him, as did promise of large sums for Visva-Bharati. This trip, too, was a disaster. He fell ill on the ship, and the Argentinean poet and editor Victoria Ocampo offered a villa for his recuperation. There Ocampo appropriated him completely Elmhirst found her quite overpowering and suspected that she was in love with Tagore. He never reached Peru or Mexico. Resisting her urgings to stay on, they got away in January 1925.[10]

Tagore had found that a disadvantage of traveling with Andrews was his unadaptability. Elmhirst recalled that "whenever Andrews and Tagore travelled together in India Tagore always had to make separate arrangement with his hosts to hear the local musicians and to see the local dances. These aspects of an artist's hunger were beyond either the sensitivity of Andrews or of his puritanical upbringing. He never could make out whether Tagore' pet name for him 'Sir Charles' was a compliment or a reflection of some shortcoming!"[11]

In 1921 Canton had asked whether this Andrews, "who wrote an article in some review about Taggory long ago," had "show[n] signs of propa Gandhism?" By 1924 Andrews was committed, heart and soul, to Gandhi' mystique of the *charka*—the spinning wheel—and homespun cloth, or *khadi*, as symbol of national identity. Tagore thought that that philosophy deprived India of access to advantages of modern science. He repudiated it in 1925, in a slashing essay, "The Cult of the Charka." Dutta and Robinson call it a "corruscating critique of what would now be called 'political correctness.' " Elmhirst remembered seeing Tagore "turn on [Andrews] with blazing anger to accuse him of being the destroyer at Santiniketan of all the things that Tagore had worked for, so that while Tagore was absent and had left Andrews in charge the institution had, as Tagore said, been turned over entirely under

ndrews from education to politics and destruction." Elmhirst thought that
over the years Gandhi tried to graft as much of Tagore as he could to his own
hought. Andrews . . . even came back from a visit to Gandhi and told me he
ad discussed Tagore's and my programme at Surul [the site of Sriniketan]
vith Gandhi and that Gandhi had said to him that nothing good for India was
kely to come from the use of foreign money. That was in 1922." Twenty-two
ears later Elmhirst challenged Gandhi with that, and Gandhi claimed "that
ndrews had wholly misrepresented him." In the mid-1920s, such muddles,
vith recurrent illness, combined to make Tagore's reactions unpredictable.
dward Thompson thought and wrote much less about devoting himself to
Sengali translation.[12]

Meanwhile, he struck his best vein of work. He turned to Indian history:
not imaginative re-creation, but factual exposition. He began *The Other Side
of the Medal,* on the 1857 Indian Mutiny, the "Uprising," from the Indian point
of view. It had accumulated tales of heroism and gallantry, many undeniably
actual, but many others the stuff of legend. However, there was nothing
egendary about its connection with the Enfield rifle. Bullets came enclosed
n greased paper, and the sepoys—Indian soldiers of the East India Company's
rmy—had to tear the paper with their teeth. If the grease were cow's
at, Hindus would lose caste; if pig's fat, Muslims would be contaminated.
Soth feared a ruse to destroy caste and religious purity and thus make them
iable to conversion to Christianity; for many years English officers had tried
o proselytize. Too late, the soldiers were told to use any other lubricant;
lisaffection was already widespread. If English officers thought such fears
hildish and irrelevant, that was a literally fatal gauge of English ignorance
bout Indian culture and custom.

Insurrectionary incidents had accumulated for some time. Hanging, flog-
ging, humiliations devised to defile caste and personal sanctities of religion,
or being blown alive from the mouths of cannon were the "necessary pun-
shments." The Punjab city of Cawnpore was not the first site of violence
by both English and Indians, but events there came to represent all the
ragedies of 1857. That June an elderly English general and four hundred
oldiers, English and Sikh, fought from behind ineffective earthworks against
he local insurgent, Nana Sahib. They held out for twenty days, but when
hey could resist no longer, Nana offered to send the survivors down the
Ganges to safety in Allahabad; instead most of them were massacred at the
hores. He imprisoned some two hundred English women and children, then
laughtered them and threw the bodies, many dismembered, into a well.
'or the English, "Cawnpore" and "well" became synonyms for unparalleled
barbarism and treachery. Many Britons had an explanation: when ungrate-
ul Indian sepoys ran amok, British discipline and bravery prevailed over
narchy, and the mutineers got what they deserved.[13]

Edward Thompson set out to explain that British reprisals had been equally barbaric, that the "Mutiny" as a live issue still burned fiercely in Indian hearts and minds. Amritsar had fanned that flame. Thus he took on one of the historian's most difficult tasks: explanation of another culture's view of bitter events embedded in the national memory. The gulf between Indian and English thinking was exemplified rather farcically in 1922 in a discussion between Tagore and Lady Lytton, wife of the Bengal Governor. Thompson heard about it from Andrews and passed that account on to Canton. Lady Lytton had insisted on "dragging in the Dyer matter & asked, 'Do Indians *want* us to clear out? If they do, we'll go tomorrow.'" Tagore disliked her bringing up Amritsar and also her idea that Indians preferred the old Mogul rulers to the British. He "said that wasn't a question that cd. be answered with a yes or no. He said, 'No one says the British Govt's a bad Govt. It isn't. We shdn't object to you if you settled down among us, & lived here. But you don't. You just pass through the country.'" Lady Lytton became very flustered. Tagore remembered that Lord Robert Cecil had also brought up the Dyer case and could not see his point, but "(T. says) he was extremely anxious to see it, & he kept at it till he did. T. says Cecil is a very fine man. But Lady Lytton cdn't see." She planned to call the next day, supposedly to see Abanindranath's pictures, but Rabindranath went instead to tea with the Y.M.C.A.[14]

In a 1924 letter to Edgar W. Thompson, Edward Thompson argued that rec onciliation was impossible until everyone had as much honest information as was available. Edgar Thompson feared that such a book risked "telling Indians more than they know already & so stirring up more hatred." What particularly horrified Edward was "the savagery wh. marks the outbursts of anti-European feeling in places wh. were prominent in our Mutiny reprisals." A war without any quarter could not pass over "unremembered & unresented. The Indian Govt. has suppressed all the evidence of resentment, remember." Edgar Thompson, eager for a "ministry" of some kind, seems to have suggested that those were resentments long gone. "No, no," Edward protested, "it is against all nature & all precedent to suppose it is as you think. And why does Andrews keep havering about the necessity of our doing prayaschitta? For what?"[15]

Edgar Thompson suggested that the Mutiny had shown the imperfection of the missionary conception of Christianity. Edward Thompson now believed that that had moved him from political moderation toward the left. He now felt "how patronising nearly all our propaganda, political & religious & educational, must seem to an Indian. I can hardly imagine an Indian accepting Xty.—an educated & thinking Indian, that is, as it comes to him today, from missionaries who've got *all* their knowledge of India from books written by British. It must make him hopping mad, as I am by the guileless remarks of

Americans about the British Empire." He saw why his first book on Tagore had annoyed some Bengalis, "& I marvel that they bore with me in my Indian days. We *are* a *gauche,* crass lot."

The missionary approach inevitably implied an us/them division: "our Indian ministry," "our educational ministry," "our ministry of salvation." "Yes," Edward wrote, "our Christianity was a bad brand. And the Punjab Govt., from first to last, has been marked by self-righteousness & hardness (to use a word kinder than I believe is due)."[*] . . . It's a very bad story. Have you read William] Russell's *Diary?*" Edward wanted "to do my bit of prayaschitta, if I [c]d." Edgar Thompson reminded him that soon Indians would begin to write their history of the British in India. "That wont *undo* what we did," Edward wrote. "I'm sick of propaganda.—we want truth, or as near truth as we can get. . . . I don't seem to have got home to you how deeply I feel about the matter. It's obsessed me of recent months."

When he began *The Other Side of the Medal,* there was already an enormous Mutiny literature, both factual accounts and fictional re-creations such as Flora Annie Steel's *On the Face of the Waters,* set during the siege of Delhi, which, she claimed, "shows conclusively how very partial the Indian Mutiny was. . . ."[16]

The Indian historian Romesh Chandra Dutt sees Punjabi politics as crucial to the general climate of suspicion in 1857. Lord Dalhousie, the Viceroy in 1848, "made the mistake, which has been made again and again by British rulers in India, of ignoring old leaders and old institutions, and trying to substitute the direct and personal rule of British officials." The resulting distrust of the East India Company's intentions contributed to the Mutiny, and the Cawnpore massacres took away much of the English people's power of impartial judgment.[17]

William Howard Russell of the *Times* was the first great war reporter. In his 1858 *Diary* Edward found one who tried to look beyond the heroics and the tragedies. Russell viewed the wreckage of Cawnpore in 1858 and reflected: "How are we to prevent its recurrence? . . . That force is the base of our rule I have no doubt; for I see nothing else but force employed in our relations with the governed." Expectations of increased revenues determined government plans for social and economic improvement: "In effect, the grave, unhappy doubt which settles on my mind is whether India is the better for our rule, so far as regards the social condition of the great mass of the people."[18]

A "pretentious and noxious" book had ignited Edward's determination to write on the Mutiny. This was *The Lost Dominion,* by "Al.Carthill," pseudonym of Bennet Christian Huntingdon Calcroft-Kennedy, published in 1924. "The Lost Dominion made me angry," Edward told Edgar Thompson. Rambling and undocumented, it charges that Indian Moderates invariably preferred European culture, that the Brahmo Samaj was an agent of this denationalization, and "a great number of pseudo-moderates" were "crypto extremists." Edward would have agreed with Carthill about dominion status but the book was glib justification for a supposedly easy way out of a complicated difficulty.[19]

Early in 1925, Lionel Curtis, imperial philosopher and organizer, whom Edward had met early in 1925, asked where to find contemporary material on the Mutiny, "that he might trace its effect today." Curtis had been one of the precocious young administrators of the South African colonies and became an evangelist for dominion-commonwealth government as a basis of world government. He had a remarkable ability to insert himself and his ideas into British politics. His biographer says that some regarded him as "an imperial crank," an international busybody who "rode his hobby horses into the highest political and academic circles." He saw his concept of dyarchy, which became firmly attached to the Montagu-Chelmsford Reforms as "radical yet simple." For many Indian nationalists it was not radical enough and was far from simple. It smacked of a condescending and cynical English intention to rearrange India.[20]

Curtis went to India in 1916, then wrote a small book, *Letters to the People of India on Responsible Government.* The title is significant. For the concept of "self-government" or Home Rule (with its contentious Irish history) he substituted "responsible" provincial electorates. But how, without direct experience, did an electorate learn to handle responsibility? The *Letters* are addressed to *"the People of India,"* but he shows little sense of his recipients' passions and prejudices. It is odd that Curtis, a tireless researcher on international issues, had to ask Edward Thompson for Mutiny information.[21]

Curtis read Edward's manuscript and thought that "it was just what he was looking for," but it needed "some summary of the other side." If Edward did not publish, Curtis would incorporate it where it would be less inflammable: in *Civitas Dei,* his massive three-volume work on empire and dominion. Edward did not want his work delayed and diluted, although anything from Curtis's hand might get more public attention. He asked Gilbert Murray's opinion and explained that he wanted to give "some psychological and intellectual reasons underlying action so passionate and so passionately resented and remembered, to indicate the different ways in which English and Indians look at certain ethical questions." Murray, too, advised some conciliatory material. Still Edward hesitated, for he had been "out of England so long that I am quite incapable of judging how such a thing affects the English reader—I should be very tempted to defer to anyone's judgement." He was pessimistic about publishers. If the Labour Party published it, "it would come out as propaganda." Perhaps "some modifying & explanatory matter" might make it "less vexing to people

rought up on orthodox views of the Mutiny— . . ." He decided to try ogarth Press.[22]
He explained to Leonard Woolf:

I wrote it last year, in anger and indignation at *The Lost Dominion*. Then I saw that publication would mean a row. Officially, I am an Orientalist, being Lecturer in Bengali to the University of Oxford, publication could do me no good, and might mean resignation, since the Indian Government pays most of the expenses of the Oriental Faculty. But what made me refrain from seeking a publisher was my feeling that the book would get into wrong hands, & be read by Indian extremists while ignored by my own people.[23]

Graves, Siegfried Sassoon, and E. M. Forster also read it. Forster wrote:

I have read it with the greatest interest—especially since I have lately been seeing Savarkar's book—and I hope that you may soon find a publisher. I don't know whether your essay will do "harm" or "good" because I never look at books from that point of view. They appeal to me only as expressions of the truth, and in that way you make an irresistible appeal.

orster assured Edward that he had not exerted influence at the Hogarth ress:

Woolf is very pleased to get your MS, and feels, as did I, that it presents no difficulties to a publisher. Its effect upon your own position at Oxford is of course a very different problem, and I think you do well to consider this seriously and to be prepared for some trouble—though one must remember that people here are more sensible, or at any rate less insolent, than they are in India.

orster added a "PRIVATE" note: would Edward care to see Vinayak Savarkar's ook, of which he had a copy, before final revision? There was a problem: the ndia Office refused access to it; if it asked for Edward's source, the situation ould become awkward. Forster wanted his name kept out of that.[24]

Edward insisted that his purpose was not to rehearse Mutiny horrors but o prove that their memory endured in Indian minds—contrary to confident ssurances from missionaries of his acquaintance. A corrosive dread, often nexpressed, still hung over the European community in India. Unease urked also in English minds in England. When in India in the winter of 1912-913 Forster had associated easily with Indians who were under government urveillance as suspected seditionists. Yet in 1925 he was plainly nervous bout Savarkar's book, *The Indian War of Independence of 1857: By an ndian Nationalist*.[25]

Vinayak Damodar Savarkar was a notoriously militant Maratha nationalist who was born in 1883 and died in 1966. Thus during his lifetime he saw the Raj out in 1947 and independence in. From 1906 to 1910 he studied law in London and associated with expatriate Indians who learned methods of sabotage and assassination from Russian anarchists in Paris, a living part of the scene that Conrad summons up in *The Secret Agent.* An unidentified firm published Savarkar's book in 1909. In 1910 he was arrested, to be returned to India for trial as seditionist, anarchist, and traitor. At Marseilles, in best Conrad fashion, he escaped from the ship but was recaptured and deported for life to the Andaman Islands. He was allowed to return to India in 1921 and released but kept under close surveillance. In 1937 he joined the Mahasabha (Great Society), which militantly claimed Hindu superiority over Muslims. In 1948, when a Mahasabha member assassinated Gandhi, Savarkar was suspect but was cleared.

Every one of its 545 pages indicates why the India Office suppressed the book. The insurgent sepoys and their supporters were "Revolutionaries." The style is dramatically, slashingly polemic and spares no details of violence and bloodshed. It hammers away at several basic points: discontent was already widespread, and secret Swarajist organizations were poised to act: the Enfield cartridges merely struck the hour. The English were naively ignorant of the strength of the "Revolution," and Nana Sahib was its First Mover. Savarkar introducing the post-Independence edition, wrote: "The nation that has no consciousness of its past has no future." He still hoped that "a patriotic and yet faithful, a more detailed and yet coherent, history of 1857 may come forward from an Indian pen. . . ."[26]

Whether Edward Thompson saw Savarkar's book in 1924 is unclear, but its authorship was an open secret. The India Office may as well have tried to stuff a genie back into a bottle. "War" and "Independence" were the inflammatory words: if kept from the public eye, perhaps Indian memories would go away. That they had not was Edward Thompson's thesis for *The Other Side of the Medal.*

Leonard Woolf read it "with very great interest. I should certainly be willing to publish it." Adding conciliatory matter "would be a great mistake, but it cannot be made conciliatory to a large number of people and if you try to make it so, you will simply blur the book." He shared Edward's fear that those who ought to read it would ignore it, and that Indian extremists would use it to their own ends. "Still that is a risk that one has to face in all these cases." Woolf's advice prevailed, and the book went forward with only minor revisions. However, Edward begged him not to mention "my Oxford connection. My colleagues are *all* ex-I.C.S men, most of them of great distinction in the service, excellent men but not sharing my views. They wd. have a right to object if I wrote as a Lecturer on the Oriental Faculty. They *will* object, in any case—but that is another matter."[27]

Lyon understood why he did not see the book until published. He would never have advised holding it back. Edward had been moderate, sincere, and convincing. "I am one of the many who have been groping for a clue to the hatred and distrust with which we are regarded by vast masses of the population in India," Lyon wrote, "but I have never gone far enough back for the root cause of it." As India gained in self-consciousness, the bitterness had grown, and Edward had done "a great thing in writing this book, and I cannot conceive that you will suffer from it." Nor could Oxford condemn him. Lyon hoped for wide controversy, although "you must not hope 'to change the attitude of every Englishman who reads it!' " No Indian could have written it, and in fact only "a convinced Christian could have done it as you have done it."[28]

Edward explained that he had not wanted to compromise Lyon's views: "You have an 'official' relation to me, as one of my employers ('Salaam, Saheb!'); &—*in case* there was any row—it was just as well for you to be 'absolutely neutral' in the stainless sheet of an alibi. I did not—& no one ever could—doubt your deep liberalism, moved consistently by the whole course of your life. Only you'll understand a proud man like myself being anxious to avoid any suspicion of taking advantage of friendship."[29]

Edward insisted that his book was not *about* the Mutiny. Many English and many Indians had acted magnanimously, often at great risk. However, a summary of English retributive horrors was essential: the executions, beatings, and bizarre tortures, the deliberate humiliations to Hindu caste and Muslim religion, the comprehensive burnings of villages and slaughters of villagers. Those were "the darkest stain on our record." Carthill's generalizations about "the Oriental" infuriated him: for instance, the statement that "[m]assacre, as part of the activities of Government, is by no means in itself abhorrent to the mind of the Oriental," and "there was nothing about it which was repugnant to the Indian." In other words, Indians did not mind being massacred and could not see why others should object to equal treatment.[30]

Edward's summary of Mutiny horrors was not "just a raking up of particularly foul mud that should be allowed to settle. But the raking up is necessary. The raking up of the mud of atrocities committed by Indians has never ceased, as any English account of the Mutiny will show, while the Indian case is not known to our people." He had not dredged the records for exceptional incidents. Indeed, he could have made the English case appear even worse. It was more important to show that shadows of the Mutiny extended to the present.[31]

After 1857, Amritsar had cast the longest shadow. At best, Dyer's worst offense was criminally bad judgement. But the British outcry revealed "the workings of imperfectly informed minds obsessed with thought of Cawnpore and of merciless, unreasoning 'devils' butchering our women." Dyer's method was Mutiny-style unthinking retribution. Indian reaction after Amritsar had proved that massacre *was* repugnant to the Indian mind.[32]

In 1925 Edward still hoped for a day when "Indian traditions and account of the Mutiny will be treated as history, not prejudice or propaganda. . . . But we shall no longer feel free to dismiss even the sack of Cawnpore with "'The justly infuriated troops took terrible vengeance.'" Untrue belief would be believed "until men train themselves to wait and think at times of excitement."[33]

The heart of his message was that the rush to credulity and the assumption that Jallianwala Bagh signaled another general mutiny had done grave harm in India. "And a great deal of this was due to the same cause as much of the bitterness felt by Indians—the feeling of powerlessness."[34]

Indians felt powerless because they were a subject people who, even with the legislative reforms, had too small a share in government. The English in India felt powerless because they "live[d] a life cut off from the main life of the great country where they are sojourning, they are ignorant as regards India, and disfranchised as regards the Empire. They have only their petty social imitations of London. . . . Their newspapers dole them out such news as the editors choose. . . ." They never realized "how deep and wide was the cleavage between them and their countrymen at home."[35]

The constant, damaging British use of the word *loyal* as all-purpose measurement for Indian character derived largely from the Mutiny classification of sepoys who were or were not loyal to Company rule. An Indian critical of the government was ipso facto dangerous and undeserving, at best uncooperative, at worst a terrorist. The word *loyal* destroyed possibilities of constructive criticism or evaluation. An Anglican chaplain, in response to a man (Thompson himself?) who was trying to explain that Tagore was an important literary figure, asked only, " 'But is he *loyal?*' . . . . [H]e accepted it as without question that he somehow exemplified a pattern wisdom and civilisation to which every Asiatic must render unquestioning obedience." Englishmen needed something better than "the servile deference which we call loyalty." Misrepresentations of Indian history and "Oriental" character had made many educated Indian Moderates question the sincerity of the reforms. Indians took revenge by misrepresenting English intentions.[36]

The Other Side of the Medal concludes with a plea to *both* sides to "cleanse this poisoned well"—*well* being that loaded word with its history of women's and children's bodies brutally discarded at Cawnpore. Many in England and in India "wish with all their hearts that the Mutiny might be passed over as quickly and as lightly as possible, and the natural kindliness of both races given a free rein. . . . Only—it must be passed over by *both* sides." Both had gone mad in 1857, and again at Amritsar in 1919. What

Indians wanted now was prayaschitta—atonement—to signify willingness to clear the record and begin anew.[37]

The book appeared in October 1925. Edward observed that Hogarth probably did not usually waste review copies on "religious people," but he wanted them "waked up, esp. those who are interested in Christian missions in India—a waste of time, so far as the [Indian] educated classes are concerned, until Indian resentment is allayed."[38]

Harcourt Brace published it in 1926. "Yes," Edward had told Leonard Woolf, "let Harcourt Bruce [*sic*] do an American edition, then. There are so many anti-British circles in the U.S.A., esp. groups of Bengalis. . . ." He wrote another preface because he was "not content to have it simply anti-British propaganda, or to feed fat Yankee self-esteem. . . . It will make a few folk see the way our Foreign Office have through the Lionel Curtises & J. R. Motts collared the missions."[39]

Edward did not want his American preface construed as blanket condemnation of England and the English: "All the same . . . I *wish* Americans would leave our sins alone . . . folk like that awful Mrs. Thompson Seton, author of 'Yes, Lady Sahib' and many other poisonous books . . . you've no notion how they drive us crazy in India with their pert self-righteousness. I'm sure my countrymen resent it savagely, though they say little."[40]

The American preface forecasts all of his later writings on Indian history. He did not want "to stir up anti-British feeling." He wanted Indian readers to "feel less despairing of a change of attitude in Englishmen when they realise how much our minds have been abused by untruthful history." He concluded with a reference to foreign missions. The best missionaries had often been "the only effective channel of protest against injustice. That channel is largely blocked today"—for foreign offices and colonial offices now petted and used them, and missionaries were foolishly flattered when called "religious statesmen." But "a gilded collar is a poor thing to take in exchange for the greatest liberty in the whole world."[41]

Edward disliked descriptions of *Medal* as "counterblast" to *A Passage to India*. Comparisons were inevitable, but he never intended a counterblast. His and Forster's intentions were the same. "The well [at Cawnpore]," Michael Edwardes wrote, "produced the material of *A Passage to India*."[42]

Edward was pleased when Tagore wrote, " 'You are in disgrace with your own countrymen at present, for wh. you have my congratulation.' " Tagore's own position was even worse, because of outspoken criticism from his countrymen. But Edward was not all that much in disgrace, for influential English and American reviewers were receptive and respectful, if not always in complete agreement: Mr. Thompson was a loyal Englishman who sincerely wished to put animosities to rest. "This little book," said the

Spectator, "contains high explosive. . . . That dangerous knowledge, which may play havoc [in India], is here urgently needed to blow away the mist that distort our judgement of the Indian situation." The English "never hear word about the atrocious reprisals which equalled and in part explained or extenuated a nationalist movement as a military mutiny." The *Times Literary Supplement* recognized that English historians failed to compare English and Indian atrocities. The *New Statesman* called the publication "an event of consequence to the British Empire, . . . rarely associated with a small piece of historical inquiry." Thompson had uncovered "the policy of terrorisation deliberately adopted by the British generals and the civil officers of the East India Company as soon as the sepoy revolt broke out."[43]

The *New York Times* noted that "now that discontent with British rule is spreading in India and constantly gathering momentum, the time has come to stop and read the handwriting on the wall. . . ." The *Saturday Review of Literature* called it "a sincere and even brave attempt to expose the cruelties of British rule in India." And the *Nation and the Athenaeum* (New York) noted that imperialism itself was the greater atrocity.[44]

The book established a friendship with the journalist and lecturer S. K. Ratcliffe, who had been acting editor of the *Statesman* in Calcutta, then of the London *Statesman.* He had been "calling attention to the tremendous importance of The Other Side of the Medal. . . . I am wondering what I shall find in America when I get there at the new year. In the United States I am frequently asked to speak on India and British policy, and it does not become easier year by year." Some belligerent expatriate Bengalis "will have been, I doubt not, making the most of the ammunition which, as you realised, you could not help supplying them with." He supplied the *Nation and the Athenaeum* with a long review in which he said that the significance of Edward's book was out of all proportion to its size, and that "it may not improbably be the most important contribution in recent years to the criticism of the British dominion in India."[45]

The book also helped Edward to define what he felt Indian studies most needed, which was

> the setting of *all* Indian history—& for that matter, literature & religion as well—on a scientific, accurate basis. As it is, missionaries when they write about Hinduism write to prove that Christianity is its "crown"; Hindus, when they write about it, write to prove that the whole world ought to go crazy in worship of Sri Krishna or to prove that their philosophy is the world's greatest achievement. But it is in the "history" books that propaganda is most pervading.[46]

In the future, he would do his best to be as accurate and precise as possible to explain without scolding; and, wherever the record was skewed, to set it straight.

17

A SUBJECT CONCLUDED

In December 1925 the Thompsons moved into Scar Top, their new house on Boars Hill, Oxford's Parnassus. The Bridges' home, Chilswell, was diagonally across the road. Also on the tree-shaded roads were the Gilbert Murrays, the John Masefields, and just beside the Bridges' property began the Youlbury Woods that belonged to the archaeologist and historian Sir Arthur Evans. In spring they were magical with bluebells, and nightingales' song filled the air. It was idyllic for Edward, who gloried in nature's variations. Theo, equally enchanted, once exclaimed to Bridges, "Weren't you lucky!" To which he "growled, 'It wasn't *luck!*' " He had chosen the spot in all deliberation, and, Edward wrote, Chilswell was "at the very heart of the enchanted country dedicated to the Gipsy Scholar."[1]

The New Year began badly. Elizabeth Thompson fell seriously ill, and family members took turns to spend time with her. Not only Elizabeth felt confined; snow fell as if it would never stop. Bridges remarked to Theo: "I used to like it when I was a boy. But I don't now." Then Rushbrooke died on 30 January. He had been a schoolmaster for fifty years when he retired in 1924. "I certainly have never known a better man," Edward wrote, as he recalled the weeks at St. Olave's while he prepared for his B.A. examinations. They had walked on the downs in search of bee-orchis. "He wasn't a fool, by any means," Edward wrote, "but v. quick to detect slack or pretentious work; but he honestly held a v. low opinion of himself, &—did any man ever have so many friends whom he valued so highly?" Rushbrooke had refused to take a Cambridge M.A., which was merely a matter of a cash payment; he called it a fraud and took the Master of Laws instead, by examination, "an 'honest' degree. That was characteristic of the way he sat loose to ordinary pedantries."[2]

Then, on 2 May 1926, William Canton died. On 4 July 1924 he had turned eighty. In 1925 Edward and others had raised a fund to supplement the Civil List Pension that he had received since 1912. Edward and Collingwood got nowhere with suggestions to revive his literary fortunes. Canton, so unequivocal when advising Edward, only turned them aside with a smile or a quip. He thought up heavily biblical projects, such as a set of "statuette groups illustrating the New Testament," which made Collingwood uneasy,

and a "Book of Saints" for schools, which made Edward uncomfortable
Canton bubbled on, not admitting discouragement, consistently stubborn
asking neither sympathy nor assistance. He joked about being behind the
times, but the jokes had begun to ring hollow. Collingwood thought Canton's
ebullience "all rather too geyser-like for real health & strength. He is one of
those people it is no use trying to control." Mrs. Collingwood found him
"much older &—she says—rather pathetic, though as chirpy as always." But
all was not well, and Edward knew how limited was the time in which to
repay his immense debt to Canton. He had poured out encouragement and
correction, joking and scolding when Edward lost perspective, nagging and
nudging him along over bad moods and rough times. Yet he had to agree
when Collingwood wrote that Canton "[was not] primarily an artist; and the
things he *has* done are all to the good. The things he hasn't done—well what
can be expected from a man who spent most of his life on newspapers? What
William Canton's opinions were, I can't make out. Sometimes he declared
he was a heathen, and then he went Bible Society. I suspect his opinions
were rather like mine—Victorian sceptic with a background of inherited
& inculcated religiosity, and a foreground of 'permitte divis cetera.' " And
Collingwood exclaimed: "What an unusual kind of man he was, in a world
of pushers and climbers." Edward recalled Canton's saying, "All my life I've
trudged—sometimes with satisfaction to myself, more often not.' Complaint
was never on his lips; he merely states truth."[3]

Edward was now forty. He spoke less about time's wingéd chariot, but
from now on he had to convey as much conviction as he could muster
He had before him Collingwood's example: "Well," he had said, "I don't ask
anybody to like Ruskin; I did, because I found him interesting—not because
I found him always right. He was extraordinarily nice to me for 30 years and
more of an all-round man than anybody I ever came across. But if you say
'here he is wrong' & 'there he is wrong'—Oh dear yes!" Belief in one's subject
was paramount. "I don't know what anybody can do at present for Ruskin,"
Collingwood wrote in 1924. "He has gone down with the sunset; and he
can't very well rise again for a generation." His publisher had flooded the
market with all sorts of editions, and "at present he is a drug." Collingwood
never doubted that "in course of time, Ruskin will be revived as a Victorian
classic, and his influence on his world will be shown, but not just yet."[4]

Was Tagore, like Ruskin, going down with the sunset? Edward's immediate
problem with *Rabindranath Tagore: Poet and Dramatist*, besides finding
a publisher, was that he addressed it to the English-reading world; a revival
then seemed unlikely. In 1921 Collingwood was "taken aback" at Edward's
still writing on Tagore, because it "seems to me a poor subject. But books
and pictures are what we make them; and if the treatment is skilful, the
subject doesn't matter: or not much. You will make him interesting—not by

what he has done, but by your analysis of what he is; and he certainly is a phenomenon, and a peg on which to hang the description of the Indian mind. That is still a matter of interest to everybody. So I don't see where the discouragement comes in."[5]

Edward knew where discouragement came in. His contradictory views of Tagore presented a dilemma. Translating for illustrations got on his already frayed nerves. He had told Mahalanobis that he knew well the shortcomings in his drafts, done against time, and "[Tagore's] abundant chatter about flutes, tears, south winds, flowers, woods, separation, smiles, boats, streams & the rest has drawn me to frequent peevish comment. Sometimes I have made a splenetic remark to relieve my own soul, with no intention of letting it go into the real draft. All this will be rank blasphemy to a fervent Rabist like you." Then there was that other Tagore, serene and dignified, as at their first meeting in 1913. "There are times," E. P. Thompson says, "when Thompson showed an excess of duty, arising from respect, less for the poem before him than for the man." In 1925 Edward had told Canton: "I am sorry to hear a persistent rumour that Tagore is dying. He has been a great fellow, the greatest in India; and his passing will be felt over there like the shadow of a God being withdrawn from the wall. Here, you have no notion of the difference he has made. You must not judge him by his poetry. He has been, & is, a very great man—not half-a-dozen in India's record have been greater."[6]

The difficulty was that in this book Edward *did* ask readers to judge Tagore by his poetry. He was not dying in 1925; Edward had heard reports of his breakdowns abroad. But something *had* died, and that was Edward's sense of mission toward Bengali literature. Tagore's inconsistencies had helped to kill it. Oxford Press had rejected the book because it was advised that "his *tag* [day] is so entirely past his *tag* over here that he won't sell 100 copies." In 1925, however, Humphrey Milford accepted it after all for Oxford. Perhaps the wide notice for *The Other Side of the Medal* encouraged the reversal.[7]

Edward's preface is an eloquent plea for a reevaluation of Tagore's work and of East-West cultural relations. It begins: "The West seems to have made up its mind about the East; a few stereotyped generalisations are applied to cover the most diverse facts." The English *Gitanjali* "was seen to be mystical and religious, expectation was satisfied—'Oriental' literature was of this kind." Critics shuffled Tagore's subsequent works into that category. Edward hoped that readers would "feel how much more vigorous and varied the poet's work is than it is taken to be, and how independent and brave and generous is his spirit."[8]

Edward's intention was even broader. The English-speaking world might not care for Tagore, or India for English poets, but "it does matter whether East and West care for each other." The English, he believed, had served India better than any other nation would have done, but they had been "very incurious as to its thought and literature. Resentment of this neglec has estranged educated Indians, and is a factor of first-rate importance in the present strained situation." Few in the West imagined the sheer exten of Tagore's works. Edward had undertaken "the appalling task" of reading through all of Tagore's works: "I wished to understand the people among whom I was living; I wrote this book in the hope of serving two races."[9]

Noel Carrington, who represented Oxford Press in India in the early 1920s, left a memoir of his time there. The first chapter is a lively profile of Thompson that captures his impatience and convictions and also his state of mind when he wrote his first draft. Edward had arrived at Carrington's office and said, " 'I will save you the trouble of asking my business because I have none except to introduce myself as Edward Thompson, lecturer in English at Bankura, a god-forsaken place you will never have heard of.' " He then talked for two hours about "the appalling state of education in India, the stimulating experiments by Tagore—Raby as he called him—of the writers of Bengali literature and finally what I ought to be doing as a representative of Oxford, 'for which University' he said grinning and chuckling, 'our babu culture has an exaggerated respect as you ought to have discovered.' He made fun of officials, missionaries, professors and politicians, but he compensated for these sallies by an occasional swipe at himself. He was one of the most compulsive talkers I had ever met." Much of it was intended deliberately to shock or to elicit a reaction or opinion. Carrington went to Bankura and found it bleak and dry, but Edward's knowledge of the countryside impressed him: "He was more responsive than most English to the moods of Nature in India, to local legends and superstitions. . . ."[10]

In the aftermath of Amritsar, Carrington wrote, "Edward Thompson had an intractable passion for justice," usually shown in historical research but with "plenty of scope in current affairs." Carrington was certain that Edward no longer regarded himself primarily as a missionary and doubted that he "had ever made a convert or even regarded it as a desirable objective." He saw also that poetry "always meant as much in Thompson's life as justice He told me that he would rather be remembered for having written one great poem than for any of his histories and novels."

As a historian of Indian affairs, "Thompson was to show that he could rise above current prejudice." Carrington thought him somewhat unrealistic about reception of *The Other Side of the Medal*. Edward believed that if the English knew the facts and saw that both sides were at fault, they would better understand Indian nationalism. "I did not think his argument very realistic." Carrington added, "Anglo India accused him of blowing on the embers of racial antagonism, and I thought his surprise at this reaction a little naive." Facts from the written records "did not prevent harsh things [being] said of him in the clubs. Even more would have been said if he had

ot won the Military Cross in Mesopotamia. At that time a good war record
was not a thing you could overlook."

He knew so much about Tagore that Carrington had to "take what Thompson said of his poetry in its native form on trust (though this never prevented
him from quoting long passages for my benefit)." Carrington himself was
drawn to Tagore's ideas "on national regeneration and on education." Edward
wanted Oxford as publisher "because he felt that the prestige of the famous
English University would help to make amends for the nation's neglect." It
was typical of Thompson that "determined as he was to do justice to Tagore,
he was not going to withhold criticism where he considered the poet had
fallen from the highest standard." Many Bengalis, of course, "could not bear
to read that their world-poet had ever failed to attain perfection. Such a
reaction, which both pained and puzzled Thompson," would recur again
and again.

Title and scope of the new book were problems, for in addition to Tagore's
enormous output of poems and plays, there was the large and important body
of short fiction and many essays and lectures of great historical significance.
Another reason for limiting his study to the poems and plays was, perhaps,
his disappointing experience of translating Tagore's short stories. They, like
the essays, deserved a study to themselves.

Thompson's epilogue contains one of his most important passages. It
applies to any account of Tagore, past, present, or future:

> To sum up, he faces both East and West, filial to both, deeply indebted to
> both. His personality hereafter will attract hardly less attention than his poetry,
> so strangely previous a figure must he seem, when posterity sees him. He has
> been both of his nation, and not of it; his genius has been born of Indian thought,
> not of poets and philosophers alone but of the common people, yet it has been
> fostered by Western thought and by English literature; he has been the mightiest
> of national voices, yet has stood aside from his own folk in more than one
> angry controversy. His poetry presents the most varied in the history of Indian
> achievement.[11]

When the book appeared late in 1926, Tagore, with Mahalanobis, was
rushing about Europe and lecturing. He had a nervous breakdown, which
became influenza. He recovered quickly but broke down again in Budapest.
Doctors told him to rest, but, unable to reject a single invitation, he often
lectured morning and evening of the same day. The outpouring of interest
astonished Mahalanobis.[12]

In August they came briefly to England and called on the Thompsons at
Boars Hill but spent most of their time with the Elmhirsts at Dartington.
As Tagore left London he sent Rothenstein one of his nostalgic letters
lamenting the passing of the leisurely days of their early acquaintance.

He adverted to that with overtones of pitiable helplessness, as if som
irresistible, impersonal force gripped him—but it was a force of his ow
creation. This time he remembered to thank Rothenstein for "the help yo
rendered unexpectedly in introducing Europe to me in whose shores, like
migratory bird, I have my second nest."[13]

There was an exchange with Bridges, who was exploring possibilities o
an honorary degree. "The degree can be proposed on October 10, and vote
on November 19," Bridges wrote, "so that you cannot hear whether yo
are accepted or not before that time." Election was admittedly uncertai
but would it be inconvenient to be " 'hanging about' during the first wee
in next month"? If so, it might be wiser to await a better time. A week o
"hanging about" would have been eminently beneficial just then, but, lik
the Sorcerer's Apprentice, Tagore had to go on rushing to and fro. He thanke
Bridges but said that coming to England was impossible.[14]

Rothenstein congratulated Edward on his book and said that one cause o
deterioration in England's attitude toward Tagore was the "changes of pla
which offend people when the good poet is in Europe. Dr. Bridges' recer
move on the subject of an Oxford degree is an example. . . . I deeply regre
his growing alienation from England; in his heart I believe he does respec
English writers & English character. But events have estranged him, & ou
policy towards educated men in India has been consistently unwise."[15]

Edward replied in four passionate pages, a lament for what might hav
been and for history's inept timing:

> It meant four [sic] years of hard work to do the Tagore book, and I rarely felt
> sure of my opinions—for how can a foreigner be sure he isn't making a fool
> of himself?—and my wife and I have grudged the time and labour, often most
> bitterly. For the mere bulk of Tagore's work was itself like a steam-roller over th
> mind, and left very little there when I had finished![16]

Rabindranath Tagore: Poet and Dramatist was prominently reviewed
Edward, unnecessarily pessimistic, wrote that "a book on an Indian subjec
cannot interest reviewers or editors unless it follows certain well-know
lines." The *Times Literary Supplement,* he thought, had been "provincia
and querulous"—the writer, who confessed that he knew nothing about th
matter, wasted his space in " 'gravely doubting' if there was any 'value' i
comparing English & Indian poets." That reviewer dragged in the old stereo
type: Tagore's charm for English readers "has lain in his serene comman
of the medium of rhythmical prose . . . and in the religious serenity of th
mind which they revealed." The poems were attractive but monotonous
and although no taste "is less exacting of change than English taste," whicl
accepts cabbage and boiled potatoes ad infinitum, even English reader
wanted more selectivity. Edward had tried to be selective, but Tagore's poeti

vocabulary was now firmly set in the public mind. "Tagore has been unlucky in this," Edward told Rothenstein, "so far as the *English* influence on his work goes he belongs to the Tennyson age, but he has the misfortune to come up for judgment by the age of T. S. Eliot & Aldous Huxley. He won't get justice now—nothing could get him justice."[17]

Leonard Woolf's review disappointed Edward, for he said that there was "not a single quotation in my book which did not seem to him altogether worthless. I know that his mind is queerly closed towards beauty—by a 'good book' he means one that is uncompromisingly hostile to the established order, & has no other test of goodness." However, Woolf wrote also that Edward's was one of several books that had helped to restore his mental digestion after reviewing *My Early Life* by the Emperor William II and F. E. Verney's *Character Study of the Prince of Wales.* Thompson gave the reader "a complete apparatus" for study of Tagore's life and artistic achievement. Woolf admitted as his own problem an inability ever "to see anything in Tagore's poetry," but Edward provided "stiff reading" and made one want more of the same.[18]

Graves reacted similarly. He confessed that "the more I read of your book curiously enough the less I like him as a poet: he seems to me the perfect example of poetry accommodating itself to social service instead of looking after itself." Undoubtedly, Tagore had done immense service to Bengali poetry, "though so far as poetry is concerned, complexity is not the final end. . . ." He added that Tagore's likeness was in every photographer's shop in Vienna: "Fine looking old fellow and certainly a ~~most~~ outstanding figure in Indian cultural development: but somehow I can't feel him as a poet of any greater integration than say Tennyson. Or am I wrong."[19]

Gaps in cultural communication were at fault. Edward told Rothenstein:

> I am sure that our worst mistake has been in caring so little about Indian thought and literature. They have a *right* to demand that we care what they think; & the fact of their political insubordination makes them resent our contempt. We have no Indian studies at Oxford, other than Sanskrit—& that less of literature than of grammar. The vernaculars are despised, are not considered serious studies—yet Sanskrit is dead, they are vigorous and developing. As a result, Indian intellectuals are turning to the Continent—they are getting increasingly out of touch with us, & are forming connections with Scandinavia, Germany, Czecho-Slovakia, Italy. This fact has even a political importance.[20]

The decline in Tagore's English popularity squandered the services of a cultural ambassador. Edward, to Rothenstein:

> My disappointment over the loss of reputation that has come to Tagore is largely because he lost the best chance India has ever had of getting a hearing

from the West. He got the ear of England—& then lost it. He lost much more than his own battle. And he need not have lost it. He is surrounded by all the adulation of a *Maître*, & shuts himself in with a conceit that his sense of humour & his vigour wd. have made impossible twenty years ago. He is not the man he was.[21]

Edward grieved also over the lost opportunity for the Oxford degree. It was a misunderstanding, he told Rothenstein: "There was no enthusiasm for him here, but the degree would have gone through all right." Bridges's letter was worded unfortunately, he thought, and "Tagore thought a *rebuff* was likely and he preferred not to risk it. It is a pity, for an occasional F[ellow o] the] R[oyal] S[ociety] or doctorate of Oxford or Cambridge wd. allay a dea of political unrest in India."[22]

A Tagore letter to Rothenstein showed how far the relationship with Thompson had deteriorated. It is mean-spirited, and meaner still because criticism that should have gone to Thompson went instead to the mutual friend. It showed again how little Tagore understood the high importance that Rothenstein attached to good relations among those who cared about India. Tagore called Thompson's new book "one of the most absurd books that I have ever read dealing with a poet's life and writings." Thompson left readers to guess about his command of Bengali, and inadequacy "prevents him from realising the atmosphere of our words and therefore the colour and music and life of them." Thompson failed to distinguish between essentials and nonessentials and therefore "jumbles together details without any consideration for their significance." Yet Tagore knew that in its earlier stages Mahalanobis had given expert help.[23]

Tagore then revealed more about his own prejudices than about Edward Thompson's. Edward's "pompous spirit of self confidence" sprang from his having been "a schoolmaster in an Indian school." Yet Tagore knew nothing about Thompson as teacher and had never seen him in the classroom. He read a reference to his own admiration for Shakespeare as a slur upon his scholarship. Thompson had written: "The Englishman finds in [the poems of Tagore's *Balaka* (Wild swans)] a "tribute from this unlikeliest of admirers." He had not realized that Tagore might take that to mean that no Indian fully understood Shakespeare. He intended a compliment to Tagore's powers of appreciation for the "Universal Poet."

Tagore's next charge was especially hurtful. If he had understood Edward's painful evolution of attitude toward the missionary vocation, and the painful process by which he came at last to reject it, he could not have assumed that his stereotype fitted Edward in 1926: "Then again, being a Christian missionary, his training makes him incapable of understanding the *Jeevan-devata* [Life-god], the limited aspect of divinity which has its unique place in the individual life, in contrast to that which belongs to the universe." Would

Thompson have treated a European poet so badly? Few in Europe could judge his book from firsthand knowledge, and this had "only made him bold and safely dogmatic, affording him impunity when he built his conclusions upon inaccurate data."

Not even this completed the discharge of Tagore's rancor. He engaged in what Harish Trivedi calls "a multiple hatchet-job [that] beggars belief, as being quite contrary to his character and image." It was indeed unworthy of the Nobel Laureate and "one of the best known and respected poet-prophets of his time in the whole world, a national leader who was in eminence next to none or only to Gandhi." He had lost both his "sense of balance and honour" and his dignity. The most shocking aspect of this whole episode, Trivedi says, was not even the "extreme violence of his reaction," but the "clandestine and apparently vindictive way in which he went about expressing, instigating and orchestrating that reaction." He wrote a venomous six-page pseudonymous review in the Bengali journal *Prabashi*. Ramananda Chatterji, editor of the *Modern Review*, echoed it in his own review there as well as in *Prabashi*, of which he was founder-editor. Trivedi says that "there can be little doubt that this piece was directly inspired by Tagore himself." He had a reviser's hand also in an article by a young Bengali that hewed to the vindictive line of his elders.[24]

Chatterji wrote also a vengeful English-language article in the *Modern Review*. Thompson, he says, had enough culture and literary appreciation to write on poets' lives and works but was too ignorant of the Bengali language and literature to write on a Bengali poet. He knew the Bengali alphabet, could use a dictionary, and could grasp the gist of a work with the help of an "educated Bengali translator." Were other lecturers in foreign languages at English universities so poorly prepared? Did he *really* read through all of Tagore's works? (He did.) Thompson cited conversations with Tagore: did he take notes on the spot? (He did.) Tagore did not recall saying such things. And did London University really accept those as scholarly documentation? If so, what was one to think of that university? Was Thompson's perhaps a "consolation" degree? Was the English Thompson jealous of Tagore's popularity among the "German-speaking peoples"? His store of insults apparently exhausted, Chatterji ended by detailing "Mr. Thompson's howlers" and asking whether he can be "believed by any stretch of the imagination to have equipped himself in that manner for his difficult task."[25]

It is an astonishingly, gratuitously destructive performance. Between the lines runs a subtext of Indian resentments boiling over, toward the very failings in cultural communication that Edward himself deplored. None of Thompson's qualifying comments about Tagore's work compares for sheer unprofessionalism with Chatterji's attack. Resenting Western failures, he and

his cohorts gave Thompson no credit, yet none of them had ever tried s
hard to interpret Bengal's great poet for readers in the West.

Dutta and Robinson pass over this episode as "too complex," as indeed
is, and refer their readers to Trivedi and E. P. Thompson. The latter concede
his father's overestimate of his powers, a brashness in his well-meant wis
to produce new translations to revolutionize the world's view of Tagore, an
his premature attempt at a comprehensive estimate of so large and varied a
oeuvre. Edward Thompson knew that his book would offend many Benga
but they damned him as doubly a sinner: he had said that Tagore's geniu
and a Bengali cultural institution were flawed. His epilogue had added insu
to injury: "I have spoken lightly of Tagorites. But after all the blasphemy
have uttered against his flutes and flowers, after all my counsels that his los
travellers, if caught, be made away with, I conclude by claiming confidentl
that his output is one of fine, and often great, poetry."[26]

Blasphemy indeed! Tagore's lines were merely "fine": not every line wa
"great." "Tagorites," among them Tagore himself, found it incomprehensible

Thompson had already begun to think about other projects concerne
with India but not with Tagore. His "Tagore period" was over.

18
WRITING ABOUT INDIA

Life on Boars Hill was frequently inconvenient, for as yet the Thompsons had no car and no telephone, but in other ways it placed them at the center of a most stimulating intellectual society. They saw the Bridges family regularly. People seemed to think of Robert Bridges, Edward told Lyon, as "eternally young, a sort of Scholar-Gypsy who has remained an undergraduate." Matthew Arnold had grieved for his fugitive scholar's bygone time when "wits were fresh and clear," but there was nothing cloudy about Bridges's wits. He maintained unspoiled enthusiasm for his theories about poetry and music, and for his Society for the Preservation of English; he would summon Edward to cross the road and go over the society's findings with him. Sometimes they walked together down the hill, keeping the university's spires in sight, to Ferry Hinksey, and so on into Oxford.[1]

Masefield had a small theater in his garden and enlisted family, friends, and neighbors as actors and producers. Mrs. Masefield asked Edward to be in one of her husband's plays. Edward declined as gracefully as possible, saying that he was too busy, but really because of "a certain reluctance to appear in a play where Christ is an actor." It was probably just as well that Edward avoided this play, *The Trial of Jesus,* which ran afoul of the Public Censor's rules about theatrical impersonations of Christ; it could be performed for private but not for public audiences. Masefield's plays were not very successful, but, like Bridges, he remained an evangelist for drama; he and Edward remained good friends, and Masefield and Bridges came into Benn's Sixpenny Poets series, of which Edward became editor.[2]

Theo did her best to keep Edward's time at home as clear as possible. He needed uninterrupted time and tranquillity because he was writing novels. He was writing novels because he hoped that they might produce a readier, more abundant income. In 1927 he published two, *An Indian Day* and *These Men, Thy Friends,* which he called his "Mespot novel." They are much more than mere potboilers. They assemble his retrospective reactions to those cardinal points in his career: Bengal and Mesopotamia.

Most of the principal characters in *An Indian Day* are traceable to Bankura people and, sometimes quite specifically, to events borrowed from descriptions in Edward's letters. Bankura becomes Vishnugram, which a passing

military man condemns as "a rotten hole" with an Indian as chief civil officia
without a club, a four at bridge impossible half the time, and redeemed on
insofar as good shooting is available. The Principal of a missionary colleg
in Bengal, denomination unspecified, is beyond a doubt modeled upo
Bankura's scientifically minded John Mitchell. A missionary named Findla
who devotes himself to the Santal hill tribes, is Bankura's Woodford. Robe
Alden teaches English literature, and he has Thompson's impatience and h
ferocious scorn for Thomas Macaulay and for "missionary statesman" typ
who write books with titles such as "The Missionary Imperative." He cann
abide gullible visiting English statesmen who patronize the missionarie
and allow themselves to be taken in by the smarmy pretensions of th
least trustworthy among the local bhadralok. He refuses to hear the bisho
who stops by to preach an abstract sermon at the height of a devastatin
famine and assures the mission staff that "the Church in India-h is grow
ing . . . and-er *growing* . . . and . . . *GROWING.*" Alden thinks with disgus
of missionaries touring England and "talking earnestly, eloquently, with ar
upraised, about the 'sacrifice' our 'brethren' were taking on themselves
but carefully avoiding details of that sacrifice. He despises American wome
who write "shallow foolish Indian travel-books" such as Thompson himse
refused to write. Alden's bursts of irrepressible hilarity at the absurdities c
pretentious ceremonial are a reprise of the younger Thompson and Owsto
Smith misbehaving at Bankura's Durbar celebration in 1911. In other word:
An Indian Day reproduces with uncomfortable accuracy Edward's famine
relief work, his troubles with fraudulent accounts, his scorn for tourin
orators, the aftermath of Amritsar, and discouragement about possibilitie
of British-Indian accord.[3]

The novel is set in the mid-1920s, which Broomfield calls one of the "tragi
decades," when Hindu-Muslim animosities increased, the more moderat
of the bhadralok lost political coherence, and the younger ones turne
to terrorism. The Montagu-Chelmsford Reforms had already increased th
number of Indian local officials, but unfortunately Vishnugram's Indian com
missioner is one Deogharia, "with absolutely unlimited opportunities fo
graft!" In the English community "the bitterness of the Dyer controversy an
of the Non-cooperation troubles smouldered. Indians thought they could run
themselves, did they? Well, they should run their own famine."[4]

Alden is principally an observer and commentator, and the protagonis
is Victor Hamar, a judge with Thompson's fierce sense of fairness (an
Mesopotamian battle experience), rusticated to Vishnugram after he freed
a group of Swarajists accused of terrorism. "The prosecution broke down,"
Hamar explains. "Government couldn't prove that those letters were authen
tic. I did my job. I dismissed the case." He does his job again at Vishnugran
after he and the chief of police discover a huge cache of arms in a cave

The English community expects him to act again like "one of those crazy pro-native folk," but this time he sentences the proven terrorists to eight years' transportation. The Indian community, where he thought he had made friends, turns on him as "a tyrant and an unscrupulous perverter of the law."[5]

Alden's pessimistic opinion about the English and Indian views of justice is that "we think first, second, and last, of doing our job; our favourite virtues are justice, firmness, integrity. To us mere kindness, as such, is weak sentimentality. But Indians don't give a bean for *our* cardinal virtues. To them any sort of harshness seems infinitely worse than the worst lapse from absolute justice. Oh, I know they often seem to assent to our code, and to accept it. But they never do." Like Fielding and Aziz, who wish for understanding but are forced apart when their horses diverge at the close of *A Passage to India*, England and India had inherited all the misunderstandings of history, multiplied during the Mutiny and exacerbated at Amritsar.[6]

As might have been expected, *An Indian Day*, like *The Other Side of the Medal*, repeatedly encountered *A Passage to India*, which had appeared in 1924. Reviewers sometimes revealed their confusion about details of the books and their authors. One American reviewer thought that both Thompson and Forster were "in the Indian service"—the I.C.S.—whereas neither had any such official connection. An English reviewer who should have known better called Forster's book *A Voyage to India*. Several, however, joined Thompson in objecting to claims for his books as "counterblast" to Forster. It seemed odd, wrote L. P Hartley, "to think of Forster's producing a 'blast' for anyone to counter." Another thought that "counter blast" was "too gross" a description of Thompson's tolerant, well-mannered book. Collingwood, a member of whose family knew Forster, commented that "he doesn't know everything" and thought that *An Indian Day* had "a very authentic air of giving, at last a real statement about the English & Indians of the present day—whereas most books of the Indian sort are either *deliberately* Tendenzgeschicte or merely tourist impressions." Sujit Mukherjee, a later critic, wrote that Forster probes more deeply than was possible with Thompson's historian's approach. Thompson knew his India better, but Forster wrote the better novel. What Thompson knew and portrayed better was the day-to-day political maneuvering at the provincial level after the reforms' tentative beginning. Nothing in *Passage* is sharper than Thompson's description of the egregious Deogharia exchanging flatteries with a visiting ex–Secretary of State for India who is writing on "The Problem of the Orient," who cannot understand why the Swarajists are still unhappy, and thinks Deogharia "the whitest Indian that ever lived," with "nothing Oriental about him but his pleasantly light colour."[7]

These Men, Thy Friends was Edward's attempt after nearly a decade to formulate a perspective upon the Mesopotamian experience. A chaplain and a doctor are at its center, and the chaplain's words, experiences, and attitudes match Edward's own. In the soldiers' talk Edward gives vent to outspoken impatience about smug and stupid generals and hangers-on at the fringes of the war who talked like front-line heroes: reporters, for instance, who only wanted to decorate their stories with something spectacular. One of them infuriates the soldiers by saying that Sannaiyat, site of crucial battles on the way to Baghdad, was "just trenches on the level." An English soldier says, with utter scorn, "It's that Indian frontier obsession again—chucking stuff at savages." That newsman was blood brother to the stage-managing cameraman in *The Leicestershires*.[8]

Edward, in the chaplain's voice, marvels anew at Indian soldiers' patience and generosity, seldom mentioned in press stories: "But doesn't it simply amaze you, that we have them here scrapping for us. They're mercenaries, when all's said and done. It isn't *their* Empire they're fighting for; and not one of them had any notion of the sheer bloody hell he was coming to. . . . They know now that the saheb and the Sirkar aren't the almighty wise folk they used to think them. . . . And we hadn't even blankets to give in return, or beds when they got cut up. . . . If we'd a brain in our heads, we'd see how perfectly bewildering it is to a lot of Asiatics—chaps whose own country has been blasted out of their hands by our guns—should be fighting and dying for us!" Another man praises the Indian troops but with imperial condescension: "It makes you proud of the Empire when you realise how it has taught these brown chaps to fight with the bayonet. With British leading they can do anything." Would the English never understand, muses a Dublin soldier, "why other races hated them?" The same smug self-satisfaction had made the Irish hate them by the slow-paced, methodically grouped executions after the Easter uprising of 1914. "Don't you know," cries the Dublin man, "what your precious military mind did? You got hold of what was a dirty slummy row, that had ruined half Dublin. . . . And you gave it dignity. You made silly murder and suicide into a martyrdom that Ireland'll never forget."[9]

Several reviewers were puzzled. Was this a travel book or history? The *Times Literary Supplement* asked, *is* it a novel? In "some more psychological parts" it was a novel, but it was difficult to say where it was not a novel: "It is a question of a greater or lesser dependence upon life and actual facts"—and there was no strict line between art and life. Still, if not an independent novel, or novel at all, it was an important book, if not an important novel. Cyril Connolly thought it "too close to history to have a plot, too close to life to have a bias": it was a narrative of "ordinary men in an extraordinary situation," an army in the process of realizing "the quite phenomenal incompetence by which it is guided from above." The *Spectator* thought it "uneven," with satire sometimes overdone: a bludgeon applied where a pinprick would do. This was true. Edward never learned

:o temper sufficiently his impotent indignation toward systems that he :hought deficient in imagination: Wesleyanism and its missions, the Indian educational establishment, the army. *These Men, Thy Friends* is a tract, a retrospective cry of protest against the idiocy and arrogance of the whole Mesopotamian campaign, tempered only by appreciations of the human capacity for friendship.[10]

He did not pause, however, to quibble about genres. He was now on many short lists as prospective contributor or author, and reviewing began :o bring in between three and four hundred pounds a year. Benn published his brief *History of India* for its Sixpenny Library, which Edward felt certain would "succeed in annoying all parties—British, Hindus, & Mohammedans—equally." Actually, he is hardest on Muslims, saying that Muslim historians measured their history by their service to Islam, and "aside from their architecture, they introduced the most sterile system that first-rate men have ever taken into their brain and blood." He recognizes that in the early years the British were simply looters of Indian riches but still believes in their capacities for eventual good and credits them with bringing new life to India: "Some of the outward gifts of British power are so familiar that they pass unnoticed; men forget how amazing it is that there should be peace and security over so vast a country."[11]

J. M. Dent asked for a series book "that tells ladies going out to India" what equipment they needed, how to get servants, and "what is the correct ettiquette on this & that occasion." Edward declined, as "unqualified to advise on these high problems." C. F. Andrews had a plan to edit a "legacy of India" collection for Oxford Press. Now Edward was more willing to credit Andrews with his selfless work for India's welfare, but he declined the request to write a literature survey for the collection because he did not want to seem to push himself ahead of other contributors on Andrews's list. However, he now found him more discriminating and with more political acumen in his relations with Indians.[12]

Instead, he entered the controversy over Katherine Mayo's *Mother India* with a review in the *Nation and the Athenaeum*. He was sharply critical of her conclusions about Indian attitudes on sex, women's position in society, and suttee, the immolation of a widow on her husband's funeral pyre. Mayo should have stopped, he thought, after the first nine chapters, which described, in harrowing detail, the physical and social disabilities of Indian women. He rejected her assumption of a "conspiracy of silence" and cited the existence of years of reports on the subject—unfortunately not always acted upon but at least on the record. He disliked her underestimate of Gandhi's courage and also a maudlin chapter on the Prince of Wales's visit to India. "She lost her case," Edward wrote, "when she wove into it a bitter conviction that the white man's rule is so overwhelmingly good for inferior breeds that it is only wickedness that makes them dissatisfied."[13]

With his own view on suttee, he returned to writing straight history. He had included a brief essay on the subject with three plays that he and Theo had published in 1927, two of which involved suttee. The essay brought the publisher so many requests for more information that he requested another, which grew into a monograph on the origins of widow-burning and British attempts to suppress it. The rite had acquired ancient religious sanction, and from early days the British were enjoined from trespass upon religious custom. Thompson documents the incidence of violations long after Regulation 17 of 1828 attempted to make the rite "culpable homicide, punishable with fine or (and) imprisonment. If drugs were administered to deprive the women of free will, the offence could be construed as murder." The gruesome business was wrapped in sanctimonious justifications of suttee as proof of the Indian wife's selfless devotion: "the widow who mounted the [husband's] pyre passed from the condition of a sinner to one of beatification; her dying curse or blessing had absolute power and unfettered course." Unlike Katherine Mayo, Edward makes no blanket indictment of Indian culture: he concentrates on the harm that Indian culture has done to itself in the eyes of the world: "It is often made a reproach against the British that, after a century and a half of predominance in India, they have not advanced the people any further along the road to fitness for self-government. I am not, I think, likely to ignore or forget the mistakes and shortcomings of our administration. But India's primary need to-day is fair judgement—from us to it and from it to us."[14]

The reviewer for the *New York Times* thought *Suttee* more valuable than *Mother India* because less sensational, the product of a long knowledge of India instead of a quick tour like Mayo's. *Suttee* would be useful to the social scientist, but there was fascination in the "sheer horror of the subject." Edward includes detailed eyewitness descriptions that are horrible indeed, but they are his proof that those who reported the events had written true history.[15]

His India publications were timely, for they coincided with the work of the Indian Statutory Commission, otherwise known as the Simon Commission. Its chairman was the austere and meticulous Sir John Simon. Its mission was to evaluate the success or nonsuccess of the Montagu-Chelmsford Reforms of 1919 and, likewise, the degree of success of Lionel Curtis's dyarchy concept. If these were to succeed, the British public must be better informed about India. It was not merely a joke that an India debate was certain to empty the parliamentary benches, and great portions of the general public had been nurtured on stereotypes of the "mysterious East." The Simon Commission would visit India in 1928 and again in the winter of 1928–1929.

In England there were plans for impressing upon the public the importance of the commission's investigation. There would be an Indian Information Centre, and Edward Thompson was on its council. Lyon observed that the government was often inarticulate and represented itself badly, and "the Centre might prove of real value if they will be careful to ascertain what the views of the other side are before they launch out into denunciation."[16]

In 1927 Edward looked, not only toward India, but westward. He had begun to think about a year's leave from Oxford; in fact, with the still-dwindling supply of I.C.S. candidates as students, there was not a great deal to leave. That June he resigned his post as Lecturer and approached Vassar College, Theo's alma mater, about a visiting appointment for 1928–1929. He told Dr. H. N. MacCracken, President of Vassar, that his Oxford job "has ceased to be an economic return for the time it takes, and especially, for the strain it leaves when one is putting in one's main effort in creative work. . . ." He did not mean to underestimate Oxford's amenities and libraries, but his books now obtained American publishers, the American market paid better than the English, and he now thought of "making a living by my pen." First, however, he wanted to see America, so that any future writing would be more than "just a stewing up of Indian memories." He added: "To the Englishman your country is as mysterious as I daresay Mesopotamia is to you. . . . I must see something of America, to us the most powerful and puzzling people in the world to-day." After some serious juggling of courses and appointments, the college offered a professorship at four thousand dollars for 1928–1929. MacCracken noted that visiting professors from England preferred class lecturing over open discussion, with which preference "we have no great sympathy, as Theo can tell you." Ratcliffe's agent asked whether Edward would be available for lecture engagements. When Edward communicated this to Dr. MacCracken and mentioned that one of Theo's relations had already asked him to speak to her women's club, MacCracken warned about the American appetite for being lectured, with the result that "an Englishman will be intoxicated by the demand for his intellectual wares" and would "be inclined to carry them to frequent markets and try to sell cheap wares at a high profit very early." In other words, the visitor accepted too many invitations from "women's clubs and the like at large rewards, from $75 to $100 without preparing and without any real respect for the intelligence of his audience." Audiences had begun to know good lectures when they heard them, "although one might not think it at times, for it is incredible that poor lectures are permitted, especially by our friends from over the sea, but this is due to the hope that springs eternal in the American breast that he may learn something from somebody. We are insatiable in this regard." Ratcliffe, an exception to that rule, could enlighten Edward on the subject.[17]

Theo was delighted that at last Edward would see America. She was proud of her New England lineage. A maternal ancestor named William Palmer, a nailer from Stepney, London, had arrived at Cape Cod on the *Fortune* in 1621, the second ship to the Plymouth Colony. Thus the Thompsons' second son was his namesake—although Edward Palmer Thompson when small thought that his name came from the Easter palms. Theo urged Edward to read *The Bent Twig,* by Dorothy Canfield, the romantic saga of a Midwestern academic family whose intelligent and independent daughter goes to New England and learns about life and love. Theo thought it the best available picture of New Englanders. He would understand "a lot about my setting & my 'past' if you read it—& it will help you to understand the girls you'll meet at Vassar. Read it for my sake—though it's not in your line."[18]

All summer there were delays in the correspondence, and Edward assumed in August that Vassar had made no final decision. Oxford wanted him to reconsider, and he had agreed to continue for another year. However, Vassar still wanted him, for 1929–1930; he should choose from the catalog the courses he wanted to teach, and professors already teaching those would "make room for you." He could use the lecture format if he wished and must not be "too good natured with students who pursue you begging to get in." Dr. MacCracken felt certain that Edward's spirit would touch "the American mind [more] than the all too rapid touring and lecturing which some visitors have indulged in." He could, of course, travel as necessary, "but it takes time to get insight into folks." Oxford agreed to his absence.[19]

With the American plan on hold, Theo went to Berne for thyroid surgery. Frank entered the Dragon School in Oxford. His father's old disappointment over his own blighted academic career came out in a letter to Theo: Frank loved examinations "as much as I used to do. *He'll* get scholarships all right." He asked questions endlessly, from a brain "working every minute." He was wilfully contrary but "incredibly good to Palmer." Frank knew just how close he could edge to a spanking, but both were delightful boys "with all their sins." Palmer, not to be outdone, was learning to read and was coping with "the caprices of our noble tongue." He complained that " 'malt' [Malt extract of Cod-liver oil] is 'a naughty word. It should have an o, not an a.' That is so.' Edward, with a trace of Wesleyan disapproval for self-indulgence, was proud of himself for keeping his temper when Palmer "loafed and loafed over a meal (he never seems hungry; he eats only for pleasure, & gets far too much pleasure out of it)." Still, Theo thought that Palmer began to grow up faster after Frank went to school.[20]

While Theo was away, Lady Mary Murray asked Edward and Palmer to lunch, and Palmer "played the part he plays so well, that of the guileless little angel; she petted him, & kept remarking on his goodness." Lady Mary the formidable daughter of the formidable Lady Carlisle, was in "her worst

moods of hauteur," twice lost her temper and was "outrageously rude" to
Edward. "It was v. painful, and after the second time I opened my own paw
and showed her a steely talon, wh. she acknowledged with a wintry smile."
Gilbert Murray, very embarrassed, asked him out for a walk. They had a "long
& *most* interesting talk," and Murray "semi-apologised" for Lady Mary, "saying
that many Labour people had such a fierce emotional feeling about Russia
that they flared up at any word that *seemed* to criticise the Bolsheviks. 'My
wife likes that. She thinks the Bolsheviks are a kind of Quakers.' " Her first and
rudest retort had come when Edward said that he "hoped the Labour Party
wd get ahead with our own problems, if they got in, instead of trying to tie up
with experiments in Russia that were no concern of ours." Perhaps Lady Mary
had tried to grill Edward on her preferred subjects, just as her mother had
grilled Murray, as her daughter's young suitor, on teetotalism, vegetarianism,
women's suffrage, Home Rule, and Liberal Party politics. Murray's biographer
says: "A price was paid for Lady Carlisle's generous financial support of her
daughter and son-in-law," and this was a particularly trying time for the
Murrays, with problems of health and uncertainties about their children's
careers. Theo had once thought that Lady Mary might be her Boars Hill
mentor. She continued to admire Lady Mary's efficiency but seems to have
dismissed the idea of mentorship.[21]

It was as well that the American year was postponed, for Elizabeth Thompson's health became ever more fragile. For some time, if she rang her bell
at night Alfred ran for a neighbor to stay with her while he went to the
doctor. She reached back in memory to milestones of their family life. In
1927 she recalled that it was just seventeen years since she and Edward had
been together in Manchester "just before you sailed for India the first time."
When she left the Letchworth house for a nursing home in 1928, she wrote,
"We have been very happy here, & poor old Alfred is very grieved at leaving
the garden. I grieve with him. . . ." But she wanted to try again at the old
address and told Theo: "I have five children, & not to live with one of them!
Why what would life be worth?" In May, her handwriting firm as ever, she
wrote to Edward and Theo: "I've been thinking, as I lay here of the many
happy holidays I have had with you and Theo, & later with Frank, & then
Palmer. . . . And we'll have happy days together yet, it may be on earth, it
will be in Heaven." There were no more holidays together. In the summer
of 1928 her long-damaged heart gave out. Her devotion and anxiety had
shaped a family; all of them knew that her hopes and Wesleyan aspirations
had formed them in ways that, even as they fretted and rebelled, remained
with them for better or for worse, for as long as they lived.[22]

Since Edward was still in England, he was able to follow more closely the
English view of the Simon Commission in India during its first fact-finding
tour from January to April 1928. It was to report and make recommendations

after its second tour. A conference, which became the three Round Tabl Conferences of 1930 to 1932, would assemble after they returned. Parli ment must approve the report and enact as law any recommendations fc constitutional changes.

The BBC asked the India Society to cooperate in "trying to make fol interested in India." It planned an "orgy of Orientalism" for 11 Januar 1929, with readings from Indian literature and songs by Indian student Edward was one of the speakers: "Then, at 10:15, when everyone has gon to sleep or switched off, I am to make a few choice remarks, for about 2 minutes, on *Peoples of India.*" He submitted a script and told Joe Ackerle the director of BBC Talks, that in the time allotted he would rather spea about Bengal. "I should, of course, make it more colloquial. I have mere tried to help folk visualise the country. One cannot go deep." Ackerle suggested a few deletions, to which Edward replied that he knew he wა prone to wandering into "trivial side-issues"—for instance, the existenc of a freshwater shark in Fiji and another in the Tigris related to the India *Carchareus gangeticus* (today called *Glyphus gangeticus*). Such digression he agreed, were irrelevant when "such grave issues as British interest in sympathy with India are forward."[23]

His Gangetic sharks would have been livelier than the talk by the Ind Society chairman, Lord Ronaldshay. Bland, boring, and insulting to India culture, it labels the Indo-Aryan people as abstract thinkers with no initiatიν until Islam arrived and set a better example. Muslims, and the British aftϵ them, had "awakened [Indians] from their apathy by imports from the viril civilization which flowed in upon them from the West. . . ." On Indian ar Ronaldshay took a note from Sir George Birdwood and pronounced th Buddha figure incomplete, without facial expression and anatomical detail.

Sir Michael Sadler arranged for Edward to speak on India to an Oxfor luncheon club. Edward heard afterward that most of the audience ha expected him to be " 'more Bolshevik' " and also more inclined to "seditio & general harmfulness," but they seemed reassured and applauded. Late however, he overheard two men discussing the speech. One had not bee present, but the other "put on a voice of *ineffable* pain & disgust. & bega 'Oh, he just wandered all over the place & said a whole lot of. . . .' " Edwar slipped away, his reputation as radical thinker quite safe.[25]

The Montagu-Chelmsford Reforms were always intended as a stopgap o the long road to increased self-determination for India, with adjustments ა ten-year intervals, or oftener, depending on Indian progress. Many Indian even many who recognized the need for more direct experience of gover ing, resented this dangling and piecemeal development of a measure so cr cial to India's future. Invariably, official response had been that Indians fir must prove themselves ready for self-government. Ostensibly, the reforn would give them that chance. But the division of powers between central and provincial governments was insulting. The provincial legislatures kept control of "transferred" duties: local self-government and administration. The central government kept the "reserved subjects": administration of justice, and control of the police, the press and books, money borrowed on provincial credit, and industrial disputes. Thus the government, in this two-tier structure called dyarchy, kept the principal instruments for controlling the exercise of civil rights.[26]

In 1952 Simon wrote that Montagu had been justified in thinking that his reforms were " 'the most momentous utterance ever made in India's chequered history,' but he cannot have anticipated, at the initial stage, the growing momentum of the forces which he then released. . . ." Nor did the Simon Commission anticipate the momentum of forces that it released in India. It stumbled badly at the start because it had no Indian members, which caused outrage in India. This was not Simon's fault. Advisers had told Lord Birkenhead, Secretary of State for India, that a "white Commission" would cause trouble, but he argued that Indians were racially inferior, and Indian opinion was so diverse that choosing a few Indian members would offend others. Simon hoped to offset Indian resentments by appointing an Indian consultative committee *after* the commission and an Indian National Congress committee had reported. Lyon believed that "we can trust Simon to keep his head and to shew a statesmanlike appreciation" for the fact that any Indians of significant influence looked for radical changes in the system of government. The crux of the whole arrangement for transfer of some powers from the central government would be the amount of "ultimate disciplinary power . . . and the final reference of problems to Parliament." The crucial issue would remain in the disposition of civil liberties.[27]

However, those liberties were abridged, not to say mangled, when the Simon Commission visited India. Objections to the "white Commission" burst out in raucous public protests. Simon acknowledged later that "the purely British composition of our own body roused resentment in many quarters in India—resentment which we did everything to allay, first by seeking the cooperation of Indian Committees (for whose aid we are deeply grateful) and later by the calling of a Representative Conference. . . ." But those gestures were too little and too late. The two-volume report and Simon's two BBC talks timed to its publication refer only obliquely to the negative reception of the commission. Indian sources are more specific. At the Bombay docks, demonstrators met them with placards inscribed "Simon go back" and "No representation, no Commission." The police dispersed them. The docks, wrote S. R. Bakshi, "had been turned into a veritable fortress for the occasion. Every entrance was guarded by armed police; squads of police, some carrying rifles and others lathis, paraded the approaches to Ballard Pier.

The authorities had fully prepared themselves for trouble, though fortunate
there was none." Huge processions, often of many thousands, carrying blac
flags and shouting "Simon go back," met the commission at almost every sto
Most of the protesters were peaceful, but their intention was unmistakabl
and police drove them back. During a Delhi hartal, five hundred studen
struck, a crowd of fifteen thousand with black flags ranged themselves alon
the station road for three-quarters of a mile, and a procession of some for
thousand formed after a mass meeting. The police protected the commissio
ers as they followed their prearranged schedule of meetings with officia
and selected nonofficials. At one point, in a travesty of hospitality, all gat
were locked and policemen stood guard at intervals of one yard around
British Association tea party for the commissioners. The boycotters "cover
the whole sky" with black kites and balloons bearing "Simon go back." It w
not an auspicious beginning for a new era of mutual understanding.[28]

19
Information Campaign

While the Simon Commission was at work, the Thompsons, with their two children and thirty-four pieces of luggage, sailed for America. The first impression at New York was not favorable. Prohibition was supposedly in force, but the city seemed "wetter than ever & hopelessly corrupt." Theo had declared a small amount of brandy. The customs agent said, " 'Here!' (v. severely), 'what are you doing? If you've anything like that, don't go telling *me*. You hide it away in some valise, quick! And don't tell me where it is, either!' " She did so. The officer opened everything else but passed that one. "He and his assistant demanded tips, but kept saying, 'Not now! not now! We couldn't get away with it.' Then, 'Now! Now we can get away with it.' " Over Edward's objections, Theo paid up.[1]

Edward, however, was on crutches and in no condition to face down a challenge. Riding was still his favorite exercise, and the leafy lanes of Boars Hill were ideal for it. In May a captious mare kicked out viciously and broke two bones in his shin. He was still in considerable pain (probably why Theo carried brandy). After three months in the hospital at home, two rounds of surgery, and insertion of a metal plate, the leg healed much too slowly. The days at sea did nothing to allay his pain. X-rays at the Brooklyn Hospital showed that osteomyelitis had set in, and the bone was "in a bowl of pus." Immediate surgery followed. English doctors had assured him that the bone was quite healthy and needed only time to heal, but at Brooklyn Edward learned that "that blamed plate" had caused long-established infection and that American doctors had long since given up plating for such injuries. One of Edward's American publishers thought the crutches " 'good publicity,' " and a reporter produced a story captioned "Oxford Lecturer to Invade Vassar on Crutches." A photographer followed, and the attention became rather tiresome, but they seemed so pleased with their story that Edward decided "it wd. be churlish for me to be peeved about it." The doctors thought that he might be able to walk unaided after three months. However, infection persisted, and his surgeon wanted to operate again at Christmas. But Edward had already had four hundred pounds' worth of surgery and felt that he could afford no more.[2]

They settled at 56 Grand Avenue, Poughkeepsie. Edward taught three literature classes. Palmer went to a public school for mornings only, and

Frank for the full day. The Poughkeepsie school was notably "better run and far more respectable" in public opinion than were tax-supported schools in England. Frank dutifully saluted the flag daily "& is much amused, in his mature fashion, by the earnest patriotism which is a large part of the curriculum."[3]

Edward told Lyon: "It is an enthusiastic people; but capricious also. I used to be annoyed when I read of American processions & meetings of anti-British protest. I now know they mean *nothing*. You can get up protest against *any*thing here. They don't remember a week." Arabs and Jews clashed in Palestine, and "[Americans] were v. excited about the Palestine riots, for 3 days; then no one cared a hang." Pain made him pessimistic, and he wondered whether Oxford wanted him back the following year:

> Everyone is kindness itself here; but I have such a feeling of futility. Americans seem so complacently sure that they have all the "idealism" that's going. And I am glad to belong to an austere civilisation—the austerest the world has seen since the Greek. We miss Scar Top; & our friends. Then, in England one is (in a v. small way) somebody, an individual. Here I am just a man whose books are never reviewed (as was the case in England, 2 years ago) & never sold. It makes a bit of difference to self-respect.[4]

This was not quite fair. His books were widely reviewed in America, and the American edition of *An Indian Day* had five impressions in 1927 and 1928. As he had told Dr. MacCracken, his better sales were American.

Edward now became a trans-Atlantic spokesman in the India information campaign. Ratcliffe, who as a professional lecturer had wide American contacts, suggested that Edward accept invitations to participate in Foreign Policy Association debates. "They pay v. badly," Edward told Lyon, "but are extremely influential. You each speak for 20 minutes, then each have 20 minutes' 'rebuttal,' then questions are put. You get about 900 audience at N. York, but ten times that number listen in; & questions are sent over the telephone."[5]

Most of his debating opponents were expatriate Indians. At Baltimore, New York, and Boston it was Sailendranath Ghose, who had fled sedition charges in 1916. Perhaps not realizing how his distortions would feed reporters' faulty information, the Foreign Policy Association gave him rare opportunities to mislead the public. The *Baltimore Sun* described him as "Leader of the Nationalist [*sic*] Congress." A news report read, "Babies in India Fed Opium at British Command, He Says." Ghose called it Britain's official policy for "emasculating the Indian people and keeping them subservient." Thompson and a distinguished American physician on the panel "hotly contested" this. It was a very old expedient, they said, for quieting babies while poor mothers worked in the fields; the practice increased after they became factory workers. Reporters ignored this. Ghose flogged two oversimplified points: everything wrong everywhere was Britain's fault, and American Independence inspired the Swarajists.[6]

In New York Ghose declared that Britain must accept blame for consequences of the freedom struggle. "Hindus May Resort to Methods of 1776" was the *New York Times* headline. Edward deplored misleading efforts to encourage Americans to see "the scenes of their own revolution enacted before their eyes [in India]."[7]

In Boston, Ghose repeated his charge that England alone was the world's troublemaker and again dragged in "your Revolutionary fathers of 1776," and Abraham Lincoln for good measure. In Philadelphia Ghose repeated this, but Thompson got a little more coverage. He said that Indians were still unready for self-government, and dominion status, not immediate Home Rule, could provide interim stability. England's domination of India was indeed an unsettling influence: "But until we can eventually settle the differences between England and India, the effect is bound to have a repercussion upon all the nations of the world." However, Ghose's simplistic declarations got the column inches.[8]

Edward debated in Chicago before twelve hundred people against a Methodist bishop (whom he did not identify) and an Indian named Nanilal Parekh, who was to appear in " 'Gandhiesque cap & costume'—not mere loincloth, I presume?)" Excited women before the meeting distributed an " 'Appeal' by Indian students. I made it waste paper; & after the meeting the Indians were very excited; and asked *me* to give them the right statistics, since I said theirs were wrong. I refused. Had I done so, the pamphlet wd. have appeared as by me!" At New York's Town Hall he debated Syed Hussein, "reputed the most brilliant [Indian] speaker in the States," Edward told Lyon. "Ratcliffe who finally refused to meet him any more says he is quite unscrupulous & diabolically clever. He is also strikingly handsome, as an Afghan colleague of his said to me, 'You may thank your stars you have never had to speak against Syed Hossain. For sex appeal, you are not in the same class with him.' The Women's Clubs are crazy about him." They met again at International House in New York. He was not clever, only "oily & dull" and in early stages of inebriation. The audience was "a lot of Indians & silly women." Hussein's admirers wanted a return appearance. Edward refused, for he thought Hussein "not worth powder and shot." Besides, he balked at spending train fare from Poughkeepsie, and his leg was very painful.[9]

Katherine Mayo's *Mother India* had had twenty-two reprints and had caused an outpouring of American indignation about sexual exploitation of Indian women. In the *Saturday Review of Literature* Edward nailed her errors, such as her statement that India had no important vernacular literatures. Still, it was true that she had shocked more thoughtful readers into realizing that "Hindu and Mohammedan thought need the same searching examination that our own thought has had, and is still getting: Indian history and politics should be handled as if neither Indian touchiness nor British pride existed." Indians should see "that they have become obsolete without realizing it, and might as well catch up with the modern world (better late than never)" and give their qualities a chance. "Miss Mayo, I believe, has denied that there are political implications in her book. But they are all over it. If she did not mean to convince the world that Indians were incorrigibly inept, what did she mean?"[10]

Ratcliffe spoke up via a *New York Times* report of his address in London to the East India Association. *Mother India,* he said, had had "a strong influence among American women and churchgoers. They welcome it as providing evidence of the superiority of Western over Oriental civilization." But perhaps educated Americans recognized "the immense difficulties of the British position in India."[11]

Andrews was in America, traveling, lecturing, and preaching. Edward thought that he was "talking a lot of bosh." Audiences and congregations accepted him as an unusual kind of Anglican clergyman, but he fell afoul of Indian expatriates because he opposed their "move to recognize Indians as 'Aryan' and therefore white." When two of them complained to Gandhi, Andrews replied that he had been quoted out of context. However, a defender admitted that "Mr. Andrews no doubt makes mistakes, sometimes terrible mistakes; being emotional by nature he can be easily deceived or misled."[12]

Tagore, too, intended to speak for India in America, but his behavior was quixotic. Sujit Mukherjee, in his careful account of Tagore's American visits, reports an "incident" at Vancouver that cut short the first to only 18–20 April 1929. He had refused earlier Canadian invitations, to protest Canada's exclusion of Indian immigrants, even though they were British subjects applying to a British dominion. He accepted in 1929 for an education conference and was then to go to the University of Southern California which wanted a six-week course on Indian philosophy and literature. He was already annoyed with America over *Mother India* and blasted it in a letter of 18 April: "The greatest indictment against America is the greedy manner in which she seized upon that vulgar book . . . the greatest collection of half-truths and outright lies yet gotten together." At the border he mislaid his passport, and the U.S. immigration official recognized Tagore but kept him standing for half an hour, then asked the stock questions: who paid his passage, had he ever been to jail, did he intend to stay in the United States. "Not surprisingly," say Dutta and Robinson, "Tagore's anti-American hackle rose." He was further irritated because the university wanted public as well as classroom appearances. He canceled the visit forthwith, pleaded poor health, and went home.[13]

It is surprising, therefore, that he returned in October 1930. The American Friends Service Committee sponsored this, his last visit to America. He had visited Russia and at New York made comments immediately construed as approval of the Soviet system and disapproval of Indian independence. His attempt at clarification only worsened matters. He had meant precisely what Lyon and Thompson believed: that Indians needed a breathing space, time to learn the ways of responsible democracy. "The mis-reporting of his views," Mukherjee says, "could not but have reawakened Tagore's old mistrust of the American press, and his public relations nearly broke down the next day" when reporters, photographers, and movie cameramen mobbed him at his residence. He refused to meet anyone. The Friends' representative argued that he had an American mission; it was unwise to alienate press and newsreels. With difficulty, he was persuaded to appear for "an orderly press conference."[14]

His American lectures were increasingly minatory, even apocryphal. A statement in Yokohama in 1929 preceded him: he had said that Indian independence was so far in the future that thinking about it now was pointless. In America he deplored "the machine-like quality of [British] administration. . . ." Indian masses had lost heart. He admired Gandhi's "sincerity, patriotism and high ideals" but doubted the practicality of his programs. He hit at the American weak spot: "You Americans seem blind to the fact, for instance, that you have your own caste system, quite as rigorous as ours, in your treatment of the negro." Americans misunderstood "the profound ethnological and historical reasons" for caste in India. The omnibus caption reads: "Tagore Sees India as a Future Power: Native Poet, on Pacific Voyage, Pictures Country Today as Apathetic in Its Misery: British System Criticized: But Britons Are Called Best of Foreign Rulers, with Natives Unready for Task."[15]

A New York interview bore another encyclopedic caption: "India's Poet Who Waits for the Dawn: 'We Are Humble and Suffer,' Says Sir Rabindranath Tagore. 'But the Morrow,' He Adds, 'Shall Be Ours.' " The interviewer, who also illustrated the article, pulled the old stop about a "wise man from the East." His portrait drawing shows Tagore much heavier, much older; he is somber, not serene, his cheeks deeply lined. Again Tagore spoke admiringly of the apparently improved condition of the Russian peasant. In another New York interview, he administered a slap unlikely to win American hearts and minds: "Had you been ruling over us you might have been worse."[16]

The Simon Commission was widely but not always accurately reported; its work must have seemed extremely remote. The *New York Times* approved of the all-British "white commission": it would benefit India more *without* Indian members, who might be " 'coerced or cajoled or otherwise swayed by the British majority.' " Indian nationalists were insulted. Were their convictions so feeble that they could not stand up to opposition? No matter what

Simon said, the belated addition of an Indian committee was a sop to India
sensibilities. In any case, Congress had already voted to boycott the Roun
Table and had demanded complete independence.[17]

Edward's response was his book *Reconstructing India,* planned to c
incide with the Simon Report and the Round Table Conference to begi
on 12 November 1930. "Yes, I have been like you wondering & ponderir
over the Indian news," he wrote to Lyon. "I am pretty sure that there w
be assassinations, esp. in Bengal. People here are friendlier to us than the
used to be over India. Our stock is higher, & the nationalists' is lower. I hav
promised to rush out a book on the situation. I believe it can do enormou
good. I want to set out the facts of defence, native states, communal trouble
& so on." He then *"slaved"* for five weeks to write eighty thousand word
while performing college duties. His leg continued to be swollen and painfu
the still-unhealed incision was three inches wide and thirteen inches long. A
the family except Edward had flu; Palmer had a mastoid operation, and Frank
tonsillectomy. Edward's "writing arm has been almost crippled with neuritis
and he had some teeth extracted. With pluck and good cheer, Theo cope
with everything. Over his objections she took on some examining work i
order to pay toward the medical bills. "No," Edward told Lyon, "we've ha
no luck in America."[18]

He *had* had luck in discovering Geoffrey Garratt, whose book, *An India*
Commentary, he had reviewed. He thought it "the best and fairest stud
of the Indian situation that has appeared in my lifetime." Garratt had bee
an Indian district officer, farmer, and later, a Calcutta businessman. He wi
well-informed and refreshingly original in his views on India.[19]

Ratcliffe read Edward's proofs and thought the book "a splendid thing
In fact, until the debates Edward had not realized how many America
drew simplistic parallels between American and Indian history and ho
shamelessly people like Ghose exploited them: American Congress an
Indian National Congress; the Fourth of July and an Indian "Independenc
Day" declared for 26 January 1930; a Stamp Act and a Salt Tax as politic
catalysts. Americans had come to believe that events in India mirrore
their own revolution, led by a frail and saintly figure. Edward pointed ot
inconsistencies in the romantic infatuation with the "Oriental": India's mea
were not always nonviolent; India was not always united in purpose; Gandl
had awesome powers but had also inconsistencies. The great question w;
whether East and West could lay aside their antipathies and accept India i
an equal partner in solving mutual concerns.[20]

Thompson most distrusted the wrapping of mysticism around issues th;
demanded pragmatic solutions. Gandhi's famous Salt March was an exampl
On 12 March 1930 he and some followers went to the Indian Ocean an
collected a symbolic and illegal scraping of salt, to protest a doubled tax o

ıe government-controlled supply. On 5 May he was arrested and interned. It as a flashpoint in relations with the British. Andrews, in a long article in the ew York Times, glorified "Gandhi's Mystic Aims in His Indian March." Those Mystic Aims" splashed across the headlines caught American attention. hompson explained that the mystique obscured some important facts. The oubled tax was for one year only. The legislative assembly at Delhi had lready twice voted it down, but the Viceroy passed it over their heads by certification." "It is hard," Thompson wrote, "to characterise the folly of ıis procedure adequately. The power of certification, like a final authority's ower of veto anywhere, was meant for use in a grave emergency." No oubt the Viceroy thought that the march threatened an emergency, but he heapened the veto and "gave colour to the Extremists' allegations that the eforms were a sham." He intimidated the more reasonable noncooperators nd "profoundly discouraged the Indian liberal who had tried amid an tmosphere of anger and contempt to work the Constitution." Thus for one ear's relatively trivial gain, the Viceroy risked his administration's integrity, trengthened the forces of irreconcilability, and made "the task of the friends f an ordered transition almost impossible."[21]

Edward pointed out that Americans were not the only sentimentalists. . British mystique glorified the "Punjab Tradition" personified in the North ıdian "martial races," a mainstay of the Indian army. It fueled "that Imperialist nthusiasm which became known the world over in the writings of Kipling. . has ministered to our pride, in recent years it has brought to some of us hame. It is now dying, but dying hard and unwillingly." Punjabi Sikhs had emained loyal during the Mutiny, were stalwart in France and Mesopotamia, nd half of the Indian deaths in the Great War were Punjabi. Therefore ıe Punjab was glorified as "the shield of India, with a modified 'martial ıw' complex." (There was a dangerously simplistic parallel with the old merican West. The Punjab, like that frontier, was supposed to be where oung Englishmen went to show their mettle.) But Amritsar had "since pread a shadow over all efforts at conciliation," and "the Punjab's superb ar effort was a double-edged achievement, a weapon that has been cutting ır hands ever since."[22]

Thompson made specific recommendations. He called again for dominion tatus like the consensual alliances with Canada, Australia, and New Zealand. ıdian history should be written better and more accurately. Indian studies ı English universities should include vernacular literatures as well as linguis-cs. Britain must stop using conferences and commissions to play for time. "It as all been largely foolery. Nothing has happened, the Commissions have ot us nowhere." If the Round Table Conference were more of the same, ıdians would rightly distrust it. But Indians had their own multiplicity of ommittees and commissions and must stop blaming their troubles on Britain and attend instead to the status of women and of Untouchables. Thompson feared "most of all the stiffening of my own people, . . . lest they shoul demand some sign of repentance for the provocation of the last ten year of folly." The true parallel with American history was that Britain again ha overlooked "the wider causes of quarrel."[23]

Edward could be pleased with the book's reception. Charles Johnson, i the *New York Times,* writing also on books by Romain Rolland and Wi Durant, thought that Thompson's "stood apart" for fairness, accuracy, an sense of humor. Geoffrey Garratt admired his ability to give Indian nationalist due credit yet be "severely critical of their leaders when they embark o actions without thinking of their outcome, or are guilty of sloppy thinkin, and unreasonableness." The *Spectator* thought no praise too high for a boo that "chastised with whips the misguided moral indignation and idealisr of freedom-proclaiming Americans." The *Times Literary Supplement* urge readers not to give up because Thompson seemed to offer few specifi suggestions for "the shaping of India's political future"; it could not be don overnight.[24]

In all, his American output was very much to the point: *his* point, tha American misconceptions of the Indian situation were dangerous. "I am ver sick of controversy," Edward wrote to Lyon. "You have no idea how unfai & lying a propaganda goes on here." He doubted whether the debates ha been useful. Undoubtedly, the traveling had done his leg no good. The famil went to Connecticut and Vermont for a retrospective view and a rest befor sailing. "But," he wrote, "it is a devilish country to make a living in." All th Thompsons looked forward to returning to Boars Hill.[25]

While Frank and Palmer raced about, wild with joy at being home, an Theo resettled domestic affairs, neither Edward nor his typewriter rested He defended American college students: sensationalist American writer falsified their image as badly as they falsified that of India. The students wer *not* "far gone in moral degeneracy, the women worse than the men. Th truth is that most of them are as attractive and straight examples of youth a the world has seen, and their good fortune failed to spoil more than a few c them." Theo was well confirmed in her belief that Edward would find Vassa women both independent and intelligent.[26]

He noted that both England and America had some reckless newspapers but he had not found them in American colleges "or the homes of peopl who want to think honestly." Americans should remember that "what to then is merely exciting news . . . is to us as perplexing a problem as we have eve faced." They should criticize Britain as they criticized France or German "and discountenance some of the acerbity now reserved for us alone."[27]

Edward regretted that his candor had "grieved many Americans, for whicl I am sorry for they were very kind to me." However, the India Office wa grateful, and even the Tory papers gave his book excellent reviews. Members of Parliament began to ask for consultation. However, he was exhausted and did not want to see even friends: "No one knows how bad things are with me, or how worn down I am in every way."[28]

Nevertheless, he had to concentrate on the Round Table Conference. Lyon thought the Simon Commission's recommendations courageous and perhaps the best to be expected "from a Commission which contained after all, a majority of Conservatives. But they fail to make the Indian ministers & Governments sufficiently responsible, and they will never learn or cease from futile railing against H.M.'s Government until they are made to realise that they are themselves fully responsible. Responsibility will teach them, quite quickly, if we can succeed in forcing them to take it." That was a large "if."[29]

The commission had a handicap that ought to have been unnecessary. On 31 October 1929 the Viceroy, on instructions from the Labour government, announced that dominion status was the solution. This was, at the very least, a discourtesy. Simon, with commendable restraint, wrote in 1952 that "a prejudgment, issued even in these vague terms, was in such circumstances embarrassing." The commissioners had not yet considered relations between British India and the Princely States, the one-fourth of India not under the Raj. Simon had some difficulty in persuading his indignant colleagues to carry on. Indian politicians, he wrote, "were quite shrewd enough to appreciate that, after this, any detailed recommendations made by the Commission, however carefully thought out, must lose much of their original force." Thus British politicians, who often criticized Indians for lack of orderly procedure, presented their own spectacle of disarray. Eventually, the gaffe was glossed over, and the work went on.[30]

Indian revenues paid the commission's principal expenses, some $146,000. For their money, Indian taxpayers got a highly provisional proposal that allowed for both hope and skepticism. An all-India federation, ideally, would include the Princely States. Burma would be cut away. Dyarchy would end. Provincial self-government would be "an experiment in the application of the British parliamentary system—with restrictions and qualifications." The central government must remain strong because "the danger of disorder in India is ever present," and "the only practical way" to protect minorities was "impartial power" for the Viceroy and provincial governors. But—what was really changed? British troops remained; Viceroy and governors kept emergency powers.[31]

Lyon received a copy of a long Government of India dispatch: "What a lot people do write! It is almost better to let them talk." Parliament talked at length but not much to the point. Many columns of the *Parliamentary Debates* contain more of uncertainty than of information. When would the commission convene in London? Would the Princely States and Opposition

British parties be represented? No one was certain. If represented, wou• they be on equal terms with other delegations? No one knew. Would Indi delegations exclude anyone who signed some other report or served (another committee? No one knew.[32]

In the public prints, few explanations really sufficed. Ratcliffe's pamphle *What the Simon Report Means,* was an exception. He stated baldly th "Dyarchy was distrusted from the outset" because it promised genuir responsibility only in theory. The commissioners' failure to explain domi ion, he said, was their way of dissociating themselves from the Viceroy premature declaration.[33]

Andrews published *India and the Simon Report,* which, like *The Oth• Side of the Medal,* set out to explain educated Indians' resentment. Unfort nately, he overdoes his apologia for Gandhi's approach to national salvatic by spinning wheel. Edward thought that it was "time [Andrews] dropp• talking about our sin . . . & tried to remember that there was more than o1 intransigent or sinning group involved." He "influenced only a certain kir of Americans." However, Andrews made two important points. First, Birke head's stubbornness, against advice, in appointing a "white" commission w a fatal mistake and a deadly insult. Second, when the English failed to secu1 cooperation from even moderate Liberals, "who had stood by the Gover ment all through the earlier non-cooperation movement," they lost India• who might have given good advice but now "stood aside on principle."[34]

Churchill, utterly opposed to tampering with the basis of empire, gru1 bled ill-naturedly that a conference should occur at all. He badgered the BB for airtime, but it refused to be commandeered. He declared that the who• Indian enterprise was in ruins; England must begin again from the beginnin On 12 December he made a "mischievous speech" before the Indian Empi1 Society, convened expressly for disapproval. "We will leave Mr. Church alone," said the Prime Minister. "But if he will take my advice he will n• repeat it."[35]

Well-wishers who believed in the saving influence of the Moderates ha seen their hopes dashed when the Indian National Congress boycotted tr conference. Of eighty-six delegates to London, fifty-seven represented Britis India, thirteen represented Britain itself, and sixteen the Princely State Garratt asked, "[W]hat on earth can one say about the Conference, so ma1 tired, so many old, so many quite declassé; and has can the whole [of] India women, though they are 9 per cent less than the men, produce no or except two"—both unofficial visitors in his view unqualified. The conferenc formally convened on 19 November 1930 with no adjustments to the list.[3]

This first conference adjourned in January 1931, to reconvene on 1 September. It had an air of dishevelment, much of it due to Gandhi. He ha met with Lord Irwin, the Viceroy, and their conversation became know•

as the Delhi Pact. It appointed Gandhi "absolute selector" of Congress delegates. He then demanded Indian independence with "a kind of semi-contractual alliance applying to the things other than war." "Semi-" was a dangling danger signal. On 17 April 1931 Lord Willingdon replaced Lord Irwin. It transpired that Gandhi selected himself to represent Congress but wavered about going. On 22 August, twenty-seven delegates sailed for London, without Gandhi. A week later he changed his mind. On 5 September a sendoff at Bombay (the *Spectator* observed sourly) resembled "a prima donna's farewell to her art."[37]

He reached London on 12 September and immediately swept off to a series of receptions. Edward observed that he "let himself be overworked," so that his usual self-possession faltered. The morning of the thirteenth he came to Boars Hill with three followers. He was already exhausted. While the others ate breakfast, Theo found him asleep over his spinning wheel in front of the drawing-room fire. After A. D. Lindsay, Michael Sadler, Gilbert Murray, Lyon, and Coupland administered "a three hours' heckling . . . a reasonably exacting ordeal" under which Edward thought him "very game and gallant," he rushed away to several peripheral meetings. "At our house," Edward wrote, "he emphasized the honour that would be India's if she won freedom without recourse to violence. I replied that it would be an equal distinction for my own people." Gandhi certainly "had exercised a restraining influence on his followers. But the last few years have seen him growingly egocentric, increasingly tolerant of lapses from the incredibly lofty ideals associated with his name. He is not the man he was."[38]

The conference now seemed set to proceed more smoothly, although Gandhi's Monday silences upset the schedule. He now called himself Commonwealth citizen, not British subject. He suggested that the communal problem—separate legislative representation and quotas for minority electorates—be set aside until the new constitution was operative, after which all problems would presumably melt away. But no constitution would work *until* the communal problem was solved. It became, and remained, the make-or-break issue.

"No, there is little chance of Hindu Nationalists accepting a communal electorates settlement—" Edward wrote to V. S. Sastri, "which is what we are going to have. The cardinal error British opinion makes, is in regarding Moslems as a 'minority'—they are *not* one, in N. Western India—& in ignoring the fact that Moslems are 'bad Indians,' i.e., are always looking outside India. On the other hand, some of the movements within the Mahasabha mean only civil war. Anyway, what can your English friends do? Tell us. I have been summoned to the great Gandhi's presence again, next Sunday. I like & admire him. But he flies off on the Muslim side. However, what sound doctrine do you want preached to him?"[39]

The Hindu delegates disagreed with one another, and Edward's limite optimism faded fast. In the second of two *Spectator* articles, he observe that Gandhi, "having come as sole Congress delegate, regretted his isolatio and pressed for the last-minute inclusion of Dr. Ansari, a moderate membe of the Muslim League." The Muslim delegates opposed him, partly becaus they resented Gandhi's maneuvering, while the press scolded the Hindus fc " 'trying to sow dissension in Muslim ranks.' " The outsider "may note furthe that Nemesis (the Hindus call it *karma*) has been over all these proceeding The Nationalists of the Hindu side began blackballing when they demande the exclusion of Sir John Simon from the Conference. Since then both side have been heresy-hunting."[40]

By November the conference had run down in discouragement and di agreements. A new constitution seemed more elusive than ever. There wei two terrorist "outrages" in India. Nothing could have sown more seriou doubts in England about India's ability to manage her own affairs. Th conference splintered still further. The Muslim delegates refused federatio until a communal settlement and allocation of electoral representative: Would a new government be responsible to a legislature at Delhi or to Secretary of State for India in London? The Moderates declared that the would not have come if they had known that they were to approve provinci autonomy without some responsibility as well for a central government; th Prime Minister must insist on responsibilities for *both* the central and th provincial legislatures. Over everything hung that premature declaration i 1929 of dominion status.

The conference's failure was plain to all, as was Gandhi's failure to tr for conciliation. He had only alienated the Indian minorities and lost som responsible English sympathies. No one knew what position he would tak when back in India. In Rome, on his way home, he announced a new boyco and noncooperation campaign. The Government of India announced h arrest. When there might be another effort at rapprochement, no one knev

20

FAREWELL AND HAIL

The irony of Edward Thompson's 1930s was that he published a novel, *A Farewell to India,* then visited India three times. The title elicited pungent comment from Gandhi:

> "They tell me, Mr. Thompson, that you have published a book entitled *A Farewell to India?*"
> "That is so, Mahatmaji."
> "Well, it seems to me that you have been wasting your time again. How do you think that you are ever going to say farewell to India? You are India's prisoner."[1]

This was true. Although he wanted to avoid just "a stewing up of old India memories," India was still the subject he knew best, and the emotional pull was still strong. India was an unfinished puzzle. He cared very much about a solution—in the intervals of venting exasperation by claiming that he wanted no more to do with India.

A Farewell to India may be read as sequel to *An Indian Day.* It rewards examination because it tells so much about his attitude toward Gandhi. It returns to Vishnugram and Robert Alden, missionary teacher of English literature; his old friend John Findlay, now, after the deaths of his wife and daughter, withdrawn to the Santal hills; Vincent Hamar, the judge, now married to Alden's sister Hilda; and Jayananda, Oxford-educated former I.C.S. man and revolutionary turned forest sannyasi and guru. There is an extremist Nationalist with the nom de guerre Dinabandhu, which means "friend of the poor." (It was also a popular name for Andrews.) Fictional time, here 1929, is identifiable from references to Gandhi's revived noncooperation and imprisonment, to the Simon Commission, to an imminent Round Table Conference, to Swarajist-inspired student strikes, and to the National Congress declaration of its Independence Day for 26 January 1929. Alden muses on the zeitgeist exactly as Thompson had done during his term as Acting Principal at Bankura:

> Say it's the hot weather, say it's the folly of trying to run education with everyone bitter and with strikes coming for every trivial thing that happens anywhere in India. But there's something stirring that's getting on our nerves. You can't use guns against it as you could do once. You have got to remain

decent, however indecent the other side is. What can you do about it? You can
fight it, you can't even see it most of the time. But it's there. We are living in
another age. We haven't a new technique, and we are afraid to use the old one
that we learnt in the age that has gone.[2]

A Farewell opens with Alden fleeing another of the pompous scho
ceremonies that always destroyed Thompson's academic composure. Farc
quickly becomes tragedy. In quick succession an enigmatic note threaten
fire; a student is beaten and another's face cruelly mutilated; kerosene
poured but not ignited in a supposedly unused hostel; and there is anothe
fire note in an unused college residence that is a meeting place for terrori
plotters. At real risk to his life, Alden discovers their bomb cache and disrup
their plan, but he knows that they will reconstitute it somewhere else.

Dinabandhu's expression is "a compound of conceit, enthusiasm, ins
lence, and uncertainty. . . ." The enthusiasm was attractive, and "at time
there came into his eyes a lofty flame of selfless vision that composed i
flaws and gave it peace." But when Alden encounters him at Jayananda
retreat, he sees only conceit and insolence. Sujit Mukherjee says, "Alde
regards Dinabandhu as emergent India's greatest danger, and the narrativ
poses them as antagonists though they do not actually join combat." But the
do have a crucial conversational combat in the presence of Jayananda an
Findlay. For Dinabandhu, full independence justifies any means. He argue
" 'The English can be fought down with their own weapons of brutality an
murder. They cannot be reasoned with.' He had flung out political India
most dangerous and tenaciously held belief." To which Alden replies: "Som
of you think you can go on murdering isolated Englishmen for ever—an
then staging wholesale agitation to have everyone accused set free." Ind
could be a dominion and "enter peaceful partnership with the rest of th
Empire" or she could turn to assassination and guerilla warfare. " 'Peacefr
partnership!' The Nationalist passed beyond all control in his anger. 'You
condescension is your worst insolence of all!' "[3]

Dinabandhu cites the Irish example. Alden asks whether the Nationalis
plan to buy their goal with their lives or with the lives of others: "I wond
which of you has the magnanimity to become India's Michael Collins. Deat
at the hands of England seems a grand going out. . . . But for some of yo
it will be death at the hands of your own side." When he says that bot
sides must sacrifice toward a peaceful solution, Dinabandhu is withering
scornful; blood acquired India and blood would free India: "Do you thin
we are afraid of being shot down by your machine-guns?" In a towering rag
he leaves.[4]

Alden sees that he has failed to make his point. Where had he gone wrong
He had argued, Jayananda says, like an old-time paternalist, and asks, "Wh

nakes you so tactless, Alden?" Dinabandhu was not a "mild Hindu" and cared nothing for Hindu beliefs. He regarded Gandhi's nonviolence as a fad "useful with the world outside, especially since America has persuaded herself into a pacifist mood and looks on Gandhi as a saint." Jayananda chides Alden: "You English never learn that the age has moved until it is too late. Your diehards are still on the old chatter about Indian agitation being the work of a few half-baked clerks." He reminds Alden of proofs in his college. Dinabandhu's followers had mutilated his student. They regarded Alden as a fool and therefore dispensable. Findlay interposes that there will be peace "when the unbragging India comes face to face with the unbragging England. . . . God help her when she comes to that council-table. For she wants to be decent and honest and fair."[5]

Belatedly, Findlay and Alden realize that they had happened in upon Dinabandhu's effort to persuade Jayananda to return as terrorist, a career begun after he left the I.C.S. and, at Lord Curzon's 1901 Durbar for the Prince of Wales, had had a shocking moment of imperial insight. That spectacle had "a kind of intangible and immaterial mockery running under the show—" It was above all humiliating: "an alien pageant, for which India was paying. On the outskirts were our multitudes of spindle-shanked and eye-sunken folk." The Viceroy's demand for their homage shamed only him, as did the English ladies showing off their finery and fussing about knighthoods for their husbands. But the Viceroy did not know that he should be ashamed, nor was he rebuked when one of the Indian princes, gorgeously robed and bejewelled, turned away abruptly after doing homage, his expression all contempt and hatred. The English saw "only conquered India that had been at pains to dress itself up in its best and most honourable. And they broke into more than tittering—it was open guffaws." Yet they saw nothing ridiculous in British high officials' elaborate official get-up of medals, plumes, and ribbons, "all the paraphernalia that your particular civilisation has sanctioned and idealised." It was then that Jayananda had turned to terrorism.[6]

Thompson has neatly transposed elements of Hardinge's 1911 coronation Durbar for George V, back in time to Curzon's grand 1901 Durbar for the Prince of Wales: the jockeying for preferred positions in the Durbar camps, a "show" for Indians on the outskirts, and the obeisance of the Maharaja of Gwalior in 1911, considered so inadequate as to require a letter of apology.

Alden and Findlay tell Jayananda of rumors that he may return to the political extremists. He is silent, "and in that silence he finally dismissed the temptation that had found him in his wilderness." Industrialized India would never return to the village and spinning wheel. " 'I tell you, Gandhiji has seen something that has frightened him.' "[7]

A Farewell to India explicates that "something" and also Thompson's own ambivalences about Gandhi's India. In the novel, Gandhi tours Bengal's educational centers, "leaving a ripple of college strikes in his wake." The president of Vishnugram's Independent Students' Association announces strike in Gandhi's honor. He intends to speak there, and Alden must kee his word to expel strikers. But "even from Mr. Gandhi's point of view wrecking the college was pointless, for it was a missionary, not a governmer institution, and the government would never miss it. Thompson thinks (Gandhi's actions that helped to disable the Round Table Conference: "Bu [Alden] knew that Mr. Gandhi was living by instinct and passion, and no by reason any longer. To him the College represented Western and moder education, which had emasculated the people."[8]

Gandhi addresses a Vishnugram gathering at the rail station, but no stu dents attend. Thompson's mixed feelings of disapproval and grudging adm ration come out in Alden's account of how he "saw and heard a man wh had ceased to be one of us, and had become an elemental being—a gus blowing up from the earth, a passion enclosed (and barely enclosed) in wisened, worn-out body."

> [Alden] listened to economics that were twenty years and more out of date, and their mistakes were as nothing beside the fact that centuries of poverty an exploitation had found a voice. Through a human reed suffering was speaking– not its own, but a nation's. . . . Behind the speaker were forces of ruin, which he was serving, though aware of them, and anxious to escape them. "The man fey," he thought. "It is no longer Gandhiji that is speaking, but something that i going to burst into the Age, and shatter it."

Alden trembles, "as a skilled oarsman might when he first heard Niagara He wished that the English could have been Gandhi's friends: "I know he' wrong, yet I daren't say he's wrong. Frankly, I don't understand what I'v been watching in India these last twenty years. I doubt if they'll understand a century from now. No, of course they won't, though they'll write about i as slickly as they do now."[9]

Was Edward among the slick writers? Gone was the cockiness of earl Bankura days, when he had preached from a biblical text thoughtless chosen, and anonymous notes about the "white-skinned Gods of the College had appeared on the notice board. That had passed off, Edward had the thought, with jokes and no hard feelings. But the incident had hidden i memory, and out it came in *A Farewell to India* with the darker shading that the younger Edward had missed. On Alden's private notice board ther appears "a virulent, ill-spelled attack on 'the white-skinned gods of th College.' When the tint of his skin was flung in his face, he knew how inflamed feelings were. . . . The students, when they came back, hung abou the corridors, with the half-defiant, half-timid, hatred-charged look that h knew too well." There had been real hatred at Bankura in 1910, but Edward had been too new to catch the signals.[10]

He attributes to Vincent Hamar almost exactly the words that he himself once wrote to Lyon: " 'Yes,' said Vincent, thinking, 'I suppose I am a bit proud to belong to the austerest tradition the world has seen since the Greeks.' " Hamar tells Hilda that there is nothing austere about Alden, but Hilda observes that Alden " 'keeps his hair-shirt out of sight.' "[11]

Some reviewers were bothered that the novel began in uncertainty and insecurity and ended with everyone feeling uncertain and insecure. That, of course, was Thompson's point. He had seen India at several stages and had arrived at "the complicated and equivocal situation in which she finds herself today." He marks the "too many unreal, factitious protestations and grievances" substituted for the real problems.[12]

A Farewell to India has the shortcomings of much of Thompson's fiction writing: a distracting dissertative quality results when the preacher overcomes the novelist. Conversations (especially women's) are often cloyingly arch and the plot sometimes too obviously contrived. But the author's sincerity and authoritativeness redeem many of the faults. In 1986 David Rubin suggested his work as a model for novelists who deal with cultural conflict in developing countries: "Edward Thompson . . . confronts the prevailing British myths regarding India and shatters them. . . . It is the attempt to avoid generalizations and to come instead to grips with experience . . . that distinguishes Thompson's fiction from that of most of his Anglo-Indian contemporaries."[13]

Even while in America, Edward had thought of visiting India again. He had heard that the Rhodes Trustees had £250 available for someone to assess the extent of intellectual cooperation there. Being neither full college Fellow nor Tutor, he doubted his eligibility for Rhodes funds. Nevertheless he applied for a traveling fellowship from December 1931 to May 1932. Lord Lothian, Secretary to the Trustees, noted his status but thought it "a good thing for a man possessed of Thompson's knowledge and experience of India and gift of writing and general outlook to visit India say next cold weather in order to give Oxford the latest information about India and to interpret it more widely through his writing to public opinion in Great Britain and elsewhere." He had neither met Thompson nor mentioned the application to the Trustees, but he asked the historian Sir Reginald Coupland to "take the opportunity of looking in on him sometime and sounding him on the subject and letting me know what his position is?" Coupland did so promptly and reported that Thompson wanted " 'to investigate the lines on which a reconstruction of Indian provincial boundaries is desirable, so as to foster the local nationalism whose emergence along with the literary activity of the eleven great vernaculars has been one of the most important (though

least noted) features of the last thirty years.' " Thompson would seek ou
Indian writers and "find out what we can do to establish genuine India
studies in the West (other than Sanskrit and Pali studies) and to convinc
Indian intellectuals that English and the English language are not doors barre
between them and the outside world but [are] open ways." Too many India
writers wasted time and energy on political propaganda " 'instead of buildin
up their own nation and literature.' " The Round Table Conference had failec
therefore let literature try. Lothian noted that there was "a good deal to b
said for encouraging Mr. Thompson," for he had written "widely and wisely
about India, and sending him would serve "partly to enable him to kee
Oxford in touch with current events and partly so that he could act as a
interpreter of these events to a wider field of readers." Coupland added tha
"Thompson helps to keep Oxford opinion sane on India, and his going woul
be good for everyone—the Indians included." He got the money.[14]

When he thanked the Trustees, Edward added, "But I know that almos
anything can be accomplished in India by private negotiation with the righ
people—which is why I feel we are getting near the limit of what can be don
by Round Table Conferences. It is now the turn of private negotiation."[15]

Perhaps, Edward told Lyon, some liaison with Indian intellectuals woul
"lighten the political atmosphere and also keep some very active people ou
of mischief." This was not a canny political insertion, but a statement of har
fact. The Dinabandhus of India, unhappy and destructively single-minded
were those "very active people," intelligent but impatient, who skewed th
situation with the less productive methods of protest such as strike, boycott
and assassination.[16]

Edward went also as special correspondent for the *Manchester Guardian*
He told C. P. Scott, its editor, "My main purpose is quite unpolitical, but
believe the political movement will be too interesting for me to keep quit
aloof. . . . I believe I can find out as much of the truth as most men, for
know most of the leaders of all parties in India." Scott requested an articl
every ten days or so.[17]

He sailed on 29 December 1931. Theo went to Beirut, while Frank wa
at Winchester on a scholarship and Palmer at the Dragon School in Oxford
Edward's journey out was already an eye-opener. Except for Geoffry Garrat
and his wife, fellow passengers also bound for India, the others struck hin
as seriously inferior individuals, a deterioration from even prewar shipboarc
society. Also on board was a *Daily Express* correspondent, "v. ignorant
& v. mischievous," who tried to pump them. Edward thought the Britisl
passengers "an appalling crowd," with the crudest views of India and Britisl
politics: "I had fooled myself into thinking these folk scarcer than they are.'
Garratt did not envy him his assignment, "traipsing around a sullen & angry
India in quest of intellectual cooperation." There was little enough of tha

on board. Everyone there had heard that the government intended to put its foot down on terrorists. "My own fear," Edward wrote, "is that it is going to put it down on a banana peel."[18]

Thompson and Garratt shared, besides experience of India and Mesopotamia, the view of India's problems as the consequence of a long series of missed opportunities for both British and Indians. Garratt's *An Indian Commentary*, which Edward had reviewed while in America, sets forth with masterly concision the misjudgments and procedural dead ends that had led to the present impasse. Garratt, as Political Secretary to the Round Table, had thought that "this wretched conference with the hand of death on it is dragging out its weary length like a moribund boa constrictor." Indians would accept only " 'safeguards for the interim period' " until key issues were resolved—an interim that could drag its own weary length into years. They agreed that Gandhi "enlisted the most incompatible forces beneath his banner of home rule, and cared little what terms they demand," with disastrous results, and also that communal electorates must go and that only the English could get rid of them. "Progress" need not necessarily follow English lines; and the British, with no goal, only stalled and drifted. The information gap was still unbridged, if not unbridgeable. Before they left England, they had proposed to Macmillan a history of modern India since the founding of the East India Company in 1599. This would become *The Rise and Fulfilment of British Rule in India,* which they would finish by 1934.[19]

Upon landing, the Garratts continued to Calcutta. Edward stayed in Bombay with M. R. Jayakar, who had been on the Round Table Conference subcommittee on federation. His hospitality was "princely." Reporters from the *Times of India* and other papers came for interviews about Edward's "mission." "The words 'cultural cooperation' have made Bombay go straight up in the air," he wrote to Scott. "I am telephoned, telegraphed, written to, & generally driven to the edge of a break-down. My desk is piled high with correspondence of all sorts, from an earnest wire from H.H. of Bikaner urging me to come & shoot some of his grouse to a wire from the Punjab Literary Society urging me to come & lecture to them." He felt himself "swiftly drifting into a false position," nervous because so many Indians seemed to view him "as an all-powerful emissary from the University of Oxford, the League of Nations, and God Almighty. It is no use saying I am only Edward Thompson making enquiries. It is pathetic, this belief that an Englishman can do what he likes, if he only has the will; & this anxiety to get respected by the outside world." The Bombay police were on the alert. As honored guests, Edward and Jayakar attended the opening of a Marathi play. The manager, his hands joined in supplication, begged them to make no speeches, for "the police had sent word that we were to keep quiet." "The Indian Governments are not wicked, as many suppose," Edward wrote, "but there is a good deal of evidence that they are sometimes half-witted." What earthly harm was there if either of them had "spoken a few words of encouragement to Marathi playwrights"? Later, he learned in Delhi that "this particular piece of stupidity had been unauthorised." It seemed trivial, but it showed how Indians had to endure government's suspicions of anything that might contribute to rapprochement.[20]

It was difficult to fend off distractions without being rude when "sullen men and women" brought manuscripts "for wh. they want English publishers" or hoped to capitalize on his *Guardian* connection. He soon learned, when signing official guest books, not to connect himself with it, after the identification as "Special Correspondent" brought "two heavy scoldings for association with a notoriously sinful paper." He had to attend a party in his honor by a Bombay dabbler in the arts, "a bitter, silly, enormously wealthy woman" who corresponded with equally silly women in England and wanted to make Edward her "English disciple & agent." At Wilson College he got a lesson in the difficulty of conveying to student audiences his message of intellectual cooperation. The young professor who invited him had deplored "my activities since *The Other Side of the Medal*"—presumably his *Spectator* articles. He said, " 'It seemed to me that it was a different Edward Thompson.' " Edward managed to give "(amid much friendly jeering and interruption) a desultory talk on the R. T. Conference, then submitted to a fierce and not always courteous heckling. It was all mad & exhausting but did not worry me." If they disagreed with him, they hissed. "When I said 'Mr. Gandhi' they shouted & shouted 'Mahatma Gandhi.' They were quite impossible." The professor scolded them "impassionedly, but they only laughed. They rather pride themselves on the fact that a hearing is now refused to everyone who is not out-and-out Congress." The principal later told Jayakar that Edward had told them much that "no one else wd or cd. have told them, & that he stood up to them magnificently." Wryly, Jayakar advised a fiery antigovernment speech as the key to real popularity. In such an atmosphere, intellectual cooperation had to fight hard for a hearing. The Bombay Students Association begged him to address them, but he declined.[21]

He attended a meeting of Congress Party workers. Mira Behn (Madeleine Slade), Gandhi's English disciple, scolded Edward severely for "bothering about 'intellectual cooperation,' when only politics matter." To do real good, she thought, he should lead a procession to a protest meeting, get arrested, and go to prison. She was bitter about his staying "with the wrong people (i.e. non-Congress), v. opinionated & bigoted as to who knew 'the real India.' Jayakar says, 'It is damned cheek of an Englishwoman to think she knows more about my country than I do.' " Later Mira Behn showed kindness, but Edward found her impervious to humor and irony. However, the Congress workers and the Bombay students were not the whole picture. Edward found that "India is keeping open house for me, only the officials being v. suspicious and aloof." He was "embarrassingly famous," the target of "letters, wires, & mss. from everywhere." It was flattering, but he began to feel like "merely another kind of missionary, more hard pressed & worked."[22]

When he got free of reporters, supplicants, Congress followers, and aspiring hostesses, he did what he had come to do. He had long talks with vernacular writers, about English aid and publicity that would benefit them. He met with a group of millionaire Parsi businessmen and spent two days with the Maharajah of Baroda, an interval of kindness so lavish as to seem humiliating. These were not frivolous diversions but time invested in possible financial contributions to scholarships and other kinds of intellectual cooperation. Jayakar insisted that Edward must travel first class when visiting such personages, but his budget did not permit that luxury; he kept to second class and arranged his own affairs.

The farther he went, the more certain he was that "what is chiefly wrong with Govt. is, it has wretched publicity. It does not publish its reasons for the innumerable arrests; & has quite failed to convince the people that it means business in the Reforms." He visited Gandhi's prison, talked with his jailer, and reported him "well and happy" and rather pleased than otherwise that "God has been good to him in causing him to be arrested just when a breakdown was imminent." Edward interviewed the Viceroy and others in the central government. He found the typical I.C.S. district officer "sane & tolerant & decent, as a rule," but higher officials were "watchful & suspicious. I have only to mention the word 'Manchester Guardian' to be immediately obstructed. If I said 'Daily Express' I shd. be helped." However, he failed "to convince any of them that they shd. negotiate with Gandhi. H[is] E[xcellency] usually referred to him as 'this little devil'—. . . ." Edward insisted on the importance of negotiation, "if only because Congress (the Bengal Congress) is up to the neck in with the terrorists, & Gandhi *shd.* be made to see that his honour is concerned in this murder campaign. However, they're sure that they are winning," and they did not trust Gandhi. Edward was certain that "this arresting of 600 people daily without any plan as to what is to be done with them later is useless."[23]

He reported to the Rhodes Trustees upon return. He had not been to South India because he had stayed longer than he had intended in the cities of North India. In general, he regarded public meetings as "practically always a waste of time," but they were unavoidable, and he addressed crowded gatherings in Baroda, Amritsar, Indore, Agra, and Calcutta, and each increased his floods of mail. At Bombay and Lahore he spoke to three consecutive meetings in one day. Publicity was essential, not for himself, but for his message. In *A Letter from India,* which appeared simultaneously with submission of his *Report,*

he wrote that Bengali Moderates "count for nothing" and had no statesmen t
stand with leaders like Jayakar and Ambedkar, the leader of the Untouchables
Moderate leaders from Bombay and Madras had "some sort of influence," bu
"Bengal, so far as Delhi is concerned, is a foreign country." Bengalis though
themselves calm and self-possessed, but Edward found the middle and uppe
classes "tense and close to hysteria." Government had no practical remedy fo
economic distress. The gulf between educated Bengalis and Anglo-Indian
was as wide as ever; yet "the two races if they mingled could not fail to fin
mutual pleasure and esteem"; instead, they saw one another through thei
own extremist newspapers. "The whole thing is villainous nonsense."[24]

Politics was his secondary concern, but its effects on the intellectual scen
were unavoidable. More than contacts with great men such as Iqbal an
Tagore, he valued his "very numerous" meetings with impatient younge
writers. He found "the writers over 35 years of age, however active they ma
have been in former political agitations, are now almost to a man anxious fo
a settlement by discussion; but the young men and the college students ar
against such a settlement, and you may take it that very few of the latter (th
college students) seriously disapprove of even political assassination. I an
by no means as optimistic about the political outlook as most people seen
to be." He had met only one government official who agreed with him.[25]

The younger Bengali writers made him very uneasy. They seemed to have
jettisoned old traditions without assessing the replacement.

> The most influential young writers are "realist." They have finished with the
> kind of literature usually considered "Oriental," poetry on the loves of Radha an
> Krishna or addressed to the goddess Durga. They write Bengali far simpler and
> more direct than has been considered good literary style hitherto. They avoid an
> detest the pictorial and the picturesque. They know European literature well an
> follow it closely. They speak English with almost absurd faultlessness and many
> of them have an "Oxford manner"; though they have been educated in Calcutta
> The authors they admire are our most modern and iconoclastic. Many of their
> writings have shocked orthodox Bengali opinion greatly, and often with justice
> Some of their group are dirty-minded, and think that the body's necessities and
> sexual habits are the only things worth writing about. Others think that only
> what is repellent or ugly is fit matter for art.[26]

What had happened in Bengal would inevitably happen elsewhere. Gu
jarat, for instance, on the western coast, "copies Bengali literature closely
and translations from Bengali pour out from Gujarat presses." A modernis
movement was "much occupied with erotic themes in poetry," with "a goo
deal of the cinema" in it, and "there will be more if these tongues do no
get any standards up to which writers can measure themselves. The revol
would be slower in Urdu because of Muslim puritanism, but even there

the *form* was changing," and "poets are disentangling themselves from the Persian models that have hitherto kept the language in a secondary position and status."[27]

His meeting with Tagore was unsatisfactory. Mrs. Garratt wanted to see him, and they found him at an exhibition of his paintings, which Edward thought were *"most absurd."* Tagore "sat in a room behind, purring as he laps up the cream of praise. We saw him, but he & I were barely on speaking terms. He has slandered me all over India, & I was not going to pretend to be enthusiastic."[28]

It was a pity that Edward and Tagore did not meet at a happier time and in a more favorable setting. Tagore was having a bad year, and his estrangement was more political than artistic. He disapproved of both Gandhi's imprisonment and his belief in fasting as political pressure. In early August, the government in London plumped for the controversial communal award: separate electorates and quotas on the Legislative Councils for representation of Hindus and Muslims and some other minorities, including the Untouchables.

Thompson and Tagore did agree wholeheartedly, while Tagore and Gandhi disagreed, about the importance of intellectual cooperation. "The root of the difference was twofold," Dutta and Robinson say. "Tagore believed educational and cultural progress to be more worthwhile than political work. Secondly, he had faith in cooperation with the West so that Indians might absorb its best aspects, including its scientific knowledge. He instinctively rejected rejection." Thompson said the same when he told the Rhodes Trustees that "the political controversy [is] a wasteful and misleading simplification."[29]

Tagore would have shared Edward's dismay about some of the younger writers. Edward thought it a "flaw in our administration that there is no sort of liaison between the Government of Bengal and this very modern school, even more that there is no suspicion in the European community [in India] that it exists. These writers are very sensitive to Western opinion and immense good would be done even politically if their self-respect could be helped by the feeling that their intellectual effort was not an isolated and unknown thing but recognised as part of the Empire's life." Thompson implies that Tagore's message failed to reach the younger writers. Like Buddhadeva Bose, many in the post-Tagore generation acknowledged his supreme influence for change and regeneration, but still younger writers were impatient, although they could not escape his influence. Bengali and other Indian writers discarded old models without tolerance for the liberation that the forebears had made possible. Here is a touching instance of history repeated: Tagore in his day had been accused of outrageous realism and of unacceptably simplifying the language. A revolution in cultural permissiveness separated his extremely oblique treatments of sexual relations from the aggressive frankness of the new writers. Still, like him, they "have brought new vigour and new subjects into Bengali literature." They wrote of the rapidly industrializing areas, of the aboriginal tribes and outcastes.[30]

Edward made seven practical suggestions: an exhibition of Indian art, to include works by living artists such as the Tagore brothers; a yearbook of Indian literature to survey the year's vernacular achievements; Oxford Press collections of vernacular verse; a "kind of Nobel Prize for India"; annual prizes for Indian writing, analogous to the Hawthornden Prize and the Prix Goncourt; lectureships at British universities; and translations of the best books from the vernaculars. Efforts to those ends had mixed results. Humphrey Milford, for Oxford Press, said that no one had ever before explained a yearbook of Indian literature "as an Imperial service"—but it must have subvention. Robert Witt wrote dubiously from the Courtauld Institute about difficulties of organization and financial support for an art exhibition. The idea of a university lecture on India fared better; the Rhodes Trustees offered support. Herbert Fisher, Warden of New College, advised that it should advance " 'the knowledge of Indian humanities.' " Edward approved, for "we have had too much of Indian religion," as of politics and Indian philology and ancient languages ("already we have these studies they are *all* we have). But the whole field of the vernacular literatures, of Indian history, nationalities, manners, is open."[31]

Edward concluded by saying that he had "written far more coldly than I feel." British-Indian relations that were only administrative and political "except for the interest of the big game hunter and of our commercial houses" were too narrow to be safe. Some obstructive old notions should be discarded, such as the belief that Tagore's honorary degree was turned down "because of prejudice against his Nationalism"; the truth was more subtle: he probably feared being turned down. Everywhere Edward had found enthusiasm for friendly contacts, and a little goodwill would mean so much to Indian writers, major and minor. At the center of their estrangement was the feeling that England had never taken them seriously.[32]

On the whole, the tone of the *Report* was somber, and the editor and scholar Humayun Kabir, when he read *A Letter from India*, thanked Edward for his concern but rebuked him for his pessimism. True, India at the moment was a "spiritual Jalianwala with the Govt. commanding the only exit." India's condition, though bad, was not hopeless. Bad laws must be exposed, if only to explode the old notion of Britain as trustee for India. He thought Edward too hard on Gandhi: "a muddleheaded politician in many ways," but always honest. Edward did not argue about Gandhi's integrity; the muddleheadedness dismayed him. Edward had cited Dyer's own excuse that he did not go to Jallianwala determined to shoot. This, Kabir insisted, left him neither less guilty nor less capable of shooting. However, they agreed that India needed "a bold and constructive policy of progress."[33]

Nevertheless. Edward *was* pessimistic. The Round Table's collapse was sufficiently dispiriting, and his tour had seemed to set him apart from India as he had known it. On shipboard he and Garratt had felt like a minority of two. At the Marathi play he was a police target. The Bombay students had openly jeered him as his more repressed Bankura students had never dared to do. His status as *Guardian* correspondent had been trampled. When Mira Behn scolded him for associating with Jayakar, whom he considered one of India's conservative but sincere well-wishers, what became of his own image as well-wisher? When with the Parsi millionaires and the Maharaja of Baroda, the imperial relationship had been turned on its head: he was the supplicant, not the one who presented demands and terms. If Bengal was a "foreign country" to the Delhi government, it now seemed even more so to him; in the political climate of estrangement, his intimate knowledge of the Bengali countryside's flora and his ability to get along with the country people counted for nothing. Relations with Tagore were more ambivalent than ever. Edward's pessimism caused Allen J. Greenberger, in *The British Image of India,* to count him among the doubters who wrote with deepening misgivings about Britain's future in South Asia, along with Forster, Candler, and an increasing number of others. Alden/Thompson knew that the Nationalists had legitimate complaints, but "he does not believe that the nationalists have the right answer. This seeing of both sides and finding them wanting is a part of the total pessimission of this period." India's prisoner had had glimpses of himself through the eyes of the tribunal, and what he saw dismayed him.[34]

21

FOLLOWING LORD METCALFE

Soon after he returned, Edward had still mo
surgery on his leg. Potentially more serious was his digestive trouble, wit
him ever since Bankura, where everyone simply assumed that "Bankura w:
notorious for dyspepsia." He was nearly ill during a visit to the Lyonses, an
Lady Mary Murray scolded him for not seeing a doctor. He had seen several, t
no effect, and one gave him a book on nervous indigestion that contradicte
everything he had heard about it. It warned of cancer. That morning he ha
noticed bleeding, not for the first time, but ascribed it to "starch indigestion
The doctor prescribed "absolute brain rest" and a medication to dissolve th
starch. Edward wished he had sought help earlier but hesitated to spen
money on himself when family needs were pressing.

Foremost among those was the need to do something about Scar To
Depression inroads on Theo's American income had made maintenance (
house and grounds too expensive. They could rent furnished or unfurnishec
Or they could sell and seek a more modest place farther from Oxford. Edwar
stipulated that it *not* be in hunting country. Elaborate shooting parties fc
dignitaries visiting India, with the game already staked out for their shot:
had exacerbated his aversion to killing, whether tigers or foxes.

There were also the costs of the boys' education. Frank did well at Wincl
ester, but no Indian parent surveying a son's future was more anxious than Ec
ward was about Palmer's chances for a preparatory school scholarship. The
tended to think his worries exaggerated; Palmer, she thought, was doing we
enough; he seemed to dawdle along cheerfully although his marks wer
below scholarship range. If that continued, Edward asked in desperatior
where would be the £250 or £300 for public-school fees? Obviously, wha
drove his worries were thoughts of the Oxbridge scholarship examination
that he had missed when uprooted for work at the detested bank. Somehow
with or without scholarships, the kind of education that their father ha
missed must be available to both Frank and Palmer.

When Theo went for her annual visit to Syria, Palmer's reports worsened
What Edward really wanted for his sons was the self-confidence of being a
Oxford graduate, an Oxford insider. Oxford people seemed so supremel
confident in their self-sufficiency. At Oriel Edward was an outsider taken i

ɔn recommendation. His official Oxford connection was the Indian Institute, ɹarrow in its original conception and narrower still in its failure to keep ɪbreast of history. He was the institute's prisoner as well as India's.

This need for decisions came at a pivotal moment in his life. He failed ɪo get a Readership in Indian History at Balliol, then a Readership at Oriel, ɪlthough he had distinguished support for both. He thought the failures his personal demerit. Canton, had he been alive, would have told him not to be so foolish and to recognize what he had already accomplished. But Canton, Richards, and Rushbrooke all were gone, and Collingwood's death in 1932 ɪad ended that succession of older friends who had scolded and criticized, cajoled and encouraged.

He concentrated on writing. At first glance, three of his four books published between 1933 and 1936 may seem only a "stewing up" of India memories. They are not that, but a rounding off. He wrote *So a Poor Ghost,* another India novel. He and Garratt finished *The Rise and Fulfilment of British Rule in India.* He wrote *Introducing the Anisons,* one of two semi-autobiographical Wesleyan narratives; and he returned to Elizabethan history—not as fantasy like *The Enchanted Lady,* but a solid biography of Sir Walter Ralegh.

So a Poor Ghost brings Philip Rattray, a London liberal writer, back to the Princely State of Ryalgarh, whose Education Department he had served before the war, now to be commissioner of education for a neighboring state. He never gets there because of local and national government politics. He realizes to his surprise that he himself is one of India's ghosts and finds that he shares this realization with a retired general who has regarded him as a meddling socialist "writin' fellow." The general ought to be—and is—a caricature of imperial pomposity. But he reveals unexpected acuteness and "kindness of manner" when he tells Rattray, " 'I believe I'm gettin' to know you, Rattray, and how you feel. I thought, from what I'd heard, that you'd come back to India because you were a bolshy and wanted to make trouble. But I know now that you and I are kindred spirits. We *have* to have an excuse for comin' back, so *I* say I come for shootin', and *you* say you come as a writin' fellow. But we really come because we've got at home in this country, and we shall never feel at home—not really, absolutely at home—anywhere else.' " The Ryalgarh prince, Rattray, the general, and Edward all are India's ghosts, who will have no place in a new India. "I *intended,*" Edward told Lothian, "a nice jolly Central Indian open air sketch, a pot-boiler—& it has turned out thoroughly seditious! Now that cannot have been my own mind, for I know how soundly conservative it is . . . & how good my purposes were."[1]

Rise and Fulfilment surveys India's history from 1599, when "The Time of Trading" began during the first Elizabeth's reign and Drake, searching for the Spice Islands, declared "rights of prior discovery." The survey ends in

the twentieth century, with the Simon Commission, the Round Table Co
ference, the failure of dyarchy, and old issues in new and more urgent form
Indian participation in the civil service, in the army, in legislative bodie
It shows the British Raj as a hasty cobbling together of apparent solutior
that were simmering fuses to political bombs both metaphorical and litera
British officials, skeptical about all change, expected the administration t
deteriorate "until some drastic remedy was needed." Neither Thompson nc
Garratt would live to see the "drastic remedy" in 1947.[2]

Introducing the Arnisons is a family saga embedded in a meditation o
Wesleyan Methodism. The Arnisons are transparently the Thompsons. Th
narrator is John Arnison, eight years old when the narrative opens and th
eldest of five. The Methodism is his widowed mother's, literal-minded an
loving but generations removed from the realities of her children's lives. Sh
never understands, because he cannot tell her, how John hates Methodism
gory imagery of conditional salvation or doom for wanderers; the awft
record of one's every sin and wicked word kept inexorably up to date i
"thy dreadful book"; the spiritual blackmail sugared over with concern fc
the soul's eternal safety: all sincere and therefore more difficult to rejec
Edward's son, much later, would call all that "the chiliasm of despair." Afte
the school he calls Grammond, John is uprooted for work at a bank and end
his narrative in a new suit, with another recruit who is hopelessly, ignorantl
philistine.[3]

The subject of *Sir Walter Ralegh: Last of the Elizabethans* had intereste
Edward for forty years; that is, since Kingswood. Ralegh was a poet and,
fitfully, an Oriel man. His religious faith, Edward says, was "deeper, sincere
than that of the multitudinous orthodox." Edward admits Ralegh's faults. H
had great gifts but had "poor success" because he was a poor judge of mer
He was thought "too clever, and too variously clever"—but in fact he hat
an inferiority complex. His death at the hands of the Stuarts sacrificed "th
greatest Englishman" of his day.[4]

With a Leverhulme Foundation grant Edward began a history of the Britisl
Raj in the early nineteenth century. He found especially attractive Sir Charle
Metcalfe, who had been the acting Governor-General of India and was ther
Governor of Jamaica, then of Canada. He at least tried to hold at bay th
growing arrogance of Britain's conquerors. "He had three natural sons b
an Indian lady," Edward told Lothian, "whom he acknowledged and hac
educated in England. One died, one blew his brains out when he hac
returned to India and learnt how his mixed blood was despised, the thir
was Dalhousie's A.D.C., and finally retired to S. Africa, where he marriec
a Dutch woman, who burnt all his father's papers after his death! . . . The
last letters of all are rather terrible to have alone with me here—they are al
about the rodent ulcer (which they called a cancer then) that ate away hi

sight and his life. He was a very brave, a very lonely, a very individual man. His family want me to write his LIFE."[5]

He had to see the original sources in India. Again he applied to the Rhodes Trustees, and again Sir Reginald Coupland seconded this. *Rise and Fulfilment,* he told Lothian, was "admirable," and "more Indian history from his pen may help substantially to a better understanding between educated Indians and Englishmen, and it is essential that his work should be academically sound & scholarly, & not open to attack as being tendencious or inadequately grounded on the evidence." His 1932 contacts had "helped to improve the atmosphere," now even more important in the "final stage of constitution-making & the relapse into an attitude of dictation by Parliament. . . ." Thompson could explain to his (Indian) friends that "British public opinion, & indeed the British Government, has not changed its intentions nor weakened in sincerity." India was not Cecil Rhodes's primary interest "but Oxford was: to facilitate Thompson's writing & teaching on India is a direct benefit to Oxford." Coupland recommended three hundred pounds.[6]

In 1935 a new resource appeared in the person of H. N. Spalding, an Oxford graduate and resident with private means. A determined idealist, he was committed to mutual understanding through study of the spiritual heritages of East and West. Like Thompson, he "dreamed that Oxford might become the centre of a new renaissance based on an Honour School of Religions and Ethics." He dreamed also of an "Asia House" to revitalize the faltering Indian Institute. Spalding saw immense improvements possible in British-Indian relations "by public recognition in Oxford of the current intellectual movement in India." He happily began to devise ways to forward Edward's suggestions to the Rhodes Trustees. He had "profound admiration for Thompson" and saw him as "the 'kingpin' of the enterprise." Britons, he said, did not "*despise* India; they are simply indifferent & ignorant about it. Yours is the pen to help," and "Eastern studies must spring from the universities themselves," Oxford leading. The Indian Institute was useless. Its building, Edward told Lothian, was "cumbrous, dark, cluttered up— such a *chawl* [slum] as the Bombay Government might have built and as you know did build. Nor will any Indian ever regard this jail-like structure with anything but horror and aversion, while it is used solely for a modicum of Indian scholarship strictly subordinated to administrative requirements. . . ."[7]

Spalding established at Oriel a Senior Research Fellowship in Indian History for Edward, at £250 a year for three years. "Oriel made history a century ago [with Keble and Newman]," Spalding wrote, "and now would do so again." This eased Edward's circumstances appreciably.[8]

Edward would be in India for nearly four months. "I have never missed you more than all day yesterday," he told Theo. "I suddenly realised that

I was already so far off that even if I hurried back I cd. not get back in less than some days." Then, as Coupland had hoped, he resolved not only to follow Lord Metcalfe; he would see as many as possible of the Indian leaders. "With the terrible threatening situation everywhere, my mind revolts from the old silly patchings up & postponements. It is moving towards the idea of trying to advise the Indian leaders, when I see them, to do something both constructive & rallying their own people. I have a queer feeling of destiny on me—that I am moving, not only to my last Indian task but to something that will be a crown as well as a finish. I hope it will so prove." All might be well if they got through the next four years without a war, but there might be another market crash in 1940. An Indian crisis might well strike in the meantime.[9]

Government services were already deteriorating. The army men on board were "more large & insolent than my worst fears. One hears the elaborate drawl (often with pipe between teeth), the indifference to what is overheard, etc. They do much, completely & insufferably, to give the impression that they have no use for any but their own caste." He wondered, was he even sliding toward communism? "I think all these assumptions of superiority, wh. go with brainlessness & privilege, wd. be tolerated by no nation but ourselves." He heard that "the Army's name is dirt in India now, but they are in debt and have issued so many worthless cheques that they have ruined the white man's *izzat* [honor]. The dirty work of putting down civil insurrections they have mainly handed over to the European volunteers, yet they are as insolvent as ever." He read the India roster and realized "what a tremendous lot of grossly underpaid jobs India has no choice but to support every Native state is a nest of them. If I can do anything to shorten the day of this iniquity, I will. These conceited, ill-mannered swine, instead of keeping together an Empire whose ruling races consist in the main of decent kindly folk, are doing everything to smash it up. I wish I cd. write a novel convincingly showing them up." With E. M. Forster's Margaret Schlegel, he might have said, "An Empire bores me, so far, but I can appreciate the heroism that builds it up."[10]

An I.C.S. officer from Bharatpur State, where Edward hoped to see important Metcalfe papers, wondered why he was on such an errand. Edward explained that Metcalfe had been very important there, but the officer had never heard of him, mispronounced *Bharatpur*—but offered to be helpful. He met also the Home Secretary to the government of Bombay, who had the characteristic ultracaution of the I.C.S. man, "who watches you all the while he is asking searching questions." This one said that "his great charge against everyone he disliked politically was that they were not 'honest.' He could not believe in Gandhi's 'honesty.' " He resented Sastri's drawing his retirement pension while he continued to criticize the Government of India.[11]

Edward's research among Bombay government records was rewarding, but the city was terribly depressing. He hated the contrast between the foul smells and the brilliance of flowers and butterflies. The bay was beautiful, but the people were poor and wretched. Again and again he mentioned "the terrible NOISE. When I knew India, the noises were Nature's: screaming of parroquets, keening of kites, yelling of jackals, tonking of coopersmiths: (a small bird that sits in the trees, & goes 'tonk-tonk-tonk.')" (He was forgetting that most of his Indian days were in semirural Bankura and before the days of heavy motor traffic.) He spent a day and a half, until Jayakar insisted that he move to his house, in a "rather swanky hotel," where the food was pretentious but not good. He particularly disliked "the crowd of starving faces, on all sides, ill-paid servants who depend mainly on tips. Every time I came their way they stood to attention & salaamed. This kind of nonsense degrades those to whom it is offered, as well as those who offer it."[12]

The older political leaders disliked one another and distrusted everyone else. Jayakar was anti-Congress, with "a boundless contempt for the Gujarati; & Gandhi, the arch-Gujarati, has a leading share of it. 'I have an immense hatred of that man,'" Jayakar said. "'He has done endless mischief.'" He rejoiced that the Viceroy had refused public interviews with Gandhi and the Congress leaders, which certainly would have been put to political use. Jayakar said: "'He [Gandhi] found us with a slave mentality, & he has given us another slave mentality; he has made us a nation of sentimentalists.'" Indians, Jayakar thought, lacked "'that burning hatred of foreign rule that one wd. expect. Our chief hatred is of one another.'" Edward felt that he never wanted to write another Indian novel: how could one write honestly about characters who existed in such a morass of apathy and antipathy?[13]

He set forth some home truths for Jayakar, about "how things were going in England & Europe. . . . I told him Indian Nationalism was losing its battle, & I told him why. He asked if I wd. address a meeting if he arranged one. I said, No. He said, 'No, I suppose it would not help yr. work.' I said, 'I am not thinking about that. It wd. not help your case. You have far too many meetings, far too many leaders, far too much publicity. And you are all the time going by old catchwords, & being run by sentimentalists. And you keep on having quarrels among yourselves. You most of you hate Ambedkar— yet he has a brain & influence which you need. And that Ass Nehru never loses a chance of slating Sastri. And the outside world does not know what yr. principles are.'" They should enter the reforms resolved to make them work and assume that the British mean what they say in alleging they want self-government for India, "*& take self-government.*" Edward did not expect Jayakar to act on his advice; he was beset with family anxieties, had not had a holiday for years, and was worn out.[14]

They motored to Poona. Jayakar's spirits rose as they entered his nativ
Maharashtra, on the Deccan plain. He thought it resembled the English Lak
District. "It was not that," Edward wrote. "But it was very lovely & variec
creeks of the sea far inland, tumbling rivers, waterfalls, fields of linseed in
yellow flower, cloud-bearing flat hilltops." Edward did not request temporar
membership in the local club, but went to a hotel. He met the Englisl
commissioner, who had lived among the Mahrattas for thirty years, knev
none of their language and no Indian history, but was "quite quite soun
and friendly." It depressed Edward, though, to confront "these images of m
generation: old, bald, spectacles, fussy, complacent, ignorant, set in groove
& jellied in clichés. That is what we, abroad and so long[,] thought of a
enthusiastic boys have become. And, moreover, these are the successfu
men, not the failures like me." People "of our class" traveled by motorcar in
India. Edward took a bus.[15]

At Satara in Mahratta country, more forcibly than ever before, Edwaro
realized how a great ignorance of India's history fed misunderstandings. The
educational system was at fault, in England as in India. "We have given these
people a pathetic kind of pseudo-education, & now they are all despairing
with the plain folly of the way the West is going & helpless in their own
country. They ask sad questions. They know next to nothing of all those
things that interest an educated man in his own country: flowers, birds, etc.
An exception was the Mahrattas' idolization of their great hero Sivaji. Bu
that icon of national identity was constricting, for it glorified a golden age
long gone.[16]

Sir Akbar Hydari, whom Edward had met during the Round Table Con
ference, invited him to see Metcalfe papers at Hyderabad. There kindness
enveloped Edward. A car took him to the famous fort at Daulatabad anc
then to the Ellora Caves with their "rock-cut (& largely Muslim-smashed
sculptures. They were far finer than I imagined. What struck me was the
happiness of the life depicted. Though it was of wars (Ramayana), it was
done in a time when they were merely legend (as I hope wars with us also
may be, some day)." Sir Akbar had arranged for him to see the Ajanta Caves
in company with a South African delegation led by Jan Hofmeyr, Minister o
Interior and a former Rhodes Scholar. He regarded Edward's *Reconstructing
India* as "the only book worth reading on Indian problems." The delegation
had a copy with them: "So I became at once their political guide!" He was
astonished at what seemed his extraordinary standing in India. He told Theo
"I entered India so quietly; now everyone is tumbling over me, as if I were
the most important man in India—I, a penniless, unpopular, unsuccessfu
scribbler! But I get so tired." The Governor of Bombay wanted to see him
but Edward replied that he had no time. He told Theo, "I am not here fo
Governors."[17]

Ajanta's wall paintings of the life of the Buddha he found wonderful
nd impressive. In a way, his visit was homage to Christiana Herringham,
ho, back in 1910, had been one of the first links in the chain of his
onnections to Tagore. The paintings dated up to at least the seventh century.
There is a marvellously lovely gorge before the Ajanta Caves, with a rushing
ream bordered by agnus cactus bushes, the Pilgrims' flower wh. borders
ordan & wh. I have seen nowhere else in India. There are lovely forests
l round. Everything unchanged since the happy life of the artist monks
vo milleniums ago, except that the woods have been shot out! Not even
eafowl, & no deer." The wall-paintings, however, were far from unchanged;
o one now sees them as the monks had created them. Successive British
ilers had not protected them from effects of damp, wild-animal droppings,
id the smoke from wandering hunters' fires. Heartbreaking stretches had
ded and peeled away.[18]

Edward's next stop, in response to repeated invitations from the Maharaja
f Bikaner, was a sorry contrast to Hyderabad's hospitality. Jayakar had
arned him that Bikaner was no longer loyal to friends, and so it seemed.
dward's room was airless and so dark that he had to switch on a light at
iidday; he realized that no respected guest stayed there. He was offered a
orse if he wished to ride; no horse materialized. He felt like "a State prisoner,
ot a State guest." In fact, he was a trophy of war, an opportunity to insult the
hole British nation. There was ancient evidence of suttee: "On the gate are
ie pathetic, & famous, hand impressions left by the *satis* when going out to
ie." The maharaja's nephew, who was Home Minister, was very charming.
Yet—he was so barbarically proud of the fact that they have *strict* purdah
or all their high-class women, including the girls studying in the College. He
espised the Mahrattas for not having it: 'Mahrattas are not gentry.' And they
re all so proud of their 'sportsmanship', i.e., of the fact that they butcher
nything they see; & they are quite openly contemptuous of an Englishman
ho like myself says he does not. They are, after all, the silliest race in India.
od did immense harm with his much overrated book." After three days of
aiting, Edward got a "cool ukase" by phone to see the maharajah. After
iat, there was no reason to linger. The glow of his youthful love affair with
idia was quite gone. The visit, he told Theo, was "an eyeopener to me: it
; shredding away the last glamour from that Order [of Princes]. So far from
eing to blame for extirpating so many of them, the British shd. have cleaned
p the lot."[19]

En route to Bikaner Edward had left the train to visit Gandhi's headquarters
t Wardha. His secretary, Mahadev Desai, brought a tonga drawn by a pitiably
eble pony that he urged on with beatings, over deep holes and steep rocks.
I expected to have my leg rebroken a hundred times." Edward insisted
n walking when the road was too steep. His distress amused Desai, a

supporter of *ahimsa* ("harmlessness"). He could not understand Edward'
willingness to walk in the sun; he said that Andrews walked out only afte
sunset. The visit was unsatisfactory because Edward saw little of Gandh
who was occupied with nursing resident patients, one of whom was Mi
Behn. Gandhi's conversation seemed to be "only tortuosities. When I aske
him why Nehru keeps on saying that India 'will not touch the Constitutior
he wd. reply, 'Well, it all depends on what you *mean* by "touch."' He answer
everything that way."[20]

At Delhi, in the intervals of his archival work, the BBC, the government
Minister of Education, and *Times* correspondents all sought Edward. I
a conversation with highly placed officers, who were eager to state th
government's position, "I stuck to my guns, that they had arrested Gandhi to
soon & that they have no chance of floating the new Constitution withou
him & that they ought to open up negotiations. But there is no doubt that he
impossible. There is even less doubt that his lieutenants never wanted peac
but had kept on preparing & waging war." Lord Willingdon, the Viceroy, "wa
very charming indeed, genuinely pleased to see me again, & as delightfull
frank as ever. He usually referred to Mahatma Gandhi as 'this little devil.'
And he went on to describe Gandhi's activities, in similar vein.[21]

As a result, Edward was not in the best of moods when he saw Lion
Fielden, of All-India Radio. When Fielden asked him to broadcast his impre
sions of India, Edward sensed that "they want only soft soap"—governmer
policy, not Fielden's. "If I *gave* my impressions," Edward told Theo, "th
place would blow up." They discussed films exported to India, which Edwar
thought a lamentable influence. A few days later he gave in and broadca
on "What films are going to do to India." Fielden was in a state of barel
controlled fury with red tape, government restrictions, and BBC Easter
Service administrators in London. He "said he had never dreamed such
kind of Englishman existed until he came here."[22]

Although Edward had always thought New Delhi an unjustifiably lavis
expense and bad example in a poverty-stricken land, he now thought it "
gloriously lovely new city, fountains, & vast green shady spaces; & at it
door *miles & miles* of magnificent ruins and wild jungles! They get th
best of both worlds." That impression collapsed when friends took him t
meet two young brothers from a family supposedly the richest in Delhi–
certainly not the kind to care about ruins and jungles. They lived in "a
enormous palace in New Delhi, with an equally vast one under the sam
ownership beside it; & all luxury everywhere." They would inherit a textil
manufacturing kingdom and were already *"rich, rich."* The wife of one wa
"pretty, v. dainty, with a pose of aloofness, v.silent, v. bored, v. brainles
just spoilt. . . . Being millionaires, they are of course Gandhi-ites," the kin
of industrial patrons who seemed so incongruous with Gandhi's gospel c

implicity. "Behind them, Edward wrote, "are the unspeakable mills, where ow *each* weaver (it was admitted in the conversation) has to run 2 looms (in pan it is six) and the noise is something unbelievable. . . . I said pityingly, t must drive them deaf.' And the ardent Gandhi-ite with a lofty smile said, On the contrary it gives them v. good hearing. They have to hear well, in ll that noise."' Not tactfully, Edward's friends tried to discuss "the appalling t of Calcutta's graduates, saying how lucky these [Delhi] boys are to have eir father's business to enter." They countered that Calcutta graduates *had* ork—as rickshaw pullers! Their solution: "'Let them all go on increasing, ntil their number sweeps away the British government!' " Edward suggested hat they might sweep away much else and was treated to a tirade about the overnment's setting Muslims and Hindus against each other. "I have heard his talk for 25 years," Edward told Theo, "& I am weary of it. I know of the ruth behind it. But *what* a set these people are to take the line that they are nere helpless tools! Only idiots wd. *let* a Govt. go on year after year setting hem at sixes and sevens. This is a country of chatterers, ruled by snobs."[23]

The wealthy English living in the great cities induced another kind of re-ulsion. Edward hated their airs of superiority, "despising [India] while they uck wealth out of it as by a mighty vacuum-cleaner, & live in luxuriousness, ood all imported, servants all humble, & drilled." He feared that he was "not uite in my right wits. I shall leave India detesting everything in this bogus ivilisation. I wish I were sailing tomorrow. What a curse it was to tie up vith India! I wish I could finish with it. It was all about *nothing.*"[24]

Tagore had promised a warm welcome at Shantiniketan, but Edward esitated because Nehru was visiting; he went there later, but Tagore was way. Edward had a touching reunion with Abanindranath in Calcutta. He urprised Mahalanobis, who insisted that he must see Brajendranath Seal. dward was "greatly loth" but went. Two years later he described the scene or Rothenstein:

> Seal broke off an ancient & deep friendship because of my earlier smaller book on Tagore. For 20 years we had nothing to do with each other. Then, 2 years ago, Prasanta Mahalanobis suddenly led me into his presence. The old man, who has had several strokes, was being fed with milk like a child, the milk shaking all over his beard. He had no idea I was coming, & he started up with a wild cry, "Ohhh! Edward Thompson!" & broke down & sobbed. The rest is something I do not care to set down in a letter.

"He has been miserable all these years, ever since we ceased to be friends," Edward told Theo. Seal had said, " 'Often & often I have thought of you.' " He had been "as like King Lear begging pardon of Cordelia as I ever saw." Their meeting was a kind of benediction on Edward's Bengal years.[25]

At Allahabad he saw the lawyer Sir Tej Bahadur Sapru, who, like Jayakar, was disgruntled at the government's suspicious treatment of the older Congress leaders, and Nehru, who was "v. frank & affectionate," a contrast to his mood when they met briefly in Oxford in 1935. There he had been "a v. tired and embittered man, just out of prison," and had just arrived from Germany where his wife was ill. He was then in Oxford to enroll Indira at Somerville College. Edward had thought her "very haughty-looking, a perfect stunner." Nehru had "talked with anger and passion of the financial hold 'London' had on India."[26]

Their correspondence began in November 1935. It did not matter, Edward wrote, whether they agreed on all points: "I want friendship between Britain and India; but even more, I want the bringing of a just social system, both here and in India." In 1936 Edward sent a list of questions for comment; they were, Edward said, what Nehru's English friends would wish to ask. He suggested that eventually the Congress Party would learn "to work the constitution," and Gandhi would "cease to be a *political* figure of first importance." Congress would then change from "what we have hitherto known it as being and therefore—as 'Congress' cease to exist." He promised to say no more about Gandhi, except that he must "discover" some new message—Civil Disobedience having nearly succeeded but nevertheless having failed. Now he risked appealing only to the radical fringe. Edward was prepared "to find that I was clean mistaken. But I did my best and some of the things will be right." Edward had suggested "lines of action for the future" but must include poverty as a problem. Must they make sacrifices and have less forceful leaders with no understanding of the real issues? It was too easy, Nehru wrote, to point out Indian follies and contradictions. Did Edward perhaps attach too much importance to British and American influences and overemphasize "idolators" of the quirkier Indian phenomena such as Aurobindo Ghose, the Pondicherry guru? "It is natural that many of our people suffering from a certain inferiority complex should welcome these persons with open arms." He urged Edward to remember that Aurobindo did not represent India. However, this was a farewell letter, and Nehru did not want Edward to leave with unpleasant memories: "Do not go away with all this bitterness for this unhappy country."[27]

Record offices and archives provided many of Edward's most rewarding contacts. Repeatedly he found valuable papers at risk because there was no money for correct translation or curatorial care and storage. But clerks who were humble and outrageously underpaid took a touching interest in his quest. Their knowledge of Indian history was shallow but sincere. At the Bombay record office he "found only babus present. When they learnt who I was they were v. forthcoming." He could not dissuade them from calling him "Sir Edward." They had everything ready, papers assembled and waiting

nce his first postal inquiry, months before. The two Brahmins in charge
ere "touchingly willing to help, coming up with little comments or with
ome book in wh. they drew my attention to some statement that Metcalfe
as in India once upon a time." He began to see "what *unlimited* stocks
xist in India, & almost everywhere." Even where he did not find anything
Metcalfeish," "all the babus seem v. excited about my 'researches.' It was v.
ouching, the way men (Brahmins of the once-proud Maratha following) kept
oming up to me with old publications, & drawing my attention to numerous
laces where they had put slips because M[etcalfe] was mentioned. They
ad painfully gone through old journals etc!" They said that a young Parsi
ad some material for him, and Edward found him waiting. He presented
utographed copies of "3 big books he had already done—done badly, but
ney are genuine research of the most illuminating kind." He had stacks
f other materials, with some "v. interesting Metcalfe items." He said that
he C'cutta Records simply abound in Metcalfe material." The young man
as mistaken about that, but if Edward had not gone there, he would have
nagined great deposits of Metcalfe information. His informant had meant
ell, but Edward now knew that "the Imperial Records Dept. is all *blague.*"
he holdings were about to go from Calcutta to Delhi, and "no one (and
ertainly not the curators) have any notion what is in them."[28]

At Poona a clerk conducted him to a room "where everything was ready
or me & Metcalfe letters (copies of them, sent here for my guidance). This
as very kind." They contained nothing new or illuminating, "but they
ade for completeness & were interesting in a mild fashion." The clerks'
fficiency allowed him time for a nap and a stroll through a "jolly open
pace" with banyan trees and "parraquets" "squabbling in the leafy tops, &
aking sudden arrow flights, just like a lot of cunieform inscriptions loosed
nrough the air." The next day the archivists helped him, since he knew no
ersian, to study Persian newsletters "written to the last Peshwa (ruler of
ne Mahrattas) by spies in different courts. The ones I was reading were
vritten by a newswriter in Metcalfe's court at Delhi. It is very funny to
ealise that while Metcalfe was solemnly going about his grave duties, every
etail of every day, omitting absolutely nothing, was being sent out to the
hiefs who paid for the intelligence." The clerks handled their materials "so
agerly under such difficulties" of understaffing and underfunding. He met
imilar kindness from record keepers at the Parasnis Historical Museum at
atara. At Hyderabad, there had been no Metcalfe papers, but records of
Iyderabad's Persian tradition were important and illuminating. The head of
Iyderabad state records had seemed an exception to the general welcome;
e was standoffish at first, but they ended on the best of terms.[29]

Edward concluded the trip with a reminder of his family's missionary past.
or his mother's sake—and for that of his Arnison family—he visited her old

mission station in Ceylon. At Kandy, where she had taught as a young lad he saw her old schoolroom. "How kind and good the missionaries are, wh[e] you meet them!" he exclaimed. He felt that he owed them the completi[on] of the Arnison chronicle "if only as compensation to people who rema[in] unfairly depicted, if that is all I have to say of them."[30]

At home again he was faithful to the resolve. He turned to *John Arniso[n]* sequel to *Introducing the Arnisons*. The young John Arnison is of cour[se] Edward Thompson in his flight from the bank. He detests the self-conscio[us] piosity of his bank associates, and as John proceeds to ministerial apprentic[e] ship Edward includes incidents both disturbing and benign from Sawtry a[nd] Stonehouse. However, John's story includes an awakening to humanitari[an] socialism, through a fortuitous encounter with a couple his own age, whi[ch] did not happen during Edward's own apprenticeship. The tribute to h[is] mother's fortitude and generosity is there, but so is his resentment of t[he] family tradition that had propelled him into missionary ministry: "One lov[es] one's father and mother. But does one love their assumption of the right [to] plan and dream on one's behalf?"[31]

The India trip had been productive, except that midway the brain a[nd] body he had thought would never tire now began to seem like those [of] an old man. He had been uncomfortable, but not altogether displease[d] with the assumptions that he represented the mighty Oxford Universi[ty] and had power and influence in India. In fact, he *was* influential, as o[ne] of that small group of India advocates that included men like Garratt a[nd] Ratcliffe: liberal, articulate, and impatient with inefficiency and inhumanit[y]. They were valuable because they so often possessed facts that constituenc[y] bound persons did not know and did not know how to obtain. They we[re] free agents and talked to whoever would talk to them. Above all, no matt[er] how pessimistic they sounded, they tried to keep a broad strain of optimist[ic] idealism.

As always, Edward was torn between optimism and pessimism. He ha[d] not expected much improvement in India, but grim reality surpassed h[is] worst anticipations. Pro- and anti-Congress politicians sniped at one anoth[er] instead of discussing their disagreements. Old routines hobbled governme[nt] services. "It is a dirty, degraded land, and I cannot tell why we are so prou[d] of what we have done." Again he was glad that he had "got the glamour [and] romance of India down in my novels, before they all faded out from me, f[or] ever. They exist no longer."[32]

22

Observing a Crisis

Edward carried his anxiety about Palmer's school marks to India and back. Theo wrote that the Dragon School was "far from despairing of Palmer. A boy who is new to boarding is always at a disadvantage. . . . We can't expect him to be as book-brilliant as Frank—and he doesn't work badly, as a rule. He has his points and we don't want to break his spirit as we were in danger of breaking Frank's." Frank, she thought, was too patient and philosophical for his age, and they had praised him insufficiently. She disliked Palmer's "self-satisfied vein" and hoped he would "quiet down and make some real friends of his own." Edward had thought about offering him money for improvement. On the other hand, Palmer had "a certain disinterestedness about reward, and I hesitate to spoil." In many ways he asked less than Frank. His marks showed occasional improvement but remained below scholarship range. That £250 or £300 for his preparatory school loomed larger than ever.[1]

Theo called on his Dragon School Tutor, who pointed out that it was still true that "a wealthy employer on the outposts of Empire" still preferred a Wykehamist or Etonion or Rugbeian: " 'Why, goodness knows, but there it is, and the boy from a small school or a less-known one, no matter how good he is does not get such a leg-up.' " The Tutor emphasized that in the next term the "sheep in his form begin to separate out from the goats. . . . Those who can't keep up fall behind."[2]

As Edward embarked for India in 1936, Palmer's marks seemed to be improving, but he must remember that "*this year is of tremendous importance. I am sure you have plenty of brains, if you were not such a slack little beggar.*" But no, he did not mean that: "No, I know it isn't exactly that; only slowness to 'react.' " Theo continued to be more optimistic. Palmer went "quite gaily" to school because now he "was going back as one of the oldest boys—he *might* be a prefect." He did not become a prefect and worried about giving his mother that news and his latest marks, but he liked the year's work. He made the rugby team. If he did not get into one of the more prestigious schools, he could go to Kingswood, whose headmaster, A. B. Sackett, wrote to press its claims as a first-rate public school. She was certain (as Edward probably was not) that he would "adore living under the shadow of his father's name." She would make no decision until Edward returned.[3]

Frank, who regretted being only a rugby substitute at Winchester, now presented his parents with a problem akin to the one that had so burdened Edward. He thought about confirmation in the Church of England. Frank had said, " 'Suppose I should want to be a Communist after a few years. shouldn't like to think that I had edged myself into a way of life and belief that was against all that sort of thing.' " Theo's approach was more emotiona

> The idea of coolly being confirmed in spite of the fact that he already has idea. that seem to be at complete variance with all that the church stands for naturall is distasteful. Most boys, I suppose, just get confirmed as they get measles—an epidemic breaks out at school each autumn. We, you and I, have been brough up to take these things seriously. The worldly-wise parents even atheistical ones just let their boys go through with it with as little bother as possible.
>
> I'm afraid I'm quite at sea about it and I, like Frank, wish you were here. It isn a question of Conformity and Non-conformity. It's a question of his joining any church at all.[4]

Edward, Theo wrote, had always been a "lone wolf," and she had alway been "pretty well cut off from what most women have in the way c background of family"; if petty, "it still is *something*." She and Edward ha been brought up to the sense of God's presence: "I still believe it." The onl reason to urge church membership "at a time when it comes naturally" wa as "a sort of defence against a rainy day! If the boys are like us they are nc going to be comfortably insensitive."

Theo's thinking went round and round and returned to the problem of wh church membership was necessary if one participated in its social efforts She had ignored the Presbyterian church in Oxford, but "I *feel* that I belong but the local church would be very surprised to hear it. Why should the boy have any more definite connection with a church than we have? I feel I hav been slack and let things slide—the thing I am so hard on the boys for." Sh worried because Frank was "taking it rather hard. I imagine it will end in hi not being confirmed. . . . I feel very useless at these things."

She had revealed more than she realized. "We were very much alone, you and I," she wrote to Edward, "and still are. But we had that sense of support— 'the everlasting arms.' " Certainly, Edward respected a divine presence bu had discarded his mother's literal sense of heavenly membership.[5]

Edward began to arrange his Metcalfe materials. The military historia John William Kaye had published a two-volume biography in 1854. Both hac the problem of presenting the man without an overload of facts from Indiar history. Edward, however, hoped to write a more compact, more compas sionate account. He hoped also to provide an overview of the tradition tha shaped Metcalfe, and of how he shaped it in his turn. "Tradition is particularl valuable in India," Edward wrote, "where so much of a man's achievemen consists in the impression left on a populace that watches with a closeness hardly paralleled in any other land."[6]

He now had a considerable accumulation from London archival sources and Metcalfe family collections. Charles Theophilus Metcalfe was born at Calcutta in 1785. Like the infant Samuel, like Edward Thompson, he was early dedicated to a cause: his father, a director of the East India Company, enrolled him at the age of three months and one week as "Minor Cadet in this establishment." Charles returned to Calcutta, a Company employee, in 1801. He was not quite sixteen. That was then more typical than unusual for India recruits. Their actual education "took place, not in England or Scotland, but in a scene of shifting and dissolving empires." Metcalfe had support in high places, but his own precocious talents for hard work and organization helped to create the India that Victorians would come to consider the jewel in the imperial crown. He consolidated the obstreperous Punjab kingdoms at a time of great fears that Napoleon's European rampage would spill over into India from Russia. In 1811 Metcalfe was Resident at Delhi, the liaison, with absolute power to rule, between the Company and the king of Delhi. This king presided over only "a tattered tapestry of an empire." Metcalfe's administration was as efficient as the king's was squalid. Then, from 1820 to 1825, Metcalfe was Resident at Hyderabad and dealt with a Nizam who was " 'a melancholy madman.' " The previous Resident had ignored him so effectively that he gave up all pretense at ruling. A poverty-stricken populace and contagious rebellions resulted. Metcalfe the reformer confronted also a firm of English merchants who drained profits out of Hyderabad investments and in effect ruled the state with the veiled approbation of Lord Hastings, the Governor-General.[7]

Impressions of Metcalfe as overbearing and overambitious began with Hyderabad and his stringent measures to cleanse that Augean stable. He most wanted appointment as Governor of a major area such as Madras, even, eventually, as Governor-General. A seat on the Supreme Council was the nearest he came to that, except for two years as Acting Governor-General while Lord Bentinck made an extended tour of India.

In 1838 Metcalfe returned to England after thirty-seven years away. Shortly thereafter the cancer that would finally kill him appeared as an ulcer on his cheek; it was treated and mistreated according to theories of the day. He was scarcely settled when he was appointed Governor of Jamaica. There he ruled conscientiously and generously, but New World cultural differences overtook him. The recently freed sugar-plantation slaves, by contrast with the wretched poor of India, seemed to him well-off and happy. Their "independence of spirit" astonished Metcalfe. They were " 'fully sensible of the rights of Freedom' " because they had "stepped into them suddenly." Gradually, lifelong habits as a figure of authority "made him incline to the proprietors' side" rather than that of the workers. His mind "was as fair a mind as ever worked," but he belonged to an age that was passing, and he "knew nothing of the underdog's troubles."[8]

In 1843 he became Governor of Canada. Like his predecessors and the London authorities, he failed to comprehend a movement toward a democracy of which he had no experience. Canadian self-assertion was as unfamiliar as the Jamaicans' self-assurance. The Canadian reformers wanted "Responsible Government" instead of the old autocratic ways. Metcalfe wanted to be tolerant but could not "free himself from dominant convictions" or "improvise ways to meet emergency." His personal emergency was the cancer that was eating away his face. He returned to England at last in 1845, but only to die.[9]

Why did Edward invest so much time and effort in this man whose career has been overshadowed in history's record? He understood Metcalfe's ambivalences about India, and he echoed Metcalfe's regrets about "the best part of my life" having been spent there. Edward understood his dread, once back in England, of being an outsider. " 'What is there in India,' " Metcalfe asked himself in 1811, " 'to recompense for such sufferings?' "[10]

Metcalfe was a man of integrity. He scrutinized every expenditure. He tried to disturb the local culture as little as possible. Patronage was the supreme principle for advancement, but he refused to employ it cynically for self-promotion. He deplored the appointment to high Indian office of men from England with no experience of India. He abominated the Permanent Settlement of 1793, which had demoralized rural Bengal; it created a kind of Indian squireocracy by giving landowners acres to which *ryots* had had ancestral rights for generations. He fell out with colleagues because of their callousness toward Indians: "The most deeply felt passages of his [1815] Report are given up to a burning indictment of the oppressions which some of them practised as they marched through his territory or visited it." Widow-burning and dacoity Metcalfe could handle, but he never learned to curb his countrymen's misbehavior.[11]

He was a true liberal (although Macaulay thought him deluded about that) on English issues that to many made him a flaming radical. He disapproved of press restrictions. He favored repeal of the Corn Laws, vote by ballot, extension of male suffrage, and equal civil rights for all men. He cherished a " 'lurking fancy' " of one day entering Parliament but refused to stoop to " 'the usual means of obtaining a seat—such as bribery and corruption, canvassing, and so forth.' " Above all, he was a man of duty. Although plainly dying, he left Canada only when his councilors said that he must go, on the chance of saving his life.[12]

With *Metcalfe* completed, Edward turned his attention to Kingswood. He wrote that "being a Methodist has meant taking a lonely course in later life." Sackett replied that the school "has influenced the nation both at the top

nd in labour circles." The old Kingswood had ignored the arts; it would
ow "produce the artists." Too many students once went automatically into
he ministry. "I should greatly deplore any return to that position," Sackett
aid, "but there is not the least danger of it." Of 324 students, over 100 were
aymen's sons. The Dragon School had placed too little emphasis on English
tudies; Mr. Sackett would see that Palmer studied plenty of English.[13]

He entered Kingswood in the autumn of 1938, and Edward was recon-
iled to the choice. Palmer, he told Theo, was "an exceptionally good boy,"
nd Kingswood would pay "dividends that we shall not get from Frank's
Winchester experience."[14]

Frank, unconfirmed, entered New College, Oxford. He and Edward had
ad a long talk about confirmation, the best about religion that they had ever
ad. That calmed Edward and helped to mitigate effects of a visit from Lady
Mary Murray, who turned up at Scar Top to pry for news (they were soon to
ell Scar Top and move to Bledlow, Buckinghamshire) and to boss Edward's
onduct of his family and professional affairs.

Some of Edward's suggestions and Spalding's efforts bore fruit. Spalding
stablished the chair for a distinguished Indian visitor at All Souls College. W.
;. S. Adams, its warden, told Lord Elton, Lothian's successor as Secretary
o the Rhodes Trustees, of "'the thrill which went through India when
adhakrishnan was appointed to the Spalding Chair at Oxford.'" In 1932
he Trustees established a Rhodes Memorial Lecture to bring persons of
nternational importance to Oxford. Elton hoped that Nehru might come and
peak on a topic such as "Internationalism," "(unless civil disobedience were
n the offing, in which case he would refuse . . ."). Would it look odd, since
he money came from the South African enterprises of the archimperialist
Cecil Rhodes, for the "Rhodes Trust, of all foundations, [to] fling its mantle
ver Congress. Would not such an invitation be taken in India to be a criticism
f the British Government?" There were other considerations. Elton observed
hat "India is thirsting for a statement of our war aims, something more
pecific and idealistic than we have yet produced. India also has considerable
epercussions on the United States. If there had been Civil Disobedience
n India at the time, the United States might have been more reluctant to
ft the embargo on arms export." Therefore a Nehru visit would be timely.
'hompson would try to persuade him to come. Thompson wrote eloquently,
ut war and "the rush of events" prevented Nehru's accepting.[15]

Edward's other suggestions for intellectual cooperation progressed fitfully
r not at all because they fell into a bureaucratic bog. The Rhodes Trustees
ffered four hundred pounds to bring "some distinguished representative
f one of the literary movements in India" as a lecturer for a year, and
dward suggested candidates. Elton told W. G. S. Adams, of All Souls, that
'hompson "argued strongly against his being brought to the Indian Institute,

which he regards as a hopeless institution"; the visitor should have an ordinary university appointment. "From then onwards," Elton wrote, "a series of mysterious delays and mischances seems to have overtaken the proposal." In 1933 the Trustees asked for a decision. The university replied that it had received no proposal—although the Trustees' files contained an acknowledgment "suggesting vaguely" a referral to the General Board of the Faculties. In March 1933 the university's Hebdobmadal Council asked for details. Thompson had already supplied details. A similar fate befell a suggestion for exchange lecturers: young Oxford dons to teach in India, and their counterparts in England. "At this point," Elton wrote, "the project seems mysteriously to have petered out." The university enquired vaguely about it in October 1933, after which it lay dormant until a query, in April 1937 about combining it with a campaign to stimulate interest in the I.C.S. Again nothing happened. What about the "expediency of taking up this obviously somewhat Sisyphean project again?" Elton asked in 1939. There Oxford' intellectual cooperation stood when England and France declared war on Germany on 3 September 1939.[16]

Information about Indian politics was fragmentary and confused. Lothian alarmed by the accelerating downfall of European governments, had already asked Edward whether he would go again to India, if the Trustees provided funds, to see his Congress Party friends "and in part for literary or historical purposes." The latter would cause no difficulty "because you naturally spout literature and history." Edward at first declined because of other work and deteriorating health, and because he had nothing specific to contribute just then. Lothian asked again as the months grew more menacing. Edward consulted Lionel Fielden, just back from India; Krishna Menon, the India League's representative in Britain; Lord Zetland, Secretary of State for India and Lord Halifax. Zetland and Halifax could say nothing official but thought his going a "good thing." Edward had said often enough that he never wanted to see India again, but Zetland promised to get air passage at once. Edward finally promised "at least to bring back firsthand impressions and information and perhaps secure a longer time before decisions are made." He feared that German bombing might begin before he returned. He agreed to go because "men whose judgment I respect wanted me to go, and could not think of any better qualified man who was not an official." Elton told Lionel Curtis that Thompson would go "officially to study literary and social movements, but also to establish contacts with his friends among the Congress leaders."[17]

Before he could leave, a family crisis beset the Thompsons. On 9 September 1939 Frank, who had turned nineteen in August, was called up for training. In a storm of misdirected phone calls, telegrams, and letters, Theo tried to get him released, since he was still underage, so that he could at least take the New College formal-entrance examinations. Frank, however

efused release. "He says he *must* stay," Theo wrote to Edward. "He gave me
many reasons. . . . But the main things are—1.) that all his friends are either
n it, or getting into it soon—2.) that he *can't*, once having got himself into
the frame of mind he achieved last week of giving up the 2 terms at College,
tc.—now making a complete *volte-face* and have the whole thing to do again
n 6 months' time or more, when he is 20." A release order came through,
nd Theo telegraphed to sanction cancellation because "he was desperately
upset at the idea of going back to Oxford. As his generation is 'for it,' it is the
ucky ones who can begin to prepare at once instead of sitting at work that
eems useless. . . ." Frank could have "a few months of service in a home
unit before going to F[rance]." In Edward's mind immediate uncertainties
mingled with memories of that other Frank lost in France. In the end Frank
tayed at New College until he turned twenty.[18]

Edward flew to India on 3 October. On the thirteenth he was in Allahabad
with Nehru, who was just back from an emergency meeting of the Congress
Working Committee at Wardha. There was indeed an emergency. On 3
eptember Lord Linlithgow, the Viceroy, had informed the people of India
hat they were at war with Germany. He did not consult with Indians or
equest Indian advice. Congress leaders sympathized with Britain but felt
etrayed and refused to fight without a promise of true independence at
nce, which had long been Nehru's position. The Congress Working Committee resolved: "A free independent India will gladly associate herself with
ther free nations for mutual defence against aggression and for economic co-
peration, but co-operation must be between equals and by mutual consent."
n 1934 an India Bill in Parliament had allowed elections that brought the
Congress Party to power in ministries of key provinces. The real power,
owever, remained with parliamentary committees. After the Viceroy's dec-
aration of Indian belligerency, those provincial ministries began to resign
n protest. The Muslim League leapt into this vacuum and on 22 December
would declare India's Day of Independence—that is, independence from
cooperation with Congress. The division began that would end with Pakistan
nd the division of India in 1947.[19]

Upon his return in November Edward submitted three reports to the
Trustees: "Personal Narrative"; "Summary and Suggestions"; and "Political
Report." The "Narrative" tells most about his schedule and reactions. An
irport incident at Poole showed what people could expect in this new
vartime: "The Censor confiscated every scrap of printed or written matter."
An Australian farmer lost a copy of Thackeray's *The Virginians* and said he
elt like "an animal going back to the burrow to die." An Australian woman lost
er English classics; the Censor demanded her prayer book as well, but she
refused flatly to surrender it." A young engineer forfeited a costly technical
ook, and everyone lost Penguins, of which there were finally "two tall

piles." Edward lost Chamberlain's speeches at the outbreak of war, which the Ministry of Information had sent express at the last minute. The Australians "left our shores angry, saying that there was no difference between us and the other totalitarian governments." They considered themselves robbed, and Britain had squandered goodwill. Edward understood the need for care but suggested that the British government replace *The Virginians* and apologize to the lady. Axis propaganda snatched at every negative scrap, and could have obtained this one from the lady's complaint to the *Times:* were her *Times* news clippings, collected during six months in England, a secret code? "Here was danger indeed!" Her *Book of Common Prayer* "really perplexed" the official, who examined it for some time. "Surely we should be allowed the solace of books on the long journey to Australia."[20]

At Allahabad Edward stayed with Sapru and understood anew conservatism's drag on India. Sapru was still a political diehard, "so desperately so that he would have seemed old-fashioned in Henry VIII's time," with a horror of Russia, which he believed was ready to devastate India by air, and "a great admiration of Mussolini and (formerly) of Hitler." He was rich and generous but "intensely worried about the Socialism of Congress and of Nehru in particular (for Nehru is dead in earnest)." His library included only "Right" books: "The 'Left' is rigidly excluded."[21]

Edward remembered that "in wartime the obscurest individual, if he suddenly flies to India, is watched and quoted." Everyone he met was long out of date. On 14 October the *Times* for 21 September was the latest its Delhi correspondent had seen. "I therefore saw officials in crowds, Members of Council, Governors, all asking what was happening in London." The press followed him as if he were a film star or politician. He had arrived "at a moment of almost unprecedented tension, and the intense loneliness in which many men have to live their lives made them feel that they had no choice but to open their minds, and they deliberately chose a man who had flown from the outside world and must fly back again." In the end he saw everyone "from Governors to ex-Government-agents and ex-terrorists," and was "astonished by the frankness with which everyone talked. This was sometimes almost embarrassing."[22]

From 13 to 16 October Edward was with Nehru, talking and talking. "From first to last his kindness to me was wonderful." On the sixteenth Edward went to Delhi and found it "not possible to overstate the isolation of New Delhi from the rest of India." He dined with English members of the Viceroy's Council and was "shocked to find that, apart from a formal handshake which one of them had had with Nehru, Inglis [the *Times* correspondent] and I were the only men who had ever met Gandhi and Nehru." He offered to introduce Nehru to one of the councilors, but the man "drew himself up and said, 'You forget, I am an official.' " Later, a Governor said that he would be " 'heart-broken when I leave India without having ever seen

Gandhi.'" Edward was astonished. Gandhi was only forty miles away, and a note would have requested a meeting. But he understood the complication: Gandhi, like the tiger, is royal game; only a Viceroy can shoot him." A Governor's visit might be misrepresented. "It is very hard luck being an official; you have to confine your friendship to people who are usually damnably dull." Nor had some officials ever met any of the princes. "I cannot think," Edward wrote, "that the absorption in files is the only thing that will keep India straight."[23]

He realized that some official complaints "were seriously meant." The British deeply resented Nehru's comments on British imperialism, taken to mean that they were no different from the Nazis. He mentioned this to Nehru, who made "a magnificently clear distinction between British Imperialism and Nazism" in a Delhi speech on 4 November.[24]

Edward talked long with Jinnah, who was greatly puzzled as to why he wanted a meeting and tried to find out "whether I had a mission from some exalted personage in London. 'I do not want to be rude,' he kept saying, but . . . why do you want to see me?'" Edward concluded that "Jinnah, of course, is nothing of a Muslim, any more than Nehru is a Hindu; he is thoroughly Europeanised." He shrugged off interest in religion. "Something rather fine," Edward thought, "has gone wrong in Jinnah," whose mind "proceeds by a chain of brittle sticks, that snap and hold nothing." At the end Jinnah said, "with long impressive pauses, 'I have a message for you. . . . Do not forget your friends. . . . They are not *all* lost. You still have friends. . . . . Choose . . . your friends.' A straightforward appeal to us to 'divide and rule'!" Edward found himself "thinking better of Jinnah than any of the evidence appears to justify. His life has been a barren one, and—I repeat—there *is* something rather fine that has got warped in Jinnah."[25]

On 21 October Edward saw the Viceroy but thought him "extraordinarily unresponsive; it was "like talking to a blank wall." Nehru had said, "'You know, I like the Viceroy. And I'll tell you why. He never once, in his last talk with me, mentioned Hindu-Muslim relations.'" Edward took the liberty of repeating this to the Viceroy: "'What Nehru meant was that he appreciated your courtesy in taking it for granted that he knew all about this difficulty, and you did not triumphantly bring it forward as a trump card to stop all progress.' There was no flicker on the impassive face, but a little later I heard him say, almost to himself, 'I didn't think Nehru spotted that!'" Edward realized later that he himself had "completely misunderstood the Indian situation in some respects." In his own defence he noted the suddenness of the crisis; he was there "because I was an Englishman who knew the Congress leaders intimately, and no one else seemed to know them." He recalled the Viceroy's last words: "'I have no hope.'" Still, with some reservations, "almost everyone, from the Viceroy downwards, spoke generously of [Congress's] effort and achievement."[26]

Nehru summoned him to Wardha, where the Congress Working Committee was with Gandhi. On the twenty-second he went, the only Englishman on the train, "in some distress of mind. I had seen the decency of both sides, and felt the tragedy of the clash that was coming. . . ." It was the more poignant because Indians along the way showed him "the most perfect courtesy and friendliness." He found Gandhi and Nehru relaxed and cheerful. Edward promised to say nothing about the resignations of the Ministries, and Gandhi promised not to " 'strike the first blow' " in the form of Civil Disobedience.[2]

On the twenty-third Edward was the only outsider allowed to meet the Working Committee. "Nehru of course arranged this exceptional experience." All was kindness and good will, and the committee decided to interview *him,* for ill-wishers would make political capital of his interviewing them immediately after seeing the Viceroy. They had a relatively lighthearted discussion of a speech by the Archbishop of Canterbury, who had reportedly said that "on the whole, Congress had not been *unduly* unfair to the minorities." Was unfairness acceptable if not excessive? Edward explained that the Archbishop was no doubt thinking "along the lines of treatment of Nonconformists . . . ."[28]

He spoke briefly with Gandhi, and Mira Behn begged for information " 'We hear nothing in India.' " Were the British armed forces really *good* and would they win the war? Meanwhile the Working Committee decided not to invoke Civil Disobedience, and Edward hoped that his report from New Delhi had had some influence. On the twenty-fourth they met again. They despaired of getting understanding from the India Office in London, "but [had] still a deep-rooted faith that if the British people could be brought to listen patiently India's feelings would be understood." Edward promised to report that to the Rhodes Trustees and to talk to Members of Parliament and answer questions when he got home. Nehru had told him that there was "tremendous pressure for action, especially from the younger men," but they had gained time. Edward believed that Civil Disobedience would come, but not before the New Year. Congress should, if it espoused neutrality, discourage army recruiting, but Edward begged them not to be precipitate, since they "cannot prevent recruiting" because there was so much unemployment. The Working Committee put it aside—for the present.[29]

On the evening of the twenty-fourth Edward, Nehru, and a few others left for Bombay. "On a high balcony was old Kalam Azad, the one silent member of the Committee, waving to us." Edward called out an Arabic greeting, "and the old man went wild with delight, and threw down his stick and shouted in return, and sent me away wth benedictions." A small episode, but of a kind that, if officialdom had only understood its value, might have made a difference over the years.[30]

On the train, Nehru answered Edward's questions for most of the night.

At every station crowds shouted "Mahatma Gandhiki jai," and "Pandit Jawaharlalki jai"—"Victory to Gandhi! Victory to Nehru!"

At Bombay Edward had a long, confidential, and frank conversation with the Governor, a cousin of Lord Zetland. On the twenty-sixth, the day the Bombay Ministry resigned, he had breakfast and "a long, stretching talk" with Ambedkar, leader of the Untouchables, and some fifteen members of the Bombay legislature. Ambedkar had just made a speech in which he had said, " 'If it is a choice between my country and myself, my country comes first. If it is a choice between my country and my community, my community comes first.' " He arrived almost in tears and did break down as he affirmed his belief in dominion status. "During this interesting scene," Edward wrote, "Nehru sat beside me on a table, swinging his legs in his schoolboy fashion and occasionally making a low comment (as when I said, 'I think religion is the greatest pest in the world.' 'I agree with you.') He was watching Ambedkar closely." Later, Edward asked what he thought, and Nehru replied that his first impression " 'was far more favourable than I ever expected.' I urged him, 'You must go on with it. There is not the slightest reason why Ambedkar should be your enemy if Congress as a body will take up the cause of the Untouchables.' " Nehru had never before met Ambedkar, which struck Edward as "very wrong," and he arranged for them to meet privately. They had a long talk, "and Ambedkar now knows that his community are sure of the support of the bravest man in India."[31]

Edward reminded the Rhodes Trustees that he could not quote from some confidential conversations, as in Calcutta with the Extremist leader, Subhaschandra Bose. There he saw Abanindranath Tagore, and Mahalanobis and his wife drove ninety miles to meet him. On 2 November at Lucknow he was again persuaded to broadcast his views, missed his train, but was driven at high speed to the next station. At Delhi, Jinnah and Nehru were meeting, and Nehru "told me what was happening." Lionel Fielden, just back from England, joined Edward there. After two days for rest at Gwalior, Edward flew home on 7 November. He had been immersed in politics, as the Rhodes Trustees expected, but he had also "learnt a lot of traditional history of old times, some of it entirely new to me and to all the books I have ever read. . . . I learnt about Indian films and the economic position of the untouchables and basic education—the new hope of India. The field of possible research in India is boundless, and is not lessening or narrowing." He had met many others well known in India but unknown in England. With many "ordinary men and women" he spoke English or Bengali: "They were all evidence." He had an Eleventh Commandment for the English in India: "Thou shalt not make a man look ridiculous."[32]

In his "Summary," Edward recalled that when at Ajanta with the South African delegation in 1936, their impression, in sad contrast to the benign

Buddhist frescoes, had been that of a country sunk in misery and squalor: "I doubt if much good was done by that visit. They disbelieved everything that officials told them, and made no bones about saying so." The Rhodes Trust could perform a service by sending to South Africa an Englishman, or better yet, a man like Nehru, to lecture on "Indian culture, history, and famous men," who could avoid controversy on the "native problem" but might accomplish much by doing as the Trustees had enabled Edward to do, meet privately with men of influence. It would be useless to send one "who whitewashed what was black, or pretended that Hinduism was very pure and noble."[33]

The Trustees could initiate programs to alleviate vernacular illiteracy, for "the westernised system of teaching through English has failed," and India needed something more suited to her poverty and material needs. India had nothing comparable to the Rhodes Trust, the Pilgrim Trust, the Leverhulme Foundation. Could there be grants for key men and women who have "discovered a thing worth doing," in science, in agriculture? Could they send a trained economist with practical experience of village life, to help Untouchables to "a position of self-respect and self-sufficiency"? Could they get Tagore's long-delayed honorary degree? Could they persuade the barristers of the Middle Temple "to restore Gandhi's name to their rolls, from which it was struck off when he was convicted for civil disobedience?" And finally, could there be a few Indian Rhodes Scholars?[34]

Edward's "Political Report" is a sober document, a catalog of chances lost or botched. He asks why, within the empire, *only* India was *told* to fight. Why, when Congress asked for independence in return for martial support, was it accused of unseemly bargaining at a time of crisis? "Congress did not consider that it was bargaining." The Viceroy had consulted with fifty-two non-Indians while Congress awaited an answer. Edward thought that "if we had gone through the formalities of asking the central assembly and the provincial assemblies, India would have come enthusiastically into the war. The trouble is, Indians like us far better than they like other foreign devils, and they keep on believing that we shall turn out better than they know we shall." Congress would have cooperated if it could have done so with self-respect. He had heard that Gandhi had wept at the thought of London bombed. Nehru told Edward that Indian opinion had been cynical about England's performance in the last war, but " 'now was different. You will have reverses, of course, and some of them will be bad ones, and there will be the old temptation to feel pleased. But everyone knows your cause is good.' "[35]

Sir Samuel Hoare, Secretary of State for India, lost a chance for amity when he listed Europeans in India as an official minority. That they, "who are birds of passage and are in India for profit, should claim to be a 'minority' arouses anger." When visiting factories Edward had noticed German and American machinery: "British business could make far better terms for itself by friendly negotiation, than by insisting on heavy legislative protection in a foreign country." British big-business firms in India were "totalitarian."[36]

Wrong turnings in Hindu-Muslim relations, especially on Pakistan, crop up throughout Edward's "Report." He records this exchange with Jinnah 'six weeks ago" (mid-November):

> "Two nations, Mr. Jinnah! Confronting each other in every province? every town? every village?"
> "Two nations, confronting each other in every province. Every town. Every village. That is the only solution."
> "That is a very terrible solution, Mr. Jinnah!"
> *Jinnah, very gravely.* "It is a terrible solution. But it is the only one."[37]

Edward was astonished to find a high official in New Delhi "seriously pushing the so-called 'Pakistan' scheme: . . . I thought he was joking at first, then I said, 'You're the first man I ever met, whose brains I respected, who supports the Pakistan scheme.' He replied that now very many were supporting it." The great Urdu poet Mohammed Iqbal, credited with originating the idea, had once told Edward that it was not his scheme; he favored a majority "Muslim Province" in the northwest, in the proposed Indian Federation. He, too, thought Pakistan would be a disaster for the British government, the people of India, and both Hindu and Muslim communities. But as the president of the Muslim League he must go along. Edward thought it too much "like the kind of thing that British M.P.'s have often said to me, about nonsense which party loyalty made them support. . . ." Pakistan he thought strategically and ethically impossible; the "only possible basis is a community of political feeling which does not exist."[38]

In one form or another the idea of an Islamic hegemony existed at many levels, from elders like Iqbal to university students. Frederick Fielden, now at the Muslim University at Aligarh, found a sullen political undercurrent, and students "over-fond of politics." For the wrong reasons, the authorities "rather welcomed this, since otherwise the students might spend their spare time in criticising their teachers and the managing authorities generally." But Fielden regretted that the university, originally the Aligarh Anglo-Oriental College, founded to bring Muslims abreast of Hindus in English-language education, now advocated an Islamic purity campaign, censorship of books, and Urdu as the medium of instruction.[39]

Edward's desire for Indian unity colors his report. He doubts "alleged Muslim solidarity," since Muslim League membership was in the hundreds of thousands, while Congress enrolled many Muslims among its four and a half million members. He cites provincial governments with Congress majorities and provinces with Muslim premiers. Nevertheless, Congress had botched opportunities to encourage "community political feeling." It "could have formed a coalition Cabinet" in Bengal but opposed coalitions on principle. In New Delhi Edward heard repeatedly that Congress was " 'arrogant, is guilty of 'hubris.' " So it sometimes was, but he heard also that the Muslim League demanded the right to vet every detail of a new constitution. Rapprochement would be possible if Jinnah were not "solely intransigent and communal." Yet Edward would not rule him out altogether, for he had been a patriot and was once a Congress man. India, Edward believed, "will have to pass through a period of coalition governments," and there would be mistakes, and "Congress is despairingly coming to realise its mistakes. . . ." In the meantime, the Muslim League, "being refused a share of power, went into opposition, and increasingly bitter opposition." This did "more than any other thing to bring about the present bitterness. . . . Pakistan, if ever formed, would not be an abutment on a kind of Muslim League regime . . . [but] would find itself a perilous island." A decade later, East Pakistan, in particular, would find this all too true.[40]

Edward then addressed the perilous question of graft in India, on which he was more broad-minded than most Englishmen—not that he approved, but he points out that generalizations needed qualification, especially in view of bad British examples in eighteenth-century administration. In the twentieth, the Bombay government, for example, seemed overloaded with Gujaratis as against Marathas: "It was not graft, it was rather racial pull." Still, the British should criticize with care, for Indians noticed the overabundance of Scots in the administration. There was no Englishman on the Viceroy's Council, and the Viceroy himself was a Scot. Eight of eleven Governors were Scots, one an Ulster Scot. The Secretary of State and Permanent Undersecretary of State, the Commander-in-Chief and the leader of the European group in the Central Assembly all were Scots. The *Times* special correspondent was a Scot. Englishmen saw nothing racial in that, but "Indians do not realise this, . . . when the Government of India has been made a close shop for one race of the three that make up Great Britain." A small thing, and perhaps not ethnologically sound, but a little care about appointments could correct a public-relations lapse that was ground for major complaints.[41]

Congress provincial governments had done good work under serious handicaps. Their ministries were too small to cope with modern procedures. Its ministers' expense accounts were too small: only 750 rupees per year; they should be 1,000. Many Congress provincial ministries had passed good agricultural, tenancy, and debt reduction acts, and had established centers for seed distribution and veterinary services. Edward could not resist including his favorite cause: game preserves. India had only one. He had already seen how the woods around Ajanta had been shot out. Whole species vere disappearing elsewhere. He had spoken to Nehru about it. He had tried to interest Gandhi, "but he merely fooled: 'We shall always have the British lion!'" (Six decades later, there is international alarm about threatened extinction of the Bengal tiger: too many distinguished visitors had gone home with tiger-skin rugs.)[42]

Nehru, Edward thought, was the key. "Nehru's honesty is almost a new quality, it is so exceptional." Everyone who got close was drawn to him, even Jinnah, who "has a contempt for Gandhi." Gandhi tied India to Britain, "but Nehru will join Hinduism and Islam. . . . Nehru's sturdy Socialism makes Jinnah trust him. . . . Gandhi has had the sense to leave Nehru to make the conversations with Jinnah, and those conversations will succeed." Edward's respect for Nehru rose even higher when he refused invitations to meet Mussolini or to go to Nuremberg.[43]

In conclusion, Edward listed three overriding problems: communalism, the princes, and Indian defense. He believed that Congress and Indian opinion would force the Muslim League to a joint Declaration of Independence. The princes could join a democratic state if they so wished. Defense was a problem because most of the army came from the Punjab, where army employment took up a population increase, but recruiters got commissions, which gave them a political hold. Bengal was "smouldering, and there will be a desperate outbreak before long." Gandhi knew little of Bengal and stayed away. Calcutta, with 75 percent of the population, paid 82 percent of taxes and had only 45 percent of representatives. The coming outbreak would be "the result of sheer misery and sense of helplessness and injustice. And in Bengal there is less contact between Indians and Europeans than anywhere else, so this outbreak will take us by surprise." It erupted in 1940 when terrorism revived after the arrest of Subhashchandra Bose and the banning of his revolutionary Forward Bloc Party.[44]

England's reputation abroad needed repair. An American editor told Edward, "'We have a simple rule, that whatever the British Government does is done from base motives.'" Could Edward cite "'a single action in all your history that was decent?'" Yes, Edward had said, England had given the South African republics independence. He was angry when the editor said "contemptuously, 'All right, we'll admit that you *once* did a good thing.'" Malcolm Cowley, who was present and took pity, pointed out that England had taken a lead in the anti–slave-trade movement.[45]

Edward had an even worse experience, a night alone with three inebriated American correspondents just back from Prague. "'You are licked,' they kept saying, 'and the whole world knows it. You are yellow, and the whole world knows it.'" Maybe, Edward wrote, but, "We are the best of a very bad lot." England had lost "a tremendous chance" in India, to achieve a high moral position. She had failed, and civil disobedience was inevitable. Britain's only chance to recover lost moral ground was, first, never again to declare India a belligerent without her consent; second, allow India to choose her own constitution; and third, make England's war aims crystal clear. British politicians may have felt that they could not declare without France, but India cared nothing for France's intentions or for England's postwar aims.[46]

Edward returned feeling "that there is one kind of thinking in this island and in the world outside quite another. This seems to me a very dangerous position. Everyone knows we are in the right, but no one is enthusiastic about us"—because the prevailing opinion was that England's ruling classes would fight to maintain the status quo.

> India is poor and miserable, and also sick of the status quo. But she is also intensely emotional, and longs to be part of an effort that has wings to it and fire within it; to be part of "war aims" that are going to remake the Empire (and not merely Europe). We need to borrow Abraham Lincoln to make two or three speeches for us! to say something that would not be merely correct—not merely about overthrowing Hitlerism, a purely negative war aim—but imaginative and emotional.

Someone who wrote plain English should "make it pikestaff clear that we mean full Dominion status (now held before India's nose for 22 years, like a carrot before a donkey . . .)." Agreement would be difficult, but not impossible. Alas, Edward Thompson feared that there would be no such statement. "Everyone who knows Indian India will bear me out in this report. But see Isaiah, LIII, 1."

"Who hath believed our report? and to whom is the arm of the Lord revealed?"[47]

23

"CHAPLAINING" AGAIN

Edward returned from India to the avalanche of disasters that marked the beginning of general war. Germany and Russia divided Poland. Russia invaded the Baltic states and attacked Finland. In March 1940 Finland fell and, in April, Denmark. In June the Western European offensive began: Germany occupied Belgium and the Netherlands. Paris fell, and the Vichy government constituted itself to represent the remainder of France. In August 1940 the Luftwaffe bombed London and the Battle of Britain began. In November Italy, puffed up over its Ethiopian success, conducted an abortive Greek campaign. Hungary, Romania, and Slovakia joined the Axis.

The United States' Lend-Lease Act, which empowered President Roosevelt to sell war materials abroad, was not operative until 1941, but there was strong American opposition to involvement in Europe's troubles. In March 1939 Ratcliffe, lecturing at Depauw University in Indiana, found himself in the backwash of American isolationism. Europe, people told him, was already a lost cause: "Every other American I talk to lets me know that the Doom has come to England and France: there *must* be war this year; Paris and London are as good as destroyed: the black empire will be established: Thy Hand Great Anarch lets the curtain fall, and universal darkness buries all."[1]

On 8 January 1940 England began food rationing. On 18 May a drive began for Local Defense Volunteers. On 1 July the government stipulated thirty-six pages a week maximum for the penny newspapers and sixty pages for the *Times.* By 9 December, in addition to sleeping space in Underground stations, London had shelter bunks for 157,200 persons. Among the sad low-priority postscripts to this bleak record was the demise of William Morris's Kelmscott Press after eighty years of elegant publishing.

Indian news had one belated bright spot: thanks to Thompson and the Rhodes Trustees, Tagore at last received his Oxford D. Litt. degree, *honoris causa.* "You will be glad to hear," Elton wrote to Edward, "that your suggestion about Rabindranath Tagore, which I passed on to the Vice-Chancellor, has borne fruit. The Council decided yesterday to revive the D. Litt. and to allow it to be conferred *in absentia.*" He felt certain that there would be no opposition in Convocation. There was none, and as a great exception to regulations the presentation took place at Shantiniketan on 7 August 1940, for Tagore was too frail to travel, even had travel been possible. Oxford graduate Sir Maurice Gwyer, Chief Justice of India, read a graceful address, and Tagore " 'replied to this volley of Latin by a volley of Sanskrit, so India held its own. . . .' " Tagore responded, in English: "In honouring me, an Indian poet, your ancient seat of learning has chosen to express its great tradition of humanity." The recognition was "a happy augury of an age to come, and though I shall not live to see it established, let me welcome this friendly gesture as a promise of better days."[2]

Otherwise, Indian news stalled on the Congress Party's demand for full independence in return for cooperation in the British war effort. A. K. Azad wrote sadly to Edward Thompson that if possible he would have avoided the Congress Party presidency, but he could not refuse his colleagues at so critical a time. He was President until 1945.[3]

The heart of the problem was that England was still largely unconcerned about India. In August 1940 Edward contributed *Enlist India for Freedom* to Victor Gollancz's Victory Books. Edward first proposed a book on Ireland, but Gollancz decided that nothing could be done about Ireland, whereas something might still be done about India. These books should have "a Left point of view," should declare that "we *must* win," and should point out that winning the war against Fascism must include "the freeing of India, followed by the willing cooperation of that country in the war effort." The style should be journalistic, "hard-hitting and easy to read." Edward produced at speed thirty thousand words and dedicated the book to the memory of Andrews, who had tried so hard to enlist England for India's freedom. Edward proceeded from basics: How was India governed? What were the National Congress and the Muslim League? What was the significance of the Viceroy's declaring India a belligerent? What could Congress do? How could England and India retrieve this most recent of lost chances? For one thing, the resigned Congress-majority provincial ministries should return enlarged, with more Muslim members. For another, there should then be "frankly Coalition Ministries for the duration of the War." This would do much to stanch Hindu-Muslim bitterness. Why should treaties of 1819, from the Napoleonic era, shackle the princely states now? With India "a willing partner" in the war, the "far Eastern flank grows safer" and Japan less of a threat. Dominion status, a "moral victory," would happen, perhaps "after a delay of a few days." It did not happen, then or later.[4]

In September 1940 Gandhi, with Congress Party approval, announced noncooperation as his nonviolent protest against the war. His leading disciple, Vinoba Bhave, and Nehru went to prison, Bhave for three months and Nehru for four years. Edward called Nehru's arrest "a piece of cold ferocity." He had hoped to go to India in October for a film project on the history f the Ganges River (Nehru was emphatic about preferring the old name, Ganga), but air passage was unavailable. Anyway, it was highly unlikely that the government would have allowed Thompson to go at such a moment. As he had predicted in his Rhodes "Political Report," terrorism erupted in Bengal with the arrest of Subhaschandra Bose. Throughout India, twenty thousand noncooperators were arrested and fourteen thousand went to jail.[5]

Nevertheless, Congress continued to demand full independence, and Edward maintained his belief in dominion as solution and a revised empire as salvation. He was both India's prisoner and prisoner of that received belief in which he had been raised and which he thought he had outgrown: the empire was a good thing and sound at heart. Some repairs to the body politic would set all to rights; better-informed legislators in Britain, corrections to the Indian educational system, more Indians on governing bodies. Unfortunately, goodwill and mechanical repairs were not enough. Edward was so often so right about Indian matters that it is disquieting, in view of his privileged knowledge, to find him embracing the solution that Congress, the dominant voice in Indian politics, had already bypassed. The fault, as he saw it, was Britain's failure to make a firm offer of dominion status: "We still keep dangling hopes of Dominion Status. Membership of the Empire has lost much of its glamour. . . . India is ceasing to listen to us—our Government is like a showman still shouting while the crowd is drifting to another booth."[6]

Ironically, he preached an obsolete doctrine when he wrote, "Either this war will shatter the Empire or it will make it something greater and nobler than time has ever dreamed any Empire could be." He sent Nehru a hopeful letter from Spalding, and Nehru replied unequivocally that government through groups of sovereign states was an unattainable ideal inside the British Empire. He was sad that the British authorities still spoke of India in imperialistic terms. British rule had done much good, but now its actions were only disruptive. Severance from Britain was essential for the " 'commonwealth of man' " that Spalding desired. Talk of conciliation made people think that Congress was not serious and was ineffective. Why was England so afraid of Indian independence "in the context of world federation"?[7]

Nevertheless, Spalding continued his efforts to broaden Oxford's outlook on Asia. In 1937 he had admitted that amalgamating Indian studies and social studies was like "pushing against locked doors—a heavy and unheartening business," but he refused to give up. When Edward wrote that " 'if war comes, then nothing else matters,' " Spalding replied, "I don't in the least agree. Everything matters, and now a hundred times more than it did before." All should "do our utmost to see that things are better this time. It is all very well for you as an Air Warden to go round nightly dowsing the glim, but what you ought surely to contribute is serious work. You are known and trusted in India." Edward should be writing and broadcasting. "Isn't this one of the unique occasions of history for effecting a final reconciliation?" Spalding still believed in the cultural approach, and Oxford must help in so critical a situation. He and Edward still wanted a School of Oriental Studies and an associated Asia House. Lothian liked the Asia House idea, but diplomacy consumed his time and energies, and he died in 1940. Spalding still cherished Edward's idea of an Oxford-India Prize. He proposed an Honours School of Religions and Ethics; both graduates and undergraduates had said that they wanted something more satisfying than the standard academic diet. That, too, could be a model for universities at home and abroad. However, Oxford's Indian program, such as it was, was winding down. Edward had left the Indian Institute in 1939, and Spalding renewed his research fellowship. After 1939 no more I.C.S. probationers came. In 1945 the last attempt to revive the Institute fizzled out. By 1947 the government had terminated all I.C.S. courses in England.[8]

Lord Elton persisted, however, with Edward's suggestion of Indian Rhodes Scholars and discussed with Sir Maurice Gwyer the wording of the qualifications. They encountered one of India's most stubborn socioethnic problems. They proposed including as eligible candidates "all full-blooded Indians resident in India" and in the princely states, "and also British subjects of mixed British and Indian blood, resident in India"—that is, Eurasians, long marginalized in Indian society. (Edward must have thought of Metcalfe's mixed-parentage son who killed himself when he discovered how the English in India despised him.) Gwyer wanted to include "the pure-blooded British resident in India," which Elton thought a mistake: "Might not the Indians say 'you gave us this new Scholarship in recognition, as you say, of India's new status and yet you have selected a substantial proportion, (as we well might find ourselves doing), of British candidates. The whole thing is another piece of hypocrisy.'" It was another of the dilemmas of imperial rule.[9]

The Thompson family had their own dilemmas. While Edward was in India, Theo sold Scar Top and found the house at Bledlow in Buckinghamshire. Margaret's daughter Barbara remembers that at first Edward did not want to be that far from Oriel, but Theo overbore his objections; she argued that the boys had passed the stage for clinging to home.[10]

Edward and his sisters had to make new arrangements for Alfred. He had worked in Letchworth at the Spirella Corset Company's factory, whose owners were Theo's American friends. He was well paid and lived with a family as paying guest. Now, Spirella needed to drop some employees. Alfred would receive twelve pounds and a gold watch, but he wanted to stay in Letchworth, where he had friends and a garden allotment and could care for his mother's grave. Strictly on a temporary basis, he moved in with Margaret's family. The arrangement was not congenial; he still had brief but blazing rages, and Charles found this more than he could stand. Barbara found lfred a place at Lincoln, but he was not happy there. At a Wesleyan residence he was told that they " 'had enough to do with people who were not mad.' " Theo proposed a room and an allotment at Chinnor in Lincolnshire, a few miles from Bledlow. He drew unemployment money and had the very small income from the trust established by the good people of Colwyn Bay, but he could not live on that. Margaret urged him to look for light work; she still shuddered when she recalled him as a youth, following his mother from room to room and saying, " 'I'm 16 years old and I can't get work—I'm 16 years old and I can't get work.' " Earning even a little, even seasonally, Edward knew, would cheer him, for "he gets terribly depressed when he broods on his uselessness. At those times, only his family can help him, and for them it is no easy job." Edward feared that Alfred would outlive him: "We can only plan for the next year or so." They would share his upkeep. Theo proposed buying a garden plot. Edward stipulated that he must *not* hire an unemployed man to dig the garden for him. He must stop buying trees for it. Above all, he must forget about being a Wesleyan local preacher and teaching Sunday School, for he had no skills with children. Thus Alfred's resettlement at Chinnor was arranged.[11]

At Kingswood, Palmer was in the lower fifth, halfway up the school, and Edward wondered whether that was too low, for the work seemed so easy. But Palmer must remember (here Edward was not tactful) that the Dragon School crammed its top boys for preparatory school scholarships, so that even ordinary boys got pulled along with them and ended somewhat beyond their depth. Palmer was not yet a "world-beater" in English and history and must get the habit of reading. He must also mind his manners. In a sudden fit of class-consciousness Edward advised Palmer to remember that "it is one of the things that mark the Englishman of class that he is careful to be correct and proper always." Edward seemed to be carrying a large wet blanket. Palmer would have a struggle to make the Kingswood rugby team "and perhaps may not manage it." A month later Edward wrote, "I am working and planning for you to come up in four years [to Cambridge]." He would see Sackett about Palmer's modern languages—at which Frank was already brilliantly adept.[12]

Buffeted by anxieties about the war and about equipping Palmer for the uncertain future, the parents continued to nudge him this way and that. If he took natural history, shouldn't he take biology? His Uncle Arthur had been only a field naturalist when so many of his competitors had solid grounding in science. Might Palmer get interested in forestry, which offered world travel? Again: "Any fool with slick pen can become an ill-paid uninfluential hack journalist. But if you know a foreign language you at once move into a small class. Please take this seriously." Edward, Theo, and Mr. Sackett combined to urge him toward the Cambridge scholarship examinations. "So it is now or never if you want Palmer to go to one of the TWO UNIVERSITIES," Theo wrote. Languages were all-important at Cambridge, especially if he wante to concentrate on English and medieval history. Palmer thought of leavir school early to work on a farm if he did not get Cambridge admission. Th alarmed Edward. He approved of farmwork during holidays, but Palmer mu remember that his father "left school at yr. age and went through 5 years serfdom, and after that whatever little I ever learnt I had to learn throug sorrow and failure."[13]

Palmer, however, was shaping his own career. His Kingswood record car describes him as of " 'independent mind' and good-naturedly impatient certain school rules." He became a prefect and had a wide variety of activitie including valuable service on the Chapel Committee "(though unable himse to subscribe to Christianity's tenets.)" He was also "highly regarded as 'very promising poet,' " which pleased his father very much. He rejoice that Palmer might "prove a poet—anyway, a man of literary and ment ability and force—so you must not get warped into anything that is—no independence, that you will always have—but eccentricity or singularit Everyone of originality gets tempted this way, and through the ages it ha produced a plentiful crop of minor folk and near-geniuses, who have to hav zestful coteries to keep their stuff alive." Palmer had sent a list of poets whos work he thought would endure. Edward disagreed strongly about Auder whose flight to America he thought inexcusable, for "it costs everything man has[,] to face the breaking of body and mind"—as true for poets a for the charlady whose son was missing at Dunkirk. Palmer must not writ a single sentence that mixed values. He must not worry about his father' criticisms, for Edward was ever ready to admit error. Palmer must not be to impatient with older people. He must "keep always firm foot on fact, while eager to welcome every doctrine." Christ's way meant peace—but that wa not the same as the church's way. Still, "Methodism is not far wrong when reminds you that your job is 'to serve the present age.' " On second thought perhaps he was mistaken about Auden, and perhaps Palmer had listed him because he considered him one of "the supreme lovers of mankind."[14]

In 1940 Kingswood, whose location at Bath was extremely vulnerable was evacuated to Uppingham in Leicestershire. Palmer now concentrate on history, but hated the assembling and reassembling of secondhand facts History probably held the better chance of a scholarship, but it was un fortunate that history was made "essentially a means to an end." Edward was now confident that Palmer would win a scholarship. So he did, and in October 1941 he entered Corpus Christi College, Cambridge, for one yea before being called up for service. Eventually, he was to be distinguished in English and history but never in languages. "Moreover," he wrote many years later, "by some mystery of inheritance which I cannot explain, all the linguistic genes which descended in superabundance upon my brother were exhausted when it came to my turn. I have never been able to command a single language with any facility."[15]

The parents, in something of a panic, had been too eager to fit him to a system that guaranteed class and educational advantages, to attach a cachet that would linger on with Frank, even after he had jettisoned conventional social and political ideologies. His frame of historical reference was already broader than Britain, in a vision of a future Europe united in purpose and prosperity, with proficiency in languages a binding factor. In 1981 Palmer himself analyzed the difference between himself and Frank as not only a difference in time but also "a gap that was enlarged by the pressure of the times." Their home was "supportive, liberal, anti-imperialist, quick with ideas and poetry and international visitors." In boyhood Palmer was Frank's supporter and protector. In their youth, Palmer excelled in the sports so important in English schools. Both wrote poetry but Frank came to it from Winchester's literary classicism, and Palmer from sources "more low-brow, moralising—perhaps even Methodistical—and self-consciously demotic." In 1981 he confessed that Winchester's "self-satisfied sense of its own excellence" had come between them in those days. In letters at least, their parents seem to have had no inkling of this.[16]

All such adjustments were the more difficult because Edward was not at home. In September 1940 he became a voluntary Y.M.C.A. worker attached to the Royal Artillery. He told Ratcliffe that he was "what they style a Wholetime Lecturer under the War Office. It has been a kind of intellectual Stop Me and Buy One man, peddling my barrow of lectures all over the place." There was no other work for him in the national effort, and it was "distressing to have lived till one was past all usefulness. However, I have done it." At first the work seemed footling and frustrating. At a camp at Bulford in Wiltshire there was much entertainment, good food, and no bombing, but he had no place to meet with the men, not even a table on which to write reports. He had brought a car that would not start, and he could not get petrol. His army pass was limited, and living quarters were elementary. The padre, an Australian, wanted him to organize small discussion groups and warned that he could expect questions such as "Why does not God stop the war?" Edward announced a lecture on "Greece and Its Importance to the World," and his audience was one man who wandered in by mistake. However, when two men turned up who said that they were dying for some intellectual conversation, the padre rather cramped their talk, for he kept interrupting and showed that he resented any such discussions if he were not in charge. The army seemed not to take the Y.M.C.A. "as anything but well-meaning chumps who do a fine job in the tea and bun line." True, its program was mostly meals (which it did well) and games. But he needed privacy in which to meet men who sought him out, such as one assigned to

India. Still, Edward was glad he had come, for he gained insight into Frank's modern military experience. He had volunteered again at twenty, after one year at New College, and reported for active duty. He, too, was with the Royal Artillery. Even in quiet Wiltshire, the war was all too real: German bombers to Coventry flew overhead.[17]

Except for battles and sermons, this was an updated version of Mesopotamia. Those inclined to snobbery were still flagrantly rank conscious. Edward saw that he would get more cooperation after his uniform came. When he requested permission to put his car in a shed, a young officer was insolent but snapped to attention when he realized that Edward was the man " 'who writes all those books.' " He offered a chair, addressed him as "Sir"; that man, Edward thought, will get ahead. Now he was asked to lecture to the whole garrison on Mesopotamia. He lectured to another unit on current history: "I had a place packed, and the level of intelligence and education was miles higher than it is here [at Bulford]." A colonel bellowed at him, wanted to know whether he had been searched and had a gun, then said that they needed a welfare officer and wanted Thompson for the job. Edward said that he was not looking for a paid job; he wanted to be where the men could talk to him. Nevertheless, he became the welfare officer and expected to write between 60 and 150 letters a day.[18]

In December he transferred to Larkhill on Salisbury Plain and had a large room with a fireplace, a shed for the car, and a request that he dress not as an officer but as a gentleman. But could he get past the sentries? He received a new pass. His commanding officer suddenly remembered *The Other Side of the Medal* and an article, perhaps in *Time and Tide*. The General at Headquarters Southern Command was upset when a Thompson lecture was canceled, supposedly by his order; he was also pleased that the mistake had occasioned their meeting. He had hoped for years to meet Edward Thompson.

The fine room at Larkhill had no equipment. This padre saw to it that the army did more than was asked: clothes, sheets, towels. The food was good; there were bomb shelters and no hardships: "The Y.M.C.A. seems like a bad dream." On 4 January 1941 he was "ordained Welfare Officer for Larkhill." The War Office decreed that welfare officers should have officer rank, and Edward resumed his old rank of captain. Perhaps, he mused, he should have stayed a chaplain: "I am a natural padre; men talk to me, and my life has had numerous disadvantages but this one great advantage, that it has enabled me to touch practically every man's life at some point." His room filled nightly, and he told them, if he were not there, to come in and sit by the fire. He found that some of these men had great respect for literature, which made his work a pleasure. Others came in great distress. A bombardier was the first to take up Edward's offer to be available at any time. His home had been bombed in November and the next-door neighbors killed. He had four little girls, aged three to eleven, and they had just been bombed again. One girl was rescued with difficulty and was still in "a state of close-on hysteria." The family had one room with one bed. "A notoriously slack office" had lost the application for family quarters. Repeated requests got no response, although the chaplain had taken up the case. Edward cut the red tape, got the only family facility available: "The man was terribly grateful." Six men came whom he encouraged to talk about their past lives, all hard ones. They were "a sort of general sink of nondescripts who do fatigues—not v. interesting." The padre, who hoped to remodel Edward as Anglo-Catholic, urged him to convince those men that they were wrong about being of no use: they contributed to the training of young officers! This padre every two months or so cleaned out the bathroom: "But that sort of thing once a two-month is a rather fine bit of religio-masochistic exercise: as a daily job not quite so exhilarating."[19]

Soon, as welfare officer and as one to be consulted, he was included in all regimental activities, and he had to learn "to keep things under my own hat as never before." Larkhill had a large cadet training unit, and a still larger survey unit with many schoolmasters and architects. Edward found the officers exceptional and had "not yet met a Blimp among them." He lectured or led discussions five nights a week. Lindsay at Balliol offered to find lecturers from Oxford, but having to "go through channels" was dampening. Salisbury Plain was a neutral area to both Bristol and Oxford, but Bristol had been bombed, and it became impossible for lecturers to travel among units. Edward thought that the army's education administrators were foolishly unrealistic: not even Francis Bacon could have covered all the subjects requested. Some of the lecturers assigned were quite unsuitable; among those was "a vast noisy Parsee" with a combatant commission, "conceited, brainless, opinionated, very anti-Congress and anti-Nehru & blustering about his 'strong imperialist views.' "[20]

Edward appealed to the BBC for publicity—not for himself, but for what was good about the army's education program. The public should know what a welfare officer did, and how complex was the job of an education officer. He had, for example, "a large isolated unit of Canadians, far away from cinemas or bus routes: a difficult audience, far less sophisticated than Americans (though there are Americans among them), but lovely fellows. . . . They are avid to know all they can about Britain, our history, antiquities, social ways, literature, everything. . . . Men are eagerly discussing Postwar Reconstruction, War Aims and Education." If the public knew more, they might get more help from "the very best men & women in civil life, visiting us, talking to us: and that the understanding between civilians & soldiers wd. be deepened."[21]

Tension was everyone's constant companion. "Everyone knows we are moving towards THE CLASH," Edward wrote to Theo, "and everyone know it will be a desperate push. Hitler will go all out with planes and u-boats, and try to get his demons across. Keep yr. U.S. flag. You may need it! (I hope this is a joke!)" The camp was bombed after he went home for a weekend; there were seventeen deaths.[22]

Welfare work increased exponentially. He needed an orderly and a tele phone. Men now came to him at all hours, and officers about their men' problems. As always, exhaustion made him pessimistic. He had signed on originally for three months with the Y.M.C.A. but now did not see how he could just walk away from the new assignment. He reflected that he was good at arranging other people's affairs, but what about Alfred, his own welfare problem? He had left all that to Theo and his sisters.

He had moments of strong feeling that Frank, now abroad, was in great danger. He thought and prayed hard for ten minutes, and the crisis feeling passed. In March 1941 Frank went with a small communications and intelli gence unit to serve in North Africa, Sicily, the Middle East, and eventually in Serbia and Bulgaria. "Thus," his brother wrote, "for over three years at an age when today's analogues might be dropping in and out of universities, he was leading an itinerant military life." In June 1941 Edward found himself hoping that if Frank were in the Libyan or the Syrian campaigns it was the Syrian, since that was a part of the world his parents knew well: cold comfort, but a connection of sorts. "Tell yr. Americans to think well of us," Edward wrote to Ratcliffe. "We may not be good or satisfactory, but we are necessary."[23]

In September 1941 Edward became the welfare officer at an R.A.F. instal lation at West Malling in Kent: "I am a pioneer missionary trying to start the first lectures that are not routine mathematical and navigation lectures I was told by everyone that the job was hopeless. This is rot," he wrote to Elton. He found those men the best he had yet met, in education and breadth of interests. "The R.A.F. level is higher than the Army's. We have few conscripts, so the physically derelict do not slip in. The keenness is immense and there is not one-tenth of the Army red tape." Most of the officers were Oxford or Cambridge men, "and I therefore cannot accept some of the breezy uplift lecturers who infest this region. We have hardly any books." That need was even greater at dispersal points where pilots passed their time between flights: "This is the front line." He had not asked for Rhodes help, as he did not want to interfere with Kent's excellent Education Service, but if there was money to spare, could the Trustees provide materials for the dispersal areas and "our hideous mess libraries"? There was no time for a library circulation system: "Our days are too precarious." He did his best singlehanded. "When I leave at the end of Oct., I shall be dead tired but deeply sorry to go."

t this same time William Rothenstein was touring R.A.F. dispersal points, s an official war artist, making portrait drawings of airmen, some the last kenesses of those who did not return.[24]

At West Malling Edward began to sag under the incessant letter writing and lso to feel that he did not want to stay on with the R.A.F. They were "not as ocile as the brutal and licentious soldiery who have learnt meekly to accept ny dud sent to them," but he began to modify some of his first impressions. he worst of it was that they referred to the army as " 'the coolies!' Shades f Quetta and Poona!" The R.A.F. began to adopt army red tape, "making lecturer fill up innumerable forms and wrangling over every penny of xpenses he claims." He was uncomfortable at a squadron party because fter two cocktails (he did not want the second) he asked for a glass of water; veryone assumed that he was drinking gin. In fact, his deteriorating health ad caught up with him: "I am not well at all and have a queer presentiment hat my strength is steadily settling down and that one way or another I am early finished." Perhaps it was just general strain "or the war and India."[25]

Indian developments—or rather, lack of them—worried him. Nehru was till in jail. Edward despaired of Gandhi's leadership: "What an ass Gandhi s! He has put the whole Indian National Movement into a bad spin." On August 1941 Tagore died. His passing ended a great career in Bengali terature, a watershed in East-West literary relations. On 14 August 1941, loosevelt and Churchill met at sea and declared the peace aims to be known s the Atlantic Charter. It stated their wish "to see sovereign rights and self-overnment restored to those who have been forcibly deprived of them.")n 9 September Churchill slapped down Indian hopes by telling the House f Commons that the charter did not apply to India, Burma, or other parts f the British Empire. Edward was beyond disgust: "Ought I perchance to tump the country addressing meetings on India? Or get put up for one of he by-elections largely on this issue? Before I end I ought to do something hat matters."[26]

He despaired about the British deficit of information on India. He had had unch in London with Herbert Morrison and thought him "a lively card." India vas not mentioned until the end of the meal, when Morrison said, " 'I know 1othing about it. It's not my department.' He thought it was merely a question f Hindu & Muslim quarrels, and 'If they do not mean Independence, why he hell can't they say so?' "—as if they had not been saying so for at least wo years! Edward had coffee with Krishna Menon, who said that Edward levin was "v. worried about India but ignorant." Edward resolved to try to ee Bevin the next week.[27]

He left the R.A.F. at the end of November 1941. On 7 December the apanese attacked Pearl Harbor, and America entered the war. The Pacific

Islands chain disintegrated, link by link. Singapore fell on 15 February 1942 and many of the sixty thousand Indian troops taken prisoner there became part of Subhaschandra Bose's Indian National Army, which intended to take up arms against the Raj. On 11 March 1942 the British-Indian impasse was only emphasized when Churchill sent Sir Stafford Cripps, leader of the House of Commons, to India with a proposal for dominion status. Provinces or states that did not wish to join could stay out, but the status quo, British control and all, would remain until after the war. Why, Gandhi asked, did he come if that was all he could offer? He advised Sir Stafford to take the first plane home and called the offer " 'a post-dated cheque on a bank that was failing.' " The Congress working committee supported him, and in the spring of 1942 Gandhi launched his last campaign, the Quit India Movement whose eventual outcome was Independence and Pakistan in 1947.[28]

On 23 April 1942 Geoffrey Garratt died in a bomb explosion in London. He had gone there to meet Cripps, who had sent for him. "Private grief is almost swallowed up in public fury at the moment," Beryl Garratt wrote to Edward. Geoffrey had already received the M.B.E. for conspicuous gallantry in another explosion incident. "What folly & selfishness has kept Geoffrey from the work till it is too late!" Foreign correspondence and relief and rescue efforts for two generations of refugees had occupied him since the Great War. He had had political aims as well: in 1925, 1929, 1931, and 1935 he had contested, as a Liberal but without success, the Cambridgeshire seat for Parliament. He had been determined not to give up when another such chance arose. In his last letter to Edward he wrote, "Somehow politics will always be a squalid game, but I do feel that there ought to be some group working to clear out the wicked old men. . . . And it can only be done by some new party prepared to fight by-elections etc. As it is they are recruiting the worst type of stock brokers, business men, and 'little brothers of the rich' into the Conservative party, and some pretty dull party hacks and trade union officials into the Labour Party. The Liberals never get a vacancy. I feel someone should be attacking personally and bitterly all the Friends of Franco, and those who sent Mussolini their sympathy and encouragement in 1936." As for India, no one, it seemed, "cares a damn— Left or Right. I rather wish I had pressed to go out, but I felt then that should only become violently rebel, and my position would have been very anomalous."[29]

Ratcliffe wrote from New York:

There can't have been many Englishmen w. emotions more instantly responsive to need, or more generous and intelligent in service. He must have seen more of human suffering than nearly all of us, and yet one felt that he had an inner spring of happiness upon which to draw. . . .

The best are falling all round us, and more and more will go as the conflict goes on and spreads over the globe.[30]

Garratt's death left Edward feeling wretched and diminished. Garratt had been one of that cherished small group, like Percy Lyon, like Ratcliffe, like the stubbornly idealistic Spalding—often like Edward Thompson himself—who prophesied against the running current and found no comfort if eventually proven right.

24
LETTERS TO THE FRONT

An unfinished typescript tells much about Ed ward's state of mind at this time. It refers to roughly the years covered in his 1939 book, *You Have Lived through All This,* but the tone is somewhat different. That earlier work surveys British thinking from 1919 to 1939, from postwar optimism and complacency to the downward slide that allowed Fascism to flourish. In this later fragment a reference to Sir Stafford Cripps' failed mission to India suggests a date of writing after March 1942. Edward may have begun the autobiography that friends and the agent Alfred Curtis Brown (with a rather backhanded compliment) had urged: "That is the only book which I would like to keep aside from Peters, for my heart has been set on getting it, as you know, for some years. I know how good it would be and how continuous a sale it would have, not necessarily because of the importance of your life, but as the expression of individuality of character."

Edward begins by writing of himself. He had become "pigeonholed as 'a man who writes about India,' " but he had had other interests: religion in his youth, and the writing of verse, "until I was close on forty." Politics then had interested him "hardly at all. I believed, in those far-off days, that the world was steadily, if slowly, moving towards a reasonably just and fair arrangement of mankind and their affairs and that it was bound so to move. We did not then talk of 'democracy' " but believed that parliamentary government would spread, "England having shown the way." The subject races had welcomed the empire as their savior from "a return of the miseries which had oppressed them before the British saved them." The Labour Party was a movement, not a political machine, and "genuine passion" had animated radicalism. When the Great War began, "We little dreamed that, having lost our brothers and friends, when we were old we were to lose sons and friends, . . . that a way of life which, with modifications such as time demanded, had served mankind for centuries, would have vanished for ever." This was all platitudes, he knew, but true.[2]

He had never belonged to a political party, and he said again: "I suppose I am really a Liberal, of the most conservative kind." But he thought the Liberal Party no longer either attractive or honest.

Probably even Gilbert Murray, who had worked so hard for the League of Nations, and the chief negotiator at the Paris Peace Conference, Lord

302

Cecil, "whose disastrous foreign policy had brought about the war," knew that appeasement would be a grave mistake. The Cripps mission had failed in "a flash of ill temper" and recriminations. But Gandhi's nonviolence and noncooperation had swung the quarrel in a wrong direction, for consistent nonviolence had proved impossible. Tagore had been right to condemn India's political mendicancy: asking for boons, then calling them inadequate. The British public did not know or care about Pakistan. (But Edward, who knew what it was and how unequivocally Jinnah was in favor, underestimated it: "It does not much interest me either, for I know that in a few years it will die away of its own innate preposterousness.") The British excuse that India could not be free because disunited would collapse once India made a start at unity. He hoped that Indian unity would not mean a complete break: "I myself, from I suppose some relic of only half-repentant Imperialism still within me, would still find myself tempted to hope that India would remain in some kind of voluntary relationship with my own people and our kindred peoples." His reasons, he told himself, were not "Imperialist" in the old possessive sense. If India and Britain reached an understanding, that would be a lesson for all the world.

In *You Have Lived through All This* he had surveyed time more easily remembered: "the last few years or so; we forget anything beyond them. . . . To anyone under forty, this book has a chance of bringing facts that they do not know, which might affect their thinking." He had concluded, "Soon we must face the alternatives, of sinking into third-rateness or reconstruction." By 1942, however, belief in the inevitable spread of parliamentary rule and stability of empire was obsolete. With British cities bombed and soldiers fighting overseas, reconstruction must be not just a change of the political guard at Westminster and Whitehall, but a comprehensive reconstitution of both government and nation.

In 1940 he had told Palmer that a new direction required "a blazing faith." Nazis, Fascists, Communists had that, and the democracies had become sloppy, "self-indulgent and dithering." The most hopeful sign was that Chamberlain was out and Churchill's coalition government in.[3]

As a conservative liberal with a tilt toward socialism, he hoped that he was among the effective ones. Now the princes were a key to British-Indian understanding. If the British understood them as a political inheritance, and more than flashing jewels and gorgeously caparisoned elephants, perhaps they would understand the complications of fitting them into twentieth-century India. To that end Edward wrote *The Making of the Indian Princes,* which traces the origins of old dynasties with their own long histories of shifting powers that became political anachronisms. Their old India originated between 1799 and 1819, two decades that put Britain in control of a new India. Edward's preface begins: "Now that India's right to independence has been acknowledged, the Princes' rights and status remain her outstanding constitutional problem. It cannot be decided by mere legal examination of their treaties with the Paramount Power." His book ends with a discussion of "paramountcy" as a doctrine of "British rights overruling the rights of all other Governments in India." Over time this had evolved as a concept of England's *duty* to rule India. "Bitterness came later in abundant measure and with frequent justification. But perhaps no conquest was ever carried through with so little of bitterness at the time, and little of bitterness clings to its memory." If this apologia was too rosy, it was still true that the Princely States were a reasonably steady element in the Indian political amalgam. The question was: what now?[4]

In 1943 E. M. Forster singled out that book in a BBC radio talk on writers on India. "You are certain," he began, "to know the name of Edward Thompson. You will be familiar with his integrity, his breadth of outlook, and the width of his interests." Forster emphasized the contrast between Metcalfe and his successors, "who may have had high principles, but were prim and self-righteous, and too obviously the products of public schools." Thompson, "who began life as a moralist, has come to believe, he tells us, that humanism is what is needed for healing of wounds, and he recommends both English and Indians to study these earlier times, when hearts were warm."[5]

The Making of the Indian Princes was widely reviewed, but two prominent notices might well have made Edward doubt whether he had punctured British complacency. One insisted that the princes' importance, psychological and political, derived from the British, who prevailed because of "superiority in organization and training" and able commanders who gave them the edge although they lacked superiority in arms. Another thought that British superiority and treaties had made the states what they became. Obviously, if there was a "Great Power," there must be "Lesser Powers." Besides, historical controversy was no key to present-day Indian problems.[6]

Edward disapproved strongly of official policy for the 650 Princely States. "When there is any suggestion of doing anything to help the subjects of the Big Princes to democracy, the official reply is always that we must not go against our treaty obligations. Last year, however, Brother Linlithgow off his own bat ukased that 300 of the smallest States shd. cease to exist . . . that they should be joined to the nearest Big State. This was a bribe to the Big Princes, our loyal supporters." The dispossessed landowners appealed to the high court, which ruled that the Viceroy's action abrogated the treaties, and the House of Commons passed a bill and made speeches calling it "a fine *democratic* deed. . . . It is anything but that, of course," Edward wrote, since it handed those people over to "far more powerful princes on whom they & their opinions can have no influence. . . ." The landowners sent the Prime Minister and Edward, and a few others, enormous and expensive cables of "pleading & protest" begging them to stop the annexations. Theo thought that Edward should reply. "No doubt this is so. But *what* reply?"[7]

In 1943 Bengal was again in the news. Food shortages, inflation, hoarding, withholding of grain stocks, shortfalls in food deliveries from neighboring governments themselves in trouble, and disastrous weather caused a catastrophic famine. There were passionate political protests in England, that such a situation should have been allowed to happen. Edward, who well remembered his famine relief work at Bankura, was on a Famine Committee in London to mobilize assistance. There was a rare disagreement with Lyon, who thought that again the trouble sprang from inexperienced administrators. "I venture to suggest," he wrote, "that some of the opinions of various authorities you quote smack of wisdom after the event, [of] which many of the actions—as to export of grain and transport arrangements etc—were dictated by the exigencies of this war, of the importance of which it is difficult for us to judge. It is in your general approach to the subject that I believe you to be in error." He cited his thirty years in Bengal and Behar administration. "The real trouble throughout this lamentable famine has been the inexperience of the ministers in Bengal & the Central Govt., due to the substitution of Indian political leaders for trained administrators." The Bengal government, thus reconstituted, had failed to foresee the famine. Indians needed responsibility, but this had been thrust upon them too soon and unfortunately at the time when Congress called out its majority provincial ministries. Inexperience had replaced experience "under the special strain of war and famine." "We must agree to differ," Lyon concluded, "and I must apologise for vaunting my experience in administration work in Bengal as opposed to your careful study of this most important question. And, in any case, I remain, as ever, your friend."[8]

Both were right. War had caught everyone unprepared. Edward had last seen his Congress friends in 1939, so that he had little firsthand report of the consequences. The I.C.S. itself was in trouble. Broomfield writes that "subordinate services in Bengal were understaffed and underpaid, and the province was an unpopular choice for recruits to the I.C.S., who generally preferred the more prosperous and politically stable provinces." In 1939, when I.C.S. recruitment ended, all leaves were suspended. Many administrators broke under the strain, and two Governors of Bengal died in office. A million and a half Bengalis died of starvation and disease.[9]

Everyone's view of events was fragmentary. Day by day and night by night Theo and Edward tried to piece together news of Frank and Palmer. In March 1941 Frank went to the Middle East as a Lieutenant in Communications and Intelligence, with a G.H.Q. Liaison Regiment known as Phantom. What they did not know was that Frank would volunteer to parachute into Serbia, then go into Bulgaria with a tiny British intelligence unit to join partisans behind the German lines. Palmer wrote cheerfully from North Africa and would eventually go into Italy with the cataclysmic assaults on Cassino. Theo hoped that he might go to the Eastern Mediterranean, for there he would inherit her friends and perhaps find some of her relatives. She was dismayed, however, because he now wanted to be known as Edward. Perhaps "some of your friends of the 'Edward' period who know you are called 'Palmer' at home . . . might be given the chance of calling you Palmer Thompson,' as they say 'You mean *Frank* Thompson.' " Mightn't Palmer Thompson be a good pen name? "It is far more distinctive than 'Edward'—you wouldn't be confused with anyone." Had she failed to convince him that it mattered to his father, Frank, and herself? Rejecting her uncle's name, did he reject his American heritage? In the army he became Edward; in his parents' letters he was Palmer.[10]

His father began to find Bledlow a refuge after all and decided that he did not want to return to Scar Top. Bledlow had a wonderful variety of meadows, downs, beechwoods, deep lanes, and juniper copses. Furthermore, Boars Hill was less satisfactory for riding, since barbed wire and fences had crept in. Besides, Oxford was depressing, with "those poor American soldiers on leave, with nixes to do, just stand against the Clarendon Hotel, or most anywhere: just stand." The afternoon cinema helped a little, "but the whole thing is ghastly. Many of them are just girl-hungry, for any girl whatsoever, and their ways are not ours, bad as ours in many ways are. War is no good to anyone." If the young men must go abroad, however, it was better to go and do it, get it over with, and go home. Oxford talked a lot but did little—including, presumably, for the stranded Americans. That supplemented what Frank had written about the "*non*-mixing of Americans"—that is, officers who preferred to frequent English officers' clubs.[11]

The Oxford Union invited Edward to speak at a debate on India and the famine. If he needed further proof of English ignorance of—and scorn for—India, he had it there. He thought the occasion "lamentable. The Left benches were almost empty: gone to worship at the Star of their God Uncle Joe; the Tory benches were packed & aggressive (as they had cause to be, for really our side did drivel—so did theirs). Those young men cared nothing whatever about India or the famine. The first speaker, who finally voted cross-bench & who privately kept on saying that he knew nothing about India &, so far as he cared, was on my side, having nixes to say spoke for 50 minutes!! Sheer inanity, not even childish prattle." An Indian Muslim opponent was "nice but ineffective." Next came "a dim surly ass who read a long screed," which someone told Edward came from the *Daily Telegraph*. Then a Jamaican made "obscure elaborate personal jests" that his opponents capitalized upon. A "rather decent Tory" took up the Jamaican's statement about color prejudice in the empire, and a flood of clichés and prejudices followed from the audience, with arguments about whether it was desirable to have a black man as the president of the Oxford Union. The Bengal famine seemed quite forgotten. After two and a half hours of this, "I the visitor spoke to a bored & nearly empty house, & felt that I must huddle all my argument up. It was NOT one of my good performances, but that does not worry me, for no one under those circ[umstances] cd. have done well." Most of the voting members had gone, and by sixty-four to fifty "the House resolved that the Govt. had done all in its power for the physical welfare & self-govt. of the Indian people—wh. both the Ind[ian] Central Govt. and the India Secretary [of State] have had to admit openly that they damn well have not." Edward left, and when he returned later found just three Tories hearing the president of the Oxford Conservative Club saying that " 'all that stood between India and Japan wd. be Gandhi's loin-cloth (laughter).' " It was indeed a lamentable occasion.[12]

Two weeks later Edward, with Krishna Menon, sampled a quite different sector of public opinion when they spoke on the Indian famine at a public meeting in Walthamstow, whose mayor presided. They tried to be "scrupulously unpolitical, then the audience took charge." An Anglican parson made "a v. red speech," after which various persons demanded the right to speak and spoke to the point that *all* was political "and lit into the Govt." Another parson, son and grandson of India missionaries and a soldier himself in India before ordination, rose to say that "he had learnt nothing at our meeting whatever, that he had hoped he wd. hear what wd. send our hearts away 'filled with love' for the people of India." Edward found Walthamstow "v. red, and the beauty of the Socialist Movemt. is that it throws up stacks of blokes who get up on their hind legs & speak & consider that they shd. But the fine thing was, this was the first Civi[c] meeting about the famine. . . ." Edward had been told that the mayor was "a big fool," and although he dropped his aitches, his pronunciation was imperfect, and his rhetoric reminiscent of the music-hall, Edward and he found common ground with cricket. His Honour had been a wicket-keeper. " 'Show me yr. hands,' I commanded sternly. Sheepishly, to the horror of his entourage, he showed them. 'Yes, they are wicketkeeper's hands. But I have seen worse.' So we formed an entente. W'stow's civic buildings are on the superbest scale, as good as they can have in any American Zenith. I had no idea we had such."[13]

Edward's contacts with valued friends were now hard stretched. Ratcliffe was still lecturing in America. He wrote in May 1942: "The public attention at present is directed at the drastic scheme for industry and business, the ceiling on incomes, and so forth. It was not possible to intensify, one would have said, the hostility of the business world towards the Govt and the New Deal, but this has certainly done it." The Republican Party no doubt rejoiced at the discontent but lacked leadership. The Klan and anti-Semites were "always ready to line up afresh against the Govt. . . . I never speak to m[e]n or women from Washington, or from any city of the interior, without hearing more about the mischievous exploitation of the always-existent anti-British sentiment." American editorials, however, had begun to speak more responsibly; this was a reaction against those expatriate Congress Party extremists in America—of whom Edward had already had enough experience—who spoke "on platforms and on the air as though nothing had happened, as though India were still struggling against the old system and the old imperialists. . . . It is essentially the same situation that you found when you were here twelve years ago: the USA in general is against the British Empire, as indeed the whole world is: not of course against England, but against British world power and influence."[14]

The Spaldings were stranded in the United States after they went there in 1939 to visit friends and give some talks. Funds from England were severely restricted, and they had much kindness from American friends but lived a wearing peripatetic life. Spalding wrote from Cambridge, Massachusetts: "Of course there must be a settlement [in India]; it is unavoidable. But who is to make it? . . . But one is left up against this horrid problem: Are men who have mishandled the affairs of their own country terribly for lack of advice capable of settling the affairs of India, let alone of taking part in world affairs? (You know that last is precisely the thing that I want to see India doing.)"[15]

Edward was annoyed with those who assumed that when the war ended the survivors would of course adopt Anglo-American blueprints: "I fancy the sufferers may have some ideas of their own, & be willing to do without our gracious governance. If they do, then much power say we." Public and editorialists seemed to assume that Indians would "accept our cause as theirs & [begin] to see that of course they shd. put aside their own affairs. As THE TIMES Special Correspondent grandly remarks, in India only 'professional politicians fuss about such a bagatelle as independence.'"[16]

Edward had said that poetry was his concern only until he was forty, but it was always on his mind, and he continued to write it. He thought that modern poetry had become trendy and tricky but was not imaginative. Palmer had sent some of his own, and Edward was pleased that he was reading traditional poetry. Palmer believed that "on the whole, poetry now should be written to be performed and not to be put in slim volumes which are read by a small public silently and to themselves. You certainly have little right to ask the working-class to be suddenly interested in stuff of this sort. It should be performed, read aloud, written as mass oratory or for songs, plays, sketches."[17]

It may not have been ideal for the times, but Edward gathered a hundred poems of his own for publication as a slim volume. He cared keenly about its reception, for this was his last word on himself as a poet. Wilfred Gibson, in the *Guardian*, liked best those from his Great War experience. The *pectator*'s reviewer read them as "poetic biography"—which they are. They show how much he had matured in the intervening years, in technique and sensitivity. Nature, nature's variations, and man's and nature's reciprocal responsibilities are still his themes.[18]

Oxford Press wanted a book on Robert Bridges, and Edward set to work at once: "It is queer; I believe I know more about him now than anyone outside his family; & I love his Shorter Poems, wh. always seem to me grand." But he found himself at odds with some of the work that Bridges valued most. He found *The Testament of Beauty* "difficult, often dull, & much of his other work null." Still, he shared with Bridges his ecstatic, even mystical reactions to natural beauty. Catherine Phillips, the biographer of Bridges, writes that they were "so powerful [that Bridges] thought they must be attributable to more than was physically evident in nature. This is an ecstasy many adolescents experience, but for most people even the memory of it fades with maturity." Edward certainly had it in adolescence and long afterward, and it was his enduring link to Bridges, along with gratitude for memories of the kindness that had welcomed him to Oxford so long ago.[19]

Others, too, preferred the lyrics and shorter poems of Bridges, as did Edward himself. Virginia Woolf, who visited Bridges in 1926, wrote in her diary: "I said how much I liked his poems—true of the short ones: but was mainly pleased & gratified to find him so obliging & easy & interested." The *Testament of Beauty* is in fact his philosophical last will and testament. He began it in an offhanded way, after the death in 1926 of his younger daughter, when Mrs. Bridges noticed a scrap of a poem dated 1924 and suggested that he might expand upon its theme. He "did not take my work on the poem very seriously" and regarded it "merely as a useful distraction—but thro these sad times there is a thanksgiving of Praises. . . ." "In effect," says Phillips, "he was doing what he felt the clergy should have been doing—attempting to construct a religion that could be reconciled with modern knowledge and attitudes." Edward certainly agreed that the clergy were out of date, and there was no doubt upon publication in 1930 that the *Testament* spoke to that postwar generation; it was reprinted repeatedly in both Britain and the United States. Some regarded it as akin to Wordsworth's *The Prelude*. Edward had reservations about the conviction of Bridges that his metrical adaptations had set poetry on a new path. However, Edward could not argue with the basic premise, that Beauty was not mere surface pleasantness: "Beauty was the very expression of God (for he never hesitated to use the term, and by it he meant a force which was personal. . . . If God be thought of as trying unceasingly to enter the world He has made and inside which He has set human free will that can be hostile and to some extent even exclude Him, then Beauty is the main spearhead of self-expression": a divine creative act that continues through the generations.[20]

Edward had always been more comfortable with shorter poetic forms, so that he leaned naturally toward the early lyrics of Bridges. He knew that he lacked the trained musician's ear and the extraordinary memory for detail that Bridges possessed. Bridges had once remarked that "of all men living [E. M. Forster] had the most brilliantly photographic mind." Edward knew that the details of his own daily action of typing a page would be a blur the next day: "the jumping letters," the white page, the light falling over his shoulder. They would not fade so rapidly, he and Bridges agreed, if he were Mr. Forster and he could set them down "vividly, in outlines which would startle my reader into attention. When Bridges pointed this out, I remembered incidents, vignettes in *A Passage to India,* pictures of things I had never seen consciously, though I spent far longer in India than Forster did—things which at once I recognized when the novelist introduced them, so that I had to exclaim, 'Yes, that's true! I have seen it, though I did not *know* I had seen it!' "[21]

Edward began to feel that his poetic philosophy was at a standstill, although his *100 Poems* quickly sold out its two thousand copies. Stephen Spender, who disliked bitterness or satire in poetry, wrote to him: "But bitterness surely means that one has succumbed to the temptation to apply a personal situation and partial experiences to the general situation and to nature. I can never understand a generalised bitterness about, say, women: because it seems to me that if one has had experiences it means that one is either wrong oneself in some way, or else has chosen the wrong woman: & the same goes with the world." He wished that Edward would write more like Laurence Binyon or Walter de la Mare. Edward retorted: "Neither of them experienced anything so tragic and wasteful as our Kut campaign or have seen at close quarters the physical misery of India, in flood and famine as well as every day. The willingness of you younger poets to admit that de la Mare and Binyon have something to them is, within my own competence to notice, something that began only yesterday." He wrote to Palmer: "I gather that he holds that a poet shd. write only about matters wh. fill him with delight, and that while I have 'a unique contribution' to make I foolishly write unlike Binyon and de la Mare. A pity, rather, but I can't help it."[22]

Palmer had his own theory about legitimate uses of poetry: experience was its material, but it needed a wider social context; just then that was the hoped-for Allied intervention in Western Europe: "But political poetry is not politics rewritten in poetic forms, it is the setting down of the genuine poetic material already in politics as in nearly every activity of life. And on the whole it must deal with issues wider than the normal hurlyburly of day to day struggle; although many of the day to day issues of today have such wide human implications . . . and the present years concentrate in them so many problems supremely important to the future of the human race, that I think even more direct political subjects than tradition allows are permissible."[23]

Edward realized that he had much less energy for poetry, indeed for crusades of any kind. Efforts to explain Indian politics seemed exhausting and redundant. Still, he kept at it. Theo tried to reassure him by saying that those who heard him knew that he did not have "the usual Oriental *penchant* for religion." He suspected that both he and his audiences were on a treadmill: "I always see the same faces before me!" he wrote to Palmer. "They go from meeting to meeting! And I shall have as chairman some Labour back-bencher (for no Labour back-bencher cares a hoot about India). However, one cannot escape one's job, I suppose. Wh. is why my advice to you is, Keep Out of Causes! Oh, you think I am writing poetry again, do you? No, I have done with all that."[24]

He spoke at another Bengal famine meeting, this time at the Central Hall in London. "I never thought to rise to speak in what is Methodism's second cathedral, though my dear mother probably hoped for it (though *not* as it has turned out). I go most unwillingly, for the truth is—I am not a natural speaker." He had learned to control his nerves by memorizing his material. No one would now believe how he loathed public platforms and how his mind was divided between such duties and those of his sons on their respective fronts: "I write light-heartedly, so does Muvver, but we know well what peril you both have to face." He wanted news of "a dropping in on Western Europe," of a landing in the Balkans, of "the inchmeal grim progress in Italy!"[25]

Not India, not even poetry could distract them from the fact that their sons were in unknown danger. They knew that Palmer was destined for that "grim progress" in Italy and that Frank had been in the Libyan campaign, to Benghazi and back. He then went to the Turkish border and to Persia, where he concentrated on learning Russian from Russian radio and conversation with transient truck drivers. His unit was in the Sicilian landings but was later withdrawn. During this interim he volunteered for the Cairo-based organization that arranged contacts with Balkan partisans. There he had parachute training and expanded his linguistic skills even more remarkably. By October 1943 he spoke nine European languages, among them Russian, Polish, Czech, Serbo-Croat, and Bulgarian, that last of primary value to the assignment, his last, to the partisans. At Oxford, with Iris Murdoch and others in a small group who saw Russia's experiment as paradigm for the future, he had embraced Communism; his affinity for the Russian experiment bound him psychologically as well as linguistically to the Slavic peoples and their languages. Of those, he found Russian the most elegant and most eloquent, "a sad, powerful language [that] flows gently off the tongue like molten gold." It was all one with his faith that Europe would have a splendid future after the conflict, and that Russia and the Slavic states would lead the way:

"Think only of the Balkans and of the beauty, gaiety and courage which their peoples have preserved through the last six hundred years, years which have brought them little else but poverty, oppression and fratricide!" The new day would see them masters of their own fate, and talk about beauty would be superfluous because beauty itself would invest their lives.[26]

By the summer of 1943 it was obvious that Edward's illness was virulent cancer, although Theo still called it his "ulcer." Doctors had given him up, but in March 1944 X rays indicated that surgery might yet be effective. Edward told Palmer that the operation had been a complete success; and without it he would not have made it through the year. He admitted that he had not felt well for a very long time but now accepted the doctors' word that he would begin to feel stronger and better. In letters to his sons he kept up—for his own and Theo's benefit as well as for theirs—anecdotes of the courageously absurd: he had heard that Indian seamen, brought before an English court, took a copy of the Koran and swore by the Buddha: "*Very* remarkable, the habits of the heathen!" An elderly parson friend was becoming a menace stripping his library of devotional books for Edward, who begged him not to do so, but the first parcel arrived inexorably. Theo felt humbled by friends' kindnesses. Religion no longer helped her to bear her thoughts, but then it had never been anything but "a rough 'rule-of-thumb.' " She wished she were more sensitive to others' concerns, "not just expecting them to understand and take an interest in mine." Palmer warned Frank that he would find both parents looking older.[27]

In August Edward was again in the hospital and told Palmer only that he had had "a small operation recently" and was "getting special treatment from a v. skilful man. We have high hopes of it." A serious setback followed swiftly, from which at first he rallied encouragingly. Theo was bitter because five weeks had been "thrown away," two in waiting for a hospital room, until friends on a hospital governing committee intervened, and three for operation and recovery, plus the "bad luck" that this surgeon disbelieved in deep radiation, which Edward should have had immediately after the first operation. The ordinary public, Theo observed bitterly, had to take doctors at their word. In any case, it was an inauspicious time for any serious illness, for medical services were desperately overstretched. A Manchester radiologist's refusal to take Edward's case shocked Theo; she was thankful to finally locate one in whom she had more faith. At first they were not hopeful, but then Edward seemed to do "surprisingly well." He told Palmer that without the operation he would have died.[28]

That same letter, however, carried the news that Frank was reported missing. "This is a sad letter to write to you, Palmer, old chap. Yesterday we recd. a wire that Major W. F. Thompson has been 'missing' since May 31. . . . We do not even know where Frank was, just as we did not know he was a major (though I guessed it). The thing we have to bear in mind, and not let up for a moment, is that there is a loophole of hope. . . ." He might be alive, or a prisoner. "He deliberately chose the most adventurous and dangerous job there was, and he did magnificently. . . . You have been simply grand, courageous[,] selfless, & you are living through trials wh. require all you can summon up of will & peace of mind. . . . We pray that Frank may yet turn up. And our deepest love & sympathy go out to you."[29]

There was a mystery about fortnightly cables, apparently from Frank, which Edward and Theo would later regard as unforgivably deceitful. The last, dated 4 September, came on 6 September. Who sent them for him? Theo thought that they came from some headquarters. She made herself believe that Frank was safe somewhere, perhaps a prisoner of war, perhaps in a hospital and without competent care, but alive: "I cannot tell you how firmly we believe this. You must too."[30]

By 22 October they had a little more information, having "wrested it with the help of two W[ar] O[ffice] departments," which had it from "a repatriated member of his mission" who was captured, then released. "There is hope, & we must cling to it," Edward told Palmer, "but, as you say, there is not a great deal. Frank was on a 'special mission'—we happen to know, but must keep it to ourselves, that it was specially risky, even for the Balkans—and 'fell into German hands' in the early part of this summer, though only on circumstantial evidence, that he did not long survive." Still, they clung to a hope that his uniform would be some salvation, for "the Germans elsewhere have usually respected British uniform." They heard that " 'there were casualties,' " into which they read their fragile hope that he was only wounded. "We agree with you," Edward wrote to Palmer, "Frank could not have done otherwise without ceasing to be Frank and, in your excellent phrase, betraying his own integrity." He seemed to slip over into acceptance of the worst when he wrote, "The deepest tragedy of what is a terrible thing for us all is that in the post-war world his value wd. have been above estimation," with his nine European languages and his integrity and courage. "Such hordes of the good & kind are so incredibly dull, so humourless, so without distinction of thought or phrase or manner," Edward wrote to Palmer. "He is irreplaceable, & the world will need him so much!"[31]

By December they knew that there remained only the "slightest possible technical' chance" that Frank was alive. They kept their hope that he was a prisoner somewhere, but both the technical chance and the hope were chimeras. On 2 June dissident partisans had captured Frank and after a precipitous show-trial shot him on 4 June. He was twenty-four years of age. A fellow officer, in a long letter to Edward and Theo, explained the special nature and dangers of their Bulgarian mission, " 'about the most difficult of any in the Balkans.' " Many years later, Palmer learned that the Cairo headquarters had abandoned the mission: it showed, it seemed, too few results. Edward and Theo were deeply bitter about those "bogus fortnightly cables sent in Frank's name," and also about a meeting with another colleague of Frank's who came to call and lulled them into a false sense of security by not telling the truth about the precariousness of Frank's situation.

Palmer thought that Frank had probably told the friend not to be too specific: "The thing is so great a tragedy that one's mind continually moves, without one's volition, to the question—'need it have happened?' How could it have been prevented? And the mind stops back along the sequence of events which lead to the final scene, and says helplessly—surely the chain could have been broken here, or here?" A tragedy, but was it necessarily a mistake? It was Frank's decision, for he had come to believe that Communism was the only way out of man's dilemma. In England, Palmer wrote, a Communist is "a man with a rather rigid order of views on the problems arising from one side of man's behaviour, and no views at all, or only textbook answers, to the problems which arise from his many other sides. Now is this not a bad state of affairs?" Communism had already brought Europe new enthusiasms and a new desire for knowledge. Frank was one of those who responded.[32]

Edward began to close down his own responses. "I am telling you everything," he wrote to Palmer, "my disease may come back at any time, in the old places or a new." Palmer must take care, for if he went too, "there is literally nothing for wh. we should want to live." The cancer returned in four new places. X-radiation seemed to check them, but they reappeared and were inoperable. Theo had been always marvelous, he told Palmer, had been gallant and vivacious and over the years had given up her own family for him. He grieved that he had continued to write to Frank notes that now seemed inexcusably trivial but were intended to save his peace of mind and also to conceal "the desperate nature of my own illness."[33]

Against such terrible odds, Edward resolved to do his best to improve, for Theo's sake more than for his own, for twice in the past year "she flatly refused to let me go through death's door," and he must be there when Palmer came home. He no longer cared about pain or death, for nothing could be worse than losing Frank, and "the utterly callous way in which we were told, then given hope, then told again" had drained his already depleted reserves.[34]

He began to write a memoir of Geoffrey Garratt but managed only four chapters. Fortunately, Alfred was reasonably secure. He had war work in a lumberyard, and his garden plot flourished. Nancy Nicholson turned up, exhausted from London fire watching but indomitable as ever, a reminder of the Thompsons' Arcadian years at Islip. Slowly, then more rapidly, the war began to wind down: 8 May 1945 was V-E day; 14 August was V-J Day. Relief mingled with regrets, and anger at the long, long waste.

Palmer's name was much on Edward's mind as well; he took up Theo's plea that he jettison "Edward" and be Palmer again. His reasoning was quite transparent. Frank's name and work had been all of a piece. Therefore Palmer must make yr. own name as Palmer: with a distinctive name like that, it wd. be folly to plump for a grim common name." E. M. Forster's friends knew him as Morgan, never as Edward. Edward J. Thompson's name had acquired some standing, so that "after my time something will remain: something, certainly, of my Indian historical work," and perhaps something of the fiction, poetry, and plays. Then his real reason came out: some reviewers did "incredible mischief" by confusing him with the poet Edward Thomas, with an Edward Thompson who wrote on Buddhism, and several others. He sometimes wished he had been called Cuthbert or Marmaduke! "Anyway, had I had a name like Palmer, with some dignity about it (I admit that Cuthbert is comic, & Marmaduke comicler) & a poetic suggestion that the bearer is a pilgrim, it wd. have helped me. People like to be able to speak of 'Morgan Forster.' You need to have all your work & life of one piece, not with a gap & hiatus." As E. P. Thompson, Palmer kept the essence of both names.[35]

Edward did not recover. With Palmer and Theo at his side, he died on 28 April 1946.

"He was primarily a poet," Herbert Margoulieth wrote in the *Oxford Magazine,* "a man of imaginative insight for whom words in due order were the natural means of expression. . . . Pressure of circumstances and of public events drove him in other directions, . . . but they never weakened the essential poet."[36]

India and the Muse had striven for his soul. His writings on Indian history, which came late (but include the Indian novels), are valuable for his effort, at a crucial juncture in British-Indian relations, to fill the blank spaces that caused such misunderstanding. "What a great gulf separated the two races," Nehru wrote, "and how they distrusted and disliked each other. But more than the distrust and dislike was the ignorance of each other, and because of this, each side was a little afraid of the other and was constantly on its guard in the other's presence." Did Nehru hope, when he invited Edward, as friend and influential writer, to the Congress Working Committee in 1939, to persuade him away from his belief in dominion status as the workable solution, although the committee unequivocally favored full independence?[37]

How to explain that stubborn "relic of half-repentant imperialism"? In subtle ways he remained a child of the age of empire, with a duty to a temporal authority that was itself ambiguous. He knew that, in many ways, imperialism was an unsound doctrine, yet like Elizabeth Thompson, whose dearest wish was her family eternally united, Edward wanted the British imperial family to remain in unity. Here are Wesleyan overtones of sin, salvation, and duty to authority. "From the outset," writes E. P. Thompson, "the Wesleyans fell ambiguously between Dissent and the Establishment, and did their utmost to make the worst of both worlds, serving as apologists for an authority in whose eyes they were an object of ridicule or condescension, but never of trust." Thus John Wesley, as well as India and his Muse, had striven for his soul. India had won.[38]

Edward Thompson feared that in embracing India he had been untrue to his Muse. He said as much in "Repentance for Political Activity," one of the *100 Poems:*

> Forgive me, Rose and Nightingale!
> The poet lays aside
> The silly wisdom that he served
> His misbelieving pride!
> . . . .
> The heart that turns from righteousness
> (As others turn from sin)
> With fierce repentance such as mine,
> No devil back shall win![39]

Edward had done his best for India. His best was very good, for at moments when connection counted he had bridged the gap between ignorance and information. If sometimes he failed, it was because the British Raj was itself history's prisoner.

NOTES

ABBREVIATIONS

eferences in lowercase letters: Edward John Thompson Papers, Western Manuscripts, Bodleian Library, Oxford University

P—Bridges Family Papers and Bodleian Library

P—Crewe Papers, Manuscripts Department, University Library, Cambridge University

/R, *Tagore*—Krishna Dutta and Andrew Robinson, *Rabindranath Tagore: The Myriad-Minded Man* (London: Bloomsbury, 1995)

IP—Hardinge Papers, Manuscripts Department, University Library, Cambridge University

E—Imperfect Encounter: Letters of William Rothenstein and Rabindranath Tagore, 1911–1941, ed. Mary Lago (Cambridge: Harvard University Press, 1972)

BB—Edward J. Thompson, *The Leicestershires beyond Baghdad* (London: Epworth Press, 1919)

IP:BL—Macmillan Papers: British Library

ld Letters—Jawarharlal Nehru, *A Bunch of Old Letters: Written Mostly to Jawaharlal Nehru and Some Written by Him* (New York: Asia Publishing House, 1960)

P:HL—Rothenstein Papers, Houghton Library, Harvard University

T—Rhodes Foundation Trustees, Records, Rhodes House, Oxford

T:LW—E. J. Thompson, *Rabindranath Tagore: His Life and Work* (Calcutta: Y.M.C.A. Publishing House; London, Oxford University Press, 1921)

T:PD—E. J. Thompson, *Rabindranath Tagore: Poet and Dramatist* (London: Humphrey Milford for Oxford University Press, 1926)

P—Thompson Papers, Western Manuscripts, Bodleian Library, Oxford University

JR—Special Materials, University of Reading

VMMS/SOAS—Methodist Church (Wesleyan Missionary Society Archives/School of Oriental and African Studies, University of London)

> CC—Chairman's Correspondence
> GC—General Correspondence
> Misc.—Miscellaneous Correspondence

1. INTRODUCING THE THOMPSONS

1. Hardinge to Sir George Clarke, 25 November 1910, HP 81/2: Various Correspondence. Diplomatic backgrounds of Hardinge and Crewe were neatly complementary. Charles Hardinge, First Baron Hardinge of Penshurst (1858–1944) and grandson of a ormer Viceroy of India, served from 1880 in Persia and Russia; he was also Permanent Undersecretary of State for Foreign Affairs from 1906 to 1910 and 1918 to 1920, and Viceroy from 1910 to 1916. Robert Crewe-Milnes, First Marquess of Crewe (1858–1945), was also Lord Lieutenant of Ireland from 1892 to 1895, Secretary of State for the Colonies rom 1908 to 1910, and Secretary of State for India from 1910 to 1915.

2. John H. Broomfield, *Elite Conflict in a Plural Society: Twentieth-Century Bengal* Berkeley and Los Angeles: University of California Press, 1968), 22–29; on *bhadralok,* see 1–20, 21–41. George Nathaniel Curzon (1859–1925) was later Lord Curzon of Kedleston,

317

Undersecretary of State for India, from 1891 to 1892, Viceroy from 1899 to 1905, an
Undersecretary of State for Foreign Affairs from 1895 to 1898 and 1919 to 1924.

3. See Victor Bailey, "The Fabrication of Deviance," in *Protest and Survival: Essay for E. P. Thompson,* ed. John Rule and Robert Malcolmson (London: Merlin Press, 1993) 222.

4. Thomas Babington Macaulay, "Minute on Education," in William Theodore de Bar et al., comps., *Sources of Indian Tradition,* Introduction to Oriental Civilizations, vol. (New York: Columbia University Press, 1958), 596–98, 601. Thomas Babington Macaula (1800–1859) in 1834 was Law Member of the Viceroy's Council and President of th Committee on Public Instruction of the East India Company. He regarded his Indi sojourn as "banishment . . . exile." He drafted the legal code, argued decisively for English language education, and left in 1838, never to see India again.

5. EJT to Elizabeth Thompson (hereafter ET), 21 December 1910, d. 2669, folios 15–17

6. EJT to ET, 4 January 1911, d. 2669, folio 20.

7. EJT to ET, 17 January 1910 [1911], folios 23–26; 1 February 1911, folios 29–30 both: d. 2669.

8. EJT to ET, 22 January [1911], d. 2669, folios 27–28.

9. On effects of censorship, see Broomfield, *Elite Conflict,* 34, 39.

10. See *The Annual Register, 1910: A Review of Public Events at Home and Abroa* (London: Longmans Green, 1911 n.s. [25 January]), 391.

11. ET, family notes, d. 2673, folio 12.

12. See J. M. Thompson, 22 April 1890, WMMS/SOAS, CC.

13. Obituary, 1894 Wesleyan Conference Minutes, in ET, family notes, d. 2673, fo lio 12.

14. J. M. Thompson, 19 October 1885, WMMS/SOAS, CC.

15. J. M. Thompson, 22 June 1889, in ibid.

16. *Wesleyan Methodist Missionary Society Report: 1885,* 90–91. Charles Bradlaugh (1833–1891) was scornful of Theosophy. Helena Blavatsky (1831–1891), a displaced Russian, claimed long-dead gurus as instructors. Annie Besant (1847–1933) supported Indian nationalism and in 1917 became President of the Indian National Congress; see Anne Taylor, *Annie Besant: A Biography* (Oxford: Oxford University Press, 1992); Walter L. Arnstein, *The Bradlaugh Case: Atheism, Sex, and Politics among the Late Victorians* (Columbia: University of Missouri Press, 1983); and Sylvia Cranston, *HPB. The Extraordinary Life and Influence of Helena Blavatsky, Founder of the Modern Theosophical Movement* (New York: Putnam, 1993).

17. J. M. Thompson, 20 May 1887, WMMS/SOAS, CC.

18. *Wesleyan Methodist Missionary Report: 1886,* 107; *1889:* 60; *1890:* 59; *1891:* 60.

19. J. M. Thompson, 22 June 1989; 22 April 1890, WMMS/SOAS, CC. Henry S. Lunn, *Friend of Missions in India: "The Cyclostyled Indian Journal"* (London: James Clarke [1890]). Henry Simpson Lunn (1859–1939) began the travel business that grew from conference arrangements for ministers. See Michael Holroyd, *Hugh Kingsmill: A Critical Biography* (London: Unicorn Press, 1964), 26.

20. Lunn, *Friend of Missions,* 7, 129, 82, 21, 43. William H. Findlay (1857–1919) was Principal of the Negapatam District and was Missionary Society Secretary from 1900 to 1910.

21. Ibid., 120, 28, 42, 107, 119, 122, 139.

22. J. M. Thompson, 22 April 1890, WMMS/SOAS, CC.

23. J. M. Thompson, 1 May 1888, WMMS/SOAS, CC.

24. J. M. Thompson, 22 April 1890, 24 December 1890, WMMS/SOAS, CC.

25. J. M. Thompson, 20 July 1891, WMMS/SOAS, CC.

26. Ibid.

27. Ibid.

28. Frederick C. Gill, *Charles Wesley, the First Methodist* (London: Lutterworth Press, 1964), 158.

29. Arnold A. Dallimore, *George Whitefield: The Life and Times of the Great Evangelist of the Eighteenth-Century Revival*, 2 vols. (Westchester, Ill.: Cornerstone Books, 1978), 2:348; see also Robert Stead, "Hazel Grove," *Cheshire Life* 39 (1973): 102-5, 107-8; and Raamah Bowers, "Growing Up in the Grove," *Cheshire Life* 43 (1977): 78-79.

30. J. M. Thompson, on thirty-nine-day voyage from 10 October 1876, c. 5351, folios 2-17; "Contrasts," missionary speech [1892?], e. 2929, folios 217-26.

2. DECISIONS

1. EJT, *Introducing the Arnisons* (London: Macmillan, 1935); EJT, preface to *John Arnison* (London: Macmillan, 1939), vii.

2. Rupert Davies and Gordon Rupp, eds., *A History of the Methodist Church in Great Britain* (London: Epworth Press, 1965), 267; Robert Moore, *Pitmen, Preachers, and Politics: The Effects of Methodism in a Durham Mining Community* (Cambridge: Cambridge University Press, 1974), 144.

3. Davies and Rupp, *History of the Methodist Church*, 62; A. G. Ives, *Kingswood School in Wesley's Day and Since* (London: Epworth Press, 1970); facsimile of Wesley, *A Short Account of the School in Kingswood near Bristol*, 13-18.

4. John Gross, *The Rise and Fall of the Man of Letters: A Study of the Idiosyncratic and the Humane in Modern Literature* (New York: Macmillan, 1969), 167.

5. EJT, *Introducing the Arnisons*, 96.

6. Ives, *Kingswood School*, 178-79, 182.

7. Ibid., 36. After Trinity College, Cambridge, Richards taught at Kingswood (1884-1920).

8. *Kingswood Magazine* 12 (1901): 30.

9. Lowther to EJT, 25 June 1906, incomplete, c. 5296, folios 27-30.

10. Ibid. Also, 16 July 1906, folios 31-34; 19 August 1906, folios 39-43; both: c. 5296.

11. Workman to Lowther, 20 February 1907 and enclosure, c. 5299, folios 161-66.

12. Lowther to EJT, 8 March 1907, folios 59-61; 8 April 1907, folios 62-64; 25 June 1906, folios 27-30; 21 October 1906, folios 39-43; 16 September 1907, folios 74-77; 1-8 December 1907, folios 87-92; all: c. 5296. "Fanatic . . . paintpot": see Hardy, *Tess of the D'Urbervilles*, chap. 123: the itinerant evangelist writes, "THY, DAMNATION, SLUMBERETH, NOT."

13. Lowther to EJT, 8-10 August 1907, folios 67-72; 17 February 1907, folios 56-58; 16 September 1907, folios 74-77; all: c. 5296.

14. Lowther to EJT, 27 April 1906, c. 5296, folios 12-19.

15. Ibid. Lowther to EJT, 10 June 1906, folios 25-26; 29 December 1906, folios 48-50; both: c. 5296.

16. Lowther to EJT, 10 June 1906, folios 25-26; 17 February 1907, folios 56-58; 29 December 1906, folios 48-50; all: c. 5296. Richmond College opened in 1843 and after 1900 was an accredited divinity school affiliated with the University of London; it is now an American center for international studies.

17. Lowther to EJT, 21 October 1906, c. 5296, folio 29.

18. EJT to Lowther, [12] June [1908], incomplete, c. 5295, folios 3-4.

19. EJT to Lowther, 22 July 1908, c. 5295, folio 5; EJT, *The Knight Mystic and Other Verses* (London: Elliot Stock, 1907).

20. ET to EJT, 12 November 1908, d. 2679, folios 5-6.

21. EJT to Lowther, 22 July 1908, incomplete, c. 5295, folio 5; ET to EJT, 5 March 1908, incomplete, d. 2679, folios 1-2.

22. EJT to Lowther, 22 July 1908, incomplete, c. 5295, folio 5; Lowther to EJT, n.c., 18 November 1907, c. 5296, folio 84. See *"The Knight Mystic and Other Verses,"*

London Quarterly Review, 109 (1911): 360-61. Published 1853-1935, primarily for Methodists, it kept them informed about literary, social, and political movements, as well as denominational history and missions.

23. EJT, "The Mass: Its Origin and Nature," *Sunday at Home* (1908-1909): 134-37.

24. Lowther to EJT, 17 January 1907, c. 5296, folios 100-101.

25. Lowther to EJT, 8 May 1908, folios 127-29; 14 June 1908, folios 136-39; 1-8 December 1907, folios 87-92; 11 January 1908, folios 97-98; 14 June 1908, folios 136-39; all: c. 5296.

26. EJT to Lowther, 9 November 1909, incomplete, c. 5295, folios 21-26. See EJT, "Eros Astray," in *Knight Mystic,* 24-26: "Love that is worthy of all trust and love / Came to me when I did not think. . . ."

27. ET to EJT, 24 November 1909, folios 9-12; 12 November 1908, folios 5-6; 2 March 1910, folios 13-16; all: d. 2679.

28. ET to EJT, 11 September 1908, d. 2679, folios 3-4.

29. Susan P. Casteras, *James Smetham: Artist, Author, Pre-Raphaelite Associate* (Aldershot: Scolar Press; Brookfield, Vt.: Ashgate, 1995).

30. See Casteras, *James Smetham,* 8; Smetham, *Letters,* ed. Sarah Smetham and William Davies (London: Macmillan, 1891, 1902), 4. See also *The Literary Works of James Smetham,* ed. William Davies (London: Macmillan, 1893); also in microform series, Eighteenth Century Sources for the Study of English Literature and Culture (Keswick, Va.: Don H. Massey), reel 365. See Lowther, "Blake and Smetham" (letter), *Academy,* 77 (1909): 378: he praises "kinship of spirit" and Smetham's "exquisite prose." See Davies, "Memoir," in Smetham, *Letters,* 15. Casteras, *James Smetham,* 4, 144, 18, 25, 27, 29. Smetham, "MS. Letters and Reminiscences," in Casteras, *James Smetham,* 29. Smetham, *Letters,* 265-66.

31. EJT, "James Smetham's Essays," *London Quarterly Review,* 5th ser., 2 (1911): 251-58.

32. Lowther to EJT, 8 August 1907, folios 67-71; 13-15 August 1908, incomplete, folios 145-46; 16 September 1907, folios 74-77; all: c. 5296. Cf. Albert C. Outler, ed., *John Wesley,* Library of Theological Thought (New York: Oxford University Press, 1964), 39.

33. Lowther to EJT, [August 1908], folio 144; 9 September 1907, folios 147-49; both c. 5296.

34. Lowther to EJT, [August 1908], c. 5296, folio 144.

35. Lowther to EJT, 31 October-7 November 1908, incomplete, c. 5296, folios 158-65 Lowther to EJT, 22 December 1909, c. 5297, folios 131-32.

36. Lowther to EJT, 28 November 1908, c. 5296, folios 171-74. Also, 31 August 1909 folios 89-90; 13 August 1909, folios 86-87; both: c. 5297.

37. Lowther to EJT, 19-20 October 1909, folios 109-16; 14 January 1909, folios 9-10 19 April 1909, folios 43-47; all: c. 5297.

38. Lowther to EJT, 13-15 August 1908, incomplete, c. 5296, folio 146; 19 April 1909 c. 5297, folios 43-49. Emily Frances Adeline Sargent (1851-1904) wrote novels with titles such as *Beyond Recall* and *Miss Betty's Mistake.* Her first, *The Story of a Repentent Soul* (1882), remained her most popular. On Davidson, see the reviews "Wesley and His Work" and "John Davidson's Last Poems," both in *Times Literary Supplement,* 15 July 1909, pages 258 and 260 respectively. *TLS* began publication in 1902, but Lowther' low opinion of contemporary reviewers kept him incurious about it. Reviewers judge Davidson's *Fleet Street and Other Poems* (London: Grant Richards, 1909) as short of greatness for "protestantism of pure negation" and the "literary brutality" in his London scenes. But see John Sloan, *John Davidson, First of the Moderns: A Literary Biography* (Oxford: Clarendon Press, 1995).

39. EJT to Lowther [undated fragment, late 1909?], c. 5295, folio 274. ET to EJT, 1 September 1908, folios 3-4; 25 March 1910, folios 19-20; 1 April 1910, folios 21-22; 1 June 1910, folios 35-38; all: d. 2679. "Many waters": see Samuel 8:7.

40. EJT to Lowther, 4 April 1910, incomplete, c. 5295, folios 70-71.
41. ET to EJT, 12 June 1910, folios 33-34; 19 June 1910, folios 35-38; both: d. 2679.

3. APPRENTICESHIP

1. EJT to ET, 14 January 1910, d. 2669, folios 2-3. See C. R. Elrington and N. M. Herbert, eds., *A History of the County of Gloucester,* Victoria History of the Counties of England, vol. 10 (London: Oxford University Press for the University of London Institute of Historical Research, 1974), 276-89, 123-39, 242-57, 289-99.

2. EJT to ET, 14 January 1910, d. 2669, folios 2-3.

3. EJT to ET, 14 January 1910, folios 2-3; 24 January 1910, folios 4-5; both: d. 2669.

4. Ibid.; EJT to Lowther, 15 March 1910, folios 60-61, c. 5295. See *Wycliffe Star* (April 1910): 175-76. The Reverend Tom Ivens (1851-1914) began as a hired local preacher, then was a district missionary. "Hundreds of conversions in the Exeter District," states his obituary, "filled him with joy, but his health was unequal to the excitement and strain of such glorious toil." When Edward Thompson knew him he was semiretired.

5. EJT to ET, 14 January 1910, d.2669, folios 2-3; EJT to Lowther, 19 February 1910, c. 5295, folios 50-53. Several Smith families still in Eastington cannot identify this Mr. Smith, who lived at Stonehouse and may have belonged to the family of Herbert Round Smith (Frank M. L. Smith, Secretary of the Old Wycliffian Society, to the author, 14 March 1995).

6. EJT to Lowther, 14 February 1910, folios 46-47; 19 February 1910, folios 50-53; both: c. 5295. Lowther crossed out or scissored passages apparently on disillusionment with the ministry. He hoped to publish some of EJT's letters; there are test proofs of a few, but nothing came of this.

7. EJT to Lowther, 19 February 1910, c. 5295, folios 50-53.

8. EJT to Lowther, 8 April 1910, c. 5295, folios 77-80.

9. EJT to Lowther, 19 February 1910, c. 5295, folios 50-53.

10. EJT to Lowther, 1 March 1910, folios 54-57; 15 March 1910, folios 60-61; both: c. 5295.

11. EJT to Lowther, 8 April 1910, folios 77-80; 2 May 1910, folios 88-91; both: c. 5295.

12. EJT to Lowther, 29 April 1910, incomplete, c. 5295, folio 87.

13. EJT to Lowther, 4 April 1910, c. 5295, folios 70-71; EJT to ET, 10 February, d. 2669, folios 6-7.

14. EJT to Lowther, 8 April 1910, c. 5295, folios 77-80.

15. EJT to Lowther, p.c. postmark 2 May 1910, folio 96; 5 May 1910, p.c. folio 97; 14 June 1910, folios 111-12; all: c. 5295. On Sawtry, see William Page, Granville Proby, and S. Inskip Ladds, eds., assisted by H. E. Morris, *The Victoria History of the County of Huntingdon,* Victoria History of the Counties of England, vol. 3 (London: St. Catherine Press for the University of London Institute of Historical Research, 1932), 203-12.

16. EJT to Lowther, 23 June 1910, c. 5295, folios 117-20.

17. EJT to Lowther, 22 July 1910, c. 5295, folios 127-28.

18. EJT to Lowther, 11 February 1910, c. 5295, folios 42-45; Canton to EJT, 4 January 1910, c. 5278, folios 1-2; Canton, *In Memory of W. V.* (London: J. M. Dent, 1901).

19. Canton, *The Invisible Playmate: A Story of the Unseen* (London: Isbister, 1894); Canton, *A History of the British and Foreign Bible Society,* 5 vols. (London: John Murray, 1904-1910).

20. EJT to Lowther, 25 May 1910, folios 103-4; 3 June 1910, folios 109-10; both: c. 5295.

21. EJT to Lowther, 17 July 1910, folios 121-24; 25 May 1910, folios 103-4; both: c. 5295.

22. ET to EJT, 4 August 1910, d. 2679, folios 41-42.

23. EJT, *The Enchanted Lady: A Comedy* (London: G. Bell and Sons, 1910).

24. Canton to EJT, 10 June 1910, c. 5278, folios 7-8.

25. EJT to Canton, 11 June 1910, folios 7-8; 19 July 1910, folios 16-17; both: c. 5278 Canton to EJT, 10 June 1910, c. 5278, folios 7-8. J. S. M. Hooper (1837-1922) was a missionary translator from Hindi and Urdu.

26. Canton to EJT, 7 June 1910, folios 5-6; 8 July 1910, folios 11-12; 18 August 1910 folios 36-37; all: c. 5278. "All for love": Spenser, The Faerie Queene, bk. 2, canto 8, st. 2

27. Canton to EJT, 18 August 1920, c. 5278, folios 36-37.

28. EJT to Canton, 30 July 1910, incomplete, c. 5276, folios 4-5.

29. EJT to Canton, 7 August 1910, c. 5276, folios 12-13.

30. Canton to EJT, 18 August 1910, c. 5276, folios 32-33; Collingwood to EJT, 12 September 1910, c. 5284, folios 145-46; W. G. Collingwood, Dutch Agnes, Her Valentine Being the Journal of the Curate of Coniston, 1616-1623 (Kendal: Thomas Wilson, 1910) William Gershom Collingwood (1854-1932) was a painter; after teaching Fine Art at Reading University he returned to the Lake Country.

31. Canton to EJT, 20 October 1910, c. 5278, folios 59-60. Sarah Smetham to Lowther 11 September 1910, folios 25-26; 9 November 1910, folios 27-28; both: c. 5315.

32. Rushbrooke to EJT, 11 June 1909, c. 5311, folios 97-103. William George Rush brooke (1849-1926) was St. Olave's headmaster from 1893 to 1922, the first Noncon formist layman to head this Church of England school chartered by Queen Elizabeth in 1571. See R. C. Cunningham, Two Schools: A History of the St. Olave's and St. Saviour's Grammar School Foundation (London: Governors of St. Olave's and St. Saviour's Gram mar School Foundation, 1971), 231.

33. Fielden to EJT, 23 August 1910, c. 5288, folios 3-6; Richards to EJT, 4 September 1910, c. 5310, folios 62-63. Frederick Joshua Fielden (1882-1955) was a Wesleyan minister's son and graduated from Gonville and Caius College, Cambridge, in 1915. He taught at the University of Lund from 1915 to 1923, then was the Principal of Bareilly College, India, from 1924 to 1925; from 1925, he was Principal and Professor of English at Agra College and, finally, at Aligarh University.

34. Collingwood to EJT, 12 September 1910, c. 5284, folios 145-46; Canton to EJT, 27 October 1910, c. 5278, folios 61-62.

35. Canton to EJT, 12 November 1910, folios 74-75; 18 November 1910, folios 76-77 both: c. 5278.

36. EJT to Canton, 3 October 1910, incomplete, c. 5276, folios 19-28.

37. Canton to EJT, 5 October 1910, c. 5278, folios 54-55.

38. EJT to Canton, 3 October 1910, c. 5276, folios 19-23.

39. Ibid. Charles Henry Monahan (1869-1951) was born in Ireland, had a brilliant career at Trinity College, Dublin, and at Richmond College, then went to India in 1893 as an educator, administrator, and translator.

40. Ibid. Frederick John Briscoe (1861-1942) served in the Transvaal and was Govern ment Advisor on "Native Affairs."

41. Canton to EJT, 8 September 1910, c. 5278, folios 43-44. As a child Flora Annie Steel (1847-1929) responded to the 1857 Indian Mutiny news by repeatedly burning and hanging in effigy the "rebel" Nana Sahib. From 1868 she lived in India, advocated education of Indian women, and in 1884 became the first Inspector of women's schools On the Face of the Waters (London: Macmillan, 1896), her version of the mutiny events was her most popular novel. See The Garden of Fidelity: Being the Autobiography of Flora Annie Steel, 1847-1929 (London: Macmillan, 1929; first published in 1896). Sir William Jones (1746-1794), a distinguished linguist, went to Calcutta in 1873 as High Court Judge. In 1874 he founded the Bengal Asiatic Society, famous for scholarly investigations and publications.

42. Canton to EJT, 12 November 1910, c. 5278, folios 74-75. See Browning, "Pippa Passes: A Drama" (1841).

43. ET to EJT, 24 November 1910, d. 2679, folios 43-44.

4. BANKURA

1. EJT to ET, 21-25 December 1910, d. 2669, folios 15-17. Except for his retirement in 1917, John Mitchell is unrecorded in the Methodist Archives.

2. Ibid.

3. ET to EJT, 9 December 1910, c. 2679, folios 51-52. See L. S. S. O'Malley, *Bengal District Gazetteer* (Calcutta: Bengal Secretariat Book Depot, 1908), 2-3, 45.

4. ET to EJT, 9 March 1911, d. 2669, folios 98-101.

5. EJT to Lowther, 2 January 1911, c. 5295, folio 142; WMMS, *The Ninety-Ninth Report* 32 (1911-1912): 105.

6. EJT to ET, 2 January 1911, d. 2669, folios 21-22.

7. Broomfield, *Elite Conflict*, 8.

8. Eric Stokes, *The English Utilitarians and India* (Oxford: Clarendon Press, 1959), 35.

9. See B. T. McCully, *English Education and the Origins of Indian Nationalism* (New York: Columbia University Press, 1940), 70. For another interpretation, see Gauri Viswanathan, *Masks of Conquest: Literary Study and British Rule in India* (London: Faber and Faber, 1990).

10. EJT to Canton, 23 July 1912, c. 5276, folio 51.

11. Tagore, "The Postmaster" ("Postmastar"), in Tagore, *Selected Short Stories,* trans. Krishna Dutta and Mary Lago (London: Macmillan, 1991), 25-32; also in *Rabindra-racanabali* (Rabindranath's works), 27 vols., 2 supp., index (Calcutta: Visva-Bharati, 1964-1966), 15:411-17.

12. Butler to Du Boulay, 28 June 1911, HP 50, vol. no. 188; January 1911, HP 48, folios 149-50. Sir (Spencer) Harcourt Butler (1869-1938) was the Lieutenant Governor of Burma and the United Provinces in 1918, and Governor, from 1921 to 1923. See Tagore, "Rashmani's Son" ("Rashmanir chhele"), in *Selected Short Stories,* 200-38; also in *Rabindra-racanabali,* 22:391-407.

13. Crewe to King George V, extract, 30 August 1911, HP 82/2, no. 135a.

14. Broomfield, *Elite Conflict,* 15-17.

15. EJT to Lowther, 26 February 1911, incomplete, folio 151; 26 March 1911, folio 152; both: c. 5295.

16. ET to EJT, 9 March 1911, c. 2679, folios 98-101. EJT to Findlay, 23 February 1911; Findlay to EJT, 31 March 1911; both: WMMS/SOAS, CC.

17. Woodford to Findlay, 14 June 1909, WMMS/SOAS, CC.

18. Ambery Smith to Hartley, 16 February 1909; Olver to Hartley, 21 April 1910; both: WMMS/SOAS, CC. F. W. Ambery Smith (1861-1929) directed a leper asylum in the Bankura Mission.

19. EJT to ET, 5 April 1911, d. 2669, folios 45-49; ET to EJT, 27-28 April 1911, d. 2679, folios 126-29.

20. WMMS, *The Ninety-Fifth Report* 31 (1909): 82-85.

21. WMMS, *The Ninety-Sixth Report* 31 (1909-1910): 103.

22. Olver to Hartley, 5 August 1909, WMMS/SOAS, CC; EJT to Lowther, 2 January 1911, c. 5295, folio 142.

23. EJT to ET, 1 February 1911, folios 29-30; 4/11 May 1911, folios 57-62; both: d. 2669.

24. EJT to Lowther, 29 January 1911, c. 5295, folio 143; ET to EJT, 12-13 October 1911, d. 2180, folios 18-25.

25. EJT to Lowther, 29 January 1911, c. 5295, folio 143.

26. EJT to Lowther, 29 July 1911, c. 5295, folios 167-68.

27. EJT to Lowther, 29 July 1910, folios 167-68; 30 July 1911, folios 171-72; 24 July 1911, folios 167-70; all: c. 5295.

28. Canton to EJT, 22 February 1911, folios 83-84; 1 March 1911, folios 85-87; both c. 5278.

29. EJT to Olver, 4 August 1911; 9 August 1911; both: WMMS/SOAS, CC.

30. EJT to Canton, 20-21 October 1911, c. 5296, folios 40-41.

31. EJT to Hartley, 21 October 1911; Hartley to EJT, 23 November 1911; Olver to Hartley, 10 August 1911; 27 September 1911; Hartley to Olver, 1 September 1911; all WMMS/SOAS, CC.

32. EJT to Lowther, 4 September 1911, c. 5295, folios 174-75.

33. EJT to Lowther, 6 December 1911, c. 5295, folios 197-98; 4 September 1911 c. 5296, folios 174-75. Canton to EJT, 5 October 1911, c. 5278, folios 117-19.

34. Olver to Hartley, 28 February 1905; Hartley to Olver, 27 August 1909; both WMMS/SOAS, CC.

5. DISCORDS

1. EJT to ET, 18 July 1911, folios 85-88; 15 November 1911, folios 123-25; both: d 2669.

2. EJT to ET, 29 December 1911, d. 2669, folios 129-32.

3. Ibid.

4. Hardinge diary, 2 November, 16 December 1911, in Robert Grant Irving, *Indian Summer: Lutyens, Baker, and Imperial Delhi* (New Haven: Yale University Press, 1981), 51. See Hardinge to King George V, 15 December 1910, no. 3a; to Sir Arthur Bigge, 26 June 1911, no. 13a; to King George V, 5 January 1911, no. 8a; all: HP 104. Arthur John Bigge (1849-1931), the King's private secretary, was later Lord Stamfordham.

5. Hardinge to King George V, 5 January 1911, no. 8a; to Bigge, 16 March 1911, no. 28; both: HP 104.

6. Hardinge to Bigge, 29 June 1911, HP 104, no. 67. Sir John Hewett (1854-1941) was in the Bengal civil service from 1877, was Lieutenant Governor of the United Provinces from 1907 to 1912, and was President of the Royal Durbar Committee in 1911. On the 1902 Durbar, see Ian Gilmour, *Curzon* (London: John Murray, 1994), 239-46.

7. Hardinge to Bigge, 28 September 1911, HP 104, no. 104.

8. Hardinge to Bigge, 1 December 1910, HP 104, no. 2c.

9. See Hardinge to Lieutenant-Governors, 8 April 1911, HP 81/2, no. 179.

10. See "The Gaekwar's Homage: A Public Apology," *Times,* 18 December 1911, 8.

11. "The Durbar at Delhi," *Spectator* 107 (1911): 1061-62.

12. "The Transfer of the Indian Capital," *Times,* 14 December 1911, 9; "The New Capital of India," *Spectator* 107 (1911): 1060-61.

13. "The Transfer of the Indian Capital," 9; "The King's Address at Delhi," *Times,* 14 December 1911, 10.

14. "A Great Imperial Announcement," *Times,* 13 December 1911, 7; "The Transfer of the Indian Capital," 9; "Durbar at Delhi," 1060-61.

15. On New Delhi, see Irving, *Indian Summer.*

16. "The Modification of the Partition," in Notes, *Modern Review* 11 (1912): 111-19.

17. EJT to ET, 21 December 1911, d. 2669, folios 143-49. Arthur Ernest Brown (1884-1952) was in Bengal for thirty-two years from 1904; then he was Bankura Principal and District Superintendent.

18. Butler to Hardinge, 30 June 1911, HP 113, pp. 44-45.

19. EJT to ET, 21 December 1911, d. 2669, folios 143-49. On 27 March 1912 the "Delhi business" had a tragic postscript. Hardinge entered the city officially, properly imperial on "the biggest elephant I have ever seen." Its elevation made him a perfect bomb target

from a rooftop. Hardinge was injured, and an attendant died. See Hardinge, *My Indian Years, 1910-1916* (London: John Murray, 1948), 79-84.

20. EJT to ET, 13 December 1911, d. 2669, folios 137-42.

21. Ibid.

22. EJT to Lowther, 12 December 1911, c. 5295, folios 199-202.

23. EJT to ET, 12 July 1911, d. 2669, folios 81-84.

24. Olver to Hartley, 10 August 1911, WMMS/SOAS, CC.

25. See Owston Smith to Hartley, 4 September 1912, WMMS/SOAS, CC.

26. See Lowther to EJT, 17-20 September 1912, c. 5299, folios 50-51.

27. EJT, "John in Prison: Three Poems Grouped as Nazarenics," *John in Prison, and Other Poems* (London: T. Fisher Unwin, 1912): vii-viii, 66-83.

28. EJT to Lowther, 19-21 August 1912, c. 5295, folio 215.

29. Ambery Smith to Hartley, 28 December 1912, WMMS/SOAS, CC. Arthur Marshman Spencer (1886-1942), EJT's Kingswood contemporary, came to Bengal in 1911.

30. See Owston Smith to Hartley, 4 December 1912; Hartley to Owston Smith, 10 January 1913; Owston Smith to Hartley, 28 January 1913; Mitchell to Hartley, 15 January 1911; Owston Smith to Hartley, 19 February 1913; Hartley to Owston Smith, 21 February 1913; Owston Smith to Hartley, 12 March 1913; Hartley to Owston Smith, 2 May 1913; Owston Smith to Hartley, 22 May 1913; Mitchell to Hartley, 24 July 1913; all: WMMS/SOAS, CC.

31. Owston Smith to Hartley, 12 March 1913, WMMS/SOAS, CC. EJT to ET, 20 March 1911, d. 2669, folios 155-56.

32. ET to EJT, 31 July-2 August 1912, d. 2681, folios 57-61.

33. ET to EJT, 27 June 1912, d. 2681, folios 14-19. William Russell Maltby (1866-1951) worked closely with the Young Layman's League and the Student Christian Movement.

34. Lowther to EJT, 7 February 1911, c. 5298, folio 86.

35. EJT to ET, 10 October 1912, d. 2669, folios 199-200.

36. See EJT, *Introducing the Arnisons*, 92. See also E. P. Thompson, *The Making of the English Working Class* (reprint, London: Victor Gollancz, 1975), 400.

37. Rushbrooke to EJT, 18 November 1912, folio 112; 22 November 1912, folios 113-14; 1 December 1912, folios 115-16; 8 December 1912, folio 117; all: c. 5311.

38. Canton to EJT, 10-13 November 1911, folios 128-29; 4 January 1912, folios 132-33; both: c. 5278. Unspaced ellipses (...) indicate ellipses that were written on the original document; letter-spaced ellipses (. . .) indicate material the author has omitted from a quotation.

39. Canton to EJT, 29 February 1912, c. 5278, folios 143-44.

40. Canton to EJT, 25 June 1912, c. 5278, folios 164-65.

41. EJT to Canton, 19 May 1912, c. 5276, folios 45-50.

42. EJT to Canton, 9 April 1912, folios 43-44; 19 November 1912, folios 55-59; both: c. 5276.

6. FORGING A CHAIN

1. Broomfield, *Elite Conflict*, 42. Thomas David Gibson-Carmichael, Fourteenth Baronet (1854-1926), was Governor of Victoria, Australia, from 1908 to 1911, of Madras, from 1911 to 1912, and of Bengal, from 1912 to 1917.

2. Crewe to Carmichael, 15 January 1912, CP, C/6.

3. See Carmichael to Crewe, 18 January 1912; 24 April 1912; 22 May 1912; 22 July 1912; all: CP, C/6. See Crewe to Hardinge, 16 February 1913, HP 56, pp. 103-4.

4. EJT to Lowther, 8 September 1912, c. 5295, folio 217.

5. Culshaw to the author, 7 October 1996. He taught at Bankura from 1934 to 1938 and 1944 to 1948 and was the chaplain of Kingswood School from 1953 to 1961. "Outsider": Edward Palmer Thompson, *Alien Homage: Edward Thompson and Rabindranath Tagore* (Delhi: Oxford University Press, 1993), 2.

6. EJT to Canton, 21 August 1912, c. 5276, folio 54.

7. On Vaishnava lyrics, see Edward C. Dimock Jr. and Denise Levertov, trans., *In Prais* of Krishna: Songs from the Bengali (Garden City, N.Y.: Doubleday, 1967), ix, 15, 82. Se also Milton Singer, ed., *Krishna: Myths, Rites, and Attitudes* (Honolulu: East-West Cente Press, 1966; and W. G. Archer, *The Loves of Krishna in Indian Painting and Poetr* (New York: Macmillan, 1957).

8. Culshaw to the author, 21 December 1996.

9. EJT to Lowther, 28 April 1912, c. 5295, folio 205.

10. Ernest Binfield Havell (1861-1934) was Superintendant of the Madras School o Art from 1884 to 1892, Principal of the Calcutta School of Art from 1896 to 1906, an Attaché of the British Legation, Copenhagen, from 1916 to 1923.

11. The chairman was Sir George Birdwood (1832-1917), who was on the Bomba Medical Staff from 1854 to 1868, when he returned to England and was Commissioner fo Indian and Colonial Exhibitions; he later served the India Office Revenue and Statistic Department from 1871 to 1902. On Havell's paper and discussion, see E. B. Havell, "Ar Administration in India," in "Proceedings," *Journal of the Royal Society of Arts* 58 (1908- 1909), 628-41. See also *IE*; and Mary Lago, *Christiana Herringham and the Edwardiar Art Scene* (Columbia: University of Missouri Press; London, Lund Humphries, 1996) 191-202.

12. William Rothenstein (1872-1945), painter and lithographer, was Britain's first Pro fessor of Civic Art, at Sheffield University, from 1917 to 1926; Principal, Royal College o Art, from 1920 to 1935; Trustee, Tate Gallery, from 1927 to 1933; and Member, Royal Fin Art Commission, from 1931 to 1938. On the 1910 meeting, see his *Men and Memories Recollections of William Rothenstein,* 2 vols. (London: Faber and Faber, 1931-1932) 2:231; also, one-volume edition abridged and annotated by Mary Lago (London: Chattc and Windus; Columbia, University of Missouri Press, 1978), 160-71. The "like-mindec friends" included A. K. Coomaraswamy and Walter Crane. A. K. Coomaraswamy (1877- 1947) was Director of the Mineral Survey of Ceylon from 1903 to 1906; Director of the Ar Section, United Provinces Exhibition, Allahabad, from 1910 to 1911; and Research Fellow in Indian, Persian, and Muhammedan Art, Museum of Fine Art, Boston, from 1917 to 1947. Walter Crane (1845-1915), who was a painter, illustrator, and socialist associate of Willam Morris, was an organizer and the first President of the Art Workers' Guild in 1884, and President of the Arts and Crafts Exhibition Society from 1888 to 1890 and 1895 to 1915. On the India Society, see Mary Lago, "No Passage from India," *TLS,* 16 April 1999, 15-16.

13. Christiana Jane Powell Herringham (1852-1929) was a daughter of Thomas Powell, a London stockbroker, and the wife of Sir Wilmot Parker Herringham, a London physician. On her career in art and art rescue, see Lago, *Christiana Herringham.*

14. See *IE*, 32; Rothenstein, *Men and Memories,* 2:249. Abanindranath (1871-1951) and Gaganendranath (1867-1938) Tagore, nephews of Rabindranath Tagore (1861-1941), who was the youngest of fifteen children of the patriarchal Maharshi Debendranath Tagore (1817-1905), Brahmo Samaj leader. On the Tagores, see D/R, *Tagore.* On Western attitudes toward Indian art, see Partha Mitter, *Much Maligned Monsters: History of Western Reactions to Indian Art* (Oxford: Clarendon Press, 1977). See also Tapati Guha-Takurta, *The Making of a New "Indian" Art: Artists, Aesthetics, and Nationalism in Bengal, c. 1850-1920* (Cambridge: Cambridge University Press, 1992).

15. Tagore, *Gitanjali,* in *Rabindra-racanabali,* 11:1-126; also *Gitanjali (Song-Offer-ing)* (London: India Society, 1912; London: Macmillan, 1913). On Rothenstein's role, see *IE*, 28-131. See also David Kopf, *The Brahmo Samaj and the Shaping of the Modern Indian Mind* (Princeton: Princeton University Press, 1979).

16. C. F. Andrews, "An Evening with Rabindra," *Modern Review* (Calcutta) (1912): 225-28. Andrews (1871-1940) had gone to Delhi after his ordination. See Hugh Tinker, *The Ordeal of Love: C. F. Andrews and India* (Delhi: Oxford University Press, 1979), 3-4.

17. Yeats, introduction to *Gitanjali,* vii-xxii; *Gitanjali* manuscript (88 folios: 106 pp.): bms Eng. 1159/61M-68 (1): RP:HL. Rothenstein's holograph note reads: "Original MS. . . . which the poet brought to me from India on his initial visit to us at Oak Hill Park London]." Items (2)-(5) are a detailed index and groups of drafts, some with revisions in other hands.

18. Rushbrooke to EJT, 18 January 1913, c. 5311, folios 121-22. Sir Brajendranath Seal (1864-1938) was a scholar and lawyer; his *Comparative Studies in Vaishnavism and Christianity* (n.p., 1899) was an early study of the subject.

19. On Lokenath Palit, see E. P. Thompson, *Alien Homage,* 26 n. 1; D/R, *Tagore,* 74-75.

20. Canton to EJT, 3 July 1913, c. 5279, folios 45-46.

21. EJT to Lowther, 21 July 1912, c. 5295, folio 212; EJT to ET, 1 January 1913, d. 2670, folio 1.

22. Canton to EJT, 17 July 1913, c. 5279, folios 13-15.

23. ET to EJT, 19 March 1913, folios 184-86; 27 March 1913, folios 187-89; both: d. 2681.

24. Canton to EJT, 6 March 1913, folios 16-17; 1 April 1913, folios 23-25; both: c. 5279. Rushbrooke to EJT, 22 August 1913, c. 5311, folio 125.

25. EJT to Lowther, 22 January 1913, c. 5275, folio 222; ET to EJT, 13 February 1913, c. 2681, folios 170-72.

26. Bridges to EJT, 5 January 1913, c. 5275, folios 24-25. See Bridges, "John Keats: A Critical Essay" (London: Lawrence and Bullen, 1895); reprinted in *Collected Essays and Papers &c. of Robert Bridges* (London: Humphrey Milford for Oxford University Press, 1929), 7:18-29. See also his *Milton's Prosody: an examination of the rules of the blank verse in Milton's later poems, with an account of the versification of Samson Agonistes, and general notes by Robert Bridges* (Oxford: Clarendon Press, 1894). After medical studies, Robert Seymour Bridges (1844-1930) joined the staff of St. Bartholomew's Hospital, London, but a prolonged severe pneumonia in 1881 turned him to poetry and a lifelong study of prosody and metrics. Stephen Phillips (1864-1915) was a poet and dramatist; he was the Editor of *Poetry Review* from 1913 to 1915.

27. Bridges to EJT, 20 April 1913, c. 5275, folios 26-27. See "A Letter to a Musician on English Prosody," *The Musical Antiquary* 1 (1909): 15-29; reprinted in *Collected Essays,* 7:55-85. On Bridges on Shelley, see Catherine Phillips, *Robert Bridges: A Biography* (New York: Oxford University Press, 1992), 139.

28. Bridges to EJT, 20 April 1913, c. 5275, folios 26-27.

29. Bridges to EJT, 24 June [1913], c. 5275, folios 28-29. Cf. D/R, *Tagore,* 173-74.

7. REQUIEM

1. Lowther to EJT, 3 December 1910, c. 5298, folio 74; 28 May 1912, c. 5299, folios 30-31; 3 February 1911, c. 5298, folios 84-85. Sir Sidney Low (1857-1932) was the Editor of the *St. James's Gazette* from 1888 to 1897 and was Literary Editor of the *Standard* from 1904.

2. Lowther to EJT, 21 June 1911, c. 5298, folio 115.

3. Lowther to EJT, 30 January 1913, c. 5299, folios 75-77.

4. Lowther to EJT, 15 September 1911, c. 5298, folios 134-35. See EJT to Lowther, 12 December 1911, c. 5295, folios 199-202. Lowther to EJT, 24 November 1911, c. 5299, folio 149.

5. Lowther to EJT, 2 February 1913, folios 78-79; 9 January 1913, folio 91; both c. 5299.

6. Lowther to EJT, 29 March 1912, folio 16; 24 April 1912, folios 56-58; 31 May 1912, folio 32; 7 November 1912, folios 60-61; all: c. 5299. See Lowther, "J. M. Synge and the Irish Revival," *Oxford and Cambridge Review* 25 (1912): 43-59.

7. Lowther to EJT, 11 November 1911, c. 5298, folio 147; Lowther to EJT, 18 July 1913, c. 5299, folio 124.

8. Lowther to EJT, 14 March 1913, folio 89; 12-15 May 1911, folios 108-9; 22 Ma 1913, folios 110-11; all: c. 5299.

9. Lowther to EJT, 29 December 1911, c. 5298, folios 154-55; 8 August 1907, c. 529(folios 67-72.

10. Lowther to EJT, 29 December 1911, c. 5298, folios 154-55; Fielden to EJT, 1' March 1912, folios 7-9; 30 June 1912, folios 10-14; both: c. 5288.

11. Fielden to EJT, 1 August 1913, folios 19-29; 26 September 1913, folios 24-26; both c. 5288.

12. Canton to EJT, 6 August 1913, folios 57-58; 16 September 1913, folios 67-72; both c. 5279.

13. See Wordsworth, "The Brothers" (1800): one of two brothers dies accidentally an is buried in Ennerdale churchyard. See also Frank Richards, "George Lowther"; and EJ1 "In Memoriam: George Lowther," both in *Kingswood Magazine* 19 (1913): 138-42.

14. EJT to ET [incomplete], 8 August 1913, d. 2670, folios 24-25.

8. EPIPHANY

1. EJT to Lowther, 28 April 1912, c. 5295, folio 205; EJT, *Ennerdale Bridge* (Londor Kelly, 1914).

2. EJT to ET, 23 April 1913, d. 2670, folio 7; Canton to EJT, 17 April 1913, c. 5279 folios 29-30.

3. EJT to Lowther, 17 June 1913, c. 5275, folios 227-32. Canton to EJT, 11 June 1913 folios 37-38; 19 June 1913, folios 39-40; 20 July 1913, folios 47-50; all: c. 5279.

4. Canton to EJT, 14-20 August 1913, c. 5279, folios 59-63.

5. C. F. Andrews, "Tagore and the Renaissance in Bengal," *Contemporary Revier* 103 (1913): 809-17. On Chandidas and Chaitanya, see J. C. Ghosh, *Bengali Literatur* (London: Geoffrey Cumberlege for Oxford University Press, 1948), 38-40, 121 ff. Se also Buddhadeva Bose, *An Acre of Green Grass: A Review of Modern Bengali Literatur* (Bombay: Orient Longmans, 1948).

6. EJT to ET, 13 August 1913, folios 17-18; 9 July 1913, folio 14; both: d. 2670.

7. EJT to ET, 8 October 1913, folios 24-25; 7 August 1913, folio 16; both: d. 2670. EJ1 "The New Laureate," *Indian Methodist Times,* August 1913, 114-15. See Phillips, *Rober Bridges,* 230-32.

8. EJT to ET, 1 October 1913, folios 22-23; 8 October 1913, folios 24-25; both: c 2670.

9. EJT to ET, 30 October 1913, d. 2670, folios 33-34. See E. P. Thompson, *Alie* Homage,* 132 n. 3. "Babu": strictly, a Bengali courtesy form of address, but also attache to clerks and others of that class, often with derogatory connotations.

10. E. P. Thompson, *Alien Homage,* 5.

11. EJT to ET, 30 October 1913, d. 2670, folios 33-34. Adi Brahmo Samaj: an "ir digenous modernization" of the Brahmo Samaj. See Kopf, *Brahmo Samaj,* 218. Tagor was "the charismatic hero" who slowed younger Brahmos' movement to "revolutionar nationalism."

12. See Tagore's parable of teaching methods, "The Parrot's Training," in *The Parrot Training and Other Stories,* trans. Marjorie Sykes (Calcutta: Visva-Bharati, 1944). Se also his *Reminiscences,* trans. unidentified (London: Macmillan, 1917), 31, 33; and "M School," in his *Personality: Lectures Delivered in America* (London: Macmillan, 1917 112.

13. See Tagore, *Glimpses of Bengal,* trans. Surendranath Tagore, rev. Thomas Sturg Moore (London: Macmillan, 1921).

14. Rothenstein to Tagore, 27 March 1913, in *IE,* 106; Tagore to Rothenstein, [1? Apr 1913], in ibid., 106-7. However, Urbana Unitarians welcomed him; their descendants an other Urbana residents sponsor an annual Tagore conference.

15. See Macmillan Reader's Reports, vol. F (November 1912), MP:BL. George Macmillan) Rothenstein, 26 November 1912, RP:HL. Charles Whibley (1859-1930) was a journalist and biographer. George A. Macmillan (1855-1936), the second son of Alexander Macmillan, the firm's founder, was Director with his elder brother, Sir Frederick Macmillan (851-1936).

16. Review of *Gitanjali, Athenaeum,* 16 November 1913, 583; a shorter review ppeared on 5 April 1913, 382. "Mr. Tagore's Poems," *TLS,* 7 November 1912, 492.

17. Ezra Pound, "Rabindranath Tagore," *Fortnightly Review,* n.s., 99 (1913): 571-79.

18. In E. P. Thompson, *Alien Homage,* 109-22 (quotations in the next few paragraphs re from this source also). On Tagore and Calcutta University, see S. K. De, "Struggle of ernaculars for Their Rightful Place in Our Universities," *Calcutta Review,* 3d ser., 154 (960): 105-22.

19. Rothenstein to Tagore, 15 November 1913, in *IE,* 139; "The Nobel Literature Prize: onour for an Indian Poet," *Times,* 14 November 1913, 8; "Swedish Tribute to Mr. Tagore," *imes,* 15 November 1913, 13. See also D/R, *Tagore,* 180-87.

20. E. P. Thompson, *Alien Homage,* 109-22.

21. Ibid.

22. Ibid., 14-15.

23. See Benita Parry, *Delusions and Discoveries: Studies on India in the British magination, 1880-1930* (Berkeley and Los Angeles: University of California Press, 972), 164-202.

24. Tagore to EJT, 18 November 1918, in E. P. Thompson, *Alien Homage,* 16.

25. EJT to ET, 26 November 1913, d. 2670, folios 47-50; Tagore to EJT, 1 January 1914, 5318, folios 16-17.

26. EJT to ET, 10 December 1913, d. 2670, folios 55-56. See also D/R, *Tagore,* 182-83.

27. Canton to EJT, 7 January 1914, c. 5279, folios 93-96.

28. Canton to EJT, 1 December 1913, c. 5279, folios 89-90.

29. EJT to ET, 10 December 1913, folios 55-56; 30 December 1913, folios 60-61; both: . 2670.

30. EJT to ET, 4 March 1914, d. 2670, folios 76-77; Canton to EJT, 26 March 1914, . 5279, folios 117-18.

31. Tagore, interview with Chandra Gupta, 23 February 1936. When *The Housewarm-ıg and Other Selected Writings of Rabindranath Tagore,* trans. Mary Lago and Tarun upta (New York: New American Library, 1965), was in progress, the translators were told) include more of "the sort of thing people expect from Tagore"—sentimental anecdotes d fables from mythology.

32. Frank O'Connor, *The Lonely Voice* (Cleveland: World Publishing, 1965), 18. 'illiam H. Peden, *The American Short Story: Front Line in the National Defense of iterature* (Boston: Houghton Mifflin, 1964), 9. See also Peter Carey, "Gathering for a alk: Literature, Politics, and Censorship in Present-Day Burma," *TLS,* 16 November 1996, 7.

33. Jyotirindranath Tagore, *Granthabali* (Library Collection) (Calcutta: Satishchandra ukhopadhyay, [n.d.]).

34. See E. P. Thompson, *Alien Homage,* 18-19.

9. INTERIM

1. ET to EJT, 8-9 May 1913, d. 2682, folios 4-8.

2. ET to EJT, 12-13 June 1913, folios 21-24; 26 June 1913, folios 29-31; both: d. 2682.

3. EJT to Hartley, 31 July 1913, WMMS/SOAS. Misc. ET to EJT, 21 August 1913, folios 71-7; 16-17 September 1913, folios 96-103; 2 October 1913, folios 109-16; 21 December)13, folios 182-87; all: d. 2682.

4. ET to EJT, 15 February 1914, folios 26-30; [February 1914], pp. 11-12 missin▪ folios 35-39; 2 April 1914, folios 62-66; all: d. 2683.

5. In Hardinge to Carmichael, 30-31 March 1914, telegram no. 153, HP 87/2.

6. See "The Pathan Raid: Indian Frontier Tribe Chastised," *Times,* 24 February 1914, Hardinge to Crewe, 22 April 1914, telegram no. 186, HP 98/2.

7. EJT to ET, 12 February 1914, d. 2670, folios 70-71.

8. On Sir Edward Marsh (1872-1953), see Christopher Hassall, *Edward Marsh, Patr▪ of the Arts: A Biography* (London: Longmans, 1959), 532, 378. Harold Monro (187▪ 1932), himself a poet, managed the bookshop from 1913 as a center for publication a▪ readings.

9. Canton to EJT, 9 January 1913, c. 5279, folios 3-6.

10. *The Letters of Ezra Pound, 1907-1941,* ed. D. D. Paige (New York: Harcou▪ Brace, 1950), 44; Yeats to Macmillan, 9 July 1916, in Simon Nowell-Smith, ed., *Letters Macmillan* (London: Macmillan, 1967), 291-92.

11. See Yeats to Macmillan, 8 July 1916, in Nowell-Smith, *Letters to Macmillan,* 29▪

12. EJT to Macmillan, 19 March 1914, UR: Macmillan 64/67.

13. Canton to EJT, 5 June 1914, folios 128-29; 11 June 1914, folios 130-31; bot▪ c. 5279.

14. See Tagore, "Living or Dead," trans. EJT, in *The Hungry Stones and Other Stor▪* (London: Macmillan, 1916), 193-212; also in his *Rabindra-racanabali,* 19:181-93.

15. Canton to EJT, 1 December 1913, c. 5279, folios 89-90.

16. Bridges to EJT, 5 June [1914], c. 5275, folios 24-27.

17. ET to EJT, 9 July 1914, folios 74-79; 23-24 July 1914, folios 87-93; both: c. 268▪

18. Mitchell to Hartley, 24 April 1914, WMMS/SOAS, CC; Hardinge to Valentine Chir▪ 29 January 1914, HP 87/2, no. 49.

19. Olver to Hartley, cablegram, 6 August 1914; 31 August 1914; both: WMMS/SOA▪ CC. Mitchell to Hartley, 23 April 1914, 26 March 1914; both: WMMS/SOAC, GC. Al▪ Rutland Spooner (1891-1978), the son of a Wesleyan minister, was at Bankura from 19▪ to 1927.

20. See "Exploits of the *Emden,*" *Times,* 23 October 1914, 6. "Commerce Protectio▪ The Task of Removing the Raiders," *Times,* 11 November 1914, 10.

21. Carmichael to Hardinge, 5 August 1914, pp. 1-4; 11 August 1914, pp. 154-59; ▪ August 1914, pp. 254-57; all: HP 62.

22. Hardinge to Chirol, 3 September 1914 (copy), HP 62, pp. 311-14.

23. Ibid.

24. ET to EJT, 6 August 1914, folios 100-103; 14 August 1914, folios 104-8; 3 Septemb▪ 1914, folios 120-26; all: d. 2683.

25. See Tagore to EJT, 18 February 1914, c. 5318, folios 29-30. Canton to EJT, ▪ November 1914, folios 152-53; 24 May 1915, folios 175-78; both: c. 5279. Tagore, *Me▪ o roudra* (Cloud and sun), in *Rabindra-racanabali,* 19:210-35.

26. Bridges, ed., *The Spirit of Man: An Anthology in English and French from t▪ Philosophers and Poets, Made by the Poet Laureate in 1915 . . .* (London: Longma▪ Green, 1917). Poems, not pages, are numbered. Cf. *IE,* 177-216.

27. Bridges to Tagore, 7 June 1914, Rabindra-Sadhana (manuscript collection), C▪ cutta.

28. Bridges to Tagore, 20 October 1914, Rabindra-Sadhana, Calcutta; to Marsh, ▪ March 1914, in Hassall, *Edward Marsh,* 293. See Humayun Kabir, *One Hundred ▪ ems of Kabir,* trans. Rabindranath Tagore and Evelyn Underhill (London: India Socie▪ 1914).

29. See Bridges, "Humdrum and Harum-Scarum," *North American Review* 216 (192▪ 647-58. Bridges's holograph note on his *Spirit of Man* file (BP): "This is the correspo▪ dence: letters from Tagore, Macmillan, Rothenstein & Thompson which resulted at last

my having permission to make verbal alterations in the English of Tagore's original poem, [*and in his translations from Kabir*—] for the Spirit of Man."

30. See Bridges to Rothenstein, 19 April [1915], in *The Selected Letters of Robert Bridges*, ed. Donald E. Stanford, 2 vols. (Newark, N.J.: University of Delaware Press, 1983–1984), 2:662–63.

31. Bridges to Yeats, 19 April [1935], in Bridges, *Selected Letters*, 2:679; and 2 October [1915] (copy), BP. Bridges to Rothenstein, 28 April 1914, BP.

32. See Thring to Bridges, 10 May 1915, BP. Bridges's penciled note on this seems to be the gist of an intended reply.

33. Rothenstein to Bridges, 12 May 1915, BP. A file at Harvard (RP:HL: bMS 1159 [21]) refers to who revised what in Tagore's original versions of poems published as *The Crescent Moon* (London: Macmillan, 1913). Others sent later from India were "more or less rewritten by Sturge Moore, not always to the advantage of Tagore's own translations, even though the English be more correct." A typescript is an intermediate version of "Thou Art the Sky" (the disputed *Gitanjali* No. 67) and also a revised typescript copy of the poem (there numbered 28 but *Gitanjali* No. 46), considerably shortened.

34. EJT to Bridges [July 1915]; 13 September 1915; both: BP. Bridges to Sir Frederick Macmillan, 24 September [1915], photocopy in BP.

35. EJT to Bridges [July 1915], BP. Crewe to Hardinge, 19 December 1914, telegram no. 685, HP 98/1. Andrews to Du Boulay, 22 March [1915], p. 547, HP 64. See Tinker, *Ordeal of Love*, 104. Sir James Houssemayne Du Boulay (1868-1945) was Hardinge's private secretary from 1910 to 1916. See "His Majesty's Birthday: List of Honours," *Times*, 3 June 1915, 9-10.

36. Canton to EJT, 23 June 1915, c. 5279, folios 179-80.

37. EJT to ET, [July 1915], d. 2671, folio 259.

38. EJT to ET, 8 July 1915, d. 2670, folio 120.

39. EJT to ET, 9 October 1915, d. 2670, folio 126.

40. EJT to ET, [24 December 1915], d. 2670, folio 127.

10. "CHAPLAINING"

1. EJT to ET, 24 March 1916, d. 2670, folios 129-31. See E. P. Thompson, *Alien Homage*, 2.

2. Lyon to EJT, 7 April 1910, c. 5301, folios 1-2. After the war, his son, Percy H. B. Lyon (1893-1937), returned to Oxford and later was one of the youngest headmasters of Rugby School.

3. EJT to ET, 24 March 1916, d. 2670, folios 129-31. Sir Jagadish Chandra Bose (1858-1937) was a botanist and the Director of the Bose Research Institute, Calcutta. Prasanta Chandra Mahalanobis (1893-1972), later a statistician of international standing, was in the Indian Educational Service from 1915 to 1948 and was head of the Department of Physics at Presidency College from 1922 to 1945. "Ramprasad," or Ramaprasada Sen (1718-1775), considered by many the greatest Vaishnava songwriter of the eighteenth century, addressed his works to the goddess Kali. These are collected in *Bengali Religious Lyrics*, trans. E. J. Thompson and A. M. Spencer (Calcutta: Association Press; London: Oxford University Press, 1923).

4. Lyon to EJT, 30 May 1916, c. 5301, folios 3-4. After retirement in 1917, Lyon (1862-1952) had posts in the home government and Oxford city government. He was a Fellow and Treasurer of Oriel College from 1918 to 1928; and he was Treasurer, from 1926 to 1932, and Chairman of the Council, from 1930 to 1935, of St. Hugh's College, Oxford.

5. Lyon to EJT, 21 June 1916, c. 5301, folios 7-8. Broomfield, *Elite Conflict*, 92, see also 93. Lyon, Note of August 1917, in Government of India, Home Political Papers, A225-32.

6. Broomfield, *Elite Conflict*, 93.

7. Ibid., 94.

8. See Lyon to EJT, 29 August 1916, c. 5301, folios 15-17.

9. See Hardinge to Butler, 18 April 1914, HP 87/2, telegram no. 169; Hardinge to Carmichael, 27 November 1914, HP 88, pp. 188-89; and 31 August 1915, HP 90/2, pp 93-95. See also Carmichael to Hardinge, 17 March 1915, HP 64, pp. 559-71. Hardinge to Meston, 29 December 1915, HP 90/2, pp. 228-29.

10. See EJT to Lyon, 28 March 1916, c. 5300, folio 6. Harihar Das (1892-1952?) wa briefly on the staff of the India Office Library, London. After Princess Victoria accepted a copy of his *Life and Letters of Toru Dutt* (London: Humphrey Milford for Oxford University Press, 1921), he was made a Fellow of the Royal Society of Literature. In 1921 he left incomplete an Oxford Ph.D. and then taught political science in India. Toru Dut (1856-1877), born in Calcutta, went with her family to France in 1869 and in 1871 to Cambridge. In 1873, back in Calcutta, she published translations from French poets as *A Sheaf Gleaned in French Fields* (London: K. Paul, Trench, 1880). See also her *Ancien Ballads and Legends of Hindustan* (London: K. Paul, Trench, 1882).

11. EJT to Lyon, 6 May 1916, c. 5300, folios 14-15; EJT to ET, [25] May 1916, d. 2670 folios 138-40; EJT to Lyon, postmark 17 April 1916, c. 5300, folio 7.

12. EJT to Hartley, 6 August 1915, WMMS/SOAS, CC.

13. ET to EJT, 20 October 1915, d. 2685, folios 12-18.

14. ET to EJT, 25 November 1915, d. 2685, folio 41.

15. ET to EJT, 1 November 1916, d. 2685, folios 210-13; EJT to ET, 23 December 1916 d. 2670, folios 205-209.

16. EJT to ET, "25?" May 1916, folios 138-40; 3 June 1916, d. 2670, folios 141-43; both d. 2670. The Student Volunteer Movement inspired Thomas J. McClelland (1873-1924 to missionary service; he went to Bengal in 1896.

17. McClelland to Hartley, 12 August 1915, WMMS/SOAS, CC.

18. EJT to ET, 11 June 1916, d. 2670, folios 144-45. EJT to Lyon, 10 June 1916, folio 27-29b; 23 June 1916, folios 33-38; both: c. 5300. Mitchell to Lyon, 17 June 1916, c. 5300 folio 32.

19. EJT to Lyon, 29 June 1916, c. 5300, folios 38b-38f.

20. Lyon to EJT, 19 June 1916, c. 5301, folios 5-6; Fielden to EJT, 15 July 1916, c. 5288 folios 46-47.

21. See Hardinge, *My Indian Years*, 144. The Right Honorable Sir (Joseph) Austen Chamberlain (1863-1937) was Secretary of State for India from 1915 to 1917; Member of the War Cabinet in 1918; Chancellor of the Exchequer from 1919 to 1921; Leader of the House of Commons from 1921 to 1922; Secretary of State for Foreign Affairs from 1924 to 1929; and First Lord of the Admiralty in 1931.

22. Quotations in this and next few paragraphs from EJT to Lyon, 29 June 1916, c. 5300 folios 65-69 (reference is to *King Lear*, act 3, scene 4, lines 32-33); and Mitchell to Lyon 17 June 1916, c. 5300, folio 32. Frank Hart (1882-1970) was an Army Chaplain in the Punjab and Northwest Frontier, then in the Bombay area, in 1916.

23. Mitchell to Hartley, 14 August 1915, WMMS/SOAS, GC.

24. ET to EJT, 28 June 1916, d. 2685, folios 157-59. EJT to Lyon, 3 June 1916, folio 19-20; 23 June 1916, folio 20; both: c. 5300.

25. Canton to EJT, [n.d. March 1916], c. 5280, folios 26-27. H. M. Margoulieth edited the first modern standard edition of Marvell (1927).

26. Canton to EJT, 27 June 1916, c. 5280, folios 55-56. See Tagore, *Mashi and Othe Stories* (London: Macmillan, 1918), 145-55.

27. Whibley's report in *IE*, 220. Canton to EJT, 7 March 1916, c. 5280, folios 14-16 [n.d., early 1916], folios 26-27; both: c. 5280.

28. EJT to Canton, 8 September 1916, c. 5276. On Tagore in Japan, see *IE*, 227-31 Stephen N. Hay, *Asian Ideas of East and West: Tagore and His Critics in Japan, China and India* (Cambridge: Harvard University Press, 1970), 12-81.

29. Summary from Barbara W. Tuchman, *The Guns of August* (New York: Macmillan, 1962), 8, 138-41. On German espionage in the Middle East, see Peter Hopkirk, *On Secret Service East of Constantinople* (London: John Murray, 1994).

30. Hardinge, *My Indian Years,* 102-3.

31. Summary from Robert Rhodes James, *Gallipoli* (New York: Macmillan, 1965), 333-47.

32. See EJT to ET, 11 June 1916, d. 2670, folios 144-48; and Chamberlain to Hardinge, 24 February 1916, HP 78, pp. 106-14. See also Sir George Buchanan, *The Tragedy of Mesopotamia* (Edinburgh: Blackwood, 1938).

33. Sir Llewyllan Woodward, *Great Britain and the War of 1914-1918* (London: Methuen, 1967), 100, 101.

34. EJT to ET, 3 June 1916, d. 2670, folios 141-43.

35. EJT to Lyon, [29 June 1916], c. 5300, folios 65-69.

11. COMBAT

1. Mulk Raj Anand, *Across the Dark Waters* (London: J. Cape, 1940), 105-9.

2. Bridges to EJT, 5 November [1916], c. 5275, folios 47-48. See Robert Graves, *Good-bye to All That,* rev. ed. (Garden City, N.Y.: Doubleday, 1957), 189-90.

3. Paul Fussell, *The Great War and Modern Memory* (New York: Oxford University Press, 1975), 8.

4. Government of India, *India's Contribution to the Great War* (Calcutta: Government Printing Office, 1923), 97, 98; *LBB,* 39; DeWitt C. Ellinwood, "The Indian Soldier, the Indian Army, and Change, 1914-1918," in *India and World War I,* ed. DeWitt C. Ellinwood and S. D. Pradhan, 177-211 (New Delhi: Manohari, 1978). Of British in Mesopotamia, 18,669 were officers, and 166,822 were other ranks. Of Indians in Mesopotamia, 9,514 were officers and warrant officers, 317,142 were other ranks, and 348,735 were non-combatants; 1,338,620 Indians and British went from India. On Indian soldiers abroad, see Ellinwood, "Indian Soldier," 179-81.

5. EJT to ET, 10 August 1916 (two letters), folios 154-56; 11 August 1916, folios 157-58; 20 August 1916, folios 167-68; 30 August 1916, folios 174-75; 17 November 1916, folio 202; 8 September 1916, folios 176-80; 20 October 1916, folios 193-95; all: d. 2670. "Another Wesleyan": Percy Cottrell Brunt (1889-1961) was with the Fourteenth Indian Division in Mesopotamia.

6. Canton to EJT, 15 August 1915, folios 63-64; 4 October 1916, folios 67-68; both: c. 5280. EJT to Canton, 28 March 1917, c. 5276, folios 118-20. EJT's diaries: 4 August 1916-June 1919, e. 2922-26.

7. EJT to Canton, 4 September 1916, c. 5276, folios 74-78.

8. EJT to Canton, 8 August 1916, folio 73; 20 December 1916, folios 96-104; both: c. 5276.

9. EJT to Lyon, 30 September 1916, c. 5300, folios 65-70. "W. Thompson": probably Edgar Wesley Thompson (1871-1963), who was an India missionary and, after 1919, was General Secretary of the Missionary Society.

10. Lyon to EJT, 15 October 1916, c. 5300, folios 18-21.

11. EJT to Canton, 11 December 1916, c. 5276, folio 93.

12. EJT to Canton, 17 November 1916, folios 89-90; 20-23 December 1916, folios 96-104; 6 January 1916, folios 107-10; all: c. 5276.

13. EJT to ET, 13 January 1917, folios 4-8; 27 January 1917, folios 15-19; both: d. 2671. Bulgaria entered the war in October 1915; the Allies had hoped that gaining Gallipoli would keep Bulgaria out of the war; see James, *Gallipoli,* 323.

14. EJT to Canton, 6 January 1917, c. 5276, folios 107-11.

15. Frank Thompson to EJT, 5 January 1916, folios 57-58; 9 August 1915, folios 59-60; both: d. 2691.

16. EJT to Lyon, 30 January 1917, folios 77-78.

17. EJT to ET, 3 February 1917, folios 24-25; 10 February 1917, folios 26-27; both: d 2670.

18. Canton to EJT, 24 January 1917, c. 5280, folios 102-3; Arthur Thompson to EJT 22 January 1917, d. 2691, folios 96-98; Margaret Pilkington-Rogers to EJT, 15 February 1917, d. 2692, folios 92-93.

19. EJT to ET, 18 February 1917, folios 28-29; 22 February 1917, folios 30-34; both d. 2671.

20. Tuchman, *Guns of August,* 116, 140-41. Sir Edward Grey, Viscount Grey o Falloden (1862-1933), was Foreign Secretary from 1905 to 1916, a historically long tenure. For his speech on 3 August 1914, justifying Britain's entry, see *Parliamentary Debates,* Commons, 5th ser., vol. 115 (3 August 1914), cols. 1809-26.

21. EJT to ET, 20 February 1917, folios 35-37; 12 March 1917, folio 38; 2 April 1917 folios 45-48; all: d. 2671.

22. EJT to ET, 26 April 1917, c. 2671, folios 54-57.

23. EJT to Canton, 25 April, folios 123-30; 3 May 1917, folios 131-40; both: c. 5276 Compare *LBB,* 70-103; he does not mention his own Military Cross.

24. *LBB,* 7.

25. Ibid., 7-8. Edmund Candler (1874-1926) taught in several Indian schools an was Principal of Mohinder Government College, Patiala, from 1904 to 1915, where E. M. Forster met him in 1912; he was *Times* Correspondent in France from 191 to 1915; Special Mesopotamian Correspondent from 1915 to 1918; *Times* Middle East Correspondent from 1918 to 1919; and Punjab Government Publicity Director from 1920 to 1921. See *LBB,* 7-8; Candler, *The Long Road to Baghdad,* 2 vols. (London: Cassell 1919); and Parry, *Delusions and Discoveries,* 310-63.

26. *LBB,* 19.

27. Xenophon: see *LLB,* 59-60, 61-62.

28. *LBB,* 78. *Euxine* is an ancient name for the Black Sea.

29. *LBB,* 48; Shakespeare, *The Life of King Henry the Fifth,* act 4, scene 3, chorus lines 46-47.

30. *LBB,* 54; *King Henry the Fifth,* act 4, scene 3, lines 16-17, 23, 33-39, 64-65.

31. *LBB,* 65-66, 67; *King Henry the Fifth,* act 4, scene 3, lines 38-39. Major Henry Molyneaux Paget Howard, Nineteenth Earl of Suffolk and Berkshire (1877-1917), com manded the Wilts[hire] Battery of the Third Wessex Brigade.

32. *LBB,* 69.

33. *LBB,* 59, 91. See Buchanan, *Tragedy of Mesopotamia,* 134.

34. *LBB,* 51.

35. Ibid., 100-101.

36. Ibid., 28-29.

37. Ibid., 119.

38. EJT to Lyon, 23 November 1916, folio 75; 29 November 1917, folio 76; both c. 5300.

39. Bridges to EJT, 29 August 1915, c. 5275, folios 45-46.

40. EJT to Canton, 3 May 1917, c. 5276, folios 131-40.

41. EJT to ET, 13 May 1917, d. 2671, folios 67-68. See *LBB,* 46.

42. EJT to Canton, 3 May 1917, folios 151-40; Canton to EJT, 13 February 1917, c. 5280 folio 168.

43. EJT to Canton, 3 June 1917, folios 154-60; 11 May 1917, folios 141-46; both c. 5276.

44. EJT to Canton, 23 July 1917, c. 5276, folios 179-80. See *LBB,* 93.

45. EJT to Canton, 25 June 1917, c. 5276, folios 166-69; H. G. Wells, *Mr. Britling See It Through* (New York: Macmillan, 1916).

12. REVISIONS

1. EJT to Lyon, 1 April 1917 c. 5300, folios 79-82. Who suggested this to EJT is unknown.

2. See Sir Thomas Holderness to Hardinge, 14 July 1914, HP 76, pp. 90-99. Holderness (1849-1934) was Secretary to the Government of India, Agriculture Department, from 1896 to 1901, and the Revenue Statistics and Commerce Department, India Office, from 1901 to 1912; then he was Undersecretary of State from 1912 to 1919. Mohammed Ali Jinnah (1876-1948) was an English-trained barrister and a Member of the Imperial Legislative Council in 1910; then he was President of the All-India Muslim League in 1916, 1920, and from 1934. He led the Muslim League Party until 1947, when Pakistan broke from India.

3. EJT to Canton, 2 August 1917, folios 181-85; 14 August 1917, folios 189-92; both: c. 5276. EJT to Lyon, 2 August 1917, c. 5300, folios 89-92.

4. EJT to Canton, 2 August 1917, c. 5276, folios 181-85; D/R, *Tagore*, 310-11, 212; Taylor, *Annie Besant*, 306. See also Broomfield, *Elite Conflict*, 135-36.

5. See Broomfield, *Elite Conflict*, 101-5. Dyarchy: see Deborah Lavin, *From Empire to International Commonwealth: A Biography of Lionel Curtis* (Oxford: Clarendon Press, 1995), 135-55, passim. The Right Honorable Edmund Samuel Montagu (1879-1924) was Undersecretary of State for India from 1910 to 1914 and Financial Secretary to the Treasury from 1914 to 1916. His sympathy for Indian political aspirations prevented his becoming Viceroy. Frederick John Napier Thesiger, First Viscount Chelmsford (1868-1933), was Governor of Queensland from 1905 to 1909, of New South Wales from 1903 to 1912, and Viceroy of India from 1916 to 1921.

6. Tagore to Rothenstein, 26 October 1917, in *IE*, 244. See also Tagore, *Nationalism* (London: Macmillan, 1917); Sujit Mukherjee, *Passage to America: The Reception of Rabindranath Tagore in the United States, 1912-1941* (Calcutta: Bookland Private, 1964), 74-85, and D/R, *Tagore*, 212.

7. George Brett to Maurice Macmillan, 11 June 1919; Macmillan to Brett, 20 May 1919, both in *IE*, 223, 222.

8. EJT to Canton, 7 August 1917, c. 5276, folios 186-88; Tagore to Rothenstein, 26 October 1917, in *IE*, 244-45; William to Albert Rothenstein, 25 November 1917, in *IE*, 245-46 n. 3.

9. EJT to Canton, 2 August 1917, c. 5276, folios 181-85.

10. EJT to Canton, 14 August 1917, c. 5376, folios 189-92; 28 February 1918, c. 5277, folios 19-29.

11. EJT to Canton, 13 November 1918, c. 5296, folios 232-33.

12. EJT to Lyon, 23 August 1917, c. 5300, folios 93-94.

13. Ibid.; EJT to Lyon, 2 August 1917, c. 5300, folios 93-94.

14. EJT to ET, 31 August 1917, folios 108-10; 30 September 1917, folios 117-18; both: d. 2671.

15. EJT to Canton, 23 September 1917, c. 5276, folios 204-5.

16. *LBB*, 125-27.

17. Ibid., 129-30.

18. Ibid., 150.

19. Candler, *Long Road to Baghdad*, 1:22-27. For more on Candler and Forster, see *Selected Letters of E. M. Forster*, ed. Mary Lago and P. N. Furbank, 2 vols. (London: Collins; Cambridge: Harvard University Press, 1983, 1985), 1:138, 194; 2:62. Some of Candler's unorthodoxy went into the character of Fielding in *A Passage to India;* see Forster, *The Hill of Devi and Other Indian Writings*, Abinger Edition, ed. Elizabeth Heine (London: Edward Arnold, 1983), 203, 205-6, 207. See also Parry, *Delusions and Discoveries*, 131-62.

20. Norfolk Regiment: see Candler, *Long Road to Baghdad*, 1:164. Some brigades were so reduced that they "had to be eked out with composite battalions . . . ; the Norfolks and Dorsets became the 'Norsets.' . . ."

21. *LBB,* 150-51.

22. EJT to ET, 21 December 1917, d. 2671, folios 149-52.

23. EJT to Lyon, 10 February 1918, c. 5300, folios 107-9.

24. EJT to Canton, 27 May 1918, folios 39-40; 28 May 1918, folios 35-38; 23 April 1918, folios 30-33; all: c. 5277.

25. Canton to EJT, 18 May 1918, c. 5280, folios 182-86; EJT to Lyon, 28 January 1918 c. 5300, folios 104-6.

26. EJT to Theodosia Jessup, 2-8 August 1918, c. 5356, folios 1-6. In 1866 the American Protestant Mission established the Syrian Protestant College, later the American Universit of Beirut, noted for scholarship, public service, and as a publishing center in English French, and Arabic. The Allies occupied Beirut; in 1920 it became the capital of Lebanon

27. Canton to EJT, 25 February 1915, folios 160-61; April 1915, folios 166-67; 2-2(April 1915, folios 169-70; 12 May 1915, folios 171-73; all: c. 5279. "Egeria": in Latin mythology, a nymph who advised a king of Rome on essential laws.

28. EJT to Theodosia Jessup, 2-8 August 1918, c. 5356, folios 1-6.

29. EJT to Canton, 18 August 1918, folios 56-57; 31 September 1918, folios 72-75 both: c. 5277.

30. EJT to Theodosia Jessup, 2-8 August 1918, c. 5356, folios 1-6; "Saturday" [October 1918], c. 5357, folios 184-85; 28 October 1918, c. 5357, folios 67-75.

31. EJT to Hartley, 30 September 1918, c. 5356, folios 67-75.

32. EJT to Theodosia Jessup, "Saturday" [September 1918], c. 5357, folios 184-85.

33. EJT to Lyon, 15 January 1919, c. 5300, folio 130.

34. Canton to EJT, 17 September 1918, folios 217-19; 25 September 1918, folios 220 21; both: c. 5280.

35. EJT to Canton, 24 September 1918, c. 5277, folios 58-60; Canton to Theodosia Jessup, 29 October 1918, c. 5280, folios 232-33.

36. EJT to Canton, 14 November 1918, folios 82-91; 13 December [1918], folios 98-101; both: c. 5277.

37. Theodosia (Jessup) Thompson (hereafter TJT) to Lyon, 11 May 1919, c. 5300, folio 140; EJT to Lyon, 29 November [1919], c. 5300, folio 153-54.

38. EJT to Lyon, 29 November [1919], c. 5300, folio 212.

39. Brown to Hartley, 11 December 1918; 28 May 1919; both: WMMS/SOAS, GC.

40. Brown to Burnet, 29 November 1919, WMMS/SOAS, GC; Correspondence, WMMS SOAS, CC. Amos Burnet (1857-1926) served in South India until appointed a Missionary Society General Secretary.

13. AMRITSAR

1. Broomfield, *Elite Conflict,* 141. See Helen Fein, *Imperial Crime and Punishment The Massacre at Jallianwala Bagh and British Judgment, 1919-1920* (Honolulu: University of Hawaii Press, 1977), 64-67.

2. Sir Michael O'Dwyer, *India as I Knew It, 1885-1925* (London: Constable, 1925) 269. O'Dwyer (1864-1940) entered the I.C.S. in 1885, was Agent to the Governor-General in Central India from 1910 to 1912, and was Lieutenant Governor of the Punjab from 191: to 1919. Rowlatt Act: see Fein, *Imperial Crime,* 24-25, 76-78, 75.

3. See Fein, *Imperial Crime,* 29; V. N. Datta, *Jallianwala Bagh* (Kurukshetra: Lyal Book Depot, 1969), 79, includes nine photographs from the scenes of 10 and 13 April 1919.

4. O'Dwyer, *India As I Knew It,* 269. On the Montagu-Chelmsford Reforms, see *Constitutional and National Development in India* (London: H. M. Stationery Office 1918), chaps. 15-18.

5. See Fein, *Imperial Crime,* 30-33.

6. O'Dwyer, *India As I Knew It,* 269, 263-317. See Raja Ram, *The Jallianwala*

Bagh Massacre: A Premeditated Plan, 2d ed. (Chandigarh: Publication Bureau, Panjab University, 1978), 128-51; a map of Jallianwala Bagh faces p. 1.

7. Dyer to the Hunter Committee, 25 August 1919, in Fein, *Imperial Crime,* 44. Reginald Edward Henry Dyer (1864-1927) was in the Indian army active service from 1886 to 1908, and in 1916 he commanded operations in southeast Persia. See Ian Colvin, *The Life of General Dyer* (Edinburgh: Blackwood, 1929).

8. Datta, *Jallianwala Bagh,* 112-13; see Fein, *Imperial Crime,* 32. Hunter Committee Report, *Report of the Committee Appointed to Investigate the Disturbances in the Punjab, Etc.,* Cmd. 681 (1920), 1-67. Amritsar District Report, *District Accounts Submitted by the Government of the Punjab,* Cmd. 534 (1920). Indian National Congress Punjab Subcommittee, *Report of the Commissioners,* 2 vols. (Bombay: Karnatak Press, 1920). See also *Parliamentary Debates,* Commons, 5th ser., vol. 131 (28 June-16 July 1920); Lords, 5th ser., vol. 41 (6 July-16 August 1920). The Honorable Lord William Hunter (1865-1957) was solicitor-general for Scotland from 1910 to 1911, and was senator of the College of Justice for Scotland from 1911 to 1936.

9. Dyer to the Hunter Committee, 25 August 1919, in Fein, *Imperial Crime,* 44.

10. Forster, *A Passage to India,* Abinger Edition, ed. Oliver Stallybrass (London: Edward Arnold, 1973), 6.

11. See Fein, *Imperial Crime,* 40-41.

12. "The Outbreak in India," *Times,* 15 April 1919, 13; "Open Rebellion in India," *Times,* 19 April 1919, 11; "The Disturbances in India," *Times,* 26 April 1919, 13.

13. EJT to Lyon, "Sunday" [after 10 April, perhaps 20th], c. 5300, folio 161.

14. Andrews to Tagore, 14 May 1919, in Tinker, *Ordeal of Love,* 155. Cf. D/R, *Tagore,* 215-18. For Andrews on Amritsar, see his letters to EJT, 22 March [1921], 22 March 1924, c. 5273, folios 62-69.

15. "Rabindranath Tagore: Why He Wishes to Resign His Title," *Manchester Guardian,* 9 July 1919, 10; also in Thompson, *Rabindranath Tagore: Poet and Dramatist* (London: Oxford University Press, 1926), 273-74.

16. Rothenstein to Tagore, 11 July 1919; Tagore to Rothenstein, 25 July 1919; both: *IE,* 255-58.

17. *RT:PD,* 274.

18. McClelland to Hartley, 12 March 1919; Hartley to McClelland, 1 May 1919; both: WMMS/SOAS, CC.

19. McClelland to Hartley, 2 April 1919; 16 April 1919, WMMS/SOAS, CC. "Missionary propaganda": McClelland most regretted losing Samuel Marinus Zwemer, *Islam: A Challenge to Faith: Studies on the Mohammedan Religion and Opportunities of the Mohammedan World from the Standpoint of Christian Missions* (New York: Student Volunteer Movement, 1908).

20. EJT to Lyon, 28 April 1920, c. 5300, folio 164; Tagore to EJT, 11 May 1920, c. 5318, folio 109.

21. Tagore, *Megh o roudra,* in *Rabindra-racanabali,* 19:210-35. James Drummond Anderson (1852-1920), a Lecturer in Bengali, EJT's Cambridge counterpart, doubted that any translation could keep the "delicate bloom" of the original. On Anderson and Tagore, see *IE,* 23-24. On derivation of "Visva-Bharati," see Krishna Kripalani, *Tagore: A Biography,* 267 n. 1.

22. Lyon to EJT, 13 June 1920, c. 5301, folios 62-64. See Fein, *Imperial Crime,* 95-96, 105-28, 130, 168-69, 177, 183-85. See also "Ten Minutes' Fire on Mob," *Times,* 15 December 1919, 13, and *Parliamentary Debates,* Commons, 5th ser., vol. 123 (16 December 1919), cols. 240-43.

23. EJT to Lyon, 20 July 1920, c. 5300, folio 166; EJT to TJT, 20 July 1919, c. 5357, folios 80-82. "Twenty-seven thousand pounds": *"An appeal for funds to present / The Saviour of the Punjab / with A Sword of Honour and a Purse is hereby made to /*

All well wishers of India, both Europeans and Indians, as a mark of gratitude to General Dyer for sparing India untold misery by arresting murder, torture, arson, loo and wholesale anarchy. . . .": in Datta, *Jallianwala Bagh*, 150-51. See also EJT, "Dye Appreciation Fund," *Statesman* (Calcutta), 13 July 1920, 7.

24. EJT to Lyon, 20 July 1920, c. 5300, folio 166. EJT to TJT, 25 July 1920, folio 87; 2(July 1919, folio 88; both: d. 5357.

25. See Forster, *Hill of Devi and other Indian writings*, xxvii.

26. Lyon to EJT, 5 October 1920, c. 5301, folios 65-67.

27. See Edmund Candler, "Probationary," in *The General Plan* (Edinburgh: Blackwood 1911), 18-23.

28. Forster, *Passage to India*, 174.

29. Lyon to EJT, 5 October 1920, folios 65-67; 12 December 1920, folios 68-70; both c. 5301.

30. EJT to Canton, 21 July 1920, c. 5277, folio 136. EJT, 19 July [1920] (letter), "Christian Principles and General Dyer," *Statesman* (Calcutta), 21 July 1920, 7-8. See also Florence Holland, "Dyer Appreciation Fund," *Statesman* (Calcutta), 7 July 1920, 7.

31. EJT to Lyon, 20 July 1920, c. 5300, folio 166.

32. Lyon to EJT, 5 October 1920, c. 5301, folios 65-67.

33. EJT to Canton, 26 July 1920, c. 5277, folio 136.

34. Canton to EJT, 25 August 1920, c. 5281, folios 122-24; EJT to Canton, [2(November 1920], c. 5277, folio 138. Haiti: U.S. Marines occupied the capital in 1915 afte a presidential assassination, ostensibly to protect American life but principally Americar sugar investments. The last marines withdrew in 1934.

35. Collingwood to EJT, 23 August 1920, c. 5284, folio 164.

14. BREAKING WITH BANKURA

1. EJT to TJT, 13 September 1920, c. 5357, folio 138.

2. EJT to TJT, 22 July 1920, folio 83; 14 August 1920, folio 110; both: c. 5357.

3. EJT to Canton, 26 July 1920, c. 5277, folio 137. Browning, "Love in a Life" (1855) "A Grammarian's Funeral" (1855).

4. EJT to Canton, 19 January 1921, c. 5277, folio 140.

5. EJT to Lyon, 12 April 1921, c. 5300, folio 171.

6. EJT to Canton, [April 1921], c. 5277, folios 299-300.

7. EJT to Committee, 1 May 1921, WMMS/SOAS, GC; EJT to Goudie, 26 May 1921 WMMS/SOAS, CC. William Goudie (1857-1922) went to the Madras District in 1882; ir 1921 he was designated Wesleyan Conference President but died before he could assume office.

8. Canton to EJT, 4 August 1921, c. 5281, folios 232-33. Goudie to EJT, 14 June 1921 WMMS/SOAS, GC. Woodford to Burnet, 11 May 1921; 22 June 1921, WMMS/SOAS, CC EJT to Canton, 11 May 1921, c. 5277, folio 146.

9. See EJT to Lyon, 25 May 1921, c. 5300, folios 172-73. See EJT to Canton, c. 5277 19 April 1921, folio 143.

10. EJT to Canton, 27 April 1921, c. 5277, folio 144.

11. Woodford to Goudie, 15 December 1921, WMMS/SOAS, CC.

12. Canton to EJT, 14 July 1920, c. 5281, folios 39-40. Ernest Rhys, *Rabindranath Tagore: A Biographical Study* (London: Macmillan, 1915), vii.

13. See Farquhar to EJT, 3 January 1921, c. 5287, folios 181-85; EJT to Canton, 3 Augus 1921, c. 5277, folio 150. John Nichol Farquhar (1861-1929) was an India missionary from 1891 to 1923; from 1924, he was Professor of Comparative Religion at the University of Manchester.

14. EJT to TJT, 20 September 1920, c. 5357, folios 146-47.

15. *RT:LW*, 1.

16. E. P. Thompson, *Alien Homage*, 40.

17. Bose, *Acre of Green Grass*, 1-3.
18. *RT:LW,* 26, 49-51; Tagore, *Kshanika* (Ephemeral), in *Rabindra-racanabali,* 7:207-332.
19. *RT:LW,* 49-51; EJT to TJT, 22 June 1921, c. 5358, folio 25.
20. EJT to Lyon, 28 December 1921, c. 5300, folio 175; EJT to Canton, 5 October 1921, c. 5277, folio 155. Seal's letter is not in his file (c. 5314).
21. See "Reviews and Notices," *Modern Review* 31 (1922): 341.
22. Tagore to EJT, 20 September 1921, c. 5318, folios 120-21. See Tagore, *Selected Letters,* ed. Krishna Dutta and Andrew Robinson (Cambridge: Cambridge University Press, 1997), 276-77.
23. EJT to Canton, 22 November 1922, folios 196-99; 18 March 1922, folio 248; 11 December 1922, folios 202-3; all: c. 5277.
24. EJT to Canton, 3 May 1922, folio 166; 12 July 1922, folio 172; both: c. 5277.
25. "Passing breeze": see *IE,* 267-91. Rothenstein had recruited as advisors H. A. L. Fisher (1865-1940), a Member of the Royal Commission on Public Services from 1912 to 1915; Vice Chancellor, Sheffield University, from 1912 to 1916; President, Board of Education, from 1916 to 1922; and President, British Academy, from 1928 to 1932; and Sir Michael Sadler (1861-1943), Vice Chancellor of Leeds University and President of the Commission to Report on Calcutta University.
26. Elmhirst diary, 18 January 1922; author's interview with Elmhirst, London, 14 August 1967. Leonard K. Elmhirst (1893-1974) was Director of the Institute of Rural Reconstruction (Sriniketan), Visva-Bharati University, from 1921 to 1924, and Founder and President of Dartington Hall. See also D/R, *Tagore,* 231.
27. See Mahalanobis to EJT, 26 July 1921, Nehru Memorial Library.
28. EJT to Canton, 3 May 1922, c. 5277, folio 166.
29. EJT to TJT, 30 April 1919, folio 61; 5 September 1920, folio 128; both: c. 5257.
30. EJT to TJT, 25 August 1921, folios 117-21; 6 September 1921, folio 140; both: c. 5358. See "The Lynching Industry, 1920," *Crisis* 21-23 (1921-1922): 160-62; and "Lynching in America," *Modern Review* 30 (1921): 243.
31. EJT to TJT, 7 September 1921, folio 141; 11 September 1921, folio 183; 14 September 1921, folio 146; all: c. 5358.
32. EJT to TJT, 25 July 1921, folios 67-68; 18 July 1921, folio 59; both: c. 5358.
33. EJT to Canton, 22 November 1922, c. 5277, folios 196-99.
34. EJT to TJT, 27 September 1920, c. 5357, folio 153. "Qualis artifex pereo!": "What an artist dies with me!" He is quoting Nero's last words.
35. EJT to TJT, 6 June 1921, folio 3; 7 June 1922, folios 4-5; both: c. 5358.
36. EJT to TJT, 15 June 1921, c. 5358, folio 15.
37. EJT to E. W. Thompson, 8 October 1922, WMMS/SOAS, GC.
38. Farquhar to E. W. Thompson, 4 January 1923, WMMS/SOAS, GC.

15. OXFORD AND ISLIP

1. E. P. Thompson, *Making of the English Working Class,* 369.
2. Richard Symonds, *Oxford and Empire: The Last Lost Cause?* (Oxford: Clarendon Press, 1991), 19-23.
3. Edward Said, *Orientalism* (London: Penguin, 1978), 19-20.
4. EJT to Canton, 25 February 1923, c. 5277, folios 215-16.
5. EJT to TJT, 23-27 February 1923, folios 29-42; 4-6 March 1923, folios 45-54; both c. 5359. Arthur Anthony MacDonell (1854-1930) was made Honorary Fellow of Balliol College and Boden Sanskrit Scholar in 1878; he was Taylorian Teacher of German from 1880 to 1900, and Deputy Professor and Emeritus Professor of Sanskrit. Arthur Lionel Smith (1850-1924) was Master of Balliol in 1916. Jean de Joinville (1224-1317) was French chronicler of the Seventh Crusade, 1248-1317; see his *Histoire de Saint-Louis,* first published 1547, reconstructed, 1874.

6. See Symonds, *Oxford and Empire*, 103-12. In 1860 Sir Monier Monier-Williams (1819-1899) became Boden Professor of Sanskrit. The Right Honorable Friedrich Max Müller (1823-1900) in 1854 became Oxford's Taylorian Professor of Modern Languages.
7. Symonds, *Oxford and Empire*, 112.
8. Ibid., 112-13. Sir (Harrington) Verney Lovett (1864-1945) entered the I.C.S. in 1884; he was on the Viceroy's Imperial Legislative Council until retirement in 1919, and then he was Oxford Reader in Indian history at Oxford from 1920 to 1932. See his *History of the Indian Nationalist Movement* (London: John Murray, 1920).
9. EJT to TJT, 23-27 February 1923, c. 5359, folios 29-42.
10. See R. C. Whiting, ed., *Oxford: Studies in the History of a University Town since 1800* (Manchester: Manchester University Press, 1993), especially D. Ian Scargill, "Responses to Growth in Modern Oxford," 110-30. Max Beerbohm, *Zuleika Dobson, or An Oxford Love Story* (London: William Heinemann, 1911).
11. EJT to TJT, 4-6 March 1923, folios 45-55; 11 March 1923, folios 58-64; both: c. 5359.
12. EJT, in Das, *Life and Letters of Toru Dutt*, 343-49.
13. Phillips, *Robert Bridges*, 192, 194, 211-12.
14. EJT to TJT, 4-6 March 1923, c. 5359, folios 45-55.
15. EJT to TJT, 20 March 1923, c. 5359, folios 74-78.
16. See Graves, *Good-bye to All That*, 291-311; on Islip, 312-19.
17. EJT to Canton, 13 August 1923, c. 5277, folio 226. See Miranda Seymour, *Robert Graves: Life on the Edge* (New York: Henry Holt, 1995), 95.
18. EJT to Canton, 13 August 1923, folio 226; 28 June 1923, folio 223; both: c. 5277.
19. EJT to Canton, 11 June 1923, folio 222; 28 June 1923, folio 223; both: c. 5277. See Richard P. Graves, *Robert Graves: The Assault Heroic, 1895-1926* (New York: Viking, 1987), 290.
20. EJT to TJT, 26 July 1923, c. 5359, folio 115; E. W. Thompson to EJT, 19 October 1923 (in possession of author).
21. EJT to Canton, 10 October 1923, c. 5277, folios 231-32.
22. TJT to EJT, 29 July 1923, folios 30-33; 26 July 1923, folios 30-33; 30 July [1923], folios 34-35; all: d. 2697.
23. EJT to TJT, 3 August 1923, c. 5359, folio 118.
24. EJT to Canton, 28 October 1923, c. 5277, folios 233-34.
25. EJT to Canton, 23 November 1923, c. 5277, folio 237.
26. EJT to Canton, 20 January 1924, c. 5277, folio 243.
27. EJT to Lyon, 22 March 1925, c. 5300, folio 200.
28. EJT to Canton, 28 October 1923, c. 5277, folios 233-34. Hack work: see Seymour, *Robert Graves*, 124. Laura Riding Jackson (1901-1991), an American poet and critic, began her career as an associate of the Southern poets, the "Fugitives." On her life with the Graveses, see Seymour, *Robert Graves*.
29. EJT to Canton, 9 March 1924, c. 5277, folios 249-50.
30. EJT to Lyon, 15 August 1923, c. 5300, folio 180.
31. EJT to Lyon, 27 November 1924, c. 5300, folios 185-87.
32. EJT to Lyon, 6 December 1924, c. 5300, folios 191-93.

16. THE OTHER SIDE OF THE MEDAL

1. Victor Alexander George Robert Bulwer-Lytton, Second Earl of Lytton (1876-1947) and son of a former Viceroy, was Parliamentary Undersecretary to the India Office, then Governor of Bengal, from 1922 to 1927, and briefly Viceroy and Acting Governor-General, in 1925. See Broomfield, *Elite Conflict*, 187-203.
2. Lyon to EJT, 16 April 1922, c. 5301, folios 73-75.

3. Lyon to L. R. Phelps, 18 August 1924, Phelps Papers, Oriel College, folios 285-86. Lancelot Ridley Phelps (1853-1936) was an authority on poor-law legislation; he was an Oriel provost from 1914 to 1929.

4. Canton to EJT, 30 June 1921, c. 5281, folios 226-27.

5. EJT to Canton, 29 August 1923, c. 5277, folio 227; EJT, *Cithaeron Dialogues* (London: G. G. Harrap, 1924).

6. EJT, *Atonement: A Play of Modern India, in Four Acts* (London: Ernest Benn, 1924).

7. EJT to Canton, 29 January 1924, c. 5277, folios 244-45.

8. See D. C. Sen to EJT, 4 April 1924, c. 5314, folios 95-96.

9. See Andrews to EJT, 12 September 1924, c. 5273, folio 70. Elmhirst to ML, 11 August 1970, author's collection. Elmhirst and his wife, Dorothy Straight Elmhirst, purchased and restored Dartington Hall, Totnes, Devon, for research in rural industry, arts, and education.

10. Author's interview, London, 13 August 1969. See D/R, *Tagore*, 253-59. Victoria Ocampo (1891-1979) was the founder of the literary journal *Sur;* she is noted for promoting foreign literatures in Argentina.

11. Elmhirst to ML, 6 October 1972, author's collection.

12. Canton to EJT, 30 June 1921, c. 5281, folios 226-27. Elmhirst to ML, 13 October 1967; 11 August 1970, author's collection. "Cult of the Charka": see D/R, *Tagore*, 261.

13. See Vincent Arthur Smith, *The Oxford History of India*, 2d ed. (Oxford: Clarendon Press, 1923), 714-21. Nana Sahib: an adopted son whom the Government of India refused to recognize as hereditary successor; such adoptions might be a ruse to assure continued rule and income. Nana's grudge fueled the Cawnpore attack.

14. EJT to Canton, 12 July 1922, c. 5277, folio 172.

15. EJT to E. W. Thompson, 26 June 1924, c. 5319, folios 68-69. Quotations in the next few paragraphs are from this source; the askerisk [*] suggests a discontinuity in the correspondence, a page lost or substituted from another letter.

16. See Steel, *The Garden of Fidelity*, 15-16; and Steel, *On the Face of the Waters*. See also J. G. Farrell, *The Siege of Krishnapur: A Novel* (Harmondsworth, Middlesex: Penguin, 1973), a modern treatment of the Cawnpore siege.

17. R[omesh] C[handra] Dutt, *India in the Victorian Age: An Economic History of the People* (London: Kegan Paul, Trench, Trübner, 1904), 88-89. Romesh Chandra Dutt (1848-1909), a cousin of Toru Dutt, in 1883 was the first Indian appointed a district officer, and in 1892 was the first Indian appointed an acting commissioner.

18. Sir William Howard Russell, *My Indian Mutiny Diary* (1860; reprint, ed. and abr. Michael Edwardes, London: Cassell, 1957). Sir William Howard Russell (1820-1907) reported also from the Crimean War, the American Civil War, the Franco-German War of 1870, and from Egypt, from 1883 to 1884, and South Africa, from 1879 to 1880.

19. "Al.Carthill" [Benet Christian Huntingdon Calcroft-Kennedy], *The Lost Dominion* (Edinburgh: Blackwood, 1924), 214-15. "Pretentious and noxious": see EJT, *Medal*, 32.

20. See Lavin, *From Empire to International Commonwealth*, 146-47.

21. See Lionel Curtis, *Letters to the Indian People on Responsible Government* (London: Macmillan, 1918); *Civitas Dei*, 3 vols. (London: Macmillan, 1934-1937; in the United States, *World Order (Civitas Dei)* (New York: Oxford University Press, 1939); he treats the Mutiny perfunctorily (558-59). Lionel George Curtis (1872-1955) in 1899 went to South Africa with the City Imperial Volunteers and in 1900 became Secretary to Alfred Milner, Governor-General for South Africa and the Cape Colony. Curtis became Assistant Colonial Secretary for Pretoria. In 1909 he returned to England to promote the British Commonwealth idea.

22. See EJT to Murray, 23 January 1925, Bodleian, MSS. Gilbert Murray, Correspondence 49, folios 18-20; 29 January 1925, ibid., 50.

23. EJT to Hogarth Press, 20 June 1925, UR: Hogarth 487.

24. E. M. Forster to EJT, 18 June 1925, folios 152-53; 24 July 1925, folios 156-57; both c. 5288.

25. [Vinayak Damodar Savarkar], *The Indian War of Independence of 1857: By an Indian Nationalist* (1909; Bombay: Phoenix Publications, 1947). On Forster and India, see P. N. Furbank, *E. M. Forster: A Life*, 2 vols. (Oxford: Oxford University Press, 1977, 1978), 1:227-29.

26. See publisher's 1947 preface, p. ix; Savarkar's introduction, pp. xxiii-xxiv. See also Savarkar, *The Story of My Transportation for Life* (Bombay: Sadbhakti Publications, 1950); Harindra Srivastava, *Five Stormy Years: Savarkar in London, June 1906-June 1911* (New Delhi: Allied Publishers, 1983).

27. Woolf to EJT, 27 June 1925; EJT to Woolf, 28 June 1925; both: Reading, Hogarth 487.

28. Lyon to EJT, 1 November 1925, c. 5301, folio 76.

29. EJT to Lyon, 5 November 1925, c. 5300, folios 201-2.

30. Ibid., p. 871; Carthill, *Lost Dominion*, 93.

31. EJT, *Medal*, 85.

32. Ibid., 96.

33. Ibid., 105, 108.

34. Ibid., 112.

35. Ibid., 113.

36. Ibid., 118-19.

37. Ibid., 129.

38. EJT to Woolf, 14 September 1925, UR: Hogarth 487.

39. EJT to Woolf, 1 January 1926, ibid.

40. EJT to Woolf, 19 January 1926, ibid. See, for example, Grace Gallatin Seton, *"Yea, Lady Saheb": A Woman's Adventurings with Mysterious India* (New York: Harper, 1925).

41. EJT, *Medal* (American edition), v-viii.

42. Michael Edwardes, "The Mutiny and Its Consequences," introduction to Russell, *Indian Mutiny Diary*, xvi.

43. Tagore to EJT, 30 December 1925, Rabindra-Bhavan (manuscript collection), Calcutta; EJT to Woolf, 19 January 1926, UR: Hogarth 487. See "The Other Side of the Medal," *Spectator* 135 (1925): 882-83; "The Indian Mutiny," *TLS*, 5 November 1925, 738; and "Shorter Notices," *New Statesman* 26 (9 January 1926): 394-95.

44. "Indian Unrest," *New York Times*, 16 May 1926, 20, 23; "The Indian Side," *Saturday Review of Literature* 2 (15 May 1926): 788; "Books in Brief," *Nation and the Athenaeum* 122 (30 June 1926): 730-31.

45. Ratcliffe to EJT, 14 December 1925, c. 5309, folio 1. See S. K. Ratcliffe, "The Mutiny," *Nation and the Athenaeum* 38 (1926): 499-500. Samuel Kerkham Ratcliffe (1868-1958) was Assistant Editor of the *Statesman* (Calcutta) from 1902 to 1907, and Editor of the *Sociological Review* from 1910 to 1917; he began his American lecture career in 1914.

46. EJT to Lyon, 5 November 1928, c. 5300, folios 291-92.

17. A SUBJECT CONCLUDED

1. EJT to Lyon, 11 January 1925, c. 5300, folios 196-97; Matthew Arnold, "The Scholar Gypsy" (1853). George Gilbert Aimé Murray (1866-1957), a classical scholar and translator, taught at New College, Oxford, from 1899 to 1936 and was a founder and Chairman of the League of Nations Union from 1923 to 1938. Sir Arthur Evans (1851-1941), a translator and archaeologist, discovered the pre-Phoenician script and excavated the prehistoric palace at Knossus.

2. EJT to Canton, 1 February 1926, folio 288; 4 February 1926, folios 289-90; both: c. 5277.

3. Collingwood to EJT, 31 October 1920, folios 165-67; 3 June 1921, folios 173-74; 14 October 1921, folios 179-80; 5 March 1923, folio 212; 4 May 1921, folio 236; 12 May 1926, folio 237; all: c. 5284. See EJT on Canton, *Dictionary of National Biography, 1922-30.* "Permitte divis cetera": "Leave the rest to the gods."

4. Collingwood to EJT, 27 April 1921, folios 171-77; 27 December 1924, folios 226-27; both: c. 5284.

5. Collingwood to EJT, 24 June 1920, folios 160-63; 19 June 1921, folios 175-76; both: c. 5284.

6. EJT to Mahalanobis, 24 March 1921, in E. P. Thompson, *Alien Homage,* 50; EJT to Canton, 15 November 1925, c. 5277, folios 280-82.

7. EJT to Canton, 13 August 1923, c. 5277, folio 226.

8. *RT:LW,* vii-ix.

9. Ibid.

10. Carrington, TS India Memoir, India Office Papers, British Library, MSS Eur. c. 392; quotations in next few paragraphs are from this source. Noel Lewis Carrington (1891-1987), after a degree from Christ Church College, Oxford, served in France with the Wiltshire Regiment from 1914 to 1918, was wounded in 1915, demobilized in 1919, and returned to Oxford. He represented Oxford University Press in India from 1919 to 1923. His authorial career included eleven books and editions, in addition to journalism.

11. EJT, *Tagore,* 303.

12. Mahalanobis to EJT, 12 December 1926, copy, Nehru Memorial Library, for. 192.

13. Tagore to Rothenstein, 7 August 1926, in *IE,* 316-17.

14. Bridges to Tagore, 10 October 1926, encl. in Mahalanobis to EJT, 12 December 1926, Nehru Memorial Library.

15. Rothenstein to EJT, 13 March 1927, c. 5311, folios 32-33.

16. EJT to Rothenstein, 16 March 1927, RP:HL.

17. "A Study of Tagore," *TLS,* 18 November 1926, 815; EJT to Rothenstein, 16 March 1927, RP:HL.

18. EJT to Rothenstein, 16 March 1927, RP:HL. See Leonard Woolf, "The World of Books: Sugar and Soap and Salt," *Nation and Athenaeum* 40 (1925): 271.

19. Graves to EJT, [October or December 1926], c. 5290, folio 163.

20. EJT to Rothenstein, 16 March 1927, RP:HL.

21. Ibid.

22. Ibid.

23. Tagore to Rothenstein, 20 April 1927, in *IE,* 320-22; quotations in next few paragraphs are from this letter.

24. Harish Trivedi, *Colonial Transactions: English Literature and India* (Bombay: Orient Longmans, 1993), 128-29.

25. Ramananda Chatterji, "Mr. Thompson's Book on Rabindranath Tagore," *Modern Review* 42 (1927): 99-103.

26. E. P. Thompson, *Alien Homage,* 47-51. See D/R, *Tagore,* 277; and *RT:PD,* 303.

18. WRITING ABOUT INDIA

1. EJT to Lyon, 11 January 1925, c. 5300, folios 196-97.

2. EJT to Lyon, 22 March 1925, c. 5300, folio 200.

3. EJT, *An Indian Day* (London: Knopf, 1927; New York: Macmillan, 1933), 168, 258-59.

4. Ibid., 14, 16; Broomfield, *Elite Conflict,* 282-315.

5. EJT, *An Indian Day,* 15-16, 252.

6. Ibid., 230-31.

7. See Robert Morss Lovett, "An Indian Day," *New Republic* 51 (1927): 317; Edwin Muir, "Fiction," *Nation and the Athenaeum* 41 (1927): 520; L. P. Hartley, "An Indian Day," *Saturday Review* 44 (1927): 26; and "By the Banyans of Bengal," *Spectator* 138 (1927): 957-58. See also Sujit Mukherjee, *Forster and Further: The Tradition of Anglo-Indian Fiction* (Hyderabad: Orient Longman, 1993), 225, 227, 231; and Collingwood to EJT, 15 June [1927], c. 5284, folio 243a. Mutual friend: Ernest H. R. Altounyan (1889-1962), a physician practicing at Aleppo, was a marriage relation of Collingwood.

8. EJT, *These Men, Thy Friends* (London: Knopf, 1927; New York: Harcourt Brace, 1928), 88-89.

9. Ibid., 127-28, 246, 187.

10. "New Novels," *TLS*, 1 December 1927, 906; Cyril Connolly, "New Novels," *New Statesman and Nation* 29 (1927): 815; R. A. T., "Fiction," *Spectator* 139 (1927): 579.

11. EJT to Lyon, 28 August 1937, c. 5300, folios 206-8; EJT, *A History of India*, Benn's Sixpenny Library, no. 18 (London: Ernest Benn, 1927), 26, 53, 77.

12. EJT to Lyon, 28 August 1927, c. 5300, folios 206-8.

13. See Katherine Mayo, *Mother India* (New York: Harcourt Brace; London: J. Cape, 1927); EJT, "Mother India," *Nation and the Athenaeum* 41 (1927): 581-82, and subsequent correspondence, 605, 631, 660, 744, 834.

14. EJT, *Suttee: A Historical and Philosophical Inquiry into the Hindu Rite of Widow-Burning* (London: Ernest Benn; Boston: Houghton Mifflin, 1928), 79, 49, 130. See "Suttee," in EJT and TJT, *Three Eastern Plays: With a Terminal Essay on "Suttee"* (London: Allen and Unwin, 1927), 111-28. See also EJT, "Prohibition of Widow-Burning in British India," *London Quarterly Review* 148 (1927): 57-66.

15. "Hindu Widow-Burning," *Sunday New York Times,* 9 September 1928, IV, p. 12. See also EJT, "Suttee among Hindus a Cenury under Ban," *New York Times,* 1 December 1929, X, p. 20.

16. Lyon to EJT, 14 August 1927, c. 5301, folios 77-79. John Alsebrook Simon, First Viscount Simon (1873-1954), was Solicitor General in 1910 and in the Home Office from 1915 to 1916. He resigned over wartime conscription and did not return to government until he was made Foreign Secretary, from 1931 to 1935, and Chancellor of the Exchequer, in 1937. He left after the 1940 Churchill landslide.

17. EJT to MacCracken, 22 January 1928; MacCracken to EJT, 2 March 1928; both: Vassar College Records. Henry Noble MacCracken (1880-1970), Vassar's fifth president, from 1915 to 1946, set standards of serious scholarship for women.

18. TJT to EJT, [March? 1928], d. 2697, folio 55; Dorothy Canfield [Fisher], *The Bent Twig* (New York: Henry Holt, 1915).

19. Amy Reed to EJT, 19 September 1928; MacCracken to EJT, 7 November 1928; both: Vassar.

20. EJT to TJT, 4 November 1928, folio 130; 1 December 1928, folio 147; Armistice Day [11 November 1928], folios 133-34; all: c. 5359. EJT to Lyon, 24 December 1928, c. 5300, folios 213-14.

21. EJT to TJT, 25-26 November 1927, c. 5359, folios 141-42. On Lady Mary Henrietta Howard (Mrs. Gilbert Murray) (1865-1956), see Duncan Wilson, *Gilbert Murray OM, 1866-1957* (Oxford: Clarendon Press, 1987), 184-85. G. B. Shaw caricatured the Howards in *Major Barbara* (1905); see Michael Holroyd, *Bernard Shaw,* 5 vols. (New York: Random House, 1988-1992), 2:100-16.

22. ET to EJT, 20 November 1927, folios 165-67; 24 May 1928, folios 209-10; both: d. 2690.

23. EJT to Lyon, 26 November 1928, c. 5300, folios 210-11; EJT to Ackerley, 21 December 1928, BBC Talks Correspondence, File 1. Joe Randolph Ackerley (1896-1967) was E. M. Forster's close friend who went to India as Secretary to the Maharaja of Chattarpur; see Joe Ackerley, *Hindoo Holiday: An Indian Journal* (London: Chatto and

Windus, 1932). He joined the BBC as Talks Producer and was Literary Editor of the *Listener,* 1935-1939.

24. Lord Ronaldshay, "India in Art and Literature," *Listener* 1 (1929): 17-18. Lawrence John Lumley Dundas, Second Marquis of Zetland and Earl of Ronaldshay (1876-1961), was on the Royal Commission for Public Services in India from 1912 to 1914, Governor of Bengal from 1917 to 1922, Secretary of State for India from 1935 to 1940 and for Burma from 1937 to 1940, and President of the India Society from 1923 to 1959.

25. EJT to TJT, 30 November 1928, folio 146; 3 December 1928, folio 149; both: c. 5359.

26. See *Indian Statutory Commission Interim Report (The Simon Commission Report)* (Cmd. 3407; London: H. M. Stationery Office, 1930), 1:148-52. See also Rt. Hon. Viscount Simon, *Two Broadcast Talks on India,* Criterion Miscellany no. 18 (London: Faber and Faber, 1930).

27. Lyon to EJT, 3 February 1929, c. 5301, folios 81-83. See Simon, *Retrospect: The Memoirs of the Rt. Hon. Viscount Simon* (London: Hutchinson, 1952), 147. Frederick Erwin Smith, First Earl of Birkenhead (1872-1930), was Secretary of State for India from 1924 to 1928, and he persuaded Simon to be the chairman of the commission but was unsympathetic to its goals and left office before it reported.

28. S. R. Bakshi, *Simon Commission and Indian Nationalism* (New Delhi: Munshiram Manohari, 1977), 64, 105.

19. INFORMATION CAMPAIGN

1. EJT to Lyon, 27 August 1929, c. 5300, folio 219.

2. Ibid. See *New York Herald,* 23 September 1929, IX, p. 18.

3. EJT to Lyon, 7 October 1929, folios 221-22; 2 November 1929, folios 221-22; both: c. 5300.

4. EJT to Lyon, 2 November 1929, folios 221-22, c. 5300.

5. EJT to Lyon, 9 February 1930, folio 224; 27 June 1929, folio 234; both: c. 5300.

6. "Babies in India Fed Opium at British Command, He Says," *Baltimore Sun,* 13 February 1930, 3.

7. "Sees World Peace in Independent India," *New York Times,* 16 February 1930, 18.

8. "India's Future Is Luncheon Topic," *Boston Evening Transcript,* 1 March 1930, I, p. 7; "Indian Independence Discussed," *New York Times,* 16 March 1930, 19. The association's archivist told this writer that he found no record of the debates. One, however, was published: *India: Discussed by Sailendra Nath Ghose and Edward Thompson,* 125th New York luncheon discussion, 15 February 1930 (New York: Foreign Policy Association [1936]).

9. EJT to Lyon, 9 June 1930, folio 225; 15 July 1920, folio 228; both: c. 5300.

10. EJT, "Mother India in the Dock," *Saturday Review of Literature* 6 (1929): 203. See also Harry Field, *After Mother India* (New York: Harcourt Brace, 1929). Katherine Mayo (d. 1940) was born in Pennsylvania and later settled in South Africa.

11. [S. K. Ratcliffe], "Says Interest in India Is Growing in America," *New York Times,* 22 October 1929, 12.

12. EJT to Lyon, 9 February 1930, c. 5300, folio 224. See Tinker, *Ordeal of Love,* 236-37.

13. Mukherjee, *Passage to America,* 95-97; D/R, *Tagore,* 284-85.

14. Mukherjee, *Passage to America,* 100-106.

15. H. L. Matthews, "Tagore Sees India . . . ," *New York Times,* 2 June 1929, II, p. 6.

16. S. J. Woolf, "India's Poet . . . ," *Sunday New York Times,* 19 October 1930, V, p. 5.

17. "Poor Judgment in India," *New York Times,* 6 February 1929, 18; "Delhi House Votes to Boycott Simon," *New York Times,* 19 February 1929, 2.

18. EJT to Lyon, 6 January 1930, folio 223; 27 June 1930, folios 226–27; 15 July 1920, folio 228; all: c. 5300.

19. Geoffrey Garratt, *An Indian Commentary* (New York: Cape and Harrison Smith, 1929). For review, see EJT, "Mother India in the Dock." Geoffrey Theodore Garratt (1888–1942) served in the I.C.S. from 1913 to 1923; he later resigned to protest the building of extravagant official residences while Indians died of famine. In the Great War, he was a *Manchester Guardian* correspondent; in World War II, at age fifty, he enrolled, with difficulty, in the Pioneer Corps and undertook a series of dangerous assignments in Europe.

20. Ratcliffe to EJT, August 1930, c. 5309, folio 42. See EJT, *Reconstructing India* (New York: Dial Press, 1930; Toronto: Longmans Green, 1933), 142–43; in Britain, *The Reconstruction of India* (London: Faber and Faber, 1930).

21. EJT, *Reconstructing India*, 161–63; C. F. Andrews, "Gandhi's Mystic Aims in His Indian March," *Sunday New York Times*, 6 April 1930, sec. X, p. 6.

22. EJT, *Reconstructing India*, 102, 109, 118.

23. Ibid., 298–300, 315–17, 321, 354.

24. Charles Johnson, "Three Contrasting Views of the Tangled Indian Question," *Sunday New York Times*, 9 November 1930, IV, p. 9; Geoffrey Garratt, "Aids to Indian Reflection," *Nation and the Athenaeum* 47 (1930): 796–97; "India in True Perspective," *Spectator* 145 (1930): 285–86; "Indian Reconstruction," *TLS*, 28 August 1930, 676.

25. EJT to Lyon, 27 June 1930, c. 5300, folios 226–27.

26. EJT, "America and India: The British Case," *Times*, 18 September 1930, 8.

27. Ibid.

28. EJT to Lyon, 2 September 1930, folio 229; 7 September 1930, folio 232; both: c. 5300.

29. Lyon to EJT, 29 July 1930, c. 5301, folio 84.

30. Simon, *Retrospect*, 150–52.

31. *Simon Commission Report*, 2:150–53.

32. Lyon to EJT, 18 November 1930, c. 5301, folio 85. See *Parliamentary Debates*, Commons, 5th ser., vol. 242 (30 July 1930), cols. 274–344.

33. S. K. Ratcliffe, *What the Simon Report Means* (London: New Statesman, 1930), 20, 27, 31.

34. C. F. Andrews, *India and the Simon Report* (London: Allen and Unwin; New York: Macmillan, 1930), 9, 33, 38.

35. "Future of India: Mr. Churchill on the Conference," *Times*, 12 December 1930, 16; Ramsay MacDonald, "Mr. MacDonald on India: Criticism of Mr. Churchill's 'Mischievous Speech,'" *Times*, 13 December 1930, 14. See also "News of the Week: The Right to Broadcast," *Spectator* 149 (1931): 203.

36. Garratt to EJT, 13 September [1930], c. 5289, folio 87. See EJT, "The Round Table Conference: 'Prologemena': What Is and Might Be," 22 November, p. 783; "The Round Table: The Economic Myth: Fact and Fancy," 29 November, p. 841; "The Round Table Conference: Unitary Government—Federation—Paramountcy," 6 December, p. 880; "The Round Table Conference," 13 December, p. 936; see also EJT (letter), "The Madras Case," 22 November 1930, p. 785; Tagore (letter), "Great Britain and India," 30 August, p. 280; all: *Spectator* 145 (1930). See also "News of the Week: The Right to Broadcast," *Spectator* 147 (1931): 203.

37. "News of the Week," *Spectator* 146 (1931): 243–44.

38. See EJT, *A Letter from India* (London: Faber and Faber, 1932), 38–39, 41. See also D/R, *Tagore*, 284, 290–91.

39. EJT to Sastri, 19 January 1931, c. 5319, folios 52–53. The Right Honorable V. S. Sastri (1869–1946) was President of the Servants of India Society from 1915 to 1917, South African Agent for the Government of India from 1927 to 1929, on the Viceroy's

Legislative Committee from 1916 to 1920, and Council of State under the Reforms in 1920.

40. EJT, "India: Federal Problems: Economic Interests, the Communal Trouble; at the R[ound] T[able] C[onference]," *Spectator* 147 (1931): 410-11; EJT, "India: The Communal Deadlock: The Depressed Classes," *Spectator* 147 (1931): 449-50. Dr. Mukhtar Ahmed Ansari (1880-1936) led a Red Crescent mission to the Balkan wars of 1912 and worked for constructive ways of reconciling nationalist Hindus and Muslims; he was President of the Muslim League in 1918 and of the Indian National Congress in 1927. E. M. Forster met him during his Indian tour of 1912-1913.

20. FAREWELL AND HAIL

1. EJT, *A Letter from India*, 32.
2. EJT, *A Farewell to India* (London: Faber and Faber, 1932), 19.
3. Ibid., 72-73, 78-79. Mukherjee, *Forster and Further*, 123.
4. EJT, *A Farewell to India*, 80-81.
5. Ibid., 83-84, 94.
6. Ibid., 235-38.
7. Ibid., 88, 91.
8. Ibid., 140-41.
9. Ibid., 143-44.
10. Ibid., 152.
11. Ibid., 286.
12. "New Novels," *TLS*, 15 January 1932, 42; I. M. Parsons, "Fiction," *Spectator* 146 (1931): 91.
13. David Rubin, *After the Raj: British Novels of India since 1947* (Hanover, N.H.: University Press of New England, 1986), 20-21.
14. Lothian to Coupland, 25 June 1931; Coupland to Rhodes Trustees, 10 July 1931; both: RT/2695. Phillip Kerr, Eleventh Marquess of Lothian (1882-1940), went to South Africa in 1904 and became Lieutenant Governor of the Transvaal. He resigned in 1922 as Private Secretary to Lloyd George, to write on imperial politics. He became Rhodes Trustees Secretary in 1925 and until 1932 was Liberal Party Representative in Ramsay MacDonald's Cabinet. As the U.S. Ambassador in 1939 he tried, through writing and broadcasting, to ease trans-Atlantic misunderstandings. Sir Reginald Coupland (1884-1952) was a Fellow and Lecturer in Ancient History at Trinity College, Oxford, from 1907 to 1914, and a Member of the Royal Commission on the Superior Civil Services in India, 1923.
15. EJT to Lothian, 12 July 1931, RT/2695.
16. EJT to Rhodes Trustees, 29 December 1931, RT/2695.
17. EJT to Scott, 2 December 1931, Rylands 715, *Guardian*, A/T17/17. Scott to EJT, 7 December 1931, in ibid., A/T17/27. *A Letter to India* includes two for the *Spectator* and one for the *Times*.
18. EJT to TJT 4 January 1932, folios 6-7; 6-7 January 1932, folios 9-13; both: c. 5360.
19. Garratt to EJT, 5 October [1931], c. 5289, folio 91; Garratt, *Indian Commentary*, 179, 182,, 205, 225, 271.
20. EJT to TJT, 15 January 1931 [1932], folio 17; 18-23 January 1932, folios 18-19; both: c. 5360. EJT, *A Letter from India*, 18-19. The Honorable Mukunda R. Jayakar (d. 1950) was a Nationalist Party leader since 1916.
21. EJT to TJT, 18 January 1932, c. 5360, folios 18-19.
22. Ibid. On Mira Behn, see EJT, *A Letter from India*, 23-29.
23. EJT, *Report*, RT/2844, 2-3. See EJT, *A Letter from India*, 65, 72-73, on Mohammed Iqbal (1873-1938), a leading Urdu poet, philosopher, and politician; he was educated in India, England, and Germany and was President of the Muslim League from 1930. Originally a supporter of Hindu-Muslim cooperation, he turned to belief in a separate Muslim state and thus is considered the father of Pakistan.

24. EJT, *Report*, RT/2844, 2. See also EJT, *A Letter from India*, 65-74. Anglo-Indian at that time, generally English living in India; now, Eurasians: persons of English-Indian heritage.

25. EJT, *Report*, RT/2844, 1-2.

26. Ibid., 2-3.

27. Ibid.

28. EJT to TJT, 29 February 1932, c. 5360, folios 27-28.

29. See D/R, *Tagore*, 308.

30. EJT, *Report*, RT/2844, 2.

31. Ibid., 3-4. EJT to Lothian, 9 June 1932; Witt to Lothian, 14 June 1932; Lothian to EJT, 12 July; 13 July 1932; EJT to Lothian, 20 July 1932; all: RT/2844.

32. EJT, *Report*, RT/2844, 6.

33. Kabir to EJT, 1 June 1932, c. 5293, folios 3-4. See EJT, *A Letter from India*, 44, 101, 102, 113, 122. Humayun Kabir (1906-1969) was a Lecturer at Calcutta University from 1933 to 1945 and an Adviser to the Government of India until 1956.

34. See Allen J. Greenberger, *The British Image of India: A Study in the Literature of Imperialism, 1880-1960* (Oxford: Oxford University Press, 1969), 149.

21. FOLLOWING LORD METCALFE

1. See EJT, *So a Poor Ghost* (London: Macmillan, 1933; New York: Knopf, 1934) 259-60.

2. EJT and G. T. Garratt, *Rise and Fulfilment of British Rule in India* (London Macmillan, 1934; reprint, Allahabad: Central Book Depot, 1965), 3, 625-26.

3. EJT, *Introducing the Arnisons*, 22-23. See E. P. Thompson, *Making of the English Working Class*, 375-76.

4. EJT, *Sir Walter Ralegh: Last of the Elizabethans* (London: Macmillan, 1935; New Haven: Yale University Press, 1936). See also EJT and TJT, *The Last Voyage* (London Macmillan, 1934); Leonard Woolf, "British in India," *New Statesman and Nation* 7 (30 June 1934): 997-98; P. Q[uennell], "Two Elizabethans," *Saturday Review* 9 (1935), 758-60; and Milton Waldman, "Last Man of an Age," *Saturday Review of Literature* 14 (26 September 1936): 12.

5. EJT to Lothian, 18 November 1935, RT/2844. "Rodent ulcer": it *is* a cancer, a basal cell invasion.

6. Coupland to Lothian, 16 July 1935, RT/2844. See Sir Reginald Coupland, *The Empire in These Days: An Interpretation* (London: Macmillan, 1935), which favors dominion status for India.

7. EJT to TJT, 21 October 1936, c. 5360, folio 41; EJT to Lothian, 23 May 1933, RT/2844. See Symonds, *Oxford and Empire*, 115-18. H. N. Spalding (1877-1953), of Scots ancestry, grew up in London and suburbs. Classics study at New College, Oxford, revealed a philosophy to embrace both modern and ancient. His interest in Eastern religions began with the Russian Orthodox, when he befriended émigrés who awoke his curiosity about other Eastern religions. He never visited India. See Symonds, *Oxford and Empire*, 118.

8. Spalding to EJT, 15 March 1936, c. 5316, folio 5.

9. EJT to TJT, 13-14 September 1936, c. 5360, folios 74-76.

10. EJT to TJT, 10 September 1936, folios 65-66; 17 September 1936, folios 83-84; 22 September 1936, folios 94-97; all: c. 5360. See Forster, *Howards End*, Abinger Edition, ed. Oliver Stallybrass (London: Edward Arnold, 1973), 110.

11. EJT to TJT, 18-19 September 1936, c. 5360, folios 88-93.

12. EJT to Palmer, 27 September 1936, d. 2701, folios 9-10.

13. EJT to TJT, 27 September 1936, folios 101-5; 24 September 1936, folios 98-103; both: c. 5360.

14. EJT to TJT, 24 September 1936, c. 5360, folios 98-100.

15. EJT to TJT, 27 September 1936, folios 103-5; 10 October 1936, folios 109-11; both: c. 5360.

16. EJT to TJT, 29-30 September 1936, c. 5360, folios 106-8. Sivaji (1627-1680) was a Mahratta chief's son raised to hate the Moguls; he was crowned the king of the Mahrattas in 1665.

17. EJT to TJT, 9 October 1936, folio 119; 14 October 1936, folios 126-27; both: c. 5360. The Right Honorable Sir Akbar Hydari (1869-1942), a State Finance Minister, led the Hyderabad delegation to the Round Table Conference, inspired founding of Osmania University, and was its Chancellor from 1925. The Right Honorable Jan Hendrick Hofmeyr (1894-1948), a Balliol graduate, was South African Minister of Interior, Public Health, and Education from 1933 to 1936; of Mines, in 1938; and of Education, from 1939 to 1948.

18. EJT to TJT, 14 October 1936, c. 5360, folios 126-27. On Ajanta, see Lago, *Christiana Herringham*, 145-247.

19. EJT to TJT, 22 October 1936, folio 129; 24 October 1936, folios 130-34; both: c. 5360. See James Tod, *Annals and Antiquities of Rajasthan, or the Central and Western Rajpoot States of India*, 2 vols. (London: Smith, Elder, 1829-1832).

20. Was EJT the "friendly Englishman" who, in a note "before 24 October 1936" asked Gandhi why he settled at Wardha, a Maratha-speaking area? Gandhi replied, "I do not belong to Gujarat, I belong to the whole of India." Wardha afforded excellent working facilities (Mahatma Gandhi, *Collected Works*, 99 vols. [Delhi: Publications Division, Ministry of Information and Broadcasting, Government of India, 1958-1984], 63:385.)

21. EJT to TJT, "Saturday 6th" [perhaps an error for 24 October], fragment, c. 5360, folio 165.

22. EJT to TJT, 26 October 1936, c. 5360, folios 135-36. Lionel Fielden (1896-1974) (no relation of F. J. Fielden) joined the BBC in 1927; he was in the General Talks Department from 1930 to 1935 and was Controller of All-India Radio from 1935 to 1940. He left the BBC in 1941. See his *The Natural Bent* (London: André Deutsch, 1944), 149-216.

23. EJT to TJT, 29 October 1936, c. 5360, folio 137; EJT, *A Letter from India*, 87-88.

24. EJT to TJT, 2-3 October 1936, c. 5360, folio 137.

25. EJT to Rothenstein, 12 August 1938, RP:HL, Bms. Eng. 1148 (1498). See also E. P. Thompson, *Alien Homage*, 95-98.

26. EJT to TJT, 5 November 1935, folio 51; 24 September 1936, folios 98-100; both: c. 5360.

27. EJT to Nehru, 26 November 1936, in *Old Letters*, 155; Nehru to EJT, 3 December 1936, c. 5305, folios 9-10. Aurobindo Ghose (1872-1980), a Bengali, lived in England for fourteen years and returned to India in 1893. After Partition protests and imprisonment he fled to Pondicherry, a French protectorate, to write in English and await transformation to perfection. See Aurobindo, *Sri Aurobindo on Himself and on the Mother* [Mme. Richard] (Pondicherry: Sri Aurobindo Ashram, 1953).

28. EJT to TJT, 27 September 1936, folios 101-5; 1 October 1936, folios 109-11; 24 September 1936, folio 99; 29-30 September 1936, folios 106-8; all: c. 5160.

29. EJT to TJT, 23 November 1936, folio 148; 26 November 1936, folios 149-51; 29 November 1936, folios 152-53; all: c. 5360.

30. EJT to TJT, 29 November 1936, c. 5360, folios 152-53.

31. EJT, *John Arnison*, 217.

32. EJT to TJT, 27 September 1936, c. 5360, folios 101-5. An undated note from Lyon (c.

5301, folio 96) would not have been cheering: "Dear Edward, your increasing friendshi
with various hide-bound reactionaries is beginning to give me serious apprehension. Yr
P.C.L." Did Lyon mean the Rhodes Trustees?

22. OBSERVING A CRISIS

1. TJT to EJT, 4 November 1935, d. 2697, folios 200-208; EJT to TJT, 25 October 1935
c. 5360, folios 41-42.

2. TJT to EJT, 21 October 1936, d. 2698, folios 61-63.

3. EJT to Palmer, 19 September 1936, d. 2701, folios 6-7; TJT to EJT, 17 Novembe
[1936], c. 2698, folios 80-85. Alfred Barrett Sackett (1895-1977) attended Kingswoo
and Merton College, Oxford; he was the Kingswood Head from 1928 to 1959.

4. TJT to EJT, 18 October 1936, folios 58-60; 27 October 1936, folios 66-69; 1
November 1936, folios 73-78; all: c. 2698; quotations in next few paragraphs are fron
these letters.

5. TJT to EJT, 18 October 1936, d. 2698, folios 58-60.

6. EJT, *The Life of Charles, Lord Metcalfe* (London: Faber and Faber, 1937), x. See Joh
William Kaye, *The Life and Correspondence of Charles, Lord Metcalfe*, 2 vols. (London
Richard Bentley, 1854).

7. EJT, *Metcalfe*, 20, 114, 189, 190.

8. Ibid., 343, 349, 350.

9. Ibid., 363.

10. EJT, *Metcalfe*, 109.

11. Ibid., 128.

12. Ibid., 356-57, 407. For Macaulay on Metcalfe, see Stokes, *English Utilitarians an
India*, 239. For a representative review, see "A Life of Public Service," *TLS*, 16 Octobe
1937, 745.

13. Sackett to EJT, 6 March 1937, folios 1-2; 9 March 1937, folios 4-5; both: c. 5312

14. EJT to TJT, 11 December 1938, c. 5360, folios 168-69.

15. Elton to Lionel Curtis, 21 November 1939; to Hailey, 2 December 1939; to Malcoln
MacDonald, 4 December 1939; all: RT/2844. EJT to Nehru, 3 December 1939, *Old Letters*
409-12. Nehru to EJT, 5 January 1940, in *Selected Works of Jawaharlal Nehru*, 23 vols.
ed. S. Gopal (New Delhi: Orient Longman, 1972-), 10:602-3. W. G. S. Adams (1874-
1966), an economist, was Warden at All Souls College from 1933 to 1945. Sir Sarpevell
Radhakrishnan (1888-1975) was Spalding Professor of Eastern Religions and Ethics from
1936 to 1952, and was Vice-President of the Republic of India from 1952 to 1962 ane
President from 1962 to 1967. Godfrey Elton, First Baron Elton of Headington (1892-1973)
a modern historian, served in Mesopotamia from 1916 to 1918, was a Lecturer in Moderr
History at Queen's College, Oxford, from 1919 to 1939, and was General Secretary of
the Rhodes Trustees from 1939 to 1959. William Malcolm Hailey, First Baron of Shahpur
(1872-1969), was in the I.C.S. in 1895 and the Indian Defence Force from 1912 to 1918
he was on the Viceroy's Executive Committee from 1919 to 1924, was Governor of the
Punjab from 1924 to 1929, and was Governor of the United Provinces from 1928 to 1930
and 1931 to 1934.

16. Elton to Adams, 21 November 1936; to Lionel Curtis, 21 November 1936; both:
RT/2844.

17. Lothian to EJT, 5 July 1939, c. 5293, folio 98. V. K. Krishna Menon (1897-
1974) was Barrister and Secretary of the India League in England from 1929; he was
High Commissioner in London from 1947 until his return to India after twenty-seven
years away. He was then High Commissioner to the Indian Parliament in 1953 and
Indian Representative to the United Nations General Assembly from 1957 to 1960.
Edward Frederick Lindley, First Earl of Halifax (1881-1959), was Lord Irwin, Viceroy
of India, from 1926 to 1931, Secretary of State for War in 1935, and Secretary of

State for Foreign Affairs from 1938 to 1940; he was the U.S. Ambassador from 1941 to 1946.

18. TJT to EJT, 13 October [1939], second letter, folios 106-7; 17 October [1939], folios 109-11; both: d. 2698.

19. Congress resolution: in Stanley Wolpert, *A New History of India*, 2d ed. (New York: Oxford University Press, 1982), 329. See also Wolpert, *Nehru: A Tryst with Destiny* (New York: Oxford University Press, 1996), 79.

20. EJT, "Narrative," RT/2844, 1. Elsie W. Danger, "Books for a Long Flight" (letter), *Times*, 16 October 1939, 9.

21. EJT, "Narrative," RT/2844, 2-4.

22. Ibid., 5-6.

23. Ibid., 9-10, 12.

24. Nehru, "The Standpoint of the Congress," 4 November 1939, in *Selected Works*, 10:220-25. See also "The Deadlock in India," *Times*, 8 November 1939, 10.

25. EJT, "Narrative," RT/2844, 12-13.

26. Ibid., 14-15, 17. Victor Alexander John Hope Linlithgow, Second Marquess (1887-1952), served in the Great War, from 1914 to 1918, and was Chairman of the Joint Select Committee on [Indian] Constitutional Reform in 1933; he was Viceroy of India from 1936 to 1943.

27. EJT, "Narrative," RT/2844, 18-19.

28. Ibid., 21, 23.

29. Ibid., 25-26.

30. Ibid., 27. Maulana Adul Kalam Azad (1888-1958), Congress Party President, 1940-1945.

31. "Narrative," RT/2844, pp. 30-31. But see Bhimrao Ramji Ambedkar, *What Congress and Gandhi Have Done to the Untouchables* (Bombay: Thacker, 1945), 208-9 n. 2 on Nehru's self-image as Brahmin. "[M]y country . . . my community"; cf. E. M. Forster, "What I Believe," in *Two Cheers for Democracy*, Abinger Edition, ed. Oliver Stallybrass (London: Edward Arnold, 1972), 65-73.

32. EJT, "Narrative," RT/2844, 36, 32.

33. EJT, "Summary," RT/2844, 1, 2.

34. EJT, "Political Report," RT/2844, 2, 3.

35. Ibid., 3.

36. Ibid., 3-4, 9.

37. Ibid., 9-10.

38. Ibid; Iqbal to EJT, 4 March 1934, c. 5291, folio 226. Sir Mohammed Iqbal (1873-1938), a philosopher and poet, educated in Cambridge and London, was called to the bar in 1908, then returned to practice in India. He was President of the All-India Muslim League when it adopted the Pakistan policy. In later years he avoided politics and tried instead to inspire Muslims with the West's practical activism as antidote to their decadent pantheism.

39. F. J. Fielden to EJT, 9 January 1939, folios 95-97; 19 May 1929, folios 100-101; both: c. 5288. On Aligarh University, see David Lelyveld, *Aligarh's First Generation: Muslim Solidarity in British India* (Princeton: Princeton University Press, 1978).

40. EJT, "Political Report," RT/2844, 10-16.

41. Ibid., 46.

42. Ibid., n.p. See EJT to Nehru, 2 January 1938, *Old Letters*, 275-76.

43. Ibid., 23, 24, 26.

44. Ibid., 31. Only a letter (30 October 1939, c. 5274, folio 191) survives, asking EJT to arrange an appointment upon arrival. Subhaschandra Bose (1897-1945) passed I.C.S. examinations but withdrew and returned to India in 1920 for political protests. He was exiled to Burma from 1924 to 1927, went to Europe, returned to India in 1936, and

became Congress Party President in 1938. Jailed in 1940, he escaped to Moscow, then t
Germany, and in 1943 to Tokyo to raise his Indian National Army, to invade India fro
Burma. He died in Japan after a plane crash.

45. Ibid., 33. Malcolm Cowley (1898-1989), an American poet and critic, was th
Editor of the *New Republic* from 1929 to 1944.

46. Ibid., 35.

47. Ibid., 36.

23. "CHAPLAINING" AGAIN

1. Ratcliffe to EJT, 1 March 1939, folio 128. "Thy Hand Great Anarch": Alexander Pop
The Dunciad, bk. 4, canto 1, l. 301.

2. Elton to EJT, 21 January 1940, c. 5287, folio 35. See D/R, *Tagore*, 352-53. Si
Maurice Linford Gwyer (1878-1952) was Chief Justice of India from 1937 to 1942 an
Vice Chancellor of Delhi University from 1939 to 1950.

3. See Azad to EJT, 28 March 1940, c. 5273.

4. Gollancz to EJT, 19 July 1940, Gollancz Papers. EJT, *Enlist India for Freedom!* Victor
Books, no. 5 (London: Victor Gollancz, 1940), 119-20. Sir Victor Gollancz (1893-1967),
liberal publisher, writer, and speaker, founded his firm in 1928. His Left Book Club aime
to expose Nazism and halt Hitler without war. His own writings concentrate on huma
need and social justice.

5. "Ganges film": see EJT to Nehru, 9 May 1940, *Old Letters*, 437-42. Vinoba Bhav
(1895-1982) was widely seen, after Gandhi's death in 1948, as his successor; he was th
instigator, in 1951, of the Bhoodan Movement for land distribution.

6. EJT, "The Outlook Now: A Summary," *Time and Tide* 21 (13 April 1940): 383-84.

7. See EJT, "The Drift to Niagara in India," *Time and Tide:* 21 (9 November 1940)
1080-81. Spalding to Nehru, 18 April 1940; forwarded by EJT. Nehru to Spalding, 22 Ma
1940, c. 5305, folios 55-57. See Nehru to EJT, 22 May 1940, c. 5305, folio 54. Nehr
rejected Spalding's ideal of economic reorganization through "such groupings as th
British Empire."

8. Spalding to EJT, 10 October 1937, folio 13; 4 September 1939, folio 45; 27 Septembe
1939, folio 46; all: c. 5316. See Symonds, *Oxford and Empire*, 119-22.

9. Elton to EJT, 8 July 1941, c. 5287, folio 37. In 1940 the Rhodes Trustees began t
appoint Indian scholars, but none actually arrived until 1947.

10. Author's interview with Barbara Sloman, London, 28 July 1997.

11. Ibid.; TJT to EJT, 15-16 November 1940, folios 123-25; 22-23 November [1940]
folios 132-48; both: c. 2698. EJT to TJT, fragment [1940], folio 13; 18 February [1941]
folio 51; both: c. 5361.

12. EJT to Palmer, 28 September 1937; 24 October 1937; both: TP.

13. EJT to Palmer, 11 November [1939]; 20 November 1939; 2 June [1940?]; all: TI
TJT to EJT, 19 November [1940], d. 2698, folio 130. See E. P. Thompson, *Beyond th
Frontier: The Politics of a Failed Mission: Bulgaria, 1944.* (Stanford: Stanford Universit
Press, 1997), 50.

14. EJT to Palmer, 14 October [1940], TP.

15. Palmer to EJT, 26 February 1940, TP. See E. P. Thompson, *Beyond the Frontier,* 50
16. E. P. Thompson, *Beyond the Frontier,* 52.

17. EJT to Ratcliffe, 18 June [1941], c. 5309, folios 191-92. EJT to TJT, 16 Novembe
[1940], c. 5361, folios 2-3.

18. EJT to TJT, 20-21 November [1940], c. 5361, folios 10-11.

19. EJT to TJT, 10 December [1940], folio 18; 9 December 1940, folio 19; 30 Decembe
1940, folio 22; 2 January 1941, folio 23; 3 January [1941], folio 24; 5 January 1941, folio
25-27; 23 January 1841, folios 40-43; 11 January [1941], folio 31; all: c. 5361.

20. EJT to TJT, 15 February [1941], folios 52-53; 13-14 January [1941], folio 32; 16 February [1941], folio 43; all: c. 5361.

21. EMF to BBC, 14 February 1941, BBC Written Archives, Thompson Talks File 2, 29-C.

22. EJT to TJT, 27 January 1941, c. 5361, folios 36-37.

23. See E. P. Thompson, *Beyond the Frontier,* 47.

24. EJT to Elton, 29 September [1941], RT/299. See William Rothenstein, *Men of the R.A.F.* (Oxford: Oxford University Press, 1942).

25. EJT to TJT, 19 October [1941], c. 5361, folio 64.

26. EJT to TJT, 23 November [1940], folios 12-13; 25 October [1941], folio 66; both: c. 5361. See "In Memory of Tagore: India Society Meeting," *Times,* 10 October 1941, 7. Speakers included EJT and Rothenstein. Churchill: see *Parliamentay Debates,* Commons, 5th ser., vol. 374 (9 September 1941), cols. 67-82.

27. EJT to TJT, 25 October [1941], c. 5361, folio 65. Herbert Stanley Morrison, Baron Morrison of Lambeth (1888-1965), was a Labour Member of Parliament from 1923 to 1956, Minister for Home Security from 1942 to 1945, and in the War Cabinet from 1942 to 1945. The Right Honorable Ernest Bevin (1881-1951) was the leader of the Dockers' Union from 1910 to 1921, General Secretary of the Transport and General Workers' Union from 1925 to 1940, Minister of Labour and National Service from 1940 to 1945, and Secretary of State for Foreign Affairs from 1945 to 1951.

28. See Wolpert, *New History of India,* 324-25. The Right Honorable Sir Stafford Cripps (1889-1952) was a Labour Member of Parliament from 1931 to 1950, Ambassador to Russia from 1940 to 1941, Leader of the House of Commons in 1942, Minister of Aircraft Production from 1942 to 1945 and for Economic Affairs in 1947, and Chancellor of the Exchequer from 1947 to 1950.

29. Garratt to EJT, 9 September 1941, c. 5289, folio 141. See "Fallen Officers (Army)," *Times,* 1 May 1942, 7.

30. Ratcliffe to EJT, 2 May 1942, c. 5309, folio 235.

24. LETTERS TO THE FRONT

1. Alfred Curtis Brown to EJT, 11 March 1945, c. 5285, folio 238; EJT, *You Have Lived through All This* (London: Victor Gollancz, 1939). Alfred Curtis Brown (1906-1980) founded his agency in 1899. Augustus Dudley Peters (1892-1973) was a literary and dramatic agent.

2. TS draft [autumn? 1942], c. 5330, folios 1-28; quotations in next few paragraphs are from this reference.

3. EJT to Palmer, 28 May 1940, TP. See EJT, *You Have Lived through All This,* 7, 288.

4. EJT, *The Making of the Indian Princes* (London: H. Milford for Oxford University Press, 1943), vi, 283, 289.

5. E. M. Forster, "Some Books," BBC Eastern Service, 12 September 1943, BBC Written Archives, Caversham Park, Reading.

6. "The Indian States: 'Princes and Politics,' " *TLS,* 28 August 1943, 418. L. F. Rushbrooke Williams, "The Princes of India," *Spectator* 171 (1943): 197.

7. EJT to Palmer and Frank, 11 March 1944, d. 2702, folio 21. See *Parliamentary Debates,* Commons, 5th ser., vol. 408 (1 March 1945), cols. 1547-48.

8. Lyon to EJT, 28 November 1943, c. 5301, folio 91. On the famine, see Broomfield, *Elite Conflict,* 304-5; and Paul R. Greenough, *Prosperity and Misery in Modern Bengal: The Famine of 1943-44* (New York: Oxford University Press, 1982).

9. See Lawrence James, *Raj: The Making and Unmaking of British India* (New York: St. Martin's Press, 1997), 578-81.

10. TJT to Palmer, [1 November 1943], folios 67-71; 16 August [1943], folios 73-75; both: d. 2701.

11. EJT to Palmer, postmark 18 October 1943, d. 2701, folio 84.

12. EJT to Palmer, 25 November 1943, d. 2701, folio 95.

13. EJT to Frank and Palmer, 6 December, postmark 1943, d. 2701, folio 97. Zenith: Sinclair Lewis, *Babbitt* (London: J. Cape, 1922).

14. Ratcliffe to EJT, 2 May 1942, c. 5309, folios 235-37.

15. Spalding to EJT, 13 September 1942, c. 5136, folios 97-100.

16. EJT to Palmer and Frank, 22 December 1943, d. 2701, folio 101.

17. Palmer to EJT, 4 June 1943, TP.

18. EJT, *100 Poems* (London: Oxford University Press, 1944). See "The Common Step Mr. Edward Thompson's Poems," *TLS,* 12 August 1944, 392; Wilfred Gibson, "Selecte Poems," *Manchester Guardian,* 2 August 1944, 3.

19. EJT to Palmer, 28 October 1943, d. 2701, folio 84; Phillips, *Robert Bridges,* 302

20. Virginia Woolf, 1 July 1926, *Diary,* ed. Anne Olivier Bell and Andrew McNeillie, vols. (London: Hogarth Press, 1977-1984), 3:92-93; Bridges, *Selected Letters,* 2:929-3(See also Phillips, *Robert Bridges,* 301, 310; and Bridges, *The Testament of Beauty: Poem in Four Books* (London: Oxford University Press, 1944).

21. On Bridges and Forster, see Phillips, *Robert Bridges,* 289-90, 292, 311-12.

22. Spender to EJT, 7 August [1942], folio 137; EJT to Spender, 1 December 1942, foli 144; both: c. 5317. EJT to Palmer, 10 December [1942], TP. Walter de la Mare (1873-1956 was a poet and author of short fiction. Laurence Binyon (1869-1943) was a poet and a historian in the Department of Prints and Drawings at the British Museum from 1895 t 1933, and deputy keeper of Oriental Prints and Drawings from 1913 to 1932).

23. Palmer to EJT, 8 January 1944, TP.

24. TJT to EJT, [1941?], d. 2699, folios 124-25; EJT to Palmer, [1942?], TP.

25. EJT to Frank and Palmer, 1 November 1943, d. 2701, folio 85.

26. In Frank Thompson, *There Is a Spirit in Europe . . . : A Memoir,* comp. TJT and I P. Thompson (London: Victor Gollancz, 1948), 16, 21.

27. TJT to Palmer, 27 March [1944], folio 4; 20-22 August, postmark 1944, folio both: d. 2702. TJT to EJT, [n.d.], d. 2699, folios 160-62. Palmer to Frank, 2 April 1944, T

28. EJT to Palmer, 20 August, postmark 1944, c. 2702, folio 9. TJT to Palmer, September 1944, folio 11; EJT to Palmer, 29 September 1944, folio 12; both: d. 2702.

29. EJT to Palmer, 29 September, postmark 1944, d. 2702, folio 12.

30. TJT to Palmer, 1 October 1944, d. 2702, folio 13.

31. EJT to Palmer, 22 October 1944, d. 2702, folio 16. See introduction (pp. 11-21 *There Is a Spirit . . . .* See also E. P. Thompson, *Beyond the Frontier.*

32. Palmer to EJT and TJT, 25 January [1945], TP.

33. EJT to Palmer, [1945?], TP.

34. EJT to Palmer, [1944?], TP.

35. EJT to Palmer, 3 April 1945, TP.

36. H. M. M[argoulieth], "Obituary: Edward John Thompson," *Oxford Magazine* 64 (May 1946): 272.

37. Nehru, *Jawaharlal Nehru: An Autobiography with Musings on Recent Events i India* (London: Bodley Head, 1958), 346.

38. E. P. Thompson, *Making of the English Working Class,* 385.

39. EJT, "Repentance for Political Activity," in *100 Poems,* 85.

BIBLIOGRAPHY

Ackerley, Joe. *Hindoo Holiday: An Indian Journal.* London: Chatto and Windus, 1932.

Ambedkar, Bhimrao Ramji. *What Congress and Gandhi Have Done to the Untouchables.* Bombay: Thacker, 1945.

Anand, Mulk Raj. *Across the Dark Waters.* London: J. Cape, 1940.

Andrews, C. F. "An Evening with Rabindra." *Modern Review* 12 (1912): 225-28.

———. "Gandhi's Mystic Aims in His Indian March." *Sunday New York Times,* 6 April 1930, sec. X, p. 6.

———. *India and the Simon Report.* London: Allen and Unwin; New York: Macmillan, 1930.

———. "Tagore and the Renaissance in Bengal." *Contemporary Review* 103 (1913): 809-17.

Archer, W. G. *The Loves of Krishna in Indian Painting and Poetry.* New York: Macmillan, 1957.

Arnstein, Walter L. *The Bradlaugh Case: Atheism, Sex, and Politics among the Late Victorians.* Columbia: University of Missouri Press, 1983.

Aurobindo. *Sri Aurobindo on Himself and on the Mother.* Pondicherry: Sri Aurobindo Ashram, 1953.

"Babies in India Fed Opium at British Command, He Says." *Baltimore Sun,* 13 February 1930, 3.

Bailey, Victor. "The Fabrication of Deviance." In *Protest and Survival: Essays for E. P. Thompson,* ed. John Rule and Robert Malcolmson, 221-56. London: Merlin Press, 1993.

Bakshi, S. R. *Simon Commission and Indian Nationalism.* New Delhi: Munshiram Manohari, 1977.

Beerbohm, Max. *Zuleika Dobson, or An Oxford Love Story.* London: William Heinemann, 1911.

"Books in Brief." *Nation and the Athenaeum* (London) 122 (30 June 1926): 730-31.

Bose, Buddhadeva. *An Acre of Green Grass: A Review of Modern Bengali Literature.* Bombay: Orient Longmans, 1948.

Bowers, Raamah. "Growing Up in the Grove." *Cheshire Life* 43 (1977): 78-79.

Bridges, Robert. *Collected Essays and Papers &c. of Robert Bridges*. 10 vols London: Humphrey Milford for Oxford University Press, 1929.

———. "John Keats: A Critical Essay." London: Lawrence and Bullen, 1895 Reprinted in *Collected Essays and Papers &c. of Robert Bridges*, 7:18–29 London: Humphrey Milford for Oxford University Press, 1929.

———. "Humdrum and Harum-Scarum." *North American Review* 21 (1922): 647–58.

———. "A Letter to a Musician on English Prosody." *The Musical Antiquary* 1 (1909): 15–29. Reprinted in *Collected Essays and Papers &c. of Robert Bridges*, 7:55–85. London: Humphrey Milford for Oxford University Press 1929.

———. *Milton's Prosody: an examination of the rules of the blank verse in Milton's later poems, with an account of the versification of Samson Agonistes, and general notes by Robert Bridges*. Oxford: Clarendon Press 1894.

———. *The Selected Letters of Robert Bridges*. Ed. Donald E. Stanford. vols. Newark, N.J.: University of Delaware Press, 1983–1984.

———. *The Testament of Beauty: A Poem in Four Books*. London: Oxford University Press, 1944.

Bridges, Robert, ed. *The Spirit of Man: An Anthology in English and French from the Philosophers and Poets, Made by the Poet Laureate in 1916 and Dedicated by Gracious Permission to His Majesty the King*. London Longmans Green, 1917.

Broomfield, John H. *Elite Conflict in a Plural Society: Twentieth-Century Bengal*. Berkeley and Los Angeles: University of California Press, 1968.

Buchanan, Sir George. *The Tragedy of Mesopotamia*. Edinburgh: Blackwood 1938.

"By the Banyans of Bengal." *Spectator* 138 (1927): 957–58.

Candler, Edmund. *The General Plan*. Edinburgh: Blackwood, 1911.

———. *The Long Road to Baghdad*. 2 vols. London: Cassell, 1919.

Canfield [Fisher], Dorothy. *The Bent Twig*. New York: Henry Holt, 1915.

Canton, William. *A History of the British and Foreign Bible Society*. 5 vols London: John Murray, 1904–1910.

———. *In Memory of W. V.* London: J. M. Dent, 1901.

———. *The Invisible Playmate: A Story of the Unseen*. London: Isbister 1894.

Carey, Peter. "Gathering for a Talk: Literature, Politics, and Censorship in Present-Day Burma." *Times Literary Supplement*, 16 November 1996, 17

Carthill, Al. [Bennet Christian Huntingdon Calcroft-Kennedy]. *The Lost Dominion*. Edinburgh: Blackwood, 1924.

Casteras, Susan P. *James Smetham: Artist, Author, Pre-Raphaelite Associate* Aldershot: Scolar Press; Brookfield, Vt.: Ashgate, 1995.

Chatterji, Ramananda. "Mr. Thompson's Book on Rabindranath Tagore." *Modern Review* 42 (1927): 99–103.

Collingwood, W. G. *Dutch Agnes, Her Valentine: Being the Journal of the Curate of Coniston, 1616–1623*. Kendal: Thomas Wilson, 1910.

Colvin, Ian. *The Life of General Dyer*. Edinburgh: Blackwood, 1929.

"Commerce Protection: The Task of Removing the Raiders." *Times,* 11 November 1914, 10.

"The Common Steps: Mr. Edward Thompson's Poems." *Times Literary Supplement,* 12 August 1944, 392.

Connolly, Cyril. "New Novels." *New Statesman and Nation* 29 (1927): 815.

Coupland, Sir Reginald. *The Empire in These Days: An Interpretation*. London: Macmillan, 1935.

Cranston, Sylvia. *HPB: The Extraordinary Life and Influence of Helena Blavatsky, Founder of the Modern Theosophical Movement*. New York: Putnam, 1993.

Cunningham, R. C. *Two Schools: A History of the St. Olave's and St. Saviour's Grammar School Foundation*. London: Governors of St. Olave's and St. Saviour's Grammar School Foundation, 1971.

Curtis, Lionel. *Civitas Dei*. 3 vols. London: Macmillan, 1934–1937. *World Order (Civitas Dei)*. New York: Oxford University Press, 1939.

———. *Letters to the Indian People on Responsible Government*. London: Macmillan, 1918.

Dallimore, Arnold A. *George Whitefield: The Life and Times of the Great Evangelist of the Eighteenth-Century Revival*. 2 vols. Westchester, Ill.: Cornerstone Books, 1978.

Danger, Elsie W. "Books for a Long Flight" (letter). *Times,* 16 October 1939, 9.

Das, Harihar. *The Life and Letters of Toru Dutt*. London: Humphrey Milford for Oxford University Press, 1921.

Datta, V. N. *Jallianwala Bagh*. Kurukshetra: Lyall Book Depot, 1969.

Davies, Rupert, and Gordon Rupp, eds. *A History of the Methodist Church in Great Britain*. London: Epworth Press, 1965.

De, S. K. "Struggle of Vernaculars for Their Rightful Place in Our Universities." *Calcutta Review,* 3d ser., 154 (1960): 105–22.

"The Deadlock in India." *Times,* 8 November 1939, 10.

De Bary, William Theodore, et al., comps. *Sources of Indian Tradition*. Introduction to Oriental Civilizations, vol. 1. New York: Columbia University Press, 1958.

"Delhi House Votes to Boycott Simon." *New York Times,* 19 February 1929, 2.

Dimock, Edward C., Jr., and Denise Levertov, trans. *In Praise of Krishna: Songs from the Bengali*. Garden City, N.Y.: Doubleday, 1967.

"The Disturbances in India." *Times,* 26 April 1919, 13.

"The Durbar at Delhi." *Spectator* 107 (1911): 1060-62.

Dutt, R[omesh] C[handra]. *India in the Victorian Age: An Economic History of the People.* London: Kegan Paul, Trench, Trübner, 1904.

Dutt, Toru. *Ancient Ballads and Legends of Hindustan.* London: K. Paul Trench, 1882.

———. *A Sheaf Gleaned in French Fields.* London: K. Paul, Trench, 1880.

Dutta, Krishna, and Andrew Robinson. *Rabindranath Tagore: The Myriad Minded Man.* London: Bloomsbury, 1995.

Ellinwood, DeWitt C. "The Indian Soldier, the Indian Army, and Change 1914-1918." In *India and World War I,* ed. DeWitt C. Ellinwood and S. D. Pradhan, 177-211. New Delhi: Manohari, 1978.

Elrington, C. R., and N. M. Herbert, eds. *A History of the County of Glouce ter.* Victoria History of the Counties of England, 11 vols. London: Oxford University Press for the University of London Institute of Historical Research, 1974.

"Exploits of the *Emden.*" *Times,* 23 October 1914, 6.

"Fallen Officers (Army)." *Times,* 1 May 1942, 7.

Farrell, J. G. *The Siege of Krishnapur: A Novel.* Harmondsworth, Middlesex: Penguin, 1973.

Fein, Helen. *Imperial Crime and Punishment: The Massacre at Jallianwala Bagh and British Judgment, 1919-1920.* Honolulu: University of Hawaii Press, 1977.

Field, Harry. *After Mother India.* New York: Harcourt Brace, 1929.

Fielden, Lionel. *The Natural Bent.* London: André Deutsch, 1944.

[Foreign Policy Association]. *India: Discussed by Sailendra Nath Ghose and Edward Thompson.* 125th New York luncheon discussion, 15 February 1930. New York: Foreign Policy Association [1936].

Forster, E. M. *The Hill of Devi and Other Indian Writings.* Abinger Edition, ed. Elizabeth Heine. London: Edward Arnold, 1983.

———. *Howards End.* Abinger Edition, ed. Oliver Stallybrass. London: Edward Arnold, 1973.

———. *A Passage to India.* Abinger Edition, ed. Oliver Stallybrass. London: Edward Arnold, 1973.

———. *Selected Letters of E. M. Forster.* Ed. Mary Lago and P. N. Furbank. 2 vols. London: Collins; Cambridge: Harvard University Press, 1983, 1985.

———. "Some Books." BBC Eastern Service, 12 September 1943. BBC Written Archives, Caversham Park, Reading.

———. *Two Cheers for Democracy.* Abinger Edition, ed. Oliver Stallybrass. London: Edward Arnold, 1972.

Furbank, P. N. *E. M. Forster: A Life.* 2 vols. Oxford: Oxford University Press, 1977, 1978.

ussell, Paul. *The Great War and Modern Memory.* New York and London: Oxford University Press, 1975.

Future of India: Mr. Churchill on the Conference." *Times,* 12 December 1930, 16.

The Gaekwar's Homage: A Public Apology." *Times,* 18 December 1911, 8.

Gandhi, Mahatma. *Collected Works.* 99 vols. Delhi: Publications Division, Ministry of Information and Broadcasting, Government of India, 1958-1984.

Garratt, Geoffrey T. "Aids to Indian Reflection." *Nation and the Athenaeum* 47 (1930): 796-97.

———. *An Indian Commentary.* New York: Cape and Harrison Smith, 1929.

Ghosh, J. C. *Bengali Literature.* London: Geoffrey Cumberlege for Oxford University Press, 1948.

Gibson, Wilfred. "Selected Poems." *Manchester Guardian,* 2 August 1944, 3.

Gill, Frederick C. *Charles Wesley, the First Methodist.* London: Lutterworth Press, 1964.

Gilmour, Ian. *Curzon.* London: John Murray, 1994.

Government of India. *India's Contribution to the Great War.* Calcutta: Government Printing Office, 1923.

Graves, Richard P. *Robert Graves: The Assault Heroic, 1895-1926.* New York: Viking, 1987.

Graves, Robert. *Good-bye to All That.* Rev. ed. Garden City, N.Y.: Doubleday, 1957.

A Great Imperial Announcement." *Times,* 13 December 1911, 7.

Greenberger, Allen J. *The British Image of India: A Study in the Literature of Imperialism, 1880-1960.* Oxford: Oxford University Press, 1969.

Greenough, Paul R. *Prosperity and Misery in Modern Bengal: The Famine of 1943-44.* New York: Oxford University Press, 1982.

Gross, John. *The Rise and Fall of the Man of Letters: A Study of the Idiosyncratic and the Humane in Modern Literature.* New York: Macmillan, 1969.

Guha-Takurta, Tapati. *The Making of a New "Indian" Art: Artists, Aesthetics, and Nationalism in Bengal, c. 1850-1920.* Cambridge: Cambridge University Press, 1992.

Hardinge of Penshurst, [Charles]. *My Indian Years, 1910-1916.* London: John Murray, 1948.

Hartley, L. P. "An Indian Day." *Saturday Review* 44 (1927): 26.

Hassall, Christopher. *Edward Marsh, Patron of the Arts: A Biography.* London: Longmans, 1959.

Havell, E. B. "Art Administration in India." In "Proceedings," *Journal of the Royal Society of Arts* 58 (1909-1910): 274-85.

Hay, Stephen N. *Asian Ideas of East and West: Tagore and His Critics i Japan, China, and India.* Cambridge: Harvard University Press, 1970.

"Hindu Widow-Burning." *Sunday New York Times,* 9 September 1928, se IV, p. 12.

"His Majesty's Birthday: List of Honours." *Times,* 3 June 1915, 9–10.

Holland, Florence. "Dyer Appreciation Fund" (letter). *Statesman* (Calcutta 13 July 1920, 7.

Holroyd, Michael. *Bernard Shaw.* 5 vols. New York: Random House, 198£ 1992.

———. *Hugh Kingsmill: A Critical Biography.* London: Unicorn Pres 1964.

"India in True Perspective." *Spectator* 145 (1930): 285–86.

"Indian Independence Discussed." *New York Times,* 16 March 1930, 19.

"The Indian Mutiny." *Times Literary Supplement,* 5 November 1925, 738.

Indian National Congress Punjab Subcommittee. *Report of the Commissio ers.* 2 vols. Bombay: Karnatak Press, 1920.

"Indian Reconstruction." *Times Literary Supplement,* 28 August 1930, 67(

"The Indian Side." *Saturday Review of Literature* 2 (15 May 1926): 788.

"The Indian States: 'Princes and Politics.' " *Times Literary Supplement,* 2 August 1943, 418.

"Indian Unrest." *New York Times,* 16 May 1926, 20, 23.

"India's Future Is Luncheon Topic." *Boston Evening Transcript,* 1 Marc 1930, sec. I, p. 7.

"In Memory of Tagore: India Society Meeting." *Times,* 10 October 1941, 7.

Irving, Robert Grant. *Indian Summer: Lutyens, Baker, and Imperial Delh* New Haven: Yale University Press, 1981.

Ives, A. G. *Kingswood School in Wesley's Day and Since.* London: Epwort Press, 1970.

James, Lawrence. *Raj: The Making and Unmaking of British India.* Nev York: St. Martin's Press, 1997.

James, Robert Rhodes. *Gallipoli.* New York: Macmillan, 1965.

"John Davidson's 'Last Poems.' " *Times Literary Supplement,* 15 July 190£ 260.

Johnson, Charles. "Three Contrasting Views of the Tangled Indian Question *Sunday New York Times,* 9 November 1930, sec. IV, p. 9.

Kabir. *One Hundred Poems of Kabir.* Trans. Rabindranath Tagore and Evely Underhill. London: India Society, 1914.

Kaye, John William. *The Life and Correspondence of Charles, Lord Metcalf* 2 vols. London: Richard Bentley, 1854.

"The King's Address at Delhi." *Times,* 14 December 1911, 10.

Kopf, David. *The Brahmo Samaj and the Shaping of the Modern Indiar Mind.* Princeton: Princeton University Press, 1979.

ιgo, Mary. *Christiana Herringham and the Edwardian Art Scene.* Columbia: University of Missouri Press; London: Lund Humphries, 1996.

———. "No Passage from India." *Times Literary Supplement,* 16 April 1999, 15-16.

ιgo, Mary, ed. *Imperfect Encounter: Letters of William Rothenstein and Rabindranath Tagore, 1911-1941.* Cambridge: Harvard University Press, 1972.

ιvin, Deborah. *From Empire to International Commonwealth: A Biography of Lionel Curtis.* Oxford: Clarendon Press, 1995.

ιlyveld, David. *Aligarh's First Generation: Muslim Solidarity in British India.* Princeton: Princeton University Press, 1978.

ιwis, Sinclair. *Babbitt.* London: J. Cape, 1922.

ιvett, Robert Morss. "An Indian Day." *New Republic* 51 (1927): 317.

ιvett, Sir Verney. *A History of the Indian Nationalist Movement.* London: John Murray, 1920.

ιwther, George. "Blake and Smetham" (letter). *Academy* 77 (1909): 378.

———. "J. M. Synge and the Irish Revival." *Oxford and Cambridge Review* 25 (1912): 43-59.

ιnn, Henry S. *Friend of Missions in India: "The Cyclostyled Indian Journal."* London: James Clarke [1890].

Lynching in America." *Modern Review* 30 (1921): 243.

The Lynching Industry, 1920." *Crisis* 21-22 (1920-1921): 160-62.

ιacDonald, Ramsay. "Mr. MacDonald on India: Criticism of Mr. Churchill's 'Mischievous Speech.' " *Times,* 13 December 1930, 14.

ι[argoulieth], H. M. "Obituary: Edward John Thompson." *Oxford Magazine* 64 (9 May 1946): 272.

ιatthews, H. L. "Tagore Sees India. . . ." *New York Times,* 2 June 1929, sec. II, p. 6.

ιayo, Katherine. *Mother India.* New York: Harcourt Brace; London: J. Cape, 1927.

ιcCully, B. T. *English Education and the Origins of Indian Nationalism.* New York: Columbia University Press, 1940.

ιitter, Partha. *Much Maligned Monsters: History of Western Reactions to Indian Art.* Oxford: Clarendon Press, 1977.

The Modification of the Partition." In Notes, *Modern Review* 11 (1912): 111-19.

ιoore, Robert. *Pitmen, Preachers, and Politics: The Effects of Methodism in a Durham Mining Community.* Cambridge: Cambridge University Press, 1974.

Mother India in the Dark." *Saturday Review of Literature* 6 (5 October 1929): 203.

Mr. Tagore's Poems." *Times Literary Supplement,* 7 November 1912, 492.

Muir, Edwin. "Fiction." *Nation and the Athenaeum* 41 (1927): 520.

Mukherjee, Sujit. *Forster and Further: The Tradition of Anglo-Indian Fi* tion. Hyderabad: Orient Longman, 1993.

Mukherjee, Sujit [Kumar]. *Passage to America: The Reception of Rabindra* nath Tagore in the United States, 1912-1941. Calcutta: Bookland Private 1964.

Nehru, Jawarhalal. *An Autobiography, with Musings on Recent Events i* India. London: Bodley Head, 1958.

———. *A Bunch of Old Letters: Written Mostly to Jawaharlal Nehru an* Some Written By Him. New York: Asia Publishing House, 1960.

———. *Selected Works of Jawarhalal Nehru.* 23 vols. Ed. S. Gopal. New Delhi: Orient Longman, 1972-.

"The New Capital of India." *Spectator* 107 (1911): 1060-61.

"News of the Week." *Spectator* 146 (1931): 243-44.

"News of the Week: The Right to Broadcast." *Spectator* 147 (1931), 203.

"The Nobel Literature Prize: Honour for an Indian Poet." *Times,* 14 November 1913, 8.

Nowell-Smith, Simon, ed. *Letters to Macmillan.* London: Macmillan, 1967.

O'Connor, Frank. *The Lonely Voice.* Cleveland: World Publishing, 1965.

O'Dwyer, Sir Michael. *India as I Knew It, 1885-1925.* London: Constable 1925.

O'Malley, L. S. S. *Bengal District Gazetteer.* Calcutta: Bengal Secretariat Boo Depot, 1908.

"Open Rebellion in India." *Times,* 19 April 1919, 11.

"The Other Side of the Medal." *Spectator* 135 (1925): 882-83.

"The Outbreak in India." *Times,* 15 April 1919, 13.

Outler, Albert C., ed. *John Wesley.* Library of Theological Thought. New York Oxford University Press, 1964.

Page, William, Granville Proby, and S. Inskip Ladds, eds., assisted by H. E Norris. *The Victoria History of the County of Huntingdon.* Victoria History of the Counties of England, vol. 3. London: St. Catherine Press for the University of London Institute of Historical Research, 1926-1932

Parry, Benita. *Delusions and Discoveries: Studies on India in the British Imagination, 1880-1930.* Berkeley and Los Angeles: University of California Press, 1972.

Parsons, I. M. "Fiction." *Spectator* 146 (1931): 91.

"The Pathan Raid: Indian Frontier Tribe Chastised." *Times,* 24 February 1914 7.

Peden, William H. *The American Short Story: Front Line in the National Defense of Literature.* Boston: Houghton Mifflin, 1964.

Phillips, Catherine. *Robert Bridges: A Biography.* New York: Oxford University sity Press, 1992.

"Poor Judgment in India." *New York Times,* 6 February 1929, 18.

Pound, Ezra. *The Letters of Ezra Pound, 1907-1941.* Ed. D. D. Paige. New York: Harcourt Brace, 1950.

———. "Rabindranath Tagore." *Fortnightly Review,* n.s., 99 (1913): 571-79.

Q[uennell]. P. "Two Elizabethans." *Saturday Review* 9 (1935): 758-60.

R. A. T. "Fiction." *Spectator* 139 (1927): 579.

Ram, Raja. *The Jallianwala Bagh Massacre: A Premeditated Plan.* 2d ed. Chandigarh: Publication Bureau, Panjab University, 1978.

Ramprasad (Ramaprasada Sen). *Bengali Religious Lyrics.* Trans. E. J. Thompson and A. M. Spencer. Calcutta: Association Press; London: Oxford University Press, 1923.

Ratcliffe, S. K. "The Mutiny." *Nation and the Athenaeum* 38 (1926): 499-500.

[———]. "Says Interest in India Is Growing in America." *New York Times,* 22 October 1929, 12.

———. *What the Simon Report Means.* London: New Statesman, 1930.

Review of *Gitanjali. Athenaeum,* 5 April 1913, 382.

Review of *Gitanjali. Athenaeum,* 16 November 1913, 583.

"Reviews and Notices." *Modern Review* 31 (1922): 341.

Rhys, Ernest. *Rabindranath Tagore: A Biographical Study.* London: Macmillan, 1915.

Richards, Frank. "George Lowther." *Kingswood Magazine* 19 (1913): 138-42.

Ronaldshay, Lord. "India in Art and Literature." *Listener* 1 (1929): 17-18.

Rothenstein, William. *Men and Memories: Recollections, 1872-1938.* Ed. and abr. Mary Lago. London: Chatto and Windus; Columbia: University of Missouri Press, 1978.

———. *Men and Memories: Recollections of William Rothenstein.* 2 vols. London: Faber and Faber, 1931-1934.

———. *Men of the R.A.F.* Oxford: Oxford University Press, 1942.

———. *Since Fifty, Men and Memories, 1922-1938: Recollections of William Rothenstein.* [Vol. 3 of *Men and Memories.*] New York: Macmillan, 1940.

Rubin, David. *After the Raj: British Novels of India since 1947.* Hanover, N.H.: University Press of New England, 1986.

Russell, Sir William Howard. *My Indian Mutiny Diary.* (Originally published as *The Indian Mutiny: A Diary.* London: George Routledge, 1860.) Reprint, ed. and abr. Michael Edwardes, London: Cassell, 1957.

Said, Edward. *Orientalism.* London: Penguin, 1978.

Savarkar, Vinayak Damodar. *The Indian War of Independence of 1857: By an Indian Nationalist.* 1909. Bombay: Phoenix Publications, 1947.

————. *The Story of My Transportation for Life.* Bombay: Sadbhakti Publi cations, 1950.

Scargill, D. Ian. "Responses to Growth in Modern Oxford." In *Oxford: Studie. in the History of a University Town since 1800,* ed. R. C. Whiting Manchester: Manchester University Press, 1993.

Seal, Brajendranath. *Comparative Studies in Vaishnavism and Christianity* N.p., 1899.

"Sees World Peace in Independent India." *New York Times,* 16 February 1930 18.

Seton, Grace Gallatin. *"Yea, Lady Saheb": A Woman's Adventurings with Mysterious India.* New York: Harper, 1925.

Seymour, Miranda. *Robert Graves: Life on the Edge.* New York: Henry Holt 1995.

"Shorter Notices." *New Statesman* 26 (9 January 1926): 394-95.

Simon, The Rt. Hon. Viscount. *Retrospect: The Memoirs of the Rt. Hon. Viscount Simon.* London: Hutchinson, 1952.

————. *Two Broadcast Talks on India.* Criterion Miscellany No. 18. London Faber and Faber, 1930.

Singer, Milton, ed. *Krishna: Myths, Rites, and Attitudes.* Honolulu: East-West Center Press, 1966.

Sloan, John. *John Davidson, First of the Moderns: A Literary Biography* Oxford: Clarendon Press, 1995.

Smetham, James. *The Literary Works of James Smetham.* Ed. William Davies. London: Macmillan, 1893. Also in reel 365, Microform Series, Eighteenth Century Sources for the Study of English Literature and Culture. Keswick, Va.: Don H. Massey.

Smith, Vincent Arthur. *The Oxford History of India.* 2d ed. Oxford: Claren don Press, 1923.

Srivastava, Harindra. *Five Stormy Years: Savarkar in London, June 1906- June 1911.* New Delhi: Allied Publishers, 1983.

Stead, Robert. "Hazel Grove." *Cheshire Life* 39 (1973): 102-5, 107-8.

Steel, Flora Annie. *The Garden of Fidelity: Being the Autobiography of Flora Annie Steel, 1847-1929.* London: Macmillan, 1929.

————. *On the Face of the Waters.* London: Macmillan, 1896.

Stokes, Eric. *The English Utilitarians and India.* Oxford: Clarendon Press, 1959.

"A Study of Tagore." *Times Literary Supplement,* 18 November 1926, 815.

"Swedish Tribute to Mr. Tagore." *Times,* 15 November 1913, 13.

Symonds, Richard. *Oxford and Empire: The Last Lost Cause?* Oxford: Claren don Press, 1991.

Tagore, Jyotirindranath. *Granthabali* (Library Collection). Calcutta: Satish chandra Mukhopadhyay, n.d.

Tagore, Rabindranath. *The Crescent Moon.* London: Macmillan, 1913.
———. *Gitanjali (Song-Offering).* London: India Society, 1912; London: Macmillan, 1913. Also, in Bengali, in *Rabindra-racanabali,* 11:1–126.
———. *Glimpses of Bengal.* Trans. Surendranath Tagore, rev. Thomas Sturge Moore. London: Macmillan, 1921.
———. "Great Britain and India" (letter). *Spectator* 145 (1930): 280.
———. *The Housewarming and Other Selected Writings of Rabindranath Tagore.* Trans. Mary Lago and Tarun Gupta. New York: New American Library, 1965.
———. *The Hungry Stones and Other Stories.* London: Macmillan, 1916.
———. *Kshanika* (Ephemeral). In *Rabindra-racanabali,* 7:207–332.
———. "Living or Dead." Trans. E. J. Thompson. In *The Hungry Stones and Other Stories,* 193–212. London: Macmillan, 1916. In *Rabindra-racanabali,* 19:181–93.
———. *Mashi and Other Stories.* London: Macmillan, 1918.
———. *Megh o roudra* (Cloud and sun). In *Rabindra-racanabali,* 19:210–35.
———. *Nationalism.* London: Macmillan, 1917.
———. "The Parrot's Training." In *The Parrot's Training and Other Stories,* trans. Marjorie Sykes. Calcutta: Visva-Bharati, 1944.
———. *Personality: Lectures Delivered in America.* London: Macmillan, 1917.
———. "Rabindranath Tagore: Why He Wishes to Resign His Title" (letter). *Manchester Guardian,* 9 July 1919, 10. Also in Thompson, *Rabindranath Tagore: Poet and Dramatist.* London: Oxford University Press, 1926, 273–74.
———. *Rabindra-racanabali* (Rabindranath's works). 27 vols., 2 supp., index. Calcutta: Visva-Bharati, 1964–1966.
———. "Rashmani's Son" ("Rashmanir chhele"). In *Selected Short Stories,* trans. Krishna Dutta and Mary Lago. London: Macmillan, 1991.
———. *Reminiscences.* Trans. unidentified. London: Macmillan, 1917.
———. *Selected Letters.* Ed. Krishna Dutta and Andrew Robinson. Cambridge: Cambridge University Press, 1997.
———. *Selected Short Stories.* Trans. Krishna Dutta and Mary Lago. London: Macmillan, 1991.
Taylor, Anne. *Annie Besant: A Biography.* Oxford: Oxford University Press, 1992.
"Ten Minutes' Fire on Mob." *Times,* 15 December 1919, 13.
Thompson, Edward John. "America and India: The British Case." *Times,* 18 September 1930, 8.
———. *Atonement: A Play of Modern India, in Four Acts.* London: Ernest Benn, 1924.

————. *Cithaeron Dialogues.* London: G. G. Harrap, 1924.

————. "Christian Principles and General Dyer" (letter). *Statesman* (Ca cutta), 21 July 1920, 7–8.

————. "The Drift to Niagara in India." *Time and Tide* 21 (9 Novembe 1940): 1080–81.

————. *The Enchanted Lady: A Comedy.* London: G. Bell and Sons, 1910.

————. *Enlist India for Freedom!* Victory Books, no. 5. London: Victo Gollancz, 1940.

————. *Ennerdale Bridge.* London: Kelly, 1914.

————. *A Farewell to India.* London: Faber and Faber, 1932.

————. *A History of India.* Benn's Sixpenny Library, no. 18. London: Ernes Benn, 1927.

————. "India: Federal Problems: Economic Interests, the Communal Trou ble; at the R[ound] T[able] C[onference]." *Spectator* 147 (1931): 410–11

————. "India: The Communal Deadlock: The Depressed Classes." *Spectato* 147 (1931): 449–50.

————. *An Indian Day.* London: Knopf, 1927; New York: Macmillan, 1933

————. "In Memoriam: George Lowther." *Kingswood Magazine* 19 (1913) 138–42.

————. *Introducing the Arnisons.* London: Macmillan, 1935.

————. "James Smetham's Essays." *London Quarterly Review,* 5th ser., (1911): 251–58.

————. *John Arnison.* London: Macmillan, 1939.

————. *John in Prison, and Other Poems,* London: T. Fisher Unwin, 1912

————. *The Knight Mystic and Other Verses.* London: Elliot Stock, 1907.

————. *The Leicestershires beyond Baghdad.* London: Epworth Press, 1919

————. *A Letter from India.* London: Faber and Faber, 1932.

————. *The Life of Charles, Lord Metcalfe.* London: Faber and Faber, 1937

————. "The Madras Case" (letter). *Spectator* 145 (1930): 785.

————. *The Making of the Indian Princes.* London: H. Milford for Oxfor University Press, 1943.

————. "The Mass: Its Origin and Nature." *Sunday at Home* (1908–1909) 134–37.

————. "Mother India." *Nation and the Athenaeum* 41 (1927): 581–82.

————. "Mother India in the Dock." *Saturday Review of Literature* 6 (1929) 203.

————. "The New Laureate." *Indian Methodist Times,* August 1913, 114–15

————. *100 Poems.* London: Oxford University Press, 1944.

————. *The Other Side of the Medal.* London: Hogarth Press, 1925.

————. "The Outlook Now: A Summary." *Time and Tide* 21 (13 April 1940) 383–84.

———. "Prohibition of Widow-Burning in British India." *London Quarterly Review* 148 (1927): 57–66.

———. *Rabindranath Tagore: His Life and Work.* Heritage of India Series. Calcutta: Y.M.C.A. Press; London: Oxford University Press, 1921.

———. *Rabindranath Tagore: Poet and Dramatist.* London: Oxford University Press, 1926. Rev. ed., Geoffrey Cumberledge for Oxford University Press, 1948.

———. *Reconstructing India.* New York: Dial Press, 1930. In Britain: *The Reconstruction of India.* London: Faber and Faber, 1930.

———. *Reports* [to the Trustees]. Rhodes Foundation, 1930, 1932, 1936.

———. "The Round Table: The Economic Myth: Fact and Fancy." *Spectator* 145 (1930): 841.

———. "The Round Table Conference." *Spectator* 145 (1930): 936.

———. "The Round Table Conference: 'Prologemena': What Is and Might Be." *Spectator* 145 (1930): 783.

———. "The Round Table Conference: Unitary Government—Federation—Paramountcy." *Spectator* 145 (1930): 880.

———. *Sir Walter Ralegh: Last of the Elizabethans.* London: Macmillan, 1935; New Haven: Yale University Press, 1936.

———. *So a Poor Ghost.* London: Macmillan, 1933; New York: Knopf, 1934.

———. *Suttee: A Historical and Philosophical Inquiry into the Hindu Rite of Widow-Burning.* London: Ernest Benn; Boston: Houghton Mifflin, 1928.

———. "Suttee among Hindus a Century under Ban." *New York Times,* 1 December 1929, sec. X, p. 20.

———. *These Men, Thy Friends.* London: Knopf, 1927; New York: Harcourt Brace, 1928.

———. *You Have Lived through All This.* London: Victor Gollancz, 1939.

Thompson, Edward John, and G. T. Garratt. *Rise and Fulfilment of British Rule in India.* London: Macmillan, 1934. Reprint, Allahabad: Central Book Depot, 1965.

Thompson, Edward John, and Theodosia Thompson. *The Last Voyage.* London: Macmillan, 1934.

———. *Three Eastern Plays: With a Terminal Essay on "Suttee."* London: G. Allen and Unwin, 1927.

Thompson, Edward Palmer. *Alien Homage: Edward Thompson and Rabindranath Tagore.* Delhi: Oxford University Press, 1993.

———. *Beyond the Frontier: The Politics of a Failed Mission: Bulgaria, 1944.* Stanford: Stanford University Press, 1997.

———. *The Making of the English Working Class.* Reprint, London: Victor Gollancz, 1975.

Thompson, Frank. *There Is a Spirit in Europe . . . : A Memoir.* Comp. The‹ dosia J. Thompson and Edward P. Thompson. London: Victor Gollanc 1948.

Tinker, Hugh. *The Ordeal of Love: C. F. Andrews and India.* Delhi: Oxfor University Press, 1979.

Tod, James. *Annals and Antiquities of Rajasthan, or the Central an Western Rajpoot States of India.* 2 vols. London: Smith, Elder, 1829-183: "The Transfer of the Indian Capital." *Times,* 14 December 1911, 9.

Trivedi, Harish. *Colonial Transactions: English Literature and India.* Bon bay: Orient Longmans, 1993.

Tuchman, Barbara W. *The Guns of August.* New York: Macmillan, 1962.

United Kingdom. Montagu-Chelmsford Report. *Constitutional and Natione Development in India.* London: H. M. Stationery Office, 1918.

United Kingdom. Parliament. Amritsar District Report. *District Accoun‹ Submitted by the Government of the Punjab.* Cmd. 534. 1920.

United Kingdom. Parliament. Simon Commission Report. *Indian Statutor Commission Interim Report.* Cmd. 3407. London: H. M. Stationery Offic‹ 1930.

United Kingdom. Parliament. Hunter Committee. *Report of the Committe Appointed to Investigate the Disturbance in the Punjab, Etc.* Cmd. 68ⅼ 1920.

Viswanathan, Gauri. *Masks of Conquest: Literary Study and British Rule i‹ India.* London: Faber and Faber, 1990.

Waldman, Milton. "Last Man of an Age." *Saturday Review of Literature* 1 (26 September 1936): 12.

Wells, H. G. *Mr. Britling Sees It Through.* New York: Macmillan, 1916.

"Wesley and His Work." *Times Literary Supplement,* 15 July 1909, 258.

Wesleyan Methodist Missionary Society Reports. London: 1885-1886, 1889 1891, 1909-1910, 1911-1912.

Whiting, R. C., ed. *Oxford: Studies in the History of a University Town sinc 1800.* Manchester: Manchester University Press, 1993.

Williams, L. F. Rushbrooke. "The Princes of India." *Spectator* 171 (1943) 197.

Wilson, Duncan. *Gilbert Murray OM, 1866-1957.* Oxford: Clarendon Press 1987.

Wolpert, Stanley. *Nehru: A Tryst with Destiny.* New York: Oxford Universit‹ Press, 1996.

———. *A New History of India.* 2d ed. New York: Oxford University Press 1982.

Woolf, Leonard. "British in India." *New Statesman and Nation* 7 (30 Jun‹ 1934): 997-98.

————. "The World of Books: Sugar and Soap and Salt." *Nation and Athenaeum* 40 (1925): 271.

Woolf, S. J. "India's Poet. . . ." *Sunday New York Times,* 19 October 1930, sec. V, p. 5.

Woolf, Virginia. *Diary.* Ed. Anne Olivier Bell and Andrew McNeillie. 5 vols. London: Hogarth Press, 1977–1984.

Zwemer, Samuel Marinus. *Islam: A Challenge to Faith: Studies on the Mohammedan Religion and Opportunities of the Mohammedan World from the Standpoint of Christian Missions.* New York: Student Volunteer Movement, 1908.

INDEX

EJT in index refers to Edward John Thompson. Page numbers in italics refer to photographs.